THE ENGLISH WITS

In the late sixteenth and early seventeenth centuries the Inns of Court and fashionable London taverns developed a culture of clubbing, urban sociability and wit. The convivial societies that emerged created rituals to define social identities and to engage in literary play and political discussion. Michelle O'Callaghan argues that the lawyer-wits, including John Hoskyns, in company with authors such as John Donne, Ben Jonson and Thomas Coryate, consciously reinvigorated humanist traditions of learned play. Their experiments with burlesque, banquet literature, parody and satire resulted in a volatile yet creative dialogue between civility and licence, and between pleasure and the violence of scurrilous words. The wits inaugurated a mode of literary fellowship that shaped the history and literature of sociability in the seventeenth century. This study will provide many new insights for historians and literary scholars of the period.

MICHELLE O'CALLAGHAN is Reader in English at the University of Reading.

William Marshall, 'Lawes of Drinking', from Blasius Multibibus (Richard Brathwaite), *A Solemne Joviall Disputation, Theoreticke and Practicke; briefly shadowing the Law of Drinking* (London, 1617), British Library, C.40.b.20

THE ENGLISH WITS

Literature and Sociability in Early Modern England

MICHELLE O'CALLAGHAN

CAMBRIDGE
UNIVERSITY PRESS

CAMBRIDGE UNIVERSITY PRESS
Cambridge, New York, Melbourne, Madrid, Cape Town, Singapore, São Paulo

Cambridge University Press
The Edinburgh Building, Cambridge CB2 2RU, UK

Published in the United States of America by Cambridge University Press, New York

www.cambridge.org
Information on this title: www.cambridge.org/9780521860840

© Michelle O'Callaghan 2007

This publication is in copyright. Subject to statutory exception
and to the provisions of relevant collective licensing agreements,
no reproduction of any part may take place without
the written permission of Cambridge University Press.

First published 2007

Printed in the United Kingdom at the University Press, Cambridge

A catalogue record for this publication is available from the British Library

Library of Congress Cataloguing in Publication data

ISBN-13 978-0-521-86084-0 hardback
ISBN-10 0-521-86084-9 hardback

Cambridge University Press has no responsibility for the persistence or accuracy of URLs for external or third-party internet websites referred to in this publication, and does not guarantee that any content on such websites is, or will remain, accurate or appropriate.

Contents

Frontispiece — *page* ii
Acknowledgements — vii
Note on the text — viii

Introduction — 1

1. Gentleman lawyers at the Inns of Court — 10
2. Ben Jonson, the lawyers and the wits — 35
3. Taverns and table talk — 60
4. Wits in the House of Commons — 81
5. *Coryats Crudities* (1611) and the sociability of print — 102
6. Traveller for the English wits — 128
7. Afterlives of the wits — 153

Notes — 178
Bibliography — 215
Index — 229

Acknowledgements

This book has benefited from its association with many people throughout its various phases. I am indebted to Martin Butler, David Colclough, Margaret Kean, Charlotte McBride, Andrew McRae, David Norbrook, Jennifer Richards, Susan Wiseman and Gillian Knight, who took the time to make constructive comments on drafts. Katie Craik read drafts, passed on references and generously shared forthcoming work. Louise Durning, Margaret Healy, Tom Healy, Erica Sheen, Cathy Shrank and Adam Smyth discussed ideas and shared thoughts on sociability. At the History of Parliament Trust, Dr Andrew Thrush gave much-needed guidance to early Stuart parliaments, offered useful snippets of information and commented on an early draft of Chapter 4. The two readers at Cambridge University Press gave supportive advice on completing the manuscript. I would also like to thank the librarians at the Bodleian Library, Corpus Christi College library, Oxford and the London Museum as well as the archivists at Hampshire Record Office and the York City Archive for their assistance.

A Leverhulme Research Award in 2003–4 enabled me to consolidate the project and bring it to fruition. The research leave funded by the School of Arts and Humanities at Oxford Brookes University was invaluable in the final stages, and I would like to thank colleagues in the English Department for their support.

Grace and Joseph have enlivened the writing of this book with their own play; it was always appreciated. This book could not have been finished without the support of Mathew Thomson. Thanks once again to all my family for continuing understanding and encouragement.

Note on the text

All conflations of u/v and i/j are routinely modernised.

Introduction

> To the High Seneschall of the right Worshipfull Fraternitie of Sireniacal Gentlemen, that meet the first Fridaie of every Moneth, at the signe of the Mere-Maide in Bread-streete in London.[1]

Thomas Coryate's letter from Ajmer, India, addressed to the Sireniacal gentleman is one of the remaining textual traces of the convivial societies that met at the Mermaid and Mitre taverns, both on Bread Street, in the first decades of the seventeenth century. Many of the Sireniacs also appeared among the diners named in a Latin poem often given the title 'Convivium Philosophicum', commemorating a banquet held at the Mitre in September 1611, and were among the wits who gathered in print to mark the publication of *Coryats Crudities* (1611). One can trace a web of references to wits frequenting the Mitre and Mermaid on Friday nights in this period through letters, account books, poems, plays and pamphlets. These early modern societies were distinguished from more informal gatherings through their rituals of association, which provided participants with a quasi-ceremonial space for recreation, play and table talk. The term 'wits' took on a more specific meaning in the late sixteenth and early seventeenth centuries that coincided with these tavern societies; its general sense as a collective noun was made particular, and attached to a distinct milieu within early modern London that cultivated a fashionable, urbane reputation. Such urbanity is the premise of Francis Beaumont's epistle from the country to Ben Jonson in the city, 'The Sun which doth the greatest comfort bring', especially when he writes of the company frequenting the Mermaid, and their convivial meetings 'when there hath been thrown / Wit able enough to justifie the Town'.[2]

William Gifford's once influential account of the 'Mermaid Club', 'a meeting of beaux esprits' presided over by Sir Walter Raleigh at the Mermaid tavern, and graced by the famous wits of the times – Ben Jonson, William Shakespeare, Francis Beamont, John Fletcher, John Donne, among others – has now been discredited.[3] This does not mean, however, that forms of clubbing did not take place at taverns in early modern London. There is evidence for established rituals of dining together among a group of Inns of Court friends and their associates in London from at least the late sixteenth into the early seventeenth century that went well beyond sharing the costs of a formal dinner at a tavern. Dining and drinking were accompanied by rituals of fellowship, extempore versifying and orations, and game-playing. Even though these performances were not always recorded for posterity, traces can be discerned in representations of an associational culture that met at the Mitre and Mermaid taverns in plays, pamphlets and poems from the late 1590s to the mid-1610s. Thomas Middleton's *Your Five Gallants*, performed around 1607, for example, is peppered with allusions to the Mitre and the Mermaid taverns as fashionable places to be seen among company in London; a reminder by one character that ''tis Miter-night', prompts the response, 'Masse 'tis indeed, Friday to day, Ide quite forgot'.[4] By collectively designating a specific day and place, meetings are turned into social events that engender their own conditions and perceptions.

Clubbing is said, in studies such as Peter Borsay's *The English Urban Renaissance*, to be a predominantly post-Restoration phenomenon, heading the development of public sociability in London and the towns. Hence the famous political clubs, like the Whig Kit-Cat club formed at the end of the seventeenth century, or the later Tory October Club, or the proliferation of coffee-house societies from the 1650s.[5] The history of sociability is seen to enter a distinct and definitive phase in the second half of the seventeenth century as it moves decisively down the high road towards the civil society of the public sphere. Peter Clark in his overview, *British Clubs and Societies, 1580–1800*, identifies the voluntary society as one of the principal engines of urbanisation, and points to the way it gives direction to processes of economic, social and political modernisation. Earlier tavern-clubbing tends to be overlooked within this modernising narrative since it is frequently equated with a court coterie culture, and thus belonging to an older, residual aristocratic culture.[6] Recent work on sixteenth- and early seventeenth-century communities, however, has drawn attention to the way that social and intellectual networks, including humanist fraternities at the Inns of Court and universities, as well as print and scribal communities, decisively re-shaped early modern associational life.[7] These studies provide a framework for re-considering the place of early tavern-clubbing in the history of sociability.

The precise composition of these early convivial societies remains shadowy, except at the points where they entered into manuscript circulation, print or other records. This is not unusual. Lists of participants in societies and records of proceedings in general were rarely made, even in the case of later seventeenth-century clubs, and very few of these have survived the passage of time.[8] One such example is the early seventeenth-century Latin poem on the 'convivium philosophicum' said to have been held at the Mitre – 'Signum mitrae erit locus, / Erit cibus, erit jocus / Optimatatissimus' ('The mitre is ye place decreed, / For witty jests, & cleanely feede, / The betterest of any').[9] It opens by listing the diners through a series of Latin puns. Those present included John Donne, his lawyer friends Christopher Brooke, John Hoskyns and Richard Martin, and other close friends and associates – Hugh Holland, Inigo Jones, the courtiers, Sir Henry Goodyer and Sir Robert Phelips, and the influential men of business, Sir Lionel Cranfield and Sir Arthur Ingram. Coryate played the part of the buffoon. I. A. Shapiro surmised that the list of well-wishers at the end of Coryate's letter to the Sireniacal gentlemen identified participants in this fraternity, many of whom were familiar from the Mitre *convivium*, although others, such as Sir Robert Cotton, the lawyer William Hakewill, and Jonson, were not. He concluded that there were, in fact, two societies, an earlier dining club that sometimes met at the Mitre, which subsequently developed into the Mermaid club. Participation in these convivial societies was probably much more fluid than this suggests. It is likely there was a core group of friends, probably those who were resident or whose business frequently kept them in London.[10] These individuals could thus serve as the memory of the society, providing the company with a degree of stability over a period of time by retaining knowledge of shared rituals and possession of cultural artefacts, such as company seals as well as poems and songs.

The personal and professional bonds, milieux and institutions these individuals have in common give a tantalising sketch of the rich fabric of associational life in late sixteenth- and early seventeenth-century London. The majority of those listed among the diners at the Mitre *convivium* and in Coryate's letters to the Sireniacs had entered either the Middle Temple or Lincoln's Inn, 'the auncient Allye, & friend of the midde Temple', in the last decades of the sixteenth century.[11] The Inns were a paradigmatic fraternity, combining men in an association held together by the bonds of civic brotherhood. They were a vital social centre in London, a place of residence for many of these men over the course of their careers, where they could meet and entertain associates during the law year or when business called them to the capital. After decades of magnificent grand revels, drama, and poetry, the Inns of Court in the late sixteenth century possessed a well-established and rich cultural tradition. Hence, Sir Benjamin Rudyerd was able to say of the 1597–8 Christmas revels, 'Never any Prince in this kingdome, or the like made soe glorious, soe rich a shew'.[12]

Networks among the élite in early modern London traversed a range of social spaces, including the Inns of Court, royal households, civic corporations and parliament. A number of those named at the Mitre *convivium* held positions at Prince Henry's court, including Sir Robert Phelips, Richard Connock and Inigo Jones, while Christopher Brooke's brother Samuel was Henry's chaplain. The predominance of Middle Temple men in the Prince's household may be explained by the presence of a senior Middle Templar, Sir Edward Phelips. He acted as the chancellor to the Duchy of Cornwall, which was in the process of being reconstituted to maintain the Prince of Wales's household and was a lucrative fund for dispensing favour.[13] It could be argued these sodalities were an aspect of a patronage culture, satellites of the court comprised of ambitious young men competing for preferment.[14] Advancement did play a part, but it does not fully determine their social function. Nor does it adequately account for the part played by the group of lawyer-wits, in particular, Hoskyns, Martin and Brooke, in these societies. All were admired by their contemporaries for their wit, although they now tend to be known through their more famous literary friends – Donne and Jonson.[15] They are cited as the leading game-makers orchestrating the literary performances identified with these convivial societies. These lawyers enjoyed Phelips's patronage; however, unlike their friend Donne, they did not seek employment at court or in aristocratic households. Instead, they secured their social identity in the civic realm through the legal profession, as members of parliament and through corporations such as the Virginia Company. The lawyers draw attention to the professional dimension of these societies and, in particular, the legacy of humanist fraternities at the Inns, which combined the profession of the law and letters with office in government, from the local magistrate to the privy councillor.[16]

These early tavern societies can be seen as early types of political clubs. They were vital spaces in which merchants, lawyers, parliamentarians, courtiers and men of letters could hold conversations on a range of issues. The political sociability practised at the tavern clubs, Pascal Brioist argues, helped to establish the foundations of the early modern public political sphere.[17] Qualifications are necessary. These fraternities were not fully-fledged political clubs, and were not politically purposeful like the later seventeenth- and eighteenth-century clubs, such as the Whig Kit-Cat club. The lawyer-wits did share a professional and ideological investment in the common law that was part of the wider transformation of political culture in the first half of the seventeenth century.[18] And political satire was one of the defining features of their literary table talk. Even so these societies were not political factions with coherent agendas.

The public image the Sireniacs cultivated was that of the wits, a complex collective and convivial identity that derived from their common educational background.[19] Coryate called the Sireniacs a 'fraternity', a term that generally described a 'company of men entered into a firm bond of society', and also commonly denoted contemporary urban fraternities, trade or craft guilds.[20] When he described the High Seneschal of the fraternity, Lawrence Whitaker, as the 'inimitable artisan of sweet elegancy', it is because his craft or profession is wit; this is the basis of his intellectual capital, like the predominantly university-educated company of 'Joviall and Mercuriall Sireniacks' (*Traveller*, p. 37). These companies had well-defined rituals based on cultures of revelling at the universities and the Inns of Court and the humanist revival of classical convivial traditions. The Sireniacs looked back to the Greek *symposium* and Roman *convivium*, as well as placing themselves in the company of the drinking societies of contemporary Europe. The safe-conduct the society composed in late October 1612 to accompany Coryate on his travels to the East offers a jocular compendium of companies of 'fellow drinkers at the crystal stream' that promiscuously ranges through various Roman military companies ending with the 'Fellowship or Fraternity'. Types of events attended by these 'fellow drinkers' are similarly eclectic, from general meetings ('cœtorum') to dining ('conviviorum') and drinking societies ('symposiorum').[21] The texts associated with the wits revive and inter-mingle classical symposiastic and convivial vocabularies to enrich the language of learned play available to them.[22] Terms of association are expansive and not as fixed as they will become later in the century when 'club' comes into common usage to denote a private society.

The humanist convivial society is the setting for recreation and civil conversations. One of its models was the humanist banquet, the ultimate *locus* for Stefano Guazzo's social ideal in his *Civile Conversation*. The occasion, 'the companie and conversation of honest and learned men', is all: it designates a privileged social space, where men can be 'private and familiar', exercise good manners and engage in learned discourse, even 'to speake freelie what he thinketh, and to call franklie for what he lacketh'.[23] The act of voluntarily entering into social contracts with one another based on trust and sodality creates a safe place for play and performance, and the discussion of philosophy and politics. Such convivial practices were intended to facilitate social exchanges among the élite and affirm social identity, designating the participants as cultivated and learned men fit to participate in the structures of governance.[24]

The transposition of the *convivium* from the aristocratic or humanist dining table to the London tavern can be identified with the development of 'new forms of public sociability' in the seventeenth and eighteenth centuries, as part of a broader process of urbanisation, which will coalesce in the public sphere of civil society.[25] The *locus* of these societies was the new metropolis, the fashionable West End of London, an area between Whitehall and the City of London. Jonson is one of the earliest dramatists of this new metropolis and puts early versions of the private society on stage in the Ladies Collegiate and the 'Wits and Braveries' of his *Epicoene*. Formed outside the jurisdiction of the state in the early modern public sphere, private societies are understood to be one of the primary mechanisms in the emergence of a civil society. The 'civilizing process', as set out by Norbert Elias, is predicated upon the pacification of social spaces that finds its ideal representation in the polite refinement of the private society. The state assumes a monopoly on violence, promulgating an ethos of moderation through the discourses of *civilité*.[26] A difficulty with Elias's thesis is that it overlooks tensions within cultures of civility, often arising out of the persistence of older honour codes alongside *civilité*. Verbal violence is legitimated within communities of honour, even as it is recognised that it transgresses the dictates of civil behaviour, thus generating debates about its place within the public realm.[27]

Clubbing at the Inns of Court in the late sixteenth century incorporated ritualised forms of aggression that, in fact, helped to constitute the social space of the convivial society, the arena in which social competence is produced and cultural value attributed.[28] The wits practised flyting, a type of verbal duelling associated with communities of honour that aggressively defined the in-group. These societies were exclusive, and developed complex vocabularies of social distinction and taste that combined the verbal violence of satire with the conviviality of banquet literature. Jonson refines this language of distinction in his early plays through game-playing as well as a satiric rhetoric of urbanity that aligns judgement with wit. By identifying his own plays and performances with humanist traditions of learned play, Jonson sought to give credibility to the professional dramatist. It was, to a certain extent, a defensive posture, a means of distinguishing himself from other dramatists and popular entertainers, such as John Taylor, who were modelling their own craft on Jonson. Coryate was a similarly troubling figure, who transgressed social distinctions through his eccentric occupations. Like Jonson, the wits had invested heavily in their intellectual capital. They used the satiric resources of the mock-encomium in the 'Panegyricke Verses' at the front of *Coryats Crudities* to set in place a convivial language of social discrimination in order to distinguish themselves from Coryate, in the guise of the lower-class buffoon, and to place themselves above the popular print marketplace. One effect was to clarify the emerging social and cultural distinctions between the élite tavern and the lower-class alehouse, illustrated so starkly in William Marshall's 1617 engraving 'The Lawes of Drinking',[29] which provided the frontispiece to Richard Brathwaite's *Solemne Joviall Disputation . . . briefly shadowing the Law of Drinking*.

The inhibition of passionate and violent words in theories of the civil society has its corollary in the concentration on principles of civic rationality as the communicative basis of the public sphere. This has meant that discourses of civic humanism and public reason are often prioritised in studies of associations and communicative practices, and alternative traditions within humanism side-lined.[30] Laughter had a recognised and strategic role to play in religious polemic and political critique. A seminal text setting out the traditions of learned play or *lusus* for humanist audiences was Erasmus's *Praise of Folly*. His letter to Martin Dorp argued that jesting was necessary because it was a vital medium for healthy frank speaking within the commonwealth: 'If you think that no one should ever speak freely or reveal the truth except when it offends no one, why do physicians heal with bitter medicines and place *aloe sacra* [holy bitters] among their most highly recommended remedies?'[31] Serious laughter, as a medium for satire and polemic, was a much-debated topic in the sixteenth and seventeenth centuries. It raised numerous questions about the limits of ridicule and the decorum of disputation that were continually revisited but not resolved. Laughter was valuable rhetorical strategy in the forum, as Cicero pointed out, because it persuaded through an appeal not to reason but to the emotions.[32] Learned play often aims to discover the limits of rational debate and favours more speculative forms of critique.

The 1597–8 Middle Temple revels, the 'Convivium Philosophicum', the 'Parliament Fart' and the 'Panegyricke Verses' before *Coryats Crudities* attest to the concerted effort to reinvigorate classically low and ludic genres, such as burlesque and the mock-encomium, and to experiment with rhetorical forms; hence Hoskyns is credited with inventing English nonsense verse.[33] Rituals of play infused the sociable practices and literary performances defining this company. The extemporised element to ritualised play permits certain freedoms and rhetorical licence, opening a space for creative manoeuvre and dissonant voices in the interstices of the cultural codes it parodies and dismantles.[34] The literary performances of the wits participate in the late humanist critique of the equation between the persuasive powers of rhetoric and civic rationality that had been the cornerstone of an earlier civic humanism.[35] Hoskyns's mock-oration delivered at the 1597–8 revels, for example, is a witty parody of humanist oratory that by separating sound and sense, matter and meaning, rhetoric and ethics produces a type of antirhetoric or nonsense. The wits parody ceremonies and traditions in which they are thoroughly acculturated to create pseudo-ceremonial spaces open to improvisation – the mock-convivium at the Mitre tavern, the House of Commons in the process of censuring a fart, and the mock-encomiastic 'Panegyricke Verses' before *Coryats Crudities*. They are attracted to literary forms that are multivocal, thus open to the sounds of dissonance. Hence, the *convivium* may have offered humanist writers a paradigmatic communal space for civil conversations governed by an ethos of moderation. Yet, the pleasures of the table could easily spill over into satire, parody and burlesque, and open an extemporised space for exploring the dimensions of laughter and pleasure, imagining forms of 'uninhibited discourse', from fantastical linguistic play to satires on the Church and State.[36] The space for this ritualised play is the private political realm. The public forum and private table were distinguished in terms of rhetorical practices. This does not mean, however, that this 'private' space did not shape political identities or influence public debate, but rather that it was an arena with its own rules of engagement.

Coryats Crudities, along with *Coryats Crambe* also published in 1611, turns the humanist book into just such a pseudo-ceremonial space. Despite the wits' resistance to print culture, Coryate's books provided subsequent writers, editors and readers with a model of print fellowship that was open to a wider readership outside the intimate circle of the coterie. The way the publication of Coryate's travels was turned into a print event illustrates how contemporary practices of sociability structured the print marketplace. Coryate improvised a persona within the tradition of orator-buffoons. He experimented with the rhetoric of presence, helping to shape a new print genre which explored analogues for live performance through the medium of print. This rhetoric of presence infuses his travel writing to produce a discourse of sight-seeing. His travel-writing partakes of the improvisatory elements of play through its curiosity which unsettles established discourses of humanist travel from within, opening travel to different communities and other ways of seeing.

I begin with the Inns of Court in the late 1590s, an associational culture providing the lawyer-wits with the ideological resources and intellectual capital that enabled them to perform effectively across a range of social arenas from the tavern to the House of Commons. The 1597–8 Middle

Temple Christmas revels are pivotal in that they initiate a tradition of clubbing in the context of the factional libellous politics of the late 1590s. Subsequent chapters trace this culture of clubbing through the composition of the 'Parliament Fart', which coincided with James's first parliament in session from 1604 to 1610, and the performance cultures and genres of tavern poetry illustrated by the 'Convivium Philosophicum' and Coryate's promotion of his *Crudities* and his travels to the Middle East and Eastern India. The 1614 'addled' parliament appears to bring to a close this phase of tavern-clubbing. Hoskyns was imprisoned for his sharp wit in this parliament, and meetings do not seem to have been revived after his release from the Tower in 1615.

The final chapter looks forward to the immediate and longer term legacy of early tavern-clubbing. The 1620s sees the reinvigoration of clubbing: fraternities proliferated in an environment unsettled and energised by the outbreak of the Thirty Years War, court scandals, corruption trials, and the recalling of parliament after almost seven years. This is the context for Jonson's creation of the 'Tribe of Ben' and his transformation of the Apollo Room at the Devil and St Dunstan tavern into a symposiastic space. The popular 'Parliament Fart' circulated widely in manuscript well into the second half of the century. It is first printed in the Royalist anthologies *Musarum Deliciæ: or, the Muses Recreation* (1655) and *Le Prince d'Amour, or the Prince of Love* (1660). *Musarum Deliciæ* assimilates the literary play of the wits to a libertine tradition of burlesque, separating it from its humanist origins. The publication of the 'Parliament Fart' in this collection of 'drollery', a new popular print genre, attests to the process of democratising previously élite modes of sociability in the second half of the seventeenth century. The 'English Wits' and early tavern-clubbing are therefore pivotal in the history of early modern sociability in Britain.

CHAPTER ONE

Gentleman lawyers at the Inns of Court

The early convivial societies were shaped at a fundamental level by the fact that many of the participants had been trained at the Inns of Court. The *convivium* held at the Mitre tavern and the Sireniacal fraternity were dominated by men from the Middle Temple and its ancient ally Lincoln's Inn.¹ That the early history of the private society is closely associated with the Inns of Court derives from their status as a voluntary professional society and a physical community that brought together a body of educated, élite men. The Inns were instrumental in the Tudor civic renaissance, which witnessed the emergence of different forms of association, including the early convivial societies.² The Inns have a unique institutional status within this history of associations. Unlike guilds or the universities, they had never been incorporated by royal charter, had no legal existence as a corporate body, nor were they bound together by a written constitution. Instead their corporate identity resided in acts of living and working together as a professional fraternity, and relied on rituals and cultural fictions to bind individuals in a voluntary contract.³ The performance of contracts of fellowship began with entry into an Inn. The student was sponsored by 'two others formerly admitted of the House, [who] enter into Bond with him, as his sureties, to observe the Orders, and dischardge the duties of the House'.⁴ The diarist John Manningham was bound with Hoskyns when he entered the Middle Temple in 1598, and this contracted fellowship gave him privileged access to Hoskyns's social circle. His diary from 1602 to 1603 assiduously records the witticisms of Hoskyns, Martin and the lawyer William Hakewill, noting the gossip about Sir Henry Neville's fortunes following the disastrous 1601 Essex rebellion, copying Donne's poems and paradoxes circulating among this group of friends, and joining in their libellous attacks on John Davies – Hoskyns had been bound with John Davies, a fellow student from Winchester and Oxford, but Davies had dramatically fallen out with both Hoskyns and Martin during the 1597–8 Christmas revels.⁵ When Donne entered Lincoln's Inn in May 1592, he was bound together with Christopher Brooke; Brooke and Donne shared chambers, and remained close friends. The particular spatial organisation, professional rituals and institutional practices of the Inns thus deeply ingrained habits of *communitas*, of sharing space, of conversation, and of entering into contracts, ranging from friendships and informal fellowships to more formal obligations.[6]

The associational culture of the Inns had clearly defined ideological foundations. A civic ideology that assimilated classical humanist theories of the *polis* to the structures and practices of the legal community had begun to emerge at the Inns in the early sixteenth century. That said, it was only during Elizabeth's reign, when the Inns embarked on an ambitious rebuilding programme and hosted a succession of magnificent entertainments, that the image of the Inns as the ideal commonwealth was consolidated in the Inns' physical and cultural fabric.[7] Hoskyns, Martin, Donne, Brooke and a number of others who participated in the early seventeenth-century societies were admitted to the Inns of Court in the 1580s and 1590s at the height of this period of institutional expansion and cultural consolidation. These men were instrumental in the promotion of civic fictions at their Inns throughout their careers, creating and executing entertainments from the Elizabethan 1597–8 Middle Temple revels to Jacobean court entertainments, magnificently exemplified by the *Memorable Masque* (1613). The distinctive civic structures and discourses of *communitas* promulgated at the Inns in the sixteenth century authorised the early convivial societies, informing their social and symbolic practices, as well as providing these men with powerful ideological resources on which they could draw as actors within and across a range of social arenas from parliament and the law courts to taverns and private tables.

That said, the 1597–8 revels are distinguished by the liberties taken in their law sports.[8] Pressure was placed on languages of association at the Inns during the late 1590s, disclosing tensions between a masculine honour culture and notions of civility, and within rhetorical traditions. The fraught, often combative expression of *communitas* during these revels, and in satires and other poems produced within this milieu, speaks to the bitter factionalism of the late 1590s. The Inns were caught up in the libellous politics of these years as Robert Devereux, Earl of Essex struggled to regain authority at court. More broadly, the culture emerging at the Inns in this period is highly responsive to tensions within humanist rhetorical traditions.[9] Ceremonial forms and oratorical traditions are subjected to critique in the 1597–8 Middle Temple revels. The 'clubbing' inaugurated during these revels is part of a process of experimentation and improvisation. Its ritualised modes of play unsettle received doctrines and, through parody and burlesque, open a space for creative manoeuvre within available discourses and ceremonial forms.[10]

'THE FOUNDATION OF A GOOD COMMON WEALE'

Gerard Legh's account of the 1561–2 Inner Temple revels in his *Accedence of Armorie* (1586) is a seminal text in the constitution of the Inns of Court as the ideal commonwealth. It is not simply a description of the revels, but a careful and elaborate cultural fiction intended to define and make manifest the philosophical basis of the Inns' customs and practices of association. Legh clearly reworks Thomas More's *Utopia* through his traveller's tale, thus magnifying the civic humanist and utopian dimension of its political vision.[11] Legh, 'Sir Herehaught', a foreign visitor to London, hears cannon shot calling the Inner Templars to commons, and questions an 'honest citizen':

> He answered me, the province was not great in quantitie, but ancient in true Nobilitie. A place said he privileged by the most excellent Princes, the high Governour of the whole land, wherein are the store of Gentlemen of the whole Realme, that repair thether to learne to rule, and obey by Law, to yeelde their fleece to their Prince and common weale, as also to use all other exercises of body and minde where-unto nature most aptly serveth, to adorne by speaking, countenance, gesture, and use of apparell the person of a Gentleman, whereby amitie is obtained and continued, that Gentlemen of all Countries in their young yeares, nourished together in one place, with such comely order, and daily conference are knit by continuall acquaintance in such unity of minds and manners, as lightly never after is severed: then which is nothing more profitable to the common weale. And after he had told me thus much of the honour of the place, I commended in mine owne conceit the pollicie of the Governour, which seemed to utter in it selfe, the foundation of a good common weale. For that the best of their people from tender yeares trayned up in precepts of Justice, it could not chuse, but yeeld forth a profitable people, to a wise common weale.[12]

Like many of his contemporaries, Legh equates the Inns of Court with the Aristotelian city state, training men to live profitably as virtuous citizens for the benefit of 'a wise common weale'.[13]

For Legh, the Inns constitute an environment in which *civitas* artfully coincides with *urbanitas*, the cultivation of mind and manners among just men that for Cicero defined the civic strength of the republic.[14] Its social type is the gentleman lawyer who combines civic office with the exercise of civility. The notion of the Inns as a place where 'Gentlemen of the whole Realme' gathered to learn the arts of gentle behaviour was commonplace by the 1560s, and speaks to their status as one of the primary centres of civility in the state, alongside the court and universities. The Inns functioned as a 'civilising' agency at a number of inter-related levels: promoting a civic discourse of the law that underpinned the notion of the civil society; through legal training disseminating an ethos of the gentleman as civil magistrate; and providing a milieu in which urbane good manners are acquired.[15] Legh's physical, social and cultural topography of the Inns illustrates how this space was negotiated through rituals and practices. It constituted a complex habitus in which young men could learn and practise ways of speaking, dressing and modes of behaviour that distinguished them within a wider society as gentlemen and thus consolidated a governing class of 'gentle' magistrates.

This is the milieu Hoskyns, Martin, Donne and Brooke entered in the last decades of the sixteenth century. Yet, none were sons of landed gentry. When Sir George Buck, in his history of the Inns, insisted that 'all those which were admitted to these houses were, and ought to be Gentlemenne, and that of three discents at least', he was reacting to the entrance of an increasing number of young men from plebeian families, resulting in what he saw as a commonly held 'error to thinke that the sonnes of Graziers, Farmers, Marchants, Tradesmen, and artificers can bee made Gentlemen, by their admittance or Matriculation in the Buttrie Hole, or in the Stewards Booke, of such a house or Inne of court'.[16] By contrast, Sir Hugh Cholmley, who attended Gray's Inn from 1618 to 1621, took it for granted that 'every man that hath but a smackering of the law though of no fortune or quallety shall bee a leader or director to the greatest and best gentlemen on the bench'.[17] Hoskyns, Martin and Brooke came from families that had profited from the civic renaissance, and therefore had a strong investment in fashioning social identities through the Inns of Court and the legal profession.[18] Hoskyns was the third son of a yeoman, and his brother Oswald, a successful London draper. Martin's father, William, an Exeter merchant, represented the city in the 1597 parliament. Brooke came from a similar background: his father, Robert, a York merchant, was twice Lord Mayor of York and sat for the city in the 1584 and 1586 parliaments, and his mother was the daughter of a York draper.[19] Donne may have traced his lineage back to an ancient Welsh line, the Dwyns of Kidwelly, yet his father was an ironmonger and citizen of London; his friends at Lincoln's Inn, Rowland and Thomas Woodward, were the sons of a London vintner of the parish of St Mary le Bow.[20] Students of the Inns of Court without armour were entitled to style themselves gentlemen by virtue of the institution. Over the course of the sixteenth century, the aristocratic community of honour had been reconfigured at the Inns through a civic humanist discourse of *vita activa*, thus enabling sons of yeomen, merchants and artisans to gain access to the 'tangible proofs of gentility'.[21]

Martin and Hoskyns were awarded leading roles in the Middle Temple 1597–8 Christmas grand revels: Martin was elected the Prince of Love, who presided over the revels, and Hoskyns took the supporting role of Clerk of Council. Although both had been disciplined in their youth for unruly behaviour, it is highly unlikely they were chosen to perform in these revels because of youthful mischief.[22] For one thing, neither were in their youth: Martin was in his late twenties and Hoskyns just over thirty. Those who led the grand revels had to be highly skilled in courtly accomplishments – singing, dancing, music – and highly proficient in rhetoric, law, and other scholastic exercises travestied in the law sports.[23] Sir Henry Helmes, the Prince of Purpoole in the Gray's Inn revels, was described as 'a very proper Man of Personage, and very active in Dancing and Revelling'. Martin's accomplishments are indicated by Davies's dedication of his *Orchestra, or a Poeme of Daucing* (1596) to him, the '*first mover and sole cause of it*'.[24]

Hoskyns had established a reputation for rhetorical brilliance at New College, Oxford; soon after these revels, he composed his *Directions for Speech and Style*, a rhetorical handbook for the use of a Middle Temple student.[25] One could speculate that Martin was chosen for the prince because of the considerable oratorical skills he brought to the practice of the law. Sir Thomas Elyot in the early sixteenth century had advanced a model for the legal profession based on the Ciceronian lawyer-orator in his *Book called The Governor*: a man 'havyng an excellent wytte . . . maye also be exactly or depely lerned in the arte of an Oratour, and also in the lawes of this realme . . . undoubtedly it should nat be impossible for hym to bring the pleadyng and reasonyng of the lawe, to the auncient fourme of noble oratours'.[26] The lawyer-orator embodied and performed the correspondence between the common law and classical civic virtues; as prince of the artificial city state during the revels, this figure personified the conjunction of justice, urbanity, and virtue in the profession of the law.

In 1603, Martin was chosen by the City of London to deliver the oration to King James on his entry into London, in recognition of his command of oratory. Like others on this occasion, Martin styled James as the '*great Augustus*'. Yet what he offered the king was artful panegyric that utilised the conventions of the 'parrhesiastic contract'.[27] By speaking frankly to James, Martin invited the king to play the role of the good and wise ruler in the parrhesiastic game:

let England *be the schoole, wherein your Majesty will practize your temperance and moderation: for here flattery will essay to undermine, or force your Majesties strongest constancie and integrity: base assertation the bane of virtuous Princes, which (like* Lazarus *dogs) licks even the Princes soares, a vice made so familiar to this age by long use, that even Pulpits are not free from that kinde of treason.*[28]

The parrhesiastic contract does not simply offer the king a model of governance, in which he is obliged to act on the advice of counsellors to avoid abuses of power, but constructs a powerful subject position for the truth-teller. Hugh Holland spoke of the 'faire example' provided by Martin, 'who, with like libertie as eloquence, was not afraid to tell the King the truth'.[29] *Parrhesia* was a privilege granted by the king only to the most honest citizen; flattery, by contrast, is a failure of *parrhesia* and the means by which citizens turn themselves into slaves, grotesquely figured by Martin in the abjection of Lazarus's dogs.[30] The emphasis is on the agency of the speaker as well as the qualities of kingship. The *parrhesiastes* is defined by his integrity, thus correlating the truth he is able to use with the way he lives his life to produce an ethical subject position. Holland will later eulogise Martin as '*oraculum Londinense*', London's Oracle, whereby the truth-telling of the just man approaches that of the gods.[31]

Martin's *parrhesiastes* is an aspect of the lawyer-orator who combines liberty of speech with the professional expertise that enables the lawyer to discern the truth.[32] Truth-telling was, of course, an aspect of service to the king. Hence, Holland elaborated Martin's example through a carefully balanced comparison: 'I will so comporte my selfe and wade warily betweene both, that I ever carry the heart of a monarchy, and the tongue of a commonwealth; the one loyall, the other liberall.'[33] It was not always an easy balance to maintain, as Holland recognised. As we shall see, tensions emerged in James's first parliament when lawyers, including Martin and Hoskyns, called on the king to act on their legal counsel, and equated the 'tongue of a commonwealth' with the parliamentary privilege of freedom of speech.[34]

The differences between the king and the lawyers that so disturbed the 1610 parliamentary sessions were resolved, if temporarily, in the civic symbolism of George Chapman's *Memorable Masque*, performed by the Middle Temple and Lincoln Inn on 15 February 1613 for the wedding of Princess Elizabeth and Frederick, Elector Palatine. Instead, it was a triumphant expression of the lawyers' loyalty and liberality. Those involved in the masque's organisation included many whose names are familiar from the Sireniacs: Inigo Jones designed the masque; Brooke was in charge of expenditure; and Sir Edward Phelips and Martin were the 'chiefe doers and undertakers'.³⁵ Prince Henry had taken command of the entertainments for his sister's marriage, and commissioned the Inns of Court masques himself. Chapman was the Prince's unofficial poet, and his *Memorable Masque*, celebrating the conversion of the indigenous Virginians to Protestantism, has been viewed as Henry's pet project, part of his promotion of the Virginian enterprise.³⁶ Yet, arguably, the *Memorable Masque* arose out of the alignment of Henry's interests with the Inns. A sizeable proportion of shareholders in the Virginia Company were members of the Middle Temple and Lincoln's Inn, including those instrumental in the masque's production: Sir Edward Phelips, his son, Robert, who was appointed to the directorship of the Company in 1613, Hoskyns, Donne, Martin and Brooke – Martin acted as the Company's legal counsel, while Brooke sat on the council from the Company's foundation in 1609 until its dissolution in 1624.³⁷ These lawyers clearly had their own investment in Virginia.

The *Memorable Masque* testified to Sir Edward Phelips's status as loyal servant to the Crown and powerbroker at the Middle Temple – he was the patron to a group of lawyers that included Martin, Hoskyns and Brooke. The youngest son of Thomas Phelips, a successful grazier in Somerset and Dorset, Phelips too was an exemplary gentleman lawyer, who had built up a highly profitable legal career as a London barrister, proving so effective in the Star Chamber that he was rewarded by Elizabeth and James. Knighted along with his son at James's accession, he was chosen the king's serjeant-meane with 'precedence before all others'; for his loyal service to the crown as Speaker in the Commons, he was appointed Chancellor to Henry's household in 1610, and gained the Mastership of the Rolls in 1611.³⁸ Around one hundred masquers met at Phelips's official residence in London, Rolls House on Chancery Lane, and from there processed through the city to the court: 'A showe at all parts so novell, conceitfull and glorious, as hath not in this land . . . beene ever before beheld.'³⁹ Phelips was wielding all the ceremonial magnificence of the progress to mark out his place within the civic landscape as a pre-eminent member of the legal profession and loyal servant to princes.

The *Memorable Masque* exploited the spectacular symbolism of the masque to create a utopian vision of the ancient, honourable and profitable place of the legal profession within the *polis*.⁴⁰ Chapman's dedication to Phelips opens by proclaiming that it renewed 'the ancient spirit, and Honor of the Innes of Court' (p. 564). The virgin priestess to the goddess Honour, the deity presiding over the masque, was '*Eunomia*, or Lawe; since none should dare accesse to Honor, but by Vertue, of which Lawe being the rule, must needes be a chiefe' (p. 570). Plutus or Riches has been perfected by his union with Honour, and through the agency of Law 'made sightly, made ingenious, made liberall' (p. 571). Riches' transformation has taken place outside the court, and since Honour and the Law had ridden in triumph from Rolls House, agency seemingly is attributed to the Inns and their patron, Phelips. The civic magistrate acts as the guardian of both the court and the commonwealth, and, since none can enter the Temple of Honour except through the Law, the legal community is conflated with the aristocratic community of honour.[41]

James was very pleased with the masque – he 'made the maskers kisse his hand at parting, and gave them many thanckes' and 'strokes the master of the rolles [Phelips] and Dick Martin'.[42] The masque consistently magnifies royal authority: James is asked to see himself as 'our Britan *Phoebus*, whose bright skie/(Enlightened with a Christian Piety)/Is never subject to black Errors night' (p. 582). That said, the symbolism implies riches are conditional upon James reforming his court, so that honour does indeed determine riches, and embracing the role of Protestant leader in Europe and an expanded empire. Martin, Brooke and Hoskyns were among those lawyers in the recent 1610 parliament who argued that royal supply for the King's household should be withheld until the Commons' concerns over impositions, taxes on imported goods, and other matters were addressed.[43] Given supply was not granted in 1610, images of Riches and his gold mines on Virginian soil would not only have been welcome at court, but wittily offered James a more 'profitable' source of income than contentious taxes. Martin and his fellow investors in the Virginia Company used the political symbolism of the masque to their advantage to present a utopian image of the colony to the court during a period when its survival hung in the balance; a year later Martin would be called on by the Company to speak to the Bill for the relief of the Virginian colonists in the 1614 parliament. The masque, like the Inns of Court revels, performs a social contract between the monarch and the legal profession, in which the prince is guided by the counsel of learned men for the good of the commonwealth.[44] The subordination of Riches to Honour and the Law offers an image of a commonwealth founded on civic principles that is to be found both in Virginia and here, in Great Britain, at the Inns of Court, and embodied in gentlemen lawyers, such as Phelips.[45]

The gentleman lawyer was a social identity that imagined a role for Inns of Court men as effective social and political actors in the commonwealth, able to perform in the law courts as well as the revels, before the king in masques and entertainments and in the House of Commons. The confidence of the legal profession was crucial to the role taken by Martin,

Hoskyns and Brooke, and many of their fellow lawyer-MPs in James's first parliament. It was a corporate identity founded in a community of interests, a series of artificial bonds between individuals based in a civic ideology, the practice of the legal profession, patronage, and shared cultural capital manifested in manners and other forms of social distinction.[46] And it infused the rituals of association and sociable practices of the convivial societies held at the London taverns. The Inns were a milieu in which associations could be formed not only to prepare the individual for civic life and to perform effectively in public arenas, but also at a more intimate and familiar level – the fraternal obligations of friendship, of voluntarily seeking out the companionship of others, and sharing each others' society over time. Civic imperatives were not suspended within these familial associations, but rather reconfigured through a discourse of friendship.

'THE DUTIES OF SOCIETIES'

The early seventeenth-century convivial societies have their origins in the coterie culture fostered at the Inns of Court. The coterie or scribal community, with 'its controlled circulation' of texts, was a vital mechanism for 'creating new communities' within the broader civic commonwealth of the Inns of Court.[47] Legh drew attention to the Inns as a familiar environment in which friendships could be formed and flourish: where men by 'daily conference are knit by continuall acquaintance in such unity of minds and manners, as lightly never after is severed' (*Accedence*, p. 216). Hoskyns, Brooke and Holland commemorated Martin following his death in 1618 with an engraved portrait and memorial poem that remembered him as 'Orbis minoris corculum', the dear heart that gave life to their circle.[48] Familiar conversation among friends necessitates the suspension of the rigid ceremonialism of courtly protocols: Michel Montaigne said of his conversations with his close male friends that he reserved 'an unaccoustomed lybertye; making truce with cerimonyes . . . and such other troublesome ordynances of our courtesie . . . there every man demeaneth himselfe as he pleaseth, and entertaynteth what his thoughtes affect . . . The ende or skope of this commerce, is principally and simplye familiarity, conference and frequentation: the excercise of mindes, without other fruite.'[49] The coterie provided a model of how civil men could socialise together, and, in this aspect, anticipates the conversational and textual practices of the private society, formed so that a civil community could talk, exercise their minds and be familiar outside the jurisdiction of the state.

Humanist coteries at the Inns of Court from the early sixteenth century had drawn on classical formulations of masculine friendship to imagine social networks and cultivate a communal ethos. The Aristotelian model of friendship, which underpinned the corporate personality of the Inns as a secular body of civil and just men, was predicated on continuity between the state and friendship, in which friendship among virtuous men was the social foundation of the *polis*.[50] Yet, Renaissance readers were also aware of the tensions between politics and friendship that could be found even in that classic study of political friendship, Cicero's *De Amicitia*: his negative examples give the impression that friendship could only survive under tyrants, and in other politically divisive environments, if distanced from the political world.[51] Donne's early verse epistles fashion a language of friendship that is intensely interested in the intimate, affective dimensions of homosocial relationships at the expense of civic virtues. Hence the speaker is not so much Cicero's good and upright friend, a man 'free from all passion, caprice, and insolence' (*De Amicitia*, v. 19), as a conflicted, impassioned figure. Friendship in Donne's familiar epistles, rather than a Ciceronian refuge for virtue in dangerous times, is itself compromised. Self-interest and conflicting obligations expose personal vulnerabilities, and can even unman.

Donne was a key player in a scribal community, connected with Cambridge University and centred at Lincoln's Inn in the 1590s, which included Rowland Woodward and his younger brother Thomas, both at Lincoln's Inn; Brooke and his younger brother Samuel, a student at Cambridge University; a 'B. B.', probably Beaupré Bell, a Cambridge man who continued to Lincoln's Inn; Everard Guilpin, a Gray's Inn and Cambridge man; and an unknown 'I. L'. Donne addressed a sonnet to 'S. B.', Samuel Brooke, probably on the occasion of his matriculation at Trinity College, Cambridge in 1592. His primary point of contact with Samuel was through his friendship with his older brother, Christopher, with whom Donne shared chambers at Lincoln's Inn; it is this relationship that has enabled Donne to act as mentor to the younger brother.[52] Within this scribal community of Cambridge and Lincoln's Inn men, Donne frequently adopts the role of the older liberal mentor, quite self-consciously positioning himself at the point of transition between interrelated institutional environments, thus opening doors for his younger friends onto new milieux. His verse epistles are 'social texts', functioning not simply to bond like-minded individuals into a group, but to create social and conceptual spaces capable of sustaining and invigorating intellectual activity.[53] They often invoke the ideals of *amicitia* – the receipt of a familiar epistle from 'T. W.' (Thomas Woodward,

Donne's young friend and fellow poet), for example, is described as nourishment for the mind and soul, 'After this banquet my soul doth say grace,/ And praise thee for it' (lines 10–11).[54] And yet, the speaker is too greedy for his letter. Temperate friendship in Donne's familiar epistles must frequently give way to the contingencies of desire, transgressing the principle of moderation governing the civil expression of *amicitia*, which demanded mastery over the passions and the suppression of affective outbursts.[55]

The civilities of friendship in Donne's verse epistles addressed to 'T. W.', in particular, are frequently compromised by the speaker's failure to manage his passions. A civic masculine self is deformed through the passionate intensity of his friendships. In 'Haste thee harsh verse as fast as thy lame measure' (line 1), 'lame measure' is both a neat take on the conventional disclaimer of unworthiness and a physical and psychological condition experienced by the speaker. The friend is 'my pain and pleasure' (line 2); the paradox captures the precariousness of the speaker's identity when invested in the absent friend. The poem is the speaker's proxy: 'I have given thee, and yet thou art too weak,/Feet, and a reasoning soul and tongue to speak' (lines 3–4). The qualifying clause weakens the line of argument testifying to the insufficiency of the speaker's own tongue and 'reasoning soul'. In both this poem and 'Pregnant again with th' old twins hope, and fear', the speaker is importunate, jealous and anxious that his letters have been met with silence. 'Pregnant again' is a study in jealousy, and the speaker is rendered womanish, undone by his passions, only momentarily able to enjoy the letter which he so craved, since he is dogged by the fear that his love is not fully reciprocated. The anguished tone of these epistles recalls the female-voiced complaint of Ovid's *Heroides*, thereby attributing an impassioned intensity and sincerity to the affective realm of male friendship. The importuning voice adopted in these epistles uneasily admits vulnerability, desire and self-interest into the bonds of friendship. In his study of Donne's letters to his male friends, David Cunnington points out how love and necessity are entwined in the letters and the 'integrity of friendship' dependent on 'civil dishonesty'.[56] Donne was fashioning a poetic language of friendship that recognised need, affective impulses and self-interest, and therefore placed intense pressure on the language of civility. Friendship is experienced as an excess of intimacy that overwhelms the speaker with its difficult commitments. These familiar epistles describe a complex social world in which individuals must constantly negotiate between their own necessities and conflicting social obligations and ideals.

The image of the 'short roll of friends writ in my heart', opening the epistle to 'I. L.', tropes a particular mode of scribal publication, the intimate circulation of verse epistles amongst an exclusive group of friends. Many of the verse epistles imagine texts exchanged from hand to hand; the physical presence attributed to the poem transmutes distance into proximity. These 'social texts' open a conceptual space for imagining an intimate milieu and exploring the dimensions of an affective homosocial community bound by 'civil dishonesties', self-interest, liabilities and obligations. The tone of the epistle to 'Mr. I. L.' is once more insistent and demanding, though less erotically charged than Donne's epistles to the young poet, 'T. W.'. The epistle relies on the urbane opposition between the city and the country, the world of office and business and that of retirement and ease, and the realms of masculine friendship and the female domestic sphere. The speaker chastises 'I. L.' for forgetting his friends at the Inns in London, seduced from their company by 'the embrace of a loved wife' (line 8) and other country pleasures. Other absent friends are made present through the exchange of letters, and the speaker chides 'I. L.' for his forgetful silence, urging him to spend 'Some hours on us your friends' (line 12). The exchange of letters will re-integrate the errant friend, and describes forms of private conviviality which bind men together in the 'duties of societies' (line 7).

These societies are exclusively male and urbane, in that they belong to the city as opposed to the country, and are explicitly defined against the embraces of a 'loved wife'. That said, the mistress does not always threaten male friendships, and instead facilitates the exchanges between men. In the epistle to 'C. B.', 'Thy friend, whom thy deserts to thee enchain', the speaker has left his mistress and friend in London, and the verse epistle binds all three into a contract. The repetition of 'thy' in the first line compounds the identity of the speaker and the friend, a compact that expands to include the mistress: 'Strong is this love which ties our hearts in one' (line 7). The verse epistle may date from Donne's courtship of Ann More – the Brooke brothers' part in the secret marriage attested to the trust and staunch loyalty that bound these friends, given that both brothers suffered imprisonment and jeopardised their careers by offending two powerful men, Sir Thomas Egerton and Sir George More.

These verse epistles circulated alongside Donne's companion poems, 'The Storm' and 'The Calm', dedicated to Brooke, and occasioned by Donne's military service under the Earl of Essex on his disastrous 1597 expedition to the Azores. These companionate poems illustrate how communities at the Inns were traversed by complex sets of social relations and obligations to friends, allies, employers and court patrons. Donne like a number of his friends at the Inns shared Essex's martial ethos. Donne and Hoskyns had been close friends of Essex's trusted secretary, Henry Wotton, since their time at Oxford – Wotton, like Hoskyns, was a Wykehamist, attending Winchester and New College, Oxford. Wotton served alongside Donne on the Azores expedition, and their friendship, often finding expression in the exchange of verse epistles, continued throughout their various careers.[57] Donne was one of the gentleman volunteers who served under Essex at Cadiz the previous year in a 'conspicuous display' of their commitment to the militarism he represented. In contrast to Cadiz, the Azores expedition was a disaster, and signalled the disintegration of Essex's career. With his position at court undermined in his absence by his powerful enemies – the Lord Treasurer, William Cecil, Lord Burghley, and his son, the Secretary of State, Sir Robert Cecil – Essex faced Elizabeth's anger while his soldiers faced financial ruin.[58]

Brooke is addressed in both poems as the trusted friend who can empathise with his despair. Essex is conspicuously absent which means that the sense of disillusionment is not overtly attached to him. The storm issues from 'England' (line 9), a jealous mother reluctant to lose her sons to war. Elizabeth had held back from fully endorsing Essex's military campaigns, and was angered by the way he dispensed knighthoods on the field to secure his soldiers' loyalty.[59] In both poems, soldiers and ships are subject to overwhelming natural forces outside their control. Yet, in 'The Calm', while martial ardour is in tatters, 'The fighting place now seamen's rags supply;/And all the tackling is a frippery' (lines 15–16), the image of the men 'meteor-like, save that we move not, hover' (line 20), is suggestive of fire, energy trapped in stasis, thus not fully quelled. Their state is analogous to Bajazet imprisoned by the lowborn tyrant, Tamburlaine, or 'like slack-sinewed Samson, his hair off' (line 34), another man of war emasculated by a woman. These poems have been read as Donne's rejection of a military career;[60] however, they have much in common with the intense frustration and sense of injustice, coupled with a vigorous honour code, maintained by Essex and his followers in the aftermath of the failed Azores expedition.

This collection of familiar poems is implicated in the turbulence of the last decade of Elizabeth's reign. Bitter rivalries between Essex and Lord Burghley and his son throughout the 1590s changed the style of the Elizabethan court to one of intense factionalism.[61] Essex and his followers relied on a doctrine that combined aristocratic and civic virtues and valued the honourable bonds of blood and friendship. But it was coupled with a Tacitean perspective that viewed the court as riven by intrigue, jealousy and ambition; a world where private behaviour and words were continually and dangerously implicated in the public world of politics.[62] Such a perspective valued *amicitia* within a community of honour, while simultaneously recognising its ideals were severely compromised in the current political climate. The fraught and impassioned expression of friendship in Donne's importuning verse epistles provided a language for imagining the complex social world of the 1590s, with its frequently conflicting and dangerous obligations to friends, patrons and principles.

LAW SPORTS

The 1597–8 Middle Temple revels, like Donne's verse epistles, were part of a wider renegotiation of associational languages at the Inns in the 1590s. The grand revels, as we have seen, were integral to the Inns' corporate image as 'the foundation of a good common weale'. Yet, revelling also belonged to the communal traditions of learned play, and such play could take a great deal of licence with the profession of the law. The 1597–8 revels experimented with burlesque, travesty and satire, as well as introducing parodic, improvised forms, such as nonsense, that will come to characterise the literary productions of the early seventeenth-century convivial societies. Such play did not seek to dismantle the civic foundations of the Inns, but rather to open spaces for improvisation and creative manoeuvre within established discourses and ceremonial forms.[63]

The revels are utopian both in their projection of an artificial city-state and generically, in that, like More's *Utopia*, they belong to a humanist tradition of *lusus*, of learned play.[64] Revelling, which included dramatic performances, orations, and other shows and devices, as well as elements of riotous behaviour, was incorporated into the pedagogic environment of grammar schools, universities and the Inns of Court. The rationale for revelling was twofold. First, extempore versifying and orations and the performance of plays provided training in rhetoric, ensuring that students had the opportunity, in the words of William Gager, the Latin dramatist and fellow of Christ Church, 'to try their voices and confirm their memories, and to frame their speech and conform it to convenient action'. Secondly, early modern theories of recreation, moralistic and medical, justified such festivities on the basis that play was a necessary restorative, ensuring that the mind and body were fit for serious study.[65] John Brinsley in his *Ludus Literarius* (1612), which set out teaching methods for grammar schools, advocated recreation for students 'as a reward of their diligence, obedience and profiting'. Leisure and pedagogy, play and study are not opposite states but dialectically related through the notion of learned play. Brinsley suggests a more organised form of play before the school break when students should be given 'a Theam to make som verses of, *ex tempore*, in the highest fourmes . . . or if time permit, to cap verses', which 'will much helpe capacitie and audacitie, memorie, right pronuntiation, to furnish with store of authorities for Poetrie, and the like'. Capping verses is considered an adversarial skill, designed 'to provoke them the most'.[66] As this suggests, *lusus* did not designate passive forms of entertainment, but was intended to be provocative in that it tested and stimulated the intellect of its audience.

Play, in all its forms, had long functioned as an expression of *communitas*, temporarily suspending hierarchies in order to make space for communal rituals.[67] Learned play at the universities and Inns of Court incorporated performers and audience into a humanist community whose primary bonds of association were those of education and intellect. Revelling thus provided these educational institutions with a means of publicly displaying collective academic capital and making claims to a cultural hegemony.[68] It opens up a ritualised space of play in which the ceremonial structures of the institution are parodied. The revellers adopted an ironised relationship to the civic rituals that constituted the artificial city-state. These rituals gave the revellers the authority to perform, and yet through parody and improvisation they asserted their mastery over its forms. Through the law sports the gentleman lawyer signified that he could afford to hold civic forms at a distance, although never out of sight, while at play precisely because of his heavy investment in these ideals.

Hoskyns's 'Fustian Answer to a Tufftaffeta Speech' performed during the 1597–8 Middle Temple revels was famed for its virtuoso performance of extempore wit: Clove's performance of fustian in Ben Jonson's *Every Man Out of his Humour*, first acted in 1599, is a piece of nonsense that pays homage to Hoskyns's mock-oration.[69] Hoskyns gave his own directions for reading his mock-oration in his *Directions for Speech and Style*: 'if yo^w will reade ov^{er} that speech, yo^w shall find most of the figures of *Rhetorick* there, meaning neither harme, nor good, but as idle as yor selfe, when yo^w are most at leisure'.[70] Leisure implies that it is a cultivated mode of learned play, an expression of cultural capital available to those who can profitably afford to spend their time idly. This does not exclude a 'serious' pedagogic element, hence Hoskyns drew a number of his examples in *Directions* from this speech. His description of *symploce* or *complexio*, the figure whereby a sequence of sentences have the same beginning and ending, points out that 'yo^w have an example of it in fustian speech about Tobacco in derision of vayne Rhetoricke' (p. 127) – '*What was the cause of the Aventine revolt, and seditious deprecation for a Tribune? it is apparent it was not* Tabacco. *What moved me to address this Expostulation to your iniquity? it is plain it is not* Tabacco.'⁷¹ Again, his account of *antimetabole* or *commutation*, a sentence in which the word order is reversed, notes that it may be 'a sharpe & wittie figure' that pricks out 'a pithy distinction of meaning', yet used 'unseasonably, it is as ridiculous as it was in the fustian oration, horse mill, mill-horse &c: but let Discrecōn bee the greatest & generall figure of figures' (p. 129).

Hoskyns's extemporised performance turns improvisation into an art form, heightening the parodic effect of fustian to display his absolute mastery of rhetoric. Such virtuosity concentrates the ear on the aural, surface quality of language. It was provoked by speech delivered by the Prince's Orator, a part played by Charles Best, described as 'ridiculous and sensles' – this may be a verdict on its quality, or it may be that Best and Hoskyns engaged in a competitive display of nonsense.⁷² Best's oration is not included in the surviving text of the revels; however, Hoskyns does describe a rhetorical device it employed in his account of *paronomasia*, the 'pleasant touch of the same letter Sillable, or word, wyth a different meaning': 'it will best become the tuff taffatta Oratorˢ to skipp upp & downe the neighbourhood of these wordes, that differ more in sence, then in sound, tending nearer to meeter, then to matter, in whose mouth longe may that phraze psper, A man not onlie fitt for the gowne, but for the gunne, for the penne but for the pike, for the booke but for the blade' (p. 130). Nonsense is a travesty of rhetoric which privileges sound over sense, resulting in a radical dissociation of style and meaning. It is a virtuoso rhetorical performance that is essentially senseless, as Hoskyns points out in a nonsensical *symploce*: 'you look for some meaning, I partly believe it; but you find none, I do not greatly respect it' (*Prince*, p. 39). David Colclough writes of Hoskyns's *Directions* that by 'treating the effect of rhetoric apart from considerations of its relation to a logically proven truth . . . persuasion [is] based upon the skill of one's language use rather than the rightness of one's argument'.⁷³ In the case of the 'Fustian Answer', rhetorical play has the potential to undermine the profitable, humanist ends of *lusus*, given that it has no ethical purpose, and the quality of its wit is not necessarily dependent on moral judgement.

An ethical dimension persists in the sense that the oration purposefully derides 'vayne Rhetoricke'. Yet, this too is largely a question of style, with Hoskyns taking rhetorical advantage of his opponent, as he contends in the neat *antimetabole*, 'even so Orator Best, is not the best Orator' (*Prince*, p. 39). The meta-rhetorical function of the oration, demonstrated by Hoskyns's later use of it in his *Directions*, produces a different form of laughter that takes its pleasure from what Kenneth Burke has described as 'pure persuasion': 'the saying of something, not for an extra-verbal advantage to be got by the saying, but because of a satisfaction intrinsic to the saying', thereby delighting in the pure form of rhetoric at the deliberate expense of sense. The oration has a purpose that is paradoxically no purpose or looks 'like a sheer frustration of purpose' if judged by persuasive rhetoric.[74] There is, as Colclough argues, a willingness in Hoskyns's writings to engage with the 'destabilizing of the relations of language and moral judgements'. One consequence is the dissociation of virtue and rhetoric that underpinned civic oratory at the Inns to produce a pragmatic and flexible political rhetoric that could be utilised by the lawyer-orator in legal and political arenas.[75] The other is a willingness to take learned play into the realms of 'pure persuasion' in which intellectual liberty is prioritised over ethical restraints and decorum.

Such liberty extends to libertinism of these revels' chivalric burlesque. Like the earlier 1561–2 Inner Temple revels, the 1597–8 revels draw on Elizabethan neo-chivalric symbolism. Legh described Pallaphilos's court as renown for 'Armes, and martiall prowesse' – the first Champions' speech in the 1597–8 revels called for the revival of 'Love and Armes, their ancient profession' (*Prince*, p. 7).[76] The earlier Inner Temple revels presented a neo-Platonic allegory of self-government, in which Desire, after an education in the virtues, married Beauty under the command of Pallas/Elizabeth. By contrast, the later Middle Temple revels staged a contest between a neo-Platonic political discourse embodied in Elizabeth, the 'true Princess *d'Amours*' (p. 13) and an Ovidian eroticised state ruled by the usurper, the Prince of Love. The combat between the two champions is suspended for the duration of the revels, thus creating a playful utopian state energised by desire and a desiring masculine subject. The Cult of Elizabeth produced an eroticised political state in which the monarch's political power was determined by her ability to direct and contain the sexual ambitions of her male subjects.[77] The aptly named Knights of the Quiver in the Middle Temple revels take their oath on Ovid's *Ars Amatoria* and the revels' ideological resistance to a neo-Platonic cult of chastity is evident in its burlesque of chivalric forms, revelling instead in phallic pleasures and sexual errancy, expressed in bawdy linguistic punning.[78] The Prince's astronomer gives the prognostication that in his reign 'distressed Ladies may (if they will) obtain such relief and bounty in the Court from the Prince and his Knights, that although they come hither empty, they may go out full of content' (p. 34). Chivalric burlesque produces a sexual libertinism, based in older notions of aristocratic licence, that subverts modes of civil behaviour and revives a playful language of gentlemanly freedom from social constraints.[79] Such freedoms are articulated within a ritualised space of play to produce a liberty of wit that resists the restraints of decorum.

The provocative libertinism of these revels is accompanied by a satiric urbanity that departs from the civilities of earlier revels.[80] If the artificial state created during the revels symbolised the conjunction of *civitas* and *urbanitas*, and locates the foundations of liberty, law and manners in the idealised city, then the satiric urbanity of the Middle Temple revels suggests the ways in which this civic discourse of *urbanitas* was reconfigured in the late 1590s. The 1597–8 revels expand and problematise the early modern vocabulary of *urbanitas* by incorporating its Ciceronian anti-type, the *urbanissimus homo*, a figure of hyper-urbanity symbolising the decline of republican virtue and civic strength. Roman hyper-urbanity was satirised in over-refined manners, effeminate dress, and affected speech.[81] The late Elizabethan gallant, a newly emergent 'urban stereotype of gentlemanly behaviour', was similarly identifiable by the way that he over-dressed his speech, as well as himself.[82] The Middle Temple revels fashioned a parodic and hyper-urbane stereotype of the Inns of Court gallant. So, for example, non-attendance at the commons is turned into an affectation: Articles 11 and 12 specify that *'all Knights of this Order be able to speak ill of Innes-a-Court-Commons'* and *'That no Knight meeting another of this Order at the Ordinary, shall ask him this question, Are you in Commons sir?'*. Article 15 stipulated *'That riding in the street after the new French fashion, he salute all his Friends with an affected Cringe; and being asked where he dined, he must not say at the Tavern or the Ordinary, but at the Miter, the Mearmaid, or the Kings-head in old Fish-street'* (p. 44). Such effete behaviour was intended to provoke ridicule, thus clarifying the proper personage of the gentleman lawyer through his anti-type – the gallant. Yet, it also suggests a complex understanding of civility, comparable to the more pragmatic and playful understanding of rhetoric displayed in Hoskyns's 'Fustian Answer' and the libertine forms of chivalric burlesque. Satiric urbanity is predicated on the dissociation of gentle manners and inner virtue, and both disdains and is fascinated by the inherent theatricality of manners.

The companion on the street in Donne's 'Satire 1' bears more than a passing resemblance to the hyper-urbane theatricality of the Knights of the Quiver. Like the Middle Temple revels, Donne uses satire to manage and negotiate social space, in particular, the transition from the study to the street, from the Inns of Court to the city.[83] The civic foundations of the Inns are destabilised in 'Satire 1' through this errant movement, which opens the older city-state to the demands of the new metropolis. The intellectual capital of the gentleman lawyer is displayed in the speaker's books – works of theology, Aristotle, and 'jolly statesmen, which teach how to tie/The sinews of a city's mystic body' (lines 7–8) – and they signify his ability, in the words of Quintilian, to 'play his part as a citizen . . . [to] guide cities by his counsel, give them a firm basis by his laws, and put them right by his judgements'.[84] These books are of no use to him on the streets where he must use a different set of co-ordinates. Loosely basing his satire on one of Horace's (1.ix), Donne significantly changes his source: whereas Horace's speaker is pursued along the streets by an unwelcome buffoon, Donne's speaker reluctantly binds himself to his inconstant friend, the 'fondling motley humorist' (line 1). 'Satire 1' is a study of friendship in which older ideals of virtuous civic-minded friendship are unfixed. Donne incorporates a lengthy prelude to the main action in which the speaker attempts to secure the agreement of his companion to a set of conditions before he leaves the certainty of his study, to 'First swear by thy best love in earnest / (If thou which lov'st all, canst love any best)/Thou wilt not leave me in the middle street' (lines 13–15). To be left on the street without a friend is to be deprived of social identity, since identity is constituted through such social contracts. Outside the study and on the streets, traditional bonds of association have no purchase; instead the primary form of social currency is dress. The speaker chastises his perspicuous friend who in reading these signs 'Dost search, and like a needy broker prize/The silk, and gold he wears, and to that rate/ So high or low, dost raise thy formal hat' (lines 30–2). Such signs are the basis for social distinction and exchange on the street, 'As though all thy companions should make thee/Jointures, and marry thy dear company' (lines 35–6).

Once on the street, the speaker is subjected to his friend's fashionable mode of walking. 'Promenade' came into usage in the mid to late sixteenth century to signify movement through the streets, either on foot or horseback, for amusement or display.[85] Everard Guilpin's close imitation of Donne's satire in the fifth satire of his *Skialetheia* (1598) imagined 'an idle City-walke' as a descent into a hellish babel, 'that hotch-potch of so many noyses' on the 'peopled streets', in which traditional signs of discrimination have no purchase.[86] Social distinctions are observed on Donne's streets, however: since they are attached to leisure and fashion they too take on a fundamental mobility symbolised by the erratic, bobbing street dance of the 'motley humourist'. The London street was part of the topography of the early modern metropolis. 'Satire 1' and the Middle Temple revels transform a specific geographical area of London around the Inns – the Strand, Fleet Street, and other streets leading to areas where the social élite congregated, such as St Paul's, or were flanked by fashionable shops and taverns – into a complex satiric *topos*. No longer a neutral space between buildings or a route through the city, the streets in the new metropolis are busy and peopled, and increasingly demarcated as a space for public displays of civility and a focus for anxieties generated by urban expansion.[87] The populous streets of London were imagined as a place where forms of social distinction were simultaneously exaggerated and placed in question, hence the satire on a type of urban chic in the 1597–8 revels, the adoption of particular styles of riding, greeting, dress, and preferred places of eating and entertainment in London. These forms of privileged knowledge functioned in the formation of urban and urbane communities, enabling individuals to identify themselves with others who shared these social codes and other signs of belonging, which in turn gained their value through restriction within the group.[88]

One of the most remarkable features of Donne's 'Satire 1' is its conclusion. Whereas Horace's speaker finally rids himself of his parasite, Donne's 'motley humourist' returns to his friend in his chambers at the Inns bruised and battered from his encounters and 'constantly a while must keep his bed' (line 112). Guilpin's version has the speaker reject his fickle companion for the constancy of his study, symbolising a profitable, virtuous world removed from the unprofitable follies of the streets; the satire concludes with the call to the commons thus reasserting the civic imperatives of *communitas*. By contrast, friendship in Donne's 'Satire 1' no longer maintains such civic certainties, and instead turns to a playful, ironic constancy – that of the friend who is only constant when physically incapacitated – which is able to tolerate if not quite accommodate personal betrayals on the street. From his satire we get the impression of a complex society in which it is frequently difficult to manage social obligations. The second half of the sixteenth century sees the transition from the concept of London as a 'capital', which resides in a 'centered, civic identity', in Vanessa Harding's words, to that of the 'polyfocal' and expansive metropolis, represented by its populous streets. Donne's 'Satire 1' participates in the invention of 'a new metropolitan culture', offering 'a way of making sense of the "burgeoning multitude of persons and behaviours that characterized early modern London"'.[89] The new metropolis placed pressure on the civic ideologies and culture of civility constituting the social make-up of the gentleman lawyer; hence Donne's complex, playful and conflicted poetic language of friendship and the theatricalised and satiric urbanity of the Middle Temple revels. Satire, parody and other modes of ritualised play offered a means of managing, renegotiating and improvising social identities and forms of *communitas* within complex and conflicted environments.[90]

CLUBBING AND COMMONING

Commoning, which has its ceremonial expression in acts of communing and eating together in the commons, becomes combative during the revels when group identity is formed, as Helen Ostovich notes, 'by provoking and indulging the aggressiveness of a particularly assertive audience'.[91] It is possible to discern the origins of the 'club', which by the mid-seventeenth century had become a relatively common term to describe a private society, in this culture of commoning at the Inns of Court and universities. This coinage is perhaps surprising since earlier meanings have little to do with sociability, and instead 'club' denoted a weapon or action of physical violence. The first recorded use of the term 'clubbing' can be found in a 1582 description of revelling recorded by Richard Madox:

we went a clubbying owt of al howses in the town, some, abowt 400, with drome, bagpipe and other melody... at Unyversytie College Latware of St. Johns welcomed us in verse with a *fyne* oration in the name of kyng Aulrede, crown*d* us with 2 fayr garlands and offered the third but I answering his oration gave hym th*e* third and crowned hym poet lawreat. So marched we up to Carfox where Sir Abbots of Bayly Colledg had an oration in prose co*mending* us for taking the savage who did ther an*swer* and yelded his hollyn club being with his... al in yvy.[92]

Clubbing appears to derive from the ceremonial holly or ivy club ceremoniously passed among the revellers. While Madox describes very orderly proceedings, such revelling could become unmannerly, and clubbing take on more violent associations, as when Oxford university students 'armed with swords and bucklers and clubs' went about the town making rough music and 'misusinge both men and women with opprobryous words'.[93] Communal lawlessness when revelling may derive from the Greek *komos*, 'the ritual drunken riot at the end of the *symposion*, performed in public' to demonstrate the drinking group's privileged relationship to the law.[94] The satiric thrust of the revels may well have functioned in a similar fashion to license the lawyers. The way the club links ritualised aggression with associational activity suggests that the emergence of the early seventeenth-century clubs, and the way that they fashioned themselves as associations, was intimately related to this culture of commoning.

Clubbing and commoning during the revels found their literary expression in satire. Those authors who chose to print volumes of satires in the late 1590s – Guilpin, Davies and John Marston – were Inns of Court men closely connected to the group gathered around Martin, Hoskyns and Donne at the Middle Temple and Lincoln's Inn. The scribal communities associated with these men were also busy circulating satires, epigrams, and libels. Satirists in this period frequently argued that satire was a privileged space for the excercise of *licentia*, free speaking: John Heath punned on the association between satire, liberty and the libertine, the freed slave, when he sent his 'free borne' satirical epigrams into the world.[95] When these authors began to define the generic parameters of satire for their generation, they did so in the context of an emergent culture of libelling. Libels and railing verses were used tactically in the skirmishes between Sir Robert Cecil and Essex in the 1590s, reaching a particular pitch in 1599 during Essex's ill-fated Irish campaign when libels were deployed to discredit Essex in his absence. When Essex was imprisoned on his return from Ireland in September, his followers responded with libels targeting his enemies at court, particularly Cecil and Raleigh.[96] Libellous politics, as we shall see in the following chapter, infused the *poetomachia* waged on stage and in pamphlets at the turn of the century: Essex complained of libellers in a letter of 12 May 1600 that 'Shortly they shall play me in what forms they list upon the stage.'[97] And this period, from 1598 to around 1603, was also a time when many of the Middle Temple wits, and their friends at other Inns, were engaged in bouts of flyting whose main target was Davies. All these verses, plays and pamphlets have in common a satiric style that has made space for often vicious personal invective alongside structures for admonition. Flyting is highly sociable: the exchange of verses on a common theme gives the appearance of a cohesive group of like-minded individuals. Yet, in contrast to the civic utopianism of *amicitia*, flyting imagines a conflicted, fraught social space.

It is not clear what caused the quarrel between Davies and Martin that climaxed so dramatically when Davies entered the Great Hall of the Middle Temple on 9 February 1598, soon after the revels, and struck Martin over the head with a bastinado until it broke. Davies was expelled, but restored in 1601 through the intervention of Sir Thomas Egerton, the Lord Keeper. Libelling seems to have been a common practice at the revels.[98] Nonetheless, Rudyerd's account of the 1597–8 revels suggests a well-orchestrated series of personal attacks on Milochius or Milorsius Stradilax, the name thought to have been taken by Davies.[99] Audiences left when he stood to deliver his speech, he gave a 'greate feaste; and insteade of grace after it, there was a libel set up against him in al famous places of the city, as Queenhive, Newgate, the Stocks' Pillory, P[issin]g Conduct (sic)', and insults continued throughout the revels. Rudyerd characterised Stradilax as a buffoon 'puft up with a poore-witted ambition', and mocked his sycophancy towards Essex that he 'would needs be cald "Exophilus", in imitation of the great Earle of the tyme' (p. 16).[100] Copies of Hoskyns's mock-oration place Raleigh at these revels, explaining in the headnote that Hoskyns 'Refused to answer at extempore' until 'importuned by ye Prince & Sr Walter Raleigh'.[101] If so, then these attacks may have been partly fuelled by factional infighting between Raleigh and Essex spilling over into the Inns. These men are known to have engaged in flyting, verbal duelling as part of their hostilities.[102] Soon after the revels, Davies sought the patronage of Cecil, Essex's enemy.

Davies has been identified with 'Mathon' satirised in a series of epigrams attributed to Rudyerd. Manningham recorded in his diary a piece of 'wit' circulating at the Middle Temple as late as 1603, originating from either Rudyerd or Sir Thomas Overbury: 'John Davys goes wadling with his arse out behinde as though he were about to make every one he meetes a wall to pisse against'.[103] Like the other 'embodied' satires mocking Davies's ugly face and clumsy gait, this libellous stigmatising of Davies's body speaks to the personalisation of politics in the 'increasingly polarised political world of the 1590s', which brought questions relating to the parameters of civil behaviour into sharp, satiric focus.[104] The flyting and libelling campaigns that engaged the Inns of Court wits from the 1590s opened a rhetorical space for ritualised violence precariously balanced between righteous satiric anger and scurrilous abuse.

Davies had jovially addressed the London wits in his *Epigrams* (1598), telling his book to 'Fall in betweene their hands that love and praise thee,/And be to them a laughter and a jest'.[105] The opening satire of Guilpin's *Skialetheia* (1598) lamented that the wits had turned their sharp satires on their own instigating a violent civil war:

> So *Englands* wits (now mounted the full height,)
> Having confounded monstrous barbarismes,
> Puft up by conquest, with selfe-wounding spight,
> Engrave themselves in civill warres *Abismes*,
> Seeking by all meanes to destroy each other,
> The unhappy children of so deere a mother.
>
> (sig. A3r–v)

Guilpin did not hestitate to enter the fray, and incorporated a satire on '*Matho*' and the lawyer, Silvio, who 'hunting for the fame/Of a wise man, studies Phylosophie' (sig. A4r).[106] Aspects of the Davies satires appear in

'Coscus' of Donne's 'Satire 2', 'Whom time . . ./Hath made a lawyer, which was (alas) of late/But scarce a poet' (lines 41, 43–4). Whether or not Davies was Donne's target, it is a study of anger and admonition within satire, which raises similar issues to those behind this bout of flyting. 'Satire 2' is an exercise in anger: although the speaker claims he is able to use discrimination in the choice of who he hates, hence only Coscus 'breeds my just offence', his anger is at such a pitch it gives the impression that he does, in fact, hate 'Perfectly all this town' (line 2) and hate all 'Equally' (line 107). Satire was available as a mode for expressing just anger on similar principles to the rhetorical equation between free speech and angry admonition.[107] That said, even within satire, the use of anger raises questions about decorum, and where just anger stops and abuse starts.

Hoskyns used the bastinado incident in his *Directions* to explain the rhetorical figure *contentio*:

shall a soldier for a blowe wth his hand given in warr to a captaine bee disgraced, & shall a lawyer for the bastinadoe given in a hall of court to his companion be advanced? we that pfesse lawes maintain outrage? & they that breake all lawes, yet in this observe civillity? where yo^w may observe every word in the latter sentence aggravated by opposicōn to eu^{er}ie word in the former. Another, did the most innocent, vouchsafe it as a pte of his glory to pray for his enemyes, and shall we the most sinfull esteeme it a blott to our reputacōn to be unrevenged on o^r brethren . . .

The bastinado incident transgressed codes of civil behaviour and civic government at the Inns, illustrating the dangers to the commonwealth when structures of preferment operate without reference to the public good. *Contentio* (to 'aggravate') is used to increase the offensiveness of the abuses the speaker discovers. This form of angry admonition is itself 'compared by contrary' with the servility of speech typifying a system 'that preffers wealthy Ignorance before chargeable study p^{re}ferrs contempt before hono^r' (*Directions*, pp. 135–6). Hoskyns draws on honour codes informing the notion of flyting as a verbal duel. Satires and libels were licensed within this culture as the rhetorical equivalent of physical aggression, and so could be employed to defend personal honour. Yet, it was also recognised that libelling compromised civil behaviour.[108] Hoskyns's description of *contentio* suggests limits to admonition: revenge should be avoided because it partakes of the passions and a corrupting personal politics rather than the observance of civility and the law. There is a similar danger that the incivility of flyting deforms the character of those seeking legitimate redress for injustice. Like Donne's study of anger in 'Satire 2', Hoskyns's description of *contentio* suggests the complex consideration of the parameters of conduct, both personal and civic, within the commonwealth that was provoked by, and fed into the fractious libellous politics of the late 1590s.

The Inns of Court had a vital role to play in the processes of civil acculturation so central to our understanding of the history of the private society. They were sites for the production and dissemination of ideologies of association from the political ideals of friendship to the civic utopianism purveyed in the revels. The associational culture of revelling and commoning at the Inns in the late sixteenth century continued to rely on the gentleman lawyer. Even so, the conjunction of chivalric burlesque and satiric urbanity in the Middle Temple revels illustrates the pressures within this communal identity, disclosing tensions between older masculine codes of honour and a culture of civility. The origins of clubbing in the revels give an alternative history of the private society in which civil acculturation exists in a fraught relationship with a masculine sociability that aggressively asserted independence, and favoured the forms of satire and libel. And it also draws attention to the traditions of learned play with its flexible social self and ritualised space of play. Through parody, satire and burlesque, the wits negotiated the plurality of the new metropolis, with its conflicted ideologies and errant trajectories, and improvised social identities and sociable practices.[109]

CHAPTER TWO

Ben Jonson, the lawyers and the wits

John Aubrey relates the story that, when Jonson was working for his bricklayer step-father 'on the garden-wall of Lincoln's Inne next to Chancerylane . . . a bencher, walking thro' and hearing him, discoursing with him, and finding him to have a witt extraordinary, gave him some exhibition to maintain him at Trinity College in Cambridge'.[1] Elements of this story, such as the bencher sending Jonson to Cambridge, are probably fabrication; nonetheless the vignette dramatises Jonson's familiarity and sense of intellectual companionship with this learned commonwealth. It is appropriate Jonson helped to maintain the physical fabric of the Inns given that his early plays, *Every Man Out of His Humour* and *Poetaster*, had their own part to play in the construction of the Inns as the ideal *polis*. Jonson found the ideal counterpart for the poet-dramatist in the lawyer-orator: he that 'can feign a commonwealth (which is the poet) can govern it with counsels, strengthen it with laws, correct it with judgements, inform it with religion and morals'.[2] This resoundingly civic paradigm was formulated in a period when Jonson was producing plays that spoke to the interests of the Inns of Court. The Inns' legal culture influenced his dramatic style. His early experiments with comical satire gave the public stage a vital role to play in the commonwealth by turning the theatre into a law court.

From his early years in London in the 1590s well into his middle age, Jonson shared the society of many of the Middle Temple and Lincoln's Inn men encountered in the previous chapter – Hoskyns, Martin, Donne, and Brooke. His friendships with these men encompassed legal aid, textual exchanges, and literary play.[3] And he shared wider concerns with these lawyer-wits: his early plays, *Every Man Out of His Humour* and *Poetaster*, defend frank speaking within the commonwealth, entering into the debates over the ethics of laughter that energised flyting at the Inns and the libellous politics of the 1590s. Jonson's revival of a humanist tradition of learned play on the public stage was stimulated not simply by an Inns of Court culture of revelling, but, more fundamentally, by the professional poet-dramatist's recognition of the improvisational and theatrical possibilities of ludic literary forms. Learned play enabled Jonson to legitimate his place, alongside Inns of Court coteries, in an increasingly diverse and theatricalised metropolitan culture.

'TO JUDGE WITH DISTINCTION'

The Jonson we know well is the court dramatist and King's poet; the significance of his association with the Inns of Court is less familiar. Tom Cain has made a strong case for viewing Jonson's early plays, especially his *Poetaster*, in terms of his associations with the 'radical circle' at the Middle Temple that included Martin, Hoskyns, Brooke and Rudyerd.[4] This was a formative period in Jonson's professional career, when he established his reputation in the public theatre. The gentleman lawyer, a man of independent judgement, skilled in the laws of the realm, and therefore well qualified to provide free and frank counsel, was an attractive figure as it enabled the aspiring dramatist to establish his own professional credibility. He was drawn to comical satire because it permitted him to extend the civic attributes of the lawyer-orator to the dramatist.

Every Man Out of His Humour, first acted in 1599, and *Poetaster*, performed late 1601, are the two early plays in which Jonson most clearly announces his indebtedness to the lawyers and the Inns of Court. The dedication of *Every Man Out* to the Inns in the 1616 folio formalised the play's well-recorded borrowings from the 1597–8 Middle Temple revels.[5] It is a key play in fashioning the Jonsonian ability 'to judge with distinction', in the words of the 'Advertisement' to the 1600 quarto. The epistle discovers the ideal judging spectator in the gentleman lawyer. When Jonson addressed the Inns as 'the Noblest Nurseries of Humanity, and Liberty, in the Kingdom', he was not simply re-stating the well-worn adage eulogising the Inns as nurseries of the nobility. Instead, he acknowledged the transformations the Inns had undergone in the course of the sixteenth century, turning this legal community into the paradigm of the learned commonwealth. Nobility does not denote the social composition of the Inns – the older notion that those admitted must be gentlemen of at least three descents – but has become modal, transmuted meritocratically into 'Humanity, and Liberty'. These gentlemen, 'being born the judges of these studies', are natural men of judgement by virtue of the humanist study of liberal arts at the Inns. Liberty, itself, is given a Roman refinement: 'when the gown and cap is off and the Lord of Liberty reigns, then to take it in your hands perhaps may make some bencher, tincted with humanity, read and not repent him'. Liberty during the revels is not a time of carnivalesque licence, but the period when liberally educated and urbane lawyers can read profitably at their leisure.[6] Jonson's equation between the law, liberty and humanity comes from the connection classical humanism made between liberty, civility and a civic society. Liberty is the condition of the civic society; only through the promotion of public good, rather than private interest, could servitude be avoided and the strength of the commonwealth ensured.[7]

The satiric *licentia* of Jonson's Asper has similarly civic foundations: 'He is of an ingenious and free spirit, eager and constant in reproof, without fear controlling the world's abuses; one in whom no servile hope of gain or frosty apprehension of danger can make to be a parasite either to time, place, or opinion' (*Characters*, lines 1–5). The satirist's frank speaking secures the health of the commonwealth because it rejects the material riches and comforts accompanying service to kings, since they enslave the mind and the tongue.[8] Asper in the Induction makes a lawyer's address to the audience under the aspect of Minerva, the Inns' symbol of their role as counsellors to the Queen. Mitis warns the 'days are dangerous, full of exception' (*Induction*, line 122) – a law term referring to objections used by a defendant to limit or bar a legal action by an accuser, in this context, the limits that can be placed on satire. Asper responds:

> But why enforce I this? As fainting? No.
> If any here chance to behold himself,
> Let him not dare to challenge me of wrong,
> For, if he shame to have his follies known,
> First he should shame to act 'em.
> (lines 138–42)

This is the classic satirist's defence. Yet the legalistic terminology – enforce, fainting or feigned action, challenge – transfers the lawyer's adversarial oratorical skills to the satirist. Just as the lawyer sets out the grounds for the accusation in court, marks his man, proves by argument, and establishes his case by testimony, so too the satirist makes and proves his case before the audience, the 'judicious friends' of *Every Man Out* (line 54). The lawyer-orator similarly lies behind the case Jonson makes in his *Discoveries* for an adversarial eloquence, proved in the heat of the public forum: 'it is one thing to be eloquent in the schools or in the hall, another at the bar or in the pulpit. There is a difference between mooting and pleading; between fencing and fighting. To make arguments in my study and confute them is easy, where I answer myself, not an adversary' (lines 431–6).

The public theatre was Jonson's analogue to the classical forum; a place where the orator-dramatist proved his eloquence and his strength of judgement, while testing the spectator's own ability to 'judge with distinction'. These civil and judicious spectators have their antitype in the Jonsonian audience from hell, derided in *The Case is Alter'd*, that 'confus'd mixture of judgement, powr'd out in the throng', in which 'the rankest stinkard of them all, will take upon him as peremptory, as if he had writ himselfe *in artibus magister*'.[9] Thomas Dekker in his *Satiromastix* was alert to – and suspicious of – the equation Jonson was making between the public theatre and the law court in this period, and took the closing arraignment in *Poetaster* to be emblematic of the play as a whole: '*Horace* hal'd his *Poetasters* to the Barre'.[10] The sixteenth century, Paul Raffield argues, witnessed the emergence of 'a poetics of the English law'; a dialogue between poetry and law, in which the lawyer became actor, author and critic. It was a dialogue made possible precisely by study of the liberal arts alongside professional legal training that Jonson so admired at the Inns. Sir Philip Sidney employed the figure of the barrister to amplify the craft of the poet: 'it is not rhyming and versing that maketh a poet (no more than a long gown maketh an advocate, who, though he pleaded in armour, should be an advocate and no soldier;) but it is feigning notable images of virtues, vices, or what else, with that delightful teaching, which must be the right describing note to know a poet by'.[11] The aptness of the figure lies in the rhetorical skills, the arts of persuasion which the poet and barrister share.

A key element in the persuasive armoury of the comical satirist was laughter. Asper leaves the audience in the Induction with the hope that the ultimate effect of his comical satire will be 'to make the circles of your eyes / Flow with distillèd laughter' (*Every Man Out*, lines 214–15). Renaissance theorists equated laughter with the energies of satire: laughter was primarily understood as an expression of scorn for the ridiculous.[12] Jonson's 'distillèd laughter' is a little more discriminating, suggesting the ethical refinement of Sidney's advice 'that all the end of the comical part be not upon such scornful matters as stir laughter only, but, mixed with it, that delightful teaching which is the end of poesy'.[13] The complexity of Jonson's laughter owes much to the extensive discussion of the forensic uses of laughter in Cicero and Quintilian. Cicero famously wrote of laughter's rhetorical advantages in the forum:

it clearly becomes an orator to raise laughter, and this on various grounds; for instance, merriment naturally wins goodwill for its author; and everyone admires acuteness ... and it shatters or obstructs or makes light of an opponent, or alarms or repulses him; and it shows the orator himself to be a man of finish, accomplishment [*urbanum*] and taste; and, best of all, it relieves dullness and tones down austerity, and, by a jest or a laugh, often dispels distasteful suggestions not easily weakened by reasonings.[14]

Jonsonian laughter, theorised in the Induction to *Every Man Out*, seeks to secure the goodwill of the audience, to lighten the austerity of the railing satirist's condemnation of the follies of the times, and, above all, to demonstrate the *urbanum* of the dramatist.

Every Man Out was performed at the height of the bitter factionalism of the late 1590s, when '*Englands* wits', as Guilpin lamented in 1598, were engaged in 'civill warres *Abismes*'. The libellous politics of these years, as we have seen in the previous chapter, raised questions about the parameters of speech and conduct within the commonwealth. Jonson developed his comical satires within this environment; like his friends and fellow satirists at the Inns of Court, he grappled with the vexed question of the ethics of laughter. The fundamental lack of consensus over this issue defines discussions of laughter, particularly the laughter of ridicule, from the ancients well into the seventeenth century, and came to the fore during the libelling campaigns of the 1590s.[15] Cicero and Quintilian may have offered clear advice on ethical restraints on laughter, but Quintilian was forced to admit there were times when even Cicero transgressed the decorum he was so noted for. Cicero's *Pro Caelio*, widely admired by the ancients for its dramatic use of comic forms, is an instructive text in this context because it expands the potential of satire through the laughter of ridicule, thus providing a classical precedent for the comic satirist, while crystallising the ethical dilemma involved in using ridicule for political or strategic ends.[16] Cicero's transformation of the law court into a comic theatre during the trial of his friend and former pupil, Caelius, was highly tactical: he was the closing speaker on the last day of the trial – also the first day of the holidays, the *Ludi Megalenses* – moreover, the accusation came from Cicero's own personal enemy, Clodius.[17] Thus implicated in the case he was defending, Cicero enlisted the devices of comic theatre to persuade the jury of the lawyer-dramatist's detachment – this section takes the form of an extended prosographia in which he speaks through historical personages and characters drawn from Terence. He does so for the purposes of satire, to accuse Clodia, the sister of his enemy, Clodius, of sexual transgressions that strategically discredit through the laughter of ridicule, rather than forensic reason, her own accusations against Caelius.

The pivotal issue in this case – and in discussions of libel and satire in the 1590s – was the distinction between accusation and abuse. Cicero argued there were no criminal charges brought against Caelius, only 'abuse and slander': 'abuse is one thing, accusation is another. Accusation requires ground for a charge, to define a fact, to mark a man, to prove by argument, to establish by testimony. The only object of slander, on the other hand, is to insult' (iii.6). Well and good, but Cicero also confounds this distinction – and his own disinterestedness – through ridicule: 'what other course is open to us who are his counsel than to refute those who attack him? And that I should do with all the more vehemence, were I not hindered by my personal enmity to that woman's husband – I meant to say brother; I always make that slip' (xiii.32). Is Cicero accusing Clodia with good grounds, or is he engaging in scurrilous personal abuse, hence the incest joke? Cicero used laughter at points where his case was the weakest, thereby relaxing the reason of the jury, and diverting attention from the facts. Laughter, in this instance, may have been brilliantly strategic, but was it ethical?

Jonson recognised this moral ambivalence in his characterisation of Cicero in *Catiline* (1611); although a virtuous man, he is an 'ambitious orator', with the suggestion that he is not above using libels against his enemies.[18] Jonson draws on *Pro Caelio* at the end of a speech in which Cicero does not make his case through argument from firm evidence, but instead uses personal invective against Catiline, accusing him of debauchery and alleging that he was 'Brought up in's sister's prostitution' (4.2.64).[19] As Caesar notes, 'You declaim/Against his manners, and corrupt your own' (lines 74–5), while Catiline recognises he has been condemned by Cicero's 'prodigious rhetoric' (line 406), not evidence: 'I hope/This Senate is more grave than to give credit/Rashly to all he vomits 'gainst a man' (lines 406–8). Yet, Catiline is guilty of conspiracy, and Cicero, for all his faults, is a virtuous man; the play suggests that the ends may well justify the means in such times.

Quintilian admitted many believed Cicero had 'no discrimination' in the forensic use of laughter, yet his reputation was secured by his 'really remarkable quality of urbanity' (*Institutio Oratoria*, vi.3.2–3). Jonson similarly seeks to resolve the difficulties posed by the laughter of ridicule in the public forum by making urbane wit key to the persona of the ethical satirist in his comical satires. As Katharine Maus points out, Jonson's satirists are not the embittered malcontents of his fellow dramatists, such as Marston, but 'are wise and virtuous men: wise and virtuous as the Roman moralists understand those terms'.[20] Cicero and Quintilian permitted the orator to engage in invective if it was delivered with an urbane wit and observed decorum, and if he did not deform himself through violent raillery. Asper, the sharp, bitter satirist of *Every Man Out*, is counselled by Cordatus (prudent and wise) and Mitis (mild and mitigating) to temper the violence of his satiric strain, to make it corrective rather than destructive. The Grex have been described as the 'stage equivalent of a marginal gloss';[21] a parallel can also usefully be drawn with the Renaissance dialogue in which meaning resides in the dialogic relationship between the interlocutors. Cordatus and Mitis mitigate Asper's onstage behaviour, counselling propriety in language and gesture. His distracted behaviour, 'Ha? What? What is 't?' (line 84) under the gentle guidance of his friends finally becomes more civil, culminating in the promise as he leaves the stage that his satire will occasion only refined laughter.

Every Man Out is highly attuned to the satiric and dramatic potential of the distinction made by Cicero and Quintilian between *urbanitas* and the decadent and hyper-urbane *urbanissimus homo*.[22] Jonson launched his invective against the hyper-urbane theatre-going gallant in one of his earliest plays, *The Case is Alter'd*, and returned to this theme in *Every Man Out*. The gallant contorts his facial features, 'his wried looks' (line 180) signify his deformed and deforming judgement.[23] It is an attribute the Jonsonian gallant shares with the Roman *scurra*, the professional parasite who wormed his way into the banquet, and abused the host's hospitality through his malicious jests. The orator's invective was sharply distinguished from the *scurra* through the ethics of moderation: 'Regard then to occasions, control and restraint of our actual raillery, and economy in bon-mots, will distinguish an orator from a buffoon [*scurra*],' Cicero advised, 'as also will the fact that we people speak with good reason, not just to be thought funny, but to gain some benefit' (*De Oratore*, ii.60.247). Carlo Buffone's character in *Every Man Out* is explicitly modelled on the Roman *scurra*: he is a 'public, scurrilous, and profane jester' and 'good feast-hound or banquet-beagle' (*Characters*, lines 23, 25).[24]

When setting out the laws for the new genre of comical satire, the laughter of ridicule provided Jonson with a vocabulary that could equate satire's invective with frank speaking, and set its civic liberties against the deformed wit of the gallant and the licentious wit of the *scurra*. Satire's frank speaking was necessary to ensure the health of the commonwealth. Hence, as we have seen, Erasmus defended his *Praise of Folly* and satiric jesting in general by equating *parrhesia* with 'bitter medicines'.[25] Just as Asper's anger must be moderated by civility, so too mild Mitis needs the critical edge of Asper's satiric wit, or else he will prove 'too timorous and full of doubt' (*Induction*, line 186). Jonson's next play, *Poetaster*, anachronistically brings together Ovid, Horace and Virgil to 'feign a commonwealth', as he says in his *Discoveries*, in which the poet-dramatist takes on the role of magistrate. The original title of the play, *The Arraignment*, Cain reminds us, would have recalled for the Elizabethan audience the very recent trial of Essex on charges of treason. Essex was a victim of libellous politics – his sympathisers responded to abuse in kind. A poetry miscellany compiled by an Inns of Court man, Richard Roberts (Bod., MS. Don.c.54), includes a collection of pro-Essex material which incorporates libels directed at his enemies – Robert Cecil, Sir Walter Raleigh, and Henry Brooke, Lord Cobham.[26] *Poetaster* was Jonson's response: he engaged in personal invective not just against rival playwrights, Marston and Dekker, but also against public figures – Lupus is said to be a thinly veiled personal attack on Lord Cobham, a magistrate instrumental in Essex's trial.[27] Jonson, like the Ciceronian comic satirist, was thus implicated in the abuse he condemned, resulting in a complex engagement with the fraught issue of where to draw the line between accusation and abuse, invective and libel.

Poetaster is a pivotal play in the so-called 'Wars of the Theatre' or 'that terrible *Poetomachia*', a term coined by Dekker in *Satiromastix*, that was played out on stage between Jonson, Marston and Dekker from 1600 to 1601. These wars arguably are a continuation of the earlier 'civil war' among the satirists at the Inns of Court, and transfer the ritualised aggression of commoning and flyting to the public stage. The 'poets' wars' at the Inns and on stage have in common a complex consideration of the ethics of serious laughter – whether personal invective can be justified within available traditions of admonition, whether it is possible to attack the man as well as the vice and not violate satiric decorum. Questions such as these energised the vibrant and volatile public sphere that emerged in the last decade of Elizabeth's reign.[28] Jonson inserts the figure of the judicious poet-dramatist, who delivers healthy admonition in the form of personal invective, into this forum. Thomas Nashe and Gabriel Harvey, in their efforts to scandalise one another in print during their 'pamphlet wars' of the early 1590s, as Alexandra Halasz has cogently argued, had similarly identified with the Ciceronian orator, whose rhetorical authority and liberty within the state resided in his reputation as a just man. Personal invective, in this context, operated as a mechanism for ensuring the health of public dialogue by discovering those individuals who would abuse its liberties.[29]

The complex pattern of accusation, misattributed accusation, counter-accusation and abuse that structures the fourth act is closely tied to the issue of true and false counsel within the libellous politics of the play. Tucca accuses Horace, 'that goat-footed envious slave', of turning 'informer' and betraying them to Caesar, so Crispinus will retaliate through libel (4.7.8–13). The confusion between true and false testimony, accusation and abuse, is resolved through the parrhesiastic contract. It is Caesar who licenses the frank speaking of Horace when he proffers his judgement on merit and detraction: 'Thanks, Horace, for thy free and wholesome sharpness, / Which pleaseth Caesar more than servile fawns. / A flattered prince soon turns the prince of fools' (5.1.94–6). The parrhesiastic contract was a moral obligation on the part of the ruler to listen to good counsel, rather than institutionally binding.[30] That said, *Poetaster* reserves its praise for states in which the royal prerogative is complemented by the law, hence *parrhesia* is simultaneously given institutional basis in the law. The play ends with Horace, the lawyer-poet, arraigning the poetasters at the bar. This situation, to an extent, is made possible by the ideal ruler, Caesar. Yet, Caesar is presented as consistently transferring his sovereignty to just men and philosopher poets, such as Virgil, and his ability to rule effectively is conditional upon his openness to wise counsel delivered by free men. Servile flattery not only transforms citizens into slaves, but also enslaves rulers.

Jonson dedicated *Poetaster* to Martin in the 1616 folio citing Martin's intervention on his behalf, probably with Chief Justice Popham, over an accusation of libel.[31] Martin, in the dedication, is Jonson's Horatian just man; as we have seen, Martin was admired as the *parrhesiastes* who was not afraid to tell kings the truth, as he did in the 1603 oration when he called on James to fulfil his own image of the virtuous philosopher-king. This particular mode of *parrhesia*, as in Jonson's *Poetaster*, combines satire with panegyric, admonition with praise. Free speech was also understood within contexts other than the encomiastic in the early seventeenth century. In the early Jacobean parliament, for example, it was accommodated to the notion of legal counsel as lawyers clarified the parameters of the parliamentary privilege of free speech. And, in fact, Martin in 1616, at the time he received Jonson's dedication, was out of favour with his prince because of his frank speech in parliament, and was struggling to dispel James's impression that he had an 'aversness or untractable humour to his Ma^{ts} desires'.[32] The figure of *parrhesia* was therefore troublingly mobile in this period.[33] It inhabited different genres and was put to a range of poetic and political uses as individuals and groups struggled to seize rhetorical initiative. One of the dangers of this volatile figure in *Poetaster* is that speaking with 'free and wholesome sharpness' could potentially sound like libel.

The laughter of ridicule is similarly difficult to control, particularly when its parameters are hotly contested. 'It sometimes happens', Quintilian warned, 'that something said against an opponent applies to the judge or also to our own client; yet one finds people who do not even avoid jests which can recoil upon themselves' (vi.3.32). Dekker's *Satiromastix* turned the tables on *Poetaster* to arraign Horace/Jonson at the bar, insisting that he pledge himself to certain conditions:

> when you Sup in Tavernes, amongst your betters, you shall sweare not to dippe your Manners in too much sawce, nor at Table to fling Epigrams, Embleames, or Play-speeches about you (lyke Hayle-stones) to keepe you out of the terrible daunger of the Shot, upon payne to sit at the upper ende of the Table, a'th left hand of Carlo Buffon. (5.2.328–32)

Dekker accused Jonson of hypocrisy: like the *scurra* he condemned, he was an inveterate libeller, even of his 'friends private vices' (1.2.227), abusing their trust and hospitality while promoting such rigid codes of civility in his plays, putting on the 'Office of an Executioner' (line 230) without a sense of his own frailties and the fact that 'we are men' (line 254). The plays engaged in 'that terrible *Poetomachia*' put into practice a public forum in which issues of satire, libel and frank speech were heatedly debated. Matthew Steggle sees the argument between Jonson and Dekker in terms of a clash between Jonson's desire for 'an inviolable text that the audience should passively accept', and Dekker's embracing of 'debate and dissent, seeing it as a process of moving towards truth'.[34] The differences between the two are not so clear-cut. Rather than requiring passivity, Jonson provokes his audience in his comical satires, demanding an active, judging spectator. Dekker and Jonson both maintained a space for debate, albeit differently configured. Jonson, in theory if not always in practice, may have insisted on ethical restraint to prevent frank speech descending into scurrility, yet he also made space within his ideal commonwealth for invective through the figure of *parrhesia*, on the basis that such liberty ensured the strength and vitality of the *polis*.

'WITS AND BRAVERIES'

The term 'wits' had long been in use, at least since the fourteenth century, to designate a social type or group. It is in the late sixteenth and early seventeenth centuries that the term takes on specialised meaning to denote a distinct speech community inhabiting a particular geographical and social space – the West End of London, around the Inns of Court, St Paul's and

Blackfriars, with their fashionable taverns and other meeting places. The 'wits' were part of a complex habitus made up of shared linguistic codes, rules for behaviour and social communication, leisure pursuits, taste in objects, songs, and ways of dressing.[35] Around the same time, the 'town', a word first coined in its modern sense as a synonym for fashionable society in Beaumont's epistle to Jonson, emerged as a category of the urban. It speaks to the transition from the older configuration of the city as the capital – a customary, centred civic space – to the heterogeneous and polyfocal metropolis.[36] The metropolis in *Every Man Out* is paced out in shifting and frequently crowded scenes, as the play travels around the city from the citizen's house to St Paul's Walk, then onto Whitehall, along the river to the Mitre tavern, and to the Counter, and finally comes within sight of the court. *Epicoene* is set not within the walls of the old city, but on the newly fashionable Strand, and participates in the fashioning of West End society as a distinct metropolitan geographical and social space.[37] This is the terrain of the gallant in the 1597–8 Middle Temple revels and Donne's 'Satire 1', which discovered in the metropolis a space for improvising social identities. Jonson takes a different tack, and articulates an ethos of urbanity that attempts to reinstate the civic foundations of the classical city, even as he exploits the theatrical potential of the metropolis.

The broad brush strokes of Jonson's stage dramatisations of these metropolitan milieux and their social arenas owe something to the classical origins of the 'wits'. This type derives from the Roman *urbanus homo*, whose own characteristics came from the qualities *urbanitas* attributed to city life. When it first emerged in Roman culture, the character of *urbanitas* was refined through the figures of the *cavillator facetus*, the clever wit, the *conviva commodus*, the agreeable dinner guest, and the *scurra*, the man-about-town. In its earliest stages of development, *urbanus* was attached not simply to modes of speech, but to a speech community. The urbane man was recognisable through the quality of his wit, and the propriety of his speech and manners. For Cicero, urbanity was at the heart of the republican ideal of a polite and learned society. 'Pray then come back', he wrote to Manius Curius, 'so that the seed of wit [*urbanitatis*] does not die along with the commonwealth.'[38]

Jonson, as we have seen, distils the urbane ideal in Roman fashion through its anti-types – the gallant and the scurrilous wit.[39] Hence, in *Every Man Out* the characters displaying a deformed wit are the *scurra*, Buffone, and the hyper-urbane types of *urbanissimus homo*. Fastidius Brisk and Saviolina, for example, are creatures of their habitus, and carry complex set of hyper-urbane metropolitan associations. Brisk is a dedicated follower of fashion: as he says in praise of the 'strange virtues' of 'rich apparel', it 'makes him that hath it without means esteemed for an excellent wit' (2.2.264–6). He holds no public office, has no estate, occupation, or any 'other designment in hand' (line 312), and instead typifies the man of leisure who is credited for his 'judicious wearing' of apparel. Just as Ciceronian hyper-urbanity was identifiable through affected speech, so too Brisk's speech is fashionably deformed; he not only borrows others' wit, 'speaks good remnants' (*Characters*, lines 35–6), he drops words from his sentences, or does not finish them at whim: 'There was a countess gave me her hand to kiss today i' the presence, 'did me more good, by Jesu, than – and yesternight sent her coach twice to my lodging to entreat me accompany her and my sweet mistress, with some two or three nameless ladies more' (2.2, lines 238–42). His mistress is Saviolina, whose humour is self-conceit, a character for whom Jonson has little to say except that her 'weightiest praise is a light wit, admired by herself and one more, her servant Brisk' (*Characters*, lines 60–1). Brisk, whose judgement is defective in any case, opines 'O, by this bright sun, she has the most acute, ready, and facetious wit that – tut, there's no spirit able to stand her' (4.5.49–51). The trick that is hatched to laugh her out of her humour – self-conceit – is to 'try [her] judgement' (5.2.101), her ability to distinguish the 'signs' of gentleman in Sogliardo, who represents the rustic clown, the classical anti-type to the urbane gentleman.

The game of wit Jonson plays with the characters – and the audience – means that Saviolina, as expected, fails the test miserably, and mistakenly 'discern[s] the gentleman' (line 72) in its anti-type, Sogliardo. The trick is a product of the times, what Elias described as the 'civilizing process': the change in behaviour and 'ways of seeing' during the Renaissance occasioned by the dissemination of civility from forms of aristocratic distinction to codes of conduct for the expanding 'gentle' classes. The civic Renaissance of the sixteenth century, in which the governing élite was augmented by educated men drawn from the middling classes, saw the diffusion of courtly modes of conduct and dress among a metropolitan community.[40] Brisk stands in for this process of diffusion, hence this 'courtier' is distanced from the court – he does not have a place, or seemingly any business there. Saviolina, the lightweight court lady, resides in rooms in the outer buildings of Whitehall, suggesting a complex geographical hierarchy of office and status. Both 'court' characters participate in a satiric economy of space attuned to the complex processes of social differentiation within the court and its environs. Other characters in the plays conduct their business and take their recreation in fashionable social meeting places outside the court in the West End – St Paul's Walk, taverns, such as the Mitre, and bowling greens. Social differentiation meant that the pressure to discern and observe often quite subtle status distinctions became more intense and integral to the conduct of social life, particularly in a crowded urban environment.[41] The vocabulary of social judgement was expanded, concentrated and, to use a Jonsonian term, 'distillèd'. The social games Jonson's comedies play work by dissolving the boundaries between on-stage action and the 'off-stage' social world.[42] The highly sophisticated language of distinction at work in these games requires the audience to judge their own place by closely scrutinising their behaviour, speech and dress, and that of their fellows. On the one hand, Jonson's game-playing invites the collusion of the audience, yet there is the risk that the audience will either resist or fall foul of the role of the judging spectator, and instead find themselves subjected to the laughter of ridicule.

Jonson's comedies are often spoken of as 'comedies of manners'. The dramatic energies of these exuberantly metropolitan plays are concentrated in conversation. 'These plays typically slacken their plots', as Jonathan Haynes notes, 'so the action unfolds at a leisurely rate leaving plenty of time for characters to stand around on stage and *talk*, venting a constant stream of social observation.'[43] Fashionable speech acts in *Epicoene* are carefully contextualised within élite cultures of recreation – the 'things wherein your fashionable men exercise themselves' – horse-racing, hunting, betting, bowling-greens, spending ostentatiously, and making social calls.[44] Metropolitan speech communities are demarcated not simply through ways of seeing, but also through hearing so acutely attuned it is able to make distinctions between different modes of wit. City talk is not intended to secure consensus on civic values, but instead addresses ephemeral issues of personal style – what to wear, how to speak, where to be seen. The play implies that older, unifying civic speech communities have become fractured, their energies dissipated. Truewit points out that city gentry cannot complain if great men neglect them since it is the 'common disease' (1.1.54) to spend their time wasting time. Clerimont in riposte says he's been reading too much of Plutarch's *Morals*, and instead should 'Talk me of pins, and feathers, and ladies, and rushes, and such things' (1.1.61–2).

Truewit, at this moment in the play, speaks in the idiom of what Lorna Hutson describes as the 'Plutarchan discourse of self-surveillance' that imagines 'oneself as one's own enemy', and has internalised the criticism of great men, rather than listening to his friends' talk. Jonson sets Plutarchan 'virile civility' against effeminising civil conversations that can only speak of womanish things.[45] The Ladies Collegiate is one of the loci in the play of effeminate wit: they 'give entertainment to all the Wits and Braveries o' the time, as they call 'em, cry down or up what they like or dislike in a brain or fashion with most masculine or rather hermaphroditical authority' (1.1.73–7).[46] Adjacent to the Ladies Collegiate are the 'Wits and Braveries'. This is one of the first recorded usages of Collegiate and Braveries in a nominative sense. While the phrase 'Ladies Collegiate' does not denote an institution as such, nonetheless this circle of women seems more formalised than a coterie gathering. It is an 'order' (1.1.72) – there is clearly defined membership and meetings are characterised by certain rituals of association and modes of discourse. The Ladies Collegiate and 'Wits and Braveries' are early instances of the private society dramatised on stage; societies formed outside the jurisdiction of the state solely for the purposes of recreation, to trade in wit and talk, and fashion new ways of socialising. Jonson explicitly depicts these companies as city-bred, 'an order between the courtiers and country madams' (1.1.72–3). The play these societies engage in has been separated from its humanist origins. In the case of the 'Wits and Braveries', male sociability is effeminised through its idle wit: its president is Sir John Daw, 'a fellow so utterly nothing, as he knows not what he would be' (2.4.141–2), and one of its members Sir Amorous La Foole, a 'precious manikin'(1.3.24), the very type of the hyper-urbane *urbanissimus homo* inhabiting fashionable areas in the town – the Strand, the china-houses, the Exchange, and Whitehall. The effeminised private societies of the town stand in for a historical process whereby the Ciceronian vocabulary of *urbanitas* and *libertas* has moved out of the public forum into the private domain, where it is reconfigured into a hyper-urbane emasculated wit.

Truewit's critical urbanity, as he recognises, 'will not take' (1.1.64) among this company, so he turns to fashionable talk of the Ladies Collegiate, albeit tempered by a jocoserious version of *querelle des femmes*. Arguably, his initial statement of the virile ethos of urbanity establishes an ethical standpoint on the subsequent action that is then left open for the judicious spectator.[47] A useful analogy can be made with the Grex in *Every Man Out*: this dramatic device reinstates the place of urbane men of judgement on stage by displacing the gallant frequently seated onstage so the audience could admire his gestures and dress, as Brisk points out, thus taking 'possession of your stage at your new play' (2.2.272). Cordatus and Mitis, who constitute the Grex – the judging spectators who remain onstage throughout the action – are intellectual rather than social types. Hence, Mitis is 'a person of no action' and therefore has 'no character' (*Characters*, line 110). Providing a dialogic critical commentary on the action, the Grex establishes a meta-urbane perspective within the play. This space is arguably occupied by 'the wits' who sit just outside the play in *Bartholomew Fair*. It opens with John Littlewit cursing

> these pretenders to wit, your Three Cranes, Mitre, and Mermaid men! Not a corn of true salt nor a grain of right mustard amongst them all. They may stand for places or so, again' the next witfall, and pay twopence in a quart more for their canary than other men. But gi' me the man can start up a justice of wit out of six-shillings beer, and give the law to all the poets and poet-suckers i' town, because they are the players' gossips.[48]

The wits are given a local habitation in contemporary fashionable London taverns – the Three Cranes, and the Mitre and Mermaid. Jonson may well be alluding to the societies meeting at these taverns in the early seventeenth century, which included many of his close friends – Martin, Hoskyns, and Holland. But he is also defining an ideal type in order to refine a set of social and cultural distinctions capable of discriminating between different modes of conviviality. There are clear educational as well as social differences distinguishing the canary-drinking wits at the fashionable London taverns from the beer-drinking pot poets at lower-class alehouses.[49] Jonson's *Bartholomew Fair*, as Phil Withington has noted, satirises the commercial, political urbanity of citizens and city corporations through his characterisations of Littlewit, the Court Proctor, Zeal-of-the-Land Busy, 'the Banbury baker and preacher', and Justice Overdo, 'the Cicero-quoting citizen-magistrate'.[50] Competing languages of urbanity emerged towards the end of the sixteenth century in the discursive repertoire of the burgeoning metropolis. Jonson claims ethical superiority for his urbane men of judgement against the effeminising urbanity of the town and the commercial urbanity of the citizens.

When Jonson invokes these societies of 'true-wits', he begins to make available a discriminating coterie social identity on stage, while insisting on its exclusivity. The 'true-wits' are, in a very humanist and ludic sense, a eu-topian community – both an ideal type and belonging to no place. Wits such as Winwife and Quarlous, for example, fall short of this ideal. The seeming ineffability of the true wits, that make fleeting yet definitive appearances in the plays, has affinities with the 'community of the same' Stanley Fish finds in Jonson's epigrams: an idealised alternate world that is paradoxically and impossibly self-sufficient, and generates a discourse of merit that authorises the autonomy of the professional poet-dramatist.[51]

PLAYING GAMES

Games are constitutive of Jonson's plays, more so than his contemporary dramatists. *The Case is Alter'd* has Peter Onion, a court servant, invite a cobbler, Juniper, to play at the 'hilts', fencing; Juniper declines since 'tis as I am fitted with the ingenuity, quantity, or quality of the cudgell' (2.7.3–4). Jonson not only registers the social distinctions between different forms of play – the élite rapier is set against the lower-class cudgel – but also associatively extends this field to incorporate other games, in this case, the wit contest in which the weapons are 'the *Anagrams* and the *Epitaphs*' (lines 7–8). The courtly games of wit the 'society of gallants' play with the court ladies occupy the stage over one long scene in *Cynthia's Revels* (1601). Games operate at a structural level: plots frequently unfold through the jest, from the convivial to the downright dangerous – Truewit warns his friends not to take a jest too far: 'Maim a man forever for a jest? What a conscience hast thou?' (*Epicoene*, 4.5.123–4). Different types of contemporary entertainments – ball-games, card games, parlour games, bowling, bear-baiting, and so forth – enrich the vocabulary of play in his comedies. And it is through the game that Jonson formulates a place for the professional poet-dramatist in theatre and other early modern performance spaces.

Games of wit and verbal ingenuity are integral to the ethics of laughter in the plays. Douglas Duncan has traced this mode of game-playing to Jonson's engagement with a Lucianic tradition of *lusus* or learned play, as it was interpreted by early humanists, particularly Erasmus in his *Praise of Folly*, and thus transmitted to Jonson. Hence, the games in *Cynthia's Revels* are conducted under the auspices of the court lady, Moria, or Folly. The intellectual balance between *jocus* and *serium* underpinning humanist *lusus* is discernible in the Jonsonian dialectic between judgement and wit.[52] Learned play, as we have seen in relation to revelling at the Inns of Court, had a pedagogic role, as well as functioning as a dimension of Renaissance civil conversations to display an individual's urbanity. His early humours comedies present satiric laughter as a 'physic of the mind' (*Every Man Out*, Induction, line 131); the well-managed jest functions to correct an imbalance of the humours, thus recreating and physicking the self. This medical discourse of laughter derives from classical and Renaissance theories of *ludus* as a necessary restorative for the mind and body. Recreation was not an alternative to study and the *vita activa*, but rather ensured the mind and body were fit for serious occupation.[53] In the context of widespread criticism of play-going as an essentially unprofitable activity, Jonson mounts a justification of the type of recreation his plays provide through Renaissance theories of healthful *lusus*, thereby drawing on traditions of learned play to define his professional status as dramatist and entertainer.

The Renaissance, it has been argued, sees the emergence of a leisure culture that was fundamentally different from an earlier medieval culture of play.[54] Leisure, the time outside public occupations in which the individual could engage in recreational pursuits, defined the social and economic élites in Renaissance society. Recreating oneself at play was a social ritual in which distinctions could be observed, alliances formed, and a group identity reinforced. Sir John Harington's 'Treatise on Playe' is particularly instructive in this context because it gives a sense of how play was reconfigured within the spaces – physical, social, and temporal – inhabited by the early modern upper-classes. Harington says his scope is *ludus* in its entirety, the '*spending of the tyme eyther in speeche or action, whose only end is a delight of the mynd or speryt*', but his main concern is recreation at court, and among those of his social status:

I cownt a little play . . . both tolerable and also commendable for worthy persons of eyther sex (specially attending in cowrt) to recreate themselves at play; and meethinkes I have observed good use therof. For it is . . . an unfittinge syght to see a presence-chamber empty more than haulfe the day, and men cannot be always discowrsing, nor women always pricking in clowts; and therefore, as I say, it is not amisse to play at some sociable game (at which more than ii may play) wherby attendawnce may seem the lesse tedious to the players, and the rest that looke on may in a sort intertayn themselves with beholding it, as daylie experience sheweth us.[55]

This is the courtly space of game-playing in *Cynthia's Revels*: Philautia proposes 'For sports sake, let's have some *riddles*, or *purposes*', Phantaste disagrees, pointing out they 'are stale', and instead suggests '*prophecies*', Philautia counters with a game called '*Substantives* and *adjectives*', which is then followed by another game known as 'A *thing done*, and, *Who did it*'.[56] These may derive from actual games played at court; above all, they are satirised by Jonson as travesties of *lusus*, indicative of a courtly milieu that has lost a sense of itself as the arbiter of morals within the commonwealth, and has degenerated into the arbiter of fashion. Given this is a point in the play where the on-stage and off-stage worlds coalesce, it is not surprising Jonson's court audience apparently did not appreciate the type of learned play, conducted under the ludic aspect of Erasmian Folly, he offered as a corrective to their 'unprofitable' play, and instead refused to collude in its forms of laughter.[57]

An expansive geography of leisure is dramatised in plays like *Epicoene*, which talks about a wealth of new places in the metropolis where the social élite could be at leisure – and be seen at one's leisure.[58] Linguistic games, such as riddles and paradoxes, were disseminated from the school room and royal court into the wider metropolis and incorporated into the civil conversations held at the table and in the private society. Sociable games were part of the social and 'psychic habitus of "civilized" people' in early modern England.[59] That said, there was a fundamental ambivalence about play that Jonson shared with many of his contemporaries.[60] The need for recreation was recognised, but it did not assuage concerns that leisure distracted the individual from civic duties. One response to this dilemma was to discriminate between different types of leisure in social and ethical terms. Harington differentiates the types of play appropriate to the different social orders, warning, somewhat ironically given his own reputation for buffoonery, that although 'to be plesawnt conseyted, to be active and musicall, are cowrtly and liberall quallyties; so, for noble personages to become jesters, tumblers, and pypers, is hateful, fond, and dishonourable' (p. 194). This distinction between high and low forms of play sets out an ideological opposition between élite profitable recreation and popular wasteful games; hence, for Harington (if not Jonson) the nobility playing cards in the presence chamber is a pleasant, productive use of time, whereas the peasant or apprentice gaming in the alehouse meant they were idle, unproductive and not at work. Jonson tends to shift the onus from the social status of participants onto ethical standards when judging the profitability of play, in order to make a place for the low-born yet high-minded poet-dramatist.

Game-playing, of course, was not just the privilege of the élite, but ubiquitous in early modern society. A heterogeneous, dynamic culture of play – intellectual, rhetorical, performative, communal and sociable – structured the everyday worlds of the sixteenth and early seventeenth centuries from the lower-class marketplace to the court. The Renaissance may have witnessed the increasing institutionalisation of play within the public theatres.[61] Yet, the richness and diversity of an older medieval culture of play persisted. Even in the Renaissance, the word 'play' was not yet reserved for drama, but had wider recreational resonances, and the player was not fixed on the stage, but performed in a wide range of social spaces.[62] The notion of the popular if employed as a synonym for the lower classes is misleading when used to define early modern entertainments. Despite the increasing social differentiation of geographical space, the professional entertainer inherited a rich culture of play that enabled him to travel across social and geographical boundaries, to perform in alehouses and the print marketplace as well as aristocratic households and at court. The celebrity clowns dominating the professional stage, Richard Tarlton and his successor William Kemp, did not confine their performances to the public theatres. Tarlton is reputed to have entertained guests with jests at the tavern he owned in Gracechurch Street, and performed in the banqueting hall before Elizabeth. Kemp's famous morris dance from London to Norwich both followed in the footsteps of the medieval travelling entertainer, albeit in changing circumstances, and, when published in the pamphlet *Nine Daies Wonder*, demonstrates the commercialisation of play in the print marketplace.[63] William Fennor was another early modern professional entertainer who continued older practices within this changing environment. A professional wit, Fennor followed the ancient craft of the jester – he styled himself the 'King's Rhyming Poet', was the author of a number of popular books of jests and pasquils, as well as publishing the orations he delivered before the King, royal family, and the court. His occupation was that of the travelling entertainer, who amused his audiences with jests and extemporised verses in praise of the nobility he visited. Richard Boyle, first Earl of Cork, recorded in his diary in 1618 that he 'gave to Mr ffennor, the King's Jester, a hackney, with bridle and saddle', probably in payment for an entertainment either delivered as part of a tour of Ireland or commissioned specifically by Boyle.[64] Fennor has many affinities with Thomas Coryate – whereas Coryate was a gentleman, Fennor made much of his claim to gentry status, and status underpinned their professional, or in Coryate's case, quasi-professional identity as entertainers.[65]

What was the place of the professional poet-dramatist in this rich and diverse culture of play? Jonson, himself, was probably employed as an actor in a travelling company as well as in the London playhouses at the start of his career. When at play on the stage, at the court, in the houses of friends and patrons, and at taverns, he participated in a vibrant culture of performance that incorporated a wide variety of entertainers, both professional and amateur, across the social spectrum, from the gentleman wit performing at private tables to the lowly ballad singer and musicians employed in taverns and the professional entertainer, like Fennor. Fennor's adoption of the title 'King's rhyming poet' takes its style from Jonson, the 'King's poet', complimenting Jonson on his superior skill, while denoting their proximity in the arena of entertainment. Jonson was notoriously hostile to rivals threatening him with this type of proximity. His sense of his own place within this arena may explain why he was both drawn to and repelled by the buffoon or *scurra*, the professional dinner guest who socialises with the élite, but is not of their class. He makes this figure central to the ethical distinctions that govern play not simply in order to make leisure productive by turning it to moral ends, but also because, as Dekker noted, he shared some of his characteristics. The buffoon spoke to Jonson's predicament: he was familiar with the men at the Inns of Court, but not of their society; in the early seventeenth century he resided in the households of the gentry and nobility, but as servant or entertainer rather than guest. Social liminality combines with ambition to fuel the energies Jonson expended on defining his identity as professional dramatist through the classical orator – a figure that gave him the authority to converse with his social superiors, while distinguishing him among his peers in the world of entertainment. It also informs his attraction to the Lucianic tradition and its forms of learned, intellectual play which could credit Jonson's own performances.

One of the most carefully realised games on stage is the game of vapours in *Bartholomew Fair*. Like the parlour games in *Cynthia's Revels*, the game of vapours is a travesty of *lusus*. Erasmus and More saw *lusus* as essentially productive, a profitable form of learned play practised among the intellectual élite to test acuteness of judgement.[66] Whereas Jonson targeted courtly game-playing in *Cynthia's Revels*, the game of vapours parodies lower-class entertainment, turning it into non-productive leisure, and distinguishing it from learned play. It is played in a tent at the fair by a motley mixture of social types: Humphrey Wasp, the tutor, Val Cutting, a roarer, Jordan Knockem, a horse-dealer, Captain Whit, a bawd. Bruce Boehrer reads this game 'as a parody of the very concept of civility' contributing 'to progressive expansion of the category of distasteful behaviour that Norbert Elias identifies as a prime element of the European history of manners'.[67] This 'distasteful behaviour' is attached by Jonson to the forms of lower-class entertainment, although it is defined as much by the absence of skill as by social class. Quarlous's judgement on the 'Game of Vapours' sounds as if it is just as concerned with participants' lack of craft as it is with incivility: 'Call you this vapours? This is such a belching of quarrel as I never heard' (4.4.76–7).[68] His standards derive from *lusus*, whose profitable and intellectual purpose is maintained over and against nasty 'nonsense' that deforms its participants.

Jonson, in fact, coins the term 'nonsense' to describe the game of vapours: this is the first recorded usage of the word to denote speech that does not convey sense (OED, 1a). It is a term that also emerges in this period to describe a particular genre of writing which puts together words in grammatically correct order, but in fact makes no sense. Hoskyns, as we have seen, was famed for his performance of 'nonsense' in his mock-oration at the 1597–8 Middle Temple revels, and again in his 'Cabalisticall verses, which by transposition of words, syllables, and letters makes excellent sense, otherwise none', before *Coryats Crudities* (1611).[69] The game of vapours is Jonson's version of nonsense, and he employs its forms in order to distance himself from the arena of lower-class entertainment by participating in a coterie game played by the wits. The game is closely related to pedagogic games, like the law sports at the Inns, which parodied rhetorical exercises. Its rules are '*every man to oppose the last man that spoke, whether it concerned him or no*' (4.4.30, stage directions), which suggest a travesty of the disputation: there is no ordering proposition and no rational debate, only nonsensical contradiction; as Wasp says, 'I have no reason, nor I will hear of no reason, nor I will look for no reason, and he is an ass that either knows any or looks for't from me' (lines 42–4).[70] By using the forms of *lusus* to parody lower-class entertainment, Jonson takes advantage of its ironic, meta-urbane standpoint to distance himself from the proceedings, identifying instead with the place of the judging spectator rather than the performer.

With its references to farts, turds and lawyers, the game echoes the flatulent premises of the 'Parliament Fart'. A humanist ludic tradition freely mixed high and low forms; the intellectual orientation of such low literary play meant that it was possible for writers, as Catherine Connors says of a Roman literature of leisure, 'to go slumming in the world of popular amusements while keeping a firm grip on the education and culture that mark them as élite'.[71] The lines attributed in the 'Parliament Fart' to the arch wit Richard Martin point out that it is hard to 'find out this figure of farting / Nor what part of speech save an interjection / This fart canne be in gramatique perfection' (Bod., MS. Mal. 23, p. 8). As a part of speech, the interjection is a 'natural ejaculation' that expresses feeling or emotion, such as anger, and does not have a grammatical connection with surrounding sentences, clauses or words.[72] This sounds like the combative nonsense of the game of vapours. Jonson was fascinated by the 'Parliament Fart': in *The Alchemist* he has Sir Epicure Mammon include those 'poets / . . . that writ so subtly of the fart' (2.2.62–4) in his hyperbolic wish-list of pleasures, and the play begins with a fart as the opening missile in the railley between Face and Subtle. The improvisational virtuosity of the fart signifies a wit that resists containment, and concentrates the ear on the aural pleasures of language. Yet, Jonson also provides a critique of nonsense in the game of vapours which insists that hearing must be accompanied by judgement. Nonsense troubles this association, undermining the profitable ends of *lusus* by effecting a radical dissociation between style and meaning, rhetoric and ethics, wit and judgement. It is just play, and therefore travesties *lusus*, privileging the *jocus* at the expense of the *serium*, and giving language too many liberties.

Despite reservations about these forms of speculative play, Jonson experimented with low literary forms alongside his fellow wits. Such low game-playing paradoxically provided a means of defining intellectual capital. He not only contributed to but helped to organise the witty front matter to *Coryats Crudities* and its sequel *Coryats Crambe*; these collections constitute one of the most concerted experiments with the mock-encomium in the early seventeenth century. It had been revived for humanist poetics by Erasmus and his *Praise of Folly* in the early sixteenth century. Jonson's 'On the Famous Voyage', a virtuoso exercise in burlesque and the mock-heroic, can be read in this tradition.[73] This exuberantly scatological mock-heroic poem tells the story of a voyage in a wherry, a small boat used by watermen, along the Fleet Ditch, a London river that by the early seventeenth century was no more than a sewer. Jonson, once again, acknowledges the influence of a recent famous fart: 'it was the intent / Of the grave fart, late let in parliament, / Had it been seconded, and not in fume / Vanished away' (lines 107–10).[74] The voyage originates at the Mermaid tavern:

> It was the day, what time the powerful moon
> Makes the poor Bankside creature wet it' shoon
> In it' own hall, when these (in worthy scorn
> Of those that put out moneys on return
> From Venice, Paris, or some inland passage
> Of six times to and fro without embassage,
> Or him that backward went to Berwick, or which
> Did dance the famous morris unto Norwich)
> At Bread Street's Mermaid having dined, and merry,
> Proposed to go to Holborn in a wherry;
> A harder task than either his to Bristo',
> Or his to Antwerp.
>
> (lines 29–40)

The poem styles itself as a coterie performance played among the canary-drinking 'truewits'. Given the theme of the wagered journey coalesces round these merry men at the Mermaid, the poem could be seen as another entry in the sociable flyting of Coryate. If so, then it only makes a very general reference to Coryate when it cites Venice and Paris, which suggest there is another site in its targets. References to wherry journeys to Bristol and Antwerp can be found in Samuel Rowland's poem before John Taylor's *The Sculler, rowing from the Tiber to the Thames*, published in early 1612, and prefaced by a sonnet addressed 'To my deere respected friend, Master Benjamin Johnson'.[75]

Recent criticism has established Taylor as a pioneering entrepreneurial popular poet.[76] This London waterman made his entry into the print marketplace in early 1612 on the back of the Coryate phenomenon with a series of pamphlets: *The Sculler* was soon followed by *Laugh and be fat, or a commentary upon the Odcombyan banket* (1612), *Odcombs Complaint: or Coriatts Funeral Epicedium* (1613) purported to be the first 'news' of Coryate since his departure, relating his 'mock' death at sea, and *The Eighth Wonder of the World: or, Coryate's escape from his supposed drowning* (1613) is the last overtly Coryate text in the series. With *The Sculler*, Taylor sought to capitalise on the recent print performance of the wits before the *Crudities*: '*I will attend the next hightide, & scramble up into* Pauls *Churchyard . . . Ile grable for Gudgeons, or fish for Flounders in the Reward of our eminent temporising Humorists, sharpe Satyrists, or Ænigmaticall Epigrammists*' (sig. A2r). At the end of *Odcombs Complaint*, he offered to school others in the type of nonsense associated with Hoskyns and the wits: 'If there be any Gentlemen, or others that are desirous to be practioners in the *Barmoodo* and *Utopian* tongues: the Professor (being the Authour hereof) dwelleth at the Old Swanne neere London Bridge, who will teach them (that are willing) to learne, with agility and facility' (p. 63). Taylor sought entry into a performance space identified with the Inns of Court wits in order to reconfigure their coterie forms of literary play for the popular print marketplace. The carnivalesque low humour of the mock-encomium and burlesque had a recreational and pedagogic role to play in humanist culture, but it also spoke the language of the marketplace.[77] Taylor's pamphlets disclose the potential of these learned low forms to function in a positive sense as genres of the working commonality.

The full title of *The Sculler* takes its cue from the *Crudities*, with its *hotch-potch, or Gallimawfrey of Sonnets, Satyres, and Epigrams*. Coryate took the term 'crudities' from the humanist language of bibliophagia, and so placed his volume within humanist traditions of the book.[78] Taylor's food metaphor appeals to less refined tastes, opening a space for literary consumption that is appreciably rougher and ruder. 'Hotch potch' and 'gallimawfrey' are cookery terms denoting stew made from odds and ends, and used to describe a confused state, or medley, or promiscuous mix of persons. 'Hotch potch' had an additional legal sense, referring to the blending of properties to ensure equality of division, especially in cases where no will had been made. These terms signify new democratising forms of literary production and authorisation. The medley was an effect of 'the general habituation to print', emerging as a popular literary form in the 1590s in response to new and diverse reading publics who were reading in new and diverse ways, not just for religious or humanist edification but also for entertainment and pleasure.[79]

Taylor admired Jonson. He reformulated the notion of intellectual labour, as Katharine Craik has noted, that Jonson himself had developed in his own works.[80] His sonnet praising Jonson before *The Sculler* plays on his 'worth', his status as the modern exemplum of the classical poet; in contrast to the learned fool Coryate, who has misspent his classical patrimony, Jonson has made good investment ensuring his own immortality. Coryate's wit is devoid of intellectual labour, wasteful rather than profitable. Jonson would probably have agreed; but he would have been less comfortable with Taylor claiming fellowship with him as a labouring poet, given his own past as a bricklayer. This presumption of fellowship may underlie his very personal antagonism towards Taylor evident in the *Discoveries*.[81] Taylor unpicked the oppositions between élite productive forms of leisure and popular wasteful forms of leisure in his verse pamphlets, in order to reconfigure the conventional relations between literature, work and social class. Jonson's sense of his own professional identity relied on these very distinctions and hierarchies being kept in place. When he engaged in forms of learned play, he did so in the company of wits whose milieu was the tavern and the private table, not the alehouse and marketplace. 'On a Famous Voyage' can be seen as a response to the proffered companionship of Taylor. Jonson's poem can be read as a full-scale travesty of a popularising *lusus* that turns the poetic labour of this self-proclaimed water poet into a 'merd-urinous load' (line 65). Jonson de-legitimates Taylor's popular forms of literary play as part of a wider burlesque of the city and its civic corporations in a similar fashion to his satire on commercial citizen urbanity in *Bartholomew Fair*.[82] That said, even as he locates the creative energies of burlesque in the realms of learned play, among the merry wits at the Mermaid, there is always the danger that its vulgar, low forms place him among the working commonality. The extreme aggression directed towards trade and commerce in this poem seems to want to insist that its author is not one of this class.

'Against an aristocratic code of *sprezzatura* that he, by birth and disposition, could never embody', says Richmond Barbour of Jonson, he 'proposed a classical ethic of deliberately cultivated skill'.[83] This may be so, but as we have seen in Jonson's response to Taylor, the image of the poet as labourer and craftsman carried its own social difficulties. There were other traditions of wit and cultures of play available in this period in which Jonson could legitimately participate, and fashion his own identity as a professional poet-wit. This ludic culture of wit enabled a fruitful satiric dialogue between liberty of speech and the forms of laughter. In the context of his friends' experiments with more speculative liberties, Jonson wanted to hold learned, intellectual play to its humanist legacy, and insist on the interdependency of judgement and wit, even as he took part in frank speaking and invective and indulged in laughter's excesses. As we shall see in the following chapter, one of the sites for this culture of performance was the tavern. Jonson, together with the Sireniacal fraternity, revitalised a classical symposiastic vocabulary and, in doing so, explored the liberties available to the canary-drinking wit.

CHAPTER THREE

Taverns and table talk

Clubbing and commoning at the Inns of Court drew on a classical tradition of banqueting literature represented by texts such as Xenophon's *Symposium* and Plutarch's *Table Talk*.[1] The revels were structured around great feasts: the frugal, spare diet of the commons gave way to sumptuous, rich banquets to celebrate the pleasures and plenitude of communal life and the liberality of the Inns. The revels were extraordinary events; even so, the everyday routine of the Inns was structured by rituals of eating together in the commons, a quotidian 'symbolisation of community, of bonding' that, as Peter Goodrich notes, was vital to maintaining and perpetuating the professional homosociality of the Inns. Pedagogic exercises, such as readings, mootings and disputations, were undertaken either during or after meals.[2] This conflation of bodily and intellectual nourishment attests to the commons' proximity to the classical *convivium*, which similarly encompassed living, drinking and eating together, and the exercise of the intellect at the table. Sharing food and drink had a civilising effect, integrating the individual into the humanist community.[3] Plutarch spoke of the 'friend-making character of the dining table', and the value of table talk since 'learned discussions' are stimulated by 'company' with the 'table and goblet before us'.[4] The mouth, the organ of both eating and speaking, was the source of numerous analogies relating the intellectual pleasures of conversation to the sensual pleasures of eating and drinking. Guazzo's *Civile Conversation* culminates with the genre of banquet literature, a symposiastic dialogue, the 'seale and conclusion of all our former talke', because other pleasures 'are nothing in comparison of that great joye and pleasure, which is felt and taken in usinge the companie and conversation of honest and learned men'.[5] The *topos* of the meal combines the corporeal and the intellectual, food and debate, also compounded in complex senses of nourishment, as both feeding and educating – table talk thus nourished the commonwealth.[6]

Convivial dining was firmly integrated into the older civic constitution of the city, and continued to provide the individual with a set of ritualised practices for negotiating complex networks of social dependency in the new metropolis. When conviviality moves from the commons and the gentleman's table and into the public drinking house in texts of the late sixteenth century, it performs a vital role in the compilation of a complex vocabulary of urbanity that heightens the theatricality of manners, enjoys play and has a predilection for satire. The tavern came to prominence in the geography of the early modern town as a fashionable site for the performance of élite masculine sociability. As we have seen, the 1597–8 Middle Temple revels designated the Mitre and Mermaid as the fashionable place for the gallant to dine, while the Gray's Inn revels of 1594–5, in a tone of light mockery, set out a programme of reading, '*Guizo*, the *French* Academy, *Galiatto* the Courtier, *Plutarch*, the *Arcadia* and Neoterical writers', that should be accompanied by 'Conference' at the tavern and 'better sort of Ord'naries' whereby the law student may 'become accomplished with Civil Conversations, and able to govern a Table with Discourse'.[7] Dekker's satiric conduct book, *Gulls Hornbook* (1609), specified the tavern – alongside St Paul's Walk, the playhouse and the ordinary – as one of the places where the would-be gallant could practise fashionable modes of urban talk, behaviour and manners. The tavern, 'which out of the question is the only rendezvous of boon company', in fact encapsulated metropolitan urbanity since it was the only place for the traveller from the country to frequent in order 'to be [accounted] a man of good reckoning in the city'.[8] Literary genres, such as epigrams, satires and symposiastic poetry, found their *topos* in the tavern. By the mid 1610s, the tavern and the table were symbolic and social spaces inhabited by convivial societies, such as the fraternity of Sireniacal gentlemen, and constituted a discursive space that was simultaneously distinguished from the public forum, while nonetheless offering an alternative arena where affairs of state and religion could be discussed among friends.

LAWS OF DRINKING

The longevity of the alehouse *topos* in early modern drama, dating at least to late medieval morality plays, attests to the established place of public drinking houses as performances space within cultures of play.[9] Stephen Gosson in his *School of Abuse* (1579) spoke of the 'twoo prose Bookes plaied at the Belsavage, where you shall finde never a woorde without wit', while George Gascoigne in his *Glass of Government* (1573) wrote scathingly 'What man hath minde to heare a merrye jest, / Or seekes to feede his eye with vayne delight / . . . Bellsavage fayre were fittest for his purse'.[10] Scenes set at drinking houses in plays and pamphlets are also notable for their careful realisation of more mundane, everyday performances of social relations. The rich texture of their dramatisation of social interactions arose out of the way drinking houses were 'indispensable social agencies': places where people met to trade news, to discuss business and politics and to be sociable, taking pleasure in company and performing social rituals that contributed to a sense of belonging within a community.[11]

Of the various drinking houses in early modern England – inns, taverns, alehouses, and ordinaries – it was the tavern where urban élites congregated and chose to fashion new practices of sociability. A clear social and legal distinction had developed between the lower-class and heavily regulated alehouse and the socially élite and self-regulating tavern in this period.[12] Hence, Jonson in *Bartholomew Fair* (1614) was able to draw carefully calibrated social distinctions between the different modes of conviviality practised by wine-drinking wits at fashionable London taverns and beer-drinking pot poets at the alehouse. Taverns provided a privileged space for social performances relatively, if not completely free from the type of surveillance and controls alehouses were subjected to. Divided into distinct public and private areas, they had private rooms available for dinners and entertainment, such as music and gaming. Drawers in George Wilkins's *Miseries of Enforced Marriage* (1607), in a scene set at the Mitre, run between the Dolphin room and the Pomegranate room bringing wine to clients such as William Scarborrow who calls for 'a full gallon of Sacke' so that Sir Francis Ilford can 'pledge it to the health of a friend of thine'.[13] These rooms, set off from the more public communal drinking areas, offered drinking companions and the more formal drinking societies, such as the Sireniacal fraternity, a space of relative privacy and exclusivity, closed to those outside its circle, to act out rituals of social intimacy and identification.

The drinking society spawned its own genre. *A Solemne Joviall Disputation, Theoreticke and Practicke; briefly shadowing the Law of Drinking* (1617) is Richard Brathwaite's very convincing imitation of the German genre of drink literature (*Trinkliteratur*). The genre had emerged out of efforts to regulate competitive social drinking, or health-pledging, among the upper classes. It exemplifies Elias's 'civilizing process' since its aim was to pacify an aggressive aristocratic honour culture through the inculcation of good manners, thus inhibiting physical violence at drinking parties.[14] Brathwaite's *Solemne Joviall Disputation* is closely related to a classic of *Trinkliteratur*, Vincentius Obsopoeus's *Ars Bibendi* (1536), a humanist conduct book that teaches the arts of drinking and accommodates the custom of health pledges to ideals of civility.[15] Obsopoeus advocated moderation, the careful choice of cultivated drinking companions from one's class, temperate speech, and good manners, such as avoiding grimacing, belching and spitting.[16] He also gave advice on 'civil dishonesties', how to deceive others and maintain face during bouts of competitive drinking. *Ars Bibendi* addressed an aristocratic audience whose social identity was invested in highly personalised and aggressive combats of honour. The translation of drinking rituals into forms of civil conversation moderated and managed the violence attendant upon heated blood, allowing a space for face-saving through artful yet honest dissimulation, whose aim was to secure assent and avoid socially destructive violent conduct.[17]

Brathwaite's *Solemne Joviall Disputation* began with the premise that social drinking was intrinsic to civility and, by tailoring his volume to the interests of a university and Inns of Court audience, shifted the orientation away from a lineage society to a society in which notions of gentility had begun to accommodate those outside the hereditary nobility with gentle education. The violence of aristocratic competitive drinking is sublimated to the imperatives of brotherhood within the drinking society, and the gentleman is a meritocratic category. Civil conversations promoted through health-pledging have become highly attuned to the social extension of credit. Drinking rituals enabled the civil gentleman to forge alliances amongst his peers, amongst the nobility, since the friendship of learned men 'far . . . from disparaging the splendor of his Nobility . . . rather it adds an ornament to his dignity' (p. 17), and even amongst merchants, who may be profitably admitted 'to their Brotherhood' for reasons of good finance: 'both in exchanging, returning, and borrowing of money, and in keeping credit, if money be not present' (p. 18). The tavern is a predominantly masculine space in keeping with the exclusive homosociality of symposiastic literature and practices.[18] Brathwaite did consider whether women could participate in drinking fraternities, and identified precedents of mixed drinking societies among the aristocracy (p. 19), but concluded that 'the title of little sister, may be with small adoe changed into the title of a Curtezan' (p. 20), warning that the presence of women at the table led to sexual rivalry among men. Women are the space onto which the sexual aggression that simultaneously threatened and affirmed the homosociality of the fraternity is projected; the civility of the proceedings was therefore predicated on their exclusion.

It would be misleading to give too sober an account of drink literature given its decided tendency towards burlesque and parody. *Ars Bibendi* introduced its ethos of moderation in mock-heroic style, 'I sing of the lawful banquet and permissible drinking.'[19] Such incongruity draws attention to the disjunction between the form, the conduct book, and the matter, drinking. Rather than simply legitimising the pleasures of the body by channelling them into forms of civility, it admits that these bodily excesses may, in fact, be vulgar yet pleasurable. *Ars Bibendi* is self-consciously artful and ludic, skilfully shifting between, and sometimes merging, the advice manual and social satire, and dancing on the line between moderation and excess, encapsulated by the oxymoron 'provident luxury' (p. 676). Banquet literature thrived on these tensions between the body and reason, pleasure and civility, 'wisdom and folly, order and disorder, moderation and excess', as Jeanneret points out, given that at 'any moment, drunken and deranged speech can invade the disciplined discourse of the diners'.[20] Brathwaite's *Solemne Joviall Disputation* delights in breaches of civility through bodily incontinence, and often burlesques the good manners to be maintained when drinking, for example, not eating one's glass or putting excrement in drinking vessels. A large part of the pleasure of the text derives from anecdotes describing the excesses of drunken behaviour in graphic detail in parodies of civil behaviour, for example, the story of a man overcome with drink who vomited in his hat out of politeness, and a young man who repeatedly urinated in his thigh boots, because the presence of women meant it was uncivil to leave the table to urinate, but then exposed himself when he stood up to propose a toast (pp. 40–3).

The humanist banquet derived much of its philosophical basis from Epicureanism. By locating the origins of a civilised society in the rituals of eating and drinking together, the banquet made a place for pleasure and the body in the formation of social identity. Ezio Pellizer argues that the *symposium* provided a ritualised space for the exercise of the passions and organisation of pleasure. An element of risk-taking was integral to these rituals: the participant put his social identity at risk in order to enjoy a state of physical and intellectual liberty balanced between the 'unregulated, violent excesses practised by the barbarians' and the 'sterile gravity of the sober'.[21] Rather than renouncing the body and its pleasures for a reasonable civility, the banquet speaks to an intellectual interest in holding conventionally opposite physical and ethical states in tension in order to open a space for a speculative liberty. The name adopted by, or possibly conferred by Coryate on, those who met at the Mermaid tavern, the 'Sireniacal gentlemen' may be a playful allusion to the Cyrenaics, a school founded by Socrates' friend Aristippus; a more hedonistic and sceptical forerunner to Epicureanism known for concentrating exclusively on bodily pleasures as the supreme good.[22] A convivial association between the Cyrenaics and the tavern societies is suggested by *Aristippus*, a private play composed by

Thomas Randolph, a Son of Ben, and performed at Cambridge in the mid 1620s, which celebrates canary wine – his play *The Drinking Academy*, set in the Apollo Room of the Devil and St Dunstan tavern, also dates from this period.²³ The early modern tavern provided a performance space for such experimentation because of the way it had been structured by social practices and a symposiastic tradition which had taken on new metropolitan dimensions in the late sixteenth and early seventeenth centuries.

TAVERN POETRY

Discussions of the poetry of drinking have tended to concentrate on the symposiastic lyric, particularly Jonson's contribution to this form. Credited with initiating an Anacreontic-Horatian tradition of moderate banqueting in English poetry, he was the 'first major writer', Joshua Scodel points out, 'to make wine's association with "wit" central to his poetic vocation'.²⁴ The symposiastic 'idiom of civility' he formulated in his lyrics and convivial conversations with the Sons of Ben inaugurated a tradition of moderate and refined 'male tavern-clubbing'.²⁵ Alongside this mode of sociability is another tradition of tavern-clubbing; it too can be glimpsed in Jonson's corpus, in his promise to Michael Drayton in his commendatory verse prefacing Drayton's *Battle of Agincourt* (1627), that he does not intend to 'raise a rhyming club / About the town' (lines 8–9). It is unclear whether this club would praise Drayton or whether it is a case of Jonson, as Dekker accused, of dipping his 'Manners in too much sawce' and flinging sharp epigrams 'lyke Hayle-stones' when he supped at taverns (*Satiromastix*, 5.2.329–31). George Puttenham posits commensality between the epigram and the tavern:

> for this *Epigramme* is but an inscription or writting made as it were upon a table, or in a windowe, or upon the wall or mantell of a chimney in some place of common resort, where it was allowed every man might come, or be sitting to chat and prate, as now in our tavernes and common tabling houses, where many merry heades meete, and scrible with ynke, with chalke, or with a cole such matters as they would every man should know, and descant upon. Afterward the same came to be put in paper and in bookes, and used as ordinarie missives, some of frendship, some of defiaunce, or as other messages of mirth: *Martiall* was the chiefe of this skil among the Latines, and at these days the best Epigrammes we finde, and of the sharpest conceit are those that have bene gathered among the reliques of the two mute *Satyres* in Rome, *Pasquill* and *Marphorir*, which in time of *Sede vacante*, when merry conceited men listed to gibe and jest at the dead Pope, or any of his Cardinales, they fastened them upon those Images which now lie in the open streets, and were tollerated, but after that terme expired were inhibited againe.²⁶

The tavern is constituted as social space that is open, 'of common resort', where men come together to write poetry that is a kind of urban graffiti, extemporised and ephemeral, scribbled with ink, chalk or coal, and intended to make its subjects common knowledge and available for public consumption. The late sixteenth century sees the emergence of a loose but distinct category of 'tavern poetry' or 'pot poetry'. Jonson's *Every Man in His Humor* (1601) jestingly refers to verses written '*extempore*' that very morning at 'the *Miter* yonder'.[27] Tavern poetry exemplifies the 'embodiedness' that Bruce Smith identifies with the 'acoustic community', ritualised performances that function to affirm group identity and are situated within the 'communal present'.[28] Extemporisation stresses the oral, aural, performative and improvisational qualities of versifying, drawing attention to the proximity between recitation and writing within sociable settings in which verses were performed, heard before an assembled company, and often written down and circulated. Like ballads, epigrams were intended to provoke response, contest and debate.[29]

Puttenham offered two primary models for the epigram, Martial and Pasquil (or Pasquin), alluding to the practice begun in fourteenth-century Rome of posting anonymous lampoons or libels initially on St Mark's day, although Puttenham attributed the practice to a designated period of misrule when the Church/State was officially without a head. Tavern poetry tended to be occasional and satiric. Tucca in Dekker's *Satiromastix* (1602) rails at Horace/Jonson that a gentleman cannot 'sneake into a Taverne with his Mermaid; but he shall be Satyr'd, and Epigram'd upon' (4.2.54–5). Many of Hoskyns's epitaphs, a form closely related to the epigram, could be said to fall into this loose category of 'merry' tavern poetry. William Camden went to the effort of collecting Hoskyns's epitaphs for his *Remaines* (1605), using them to season his book:

> But I feare now I have overcharged the Readers minde, with dolefull, dumpish, and uncomfortable lines. I will therefore for his recomfort, end this part with a few conceited, merry, and laughing Epitaphes, the most of them composed by maister *John Hostines* [sic] when he was young, and will begin with the Bellowes maker of *Oxford*.

> *Here lyeth* John Cruker *a maker of Bellowes,*
> *His craftes-master and King of good-fellowes;*
> *Yet when he came to the hower of his death,*
> *He that made Bellowes, could not make breath.*[30]

Hoskyns's epitaphs were popular, appearing regularly in the university manuscript miscellanies of the 1620s and 1630s.[31] Here, they are often copied alongside libels on Salisbury, the Earl and Countess of Somerset, and other victims. It is impossible to attribute these libels to Hoskyns or his fellow wits definitively, since libels are anonymous, and rarely owned. That said, the only known manuscript verse attributed to Martin is a libellous epitaph on Bishop Fletcher occasioned by his marriage to Lady Baker in February 1595, 'The Roman Tarquin in his folly blind / Will now be truly bishop pricked she saith'.[32] Hoskyns was also credited with the authorship of an epitaph on Fletcher, 'I was the first that made Christendom see / a Bishop to marry a Ladie'.[33] Given the sociable flyting of Davies at the Inns, it is credible that many other libels were produced by these men and circulated anonymously. Donne noted the epigrammatic quality of libels written on Salisbury soon after his death: 'witty and sharp libels made which not onely for liberty of speaking, but for the elegancie, and composition, would take deep root, and make durable impressions in the memory'.[34]

Libels – written on walls, posted on doors, and thrown through windows – as Andrew Gordon argues, ruptured the civic fabric of the early modern state.[35] Puttenham's account of pasquils incorporates libels into the burlesque ceremonialism of the city, a ritualised space of play that had the generic credibility of a tradition stretching back to Virgil and ancient Rome. For Puttenham, libels are a sub-genre of the epigram, and both forms have a vital role to play in ensuring the continued health of the commonwealth through the ritualised expression of just anger. The epigram originated out of the recognition 'that men would and must need utter their splenes in all ordinarie matters . . . or else it seemed their bowels would burst' (p. 68). Epigrams and libels within this medical idiom, like the bitter medicine of Erasmus's *parrhesia*, were thus necessary purgatives in the state, and since they could not be prevented by any 'civill ordinance', they were a mode of writing that raised particular kinds of questions about violent words, civility and its limits.

The commensality of the tavern and libels, the way that place and genre were elaborated in close proximity, meant that it was possible to imagine libels issuing not from only below, but from within the socially élite space of the tavern.[36] This configuration of the tavern opened an imaginative space for élite oppositional cultures, and decisively shaped their cultural presence in London in the late sixteenth and early seventeenth centuries. Although taverns did not suffer the same level of legislation as alehouses, considered hotbeds of popular disorder and sedition, nonetheless there was concern they fostered riotous behaviour among the élite.[37] The poem 'Precepts of Urbanity', a type of versified conduct book, presents the tavern as an analogous space to the alehouse in its section headed 'Ryot':

> If taverne or the alehouse thou dost haunt
> Wit, credit, health, & wealth thou soone shalt want;
> these frutes they yeld y^t be surchargd wth drinke,
> they brawle & fight, yea stagger, spue & stinke.[38]

Libels and satiric epigrams were condemned in this period as riotous or seditious *and* viewed as means of channelling riot and violent words into socially healthy forms by administering necessary purgatives.

Despite the blanket condemnation of all drinking establishments in the 'Precepts of Urbanity', there were increasingly subtle social and ideological differences between the way that the alehouse and tavern were imagined. In the early seventeenth century, a new element came to the fore in the representation of the tavern. 'Merry heades' were still writing libels and epigrams, but they were also composing lyric poetry. George Wither cast the tavern in a symposiastic role when he evoked a friendly bout of poetic composition at the Devil and St Dunstan tavern in Fleet Street around 1613:

> ... CUDDY, *Thou*, and I,
> Each the others' skill to try,
> At Saint *Dunstanes* charmed Well,
> (As some present there can tell)
> Sang upon a sudden theame,
> Sitting by the Crimson streame.[39]

The tavern is now dedicated to the Muses. The Mermaid in Beaumont's verse epistle 'The Sun which doth the greatest comfort bring' is imagined in very similar circumstances. Describing the innocent virtues of the country to Jonson, the urbane gentleman in the city, the poet suddenly realises what the country lacks is the wit and good wine only to be found in the 'Town' and at the Mermaid:

> what things have we seen
> Done at the *Mermaid*? Hard words that have been
> So nimble, and so full of subtill flame,
> As if that every one from whence they came
> Had meant to put his whole wit in a Jest,
> And had resolv'd to live a foole the rest
> Of his dull life; then when there hath been thrown
> Wit able enough to justifie the Town

> For three daies past, wit that might warrant be
> For the whole City to take foolishly
> Till that were cancell'd, and when that was gone
> We left an aire behind us, which alone
> Was able to make the two next Companies
> Right witty, though but down-right fooles more wise.[40]
>
> (*Poems*, sig. L6r–v)

Beaumont's rhapsodic eulogy to the Mermaid draws on the classic symposiastic notion of *in vino veritas*, which combines Dionysian inspiration with neo-Platonism: drinking wine gives privileged access to truth, inducing a state akin to the divine possession of *furor poeticus*.[41] The tavern is transformed into the feast-place of the gods; it is not so much good food or wine that inspires the poet, but the *energeia* of wit, intensifying pleasure into poetic rapture and constituting the Mermaid as the poetic *locus* of plenitude. The tavern becomes the habitus not of the gallant but of the wit, or rather subtle distinctions have been introduced whereby wit has predominantly positive social connotations, just as the fashionable town is no longer viewed through a moralising satire on consumption.

William Marshall's engraving 'The Lawes of Drinking', which provided the frontispiece to Brathwaite's *Solemne Joviall Disputation*, sets up an iconographic dialectic between the tavern and the alehouse which spells out the ramifications of this assimilation of the tavern to the classical *symposium* (see frontispiece). The alehouse and tavern are carefully demarcated along class lines: the cultural markers of the leisured quality constitute the social space of the tavern, while the alehouse is imagined through objects and signs belonging to the working commonality. The lower-class alehouse at the bottom of the engraving depicts men and women wearing coarse plain dress appropriate to their class, drinking together outside on benches, near a public conduit labelled 'Puddlewharf'. Although there is some familiarity between the men and women – a man in the foreground holds a woman's arm – it is an orderly gathering, not without civilities, hence one man salutes another with his cup in a health-pledge, and another plays the bagpipes while the other jigs. Above, at the tavern, the exclusively male gathering drinks indoors in a private room. The furniture is noticeably more expensive: there are carved chairs rather than benches, goblets instead of tankards, and a classical column, suggesting costly ornamentation, frames the interior. The men are fashionably and expensively dressed, sporting lace collars, capes, and hats, and 'drinking' tobacco. The most graphic difference between the two spaces is the way the tavern is now a classical symposiastic space. The gentlemen are served by Bacchus holding a lyre in one hand and wine in other, an association clarified by the Latin tag 'Nectar ut ingenium' and the wine flowing from the Helicon inspires the wits gathered at the table. The tavern sign depicts a fish framed by the motto 'Poets impalled wth Lawrell Coranets' – it is possible this was the sign adopted by the Sireniacs.[42] Poetry is an activity around which other class markers are organised within this complex codification of space. Proclaiming its distance from economic necessity, since it is sharply distinguished from the forms of popular lower-class leisure, poetry starts to become part of an aesthetic sense, functioning alongside other social practices and objects of consumption as a 'distinctive expression of a privileged position in social space'.[43] This 'privileged position' is configured through a class distinction between private and public spaces; it is noticeable that the élite space of the tavern is indoors, whereby an association is being made between private space and notions of social exclusivity and cultural refinement, whereas the lower-class drinkers at the alehouse consort commonly in public, in the open air.

THE BANQUET OF THE WITS

Shapiro has credibly dated the *convivium philosophicum* held at the Mitre tavern to September 1611.[44] The cashbook of Sir Lionel Cranfield, a diner at the Mitre *convivium*, records ten shillings 'paid at the Mitre' on Bread Street Hill on 11 May 1611 – possibly Cranfield's contribution to an earlier 'banquet of wits'. This was the year Coryate published his *Crudities*, and was preparing for his Eastern travels. Cranfield was his banker, and hosted dinners at which Coryate was a guest.[45] Coryate's letters from Ajmer allude to monthly meetings of the Sireniacal gentlemen at the Mermaid, which presumably coincided with the period between his return from his European travels in October 1608 and his departure for Constantinople in late 1612. A transcription of the safe-conduct the Sireniacs provided for Coryate on his travels survives in a copy of his *Crudities*. Written during a dinner held at the Mermaid on 31 October 1612, it describes a society of wits that met regularly, and engaged in the witty civilities and learned jesting familiar from Brathwaite's *Solemne Joviall Disputation*.

The safe-conduct opens with a playful address to fellow drinkers, setting out the Sireniacs' own place within a classical and European symposiastic tradition:

To all our kindred spirits each and every one, our companions in witty conceits and fellow drinkers at the crystal stream, battling beneath the banners of Jove, Mercury, Bacchus, Pallas, Ceres and Venus in companies, groups, squadrons, battalions, bodies, lodges, colleges, orders, brotherhoods or fraternities, to all presidents and masters of ceremonies individually and collectively, to all the fastidious, and every chairman, steward, butler and waiter at meetings, feasts, banquets and drinking parties.

The society had its own seal, and both the safe-conduct and Coryate's letters from Ajmer refer to various officers: Coryate is assigned the role of the Beadle or official buffoon and Lawrence Whitaker is repeatedly referred to as the High Seneschal or Chief Steward, although it is not recorded who held the post of Clerk of Purse.[46] This mock-state closely correlates with the ludic artificial state created during the revels. Since there were at least twenty-four joint and separate references to the Mitre and Mermaid taverns in plays, poems, pamphlets and letters across a period from the 1597–8 Middle Temple revels to around 1614 – only a couple of allusions occur outside these years – it would suggest that the clubbing initiated at these revels relocated to these taverns soon after the festivities ended, where it continued until the climactic 1614 'addled' parliament.[47] The surviving poems closely associated with these drinking societies – the 'Convivium Philosophicum', the 'Parliament Fart', and the mock-encomiastic poems before the *Crudities* – belong to the genres of learned play, and one can surmise that these societies conducted extempore orations and versifying on chosen themes, and other forms of game-playing, such as the writing of paradoxes and nonsense, an emergent genre closely associated with Hoskyns and his merry crew.

Despite the core of elected officers, participation in these companies was apparently relatively fluid given that many of those at the Mitre *convivium* also appear among the Sireniacs. This may not correlate with the fixed membership of the eighteenth-century gentlemen's club, but it does indicate well-confirmed habits of formal socialising among a wide section of friends and associates in the West End of early seventeenth-century London. Jean Beaulieu, secretary to the English ambassador in France, Sir Thomas Edmondes, wrote to the diplomat William Trumbull in November 1609: 'Yesterday all the "holy crew" together with Mr. Monger, Mr. Calvert and us three champions of this house had a meeting at the "*Mayre Made*" in Bread Street to celebrate your health.'[48] Mr. Calvert was presumably Samuel Calvert, clerk of the Virginia Company; his brother, George, was the secretary to Salisbury, and at that time sitting in the Commons; James Monger was a London merchant. Who were the 'holy crew'? The phrasing suggests a well-defined group, possibly with elected officers, that Trumbull would know easily by the nomenclature. The impression is given that the 'holy crew' met regularly and, on this occasion, were joined by Edmondes, Beaulieu, Monger and Calvert, and others, to practise the sacred rites of friendship by toasting an absent friend, thus momentarily restoring him to their society. In the early years of James's reign, a circle that included Edmondes, John Chamberlain and Ralph Winwood held their convivial meetings at the Mermaid. All had patronage and institutional affiliations that intersected with those present at the Mitre *convivium*. Beaulieu's 'three champions' is reminiscent of the neo-chivalric language of the Inns of Court revels, and it is possible he is describing a society closely connected to the Sireniacs, who also met at the Mermaid. In February 1612, three years after this Mermaid meeting at which he had been present, Samuel Calvert sent a letter to Trumbull containing 'a Banquet of the Wits by Hoskins of the Temple', a copy of the 'Convivium Philosophicum'.[49]

This Latin poem explicitly invoked a humanist tradition of learned and cultivated dining when it designated the meeting a *convivium philosophicum*. The Mitre *convivium* brought together men of varied social origins and rank within the élite: Inns of Court gentlemen, courtiers and officials in Prince Henry's household, barristers and the prominent businessmen Sir Lionel Cranfield and Sir Arthur Ingram, partners in various speculations and ventures.[50] These early seventeenth-century societies were a nodal point within a wider network of associational relations. The civic associations that structured the city commonwealth, alliances formed at Prince Henry's court, and the sociable practices of the metropolis coalesced in these convivial societies. The *convivium* enabled the creation of communities organised by horizontal relationships, epitomised by friendship, rather than the vertical hierarchies of status and rank.[51] The order of guests at the banquet does not seem at all inclined to follow the requirements of social status: Brooke is named first, followed by Donne, Cranfield, Ingram, Sir Robert Phelips, Sir Henry Neville, Richard Connock, Hoskyns, Martin, Sir Henry Goodyer, John West, Holland, Inigo Jones and Coryate. Brathwaite's *Solemne Joviall Disputation*, as we have seen, subsumed social competition to the dictates of friendship: social drinking arose out of a '*Liberalitie* [that] is occasioned either out of *pure affection*, as mutuall courtesies are shewne among friends for no other cause than meerely for friendship' (p. 3). Social rituals previously the preserve of the aristocracy were reconfigured through the dissemination of a civil notion of fraternity. And like the gentleman wits depicted in the engraving 'Laws of Drinking', those gathered at the tavern were making poetry; such aesthetic capital was at the heart of their status as a company of urbane gentlemen.

Symposiastic literature, and poetry in particular, gave these early modern drinking societies a vocabulary with which to delineate and perform male sociability. Jonson's 'Inviting a Friend to Supper' was probably composed some time between 1607 and 1612, and is therefore contemporaneous with the 'Convivium Philosophicum'.[52] They can be read as companion poems since both draw on a symposiastic tradition and were part of the same circuit of socialising. A number of these men, particularly Hoskyns, Martin, Holland and Jones, were close associates of Jonson; although Jonson was not listed among the diners at the Mitre *convivium*, he did help to orchestrate that other gathering of the wits before *Coryats Crudities*. That said, there are distinct differences between the moderate banqueting idealised in 'Inviting a Friend' and the satiric feast served up at the 'Convivium Philosophicum'. The 'Convivium Philosophicum' looks back to an alternative satiric and burlesque strand within the symposiastic tradition to the Anacreontic-Horatian symposiastic lyric favoured by Jonson.[53] Unlike Jonson's 'Invitation to Supper', and belying its title, this 'Convivium Philosophicum' does not hold to the principle of moderation: 'Quisquis hic vult esse prudens, / Adsit, nihil aliud studens / Quam potare plene' (Whosoe will be counted prudent / Let him be no other student / But to drink profoundly).[54] What is served at this table at the Mitre is jesting and satire. The poem has three distinct sections denoting the various courses: the first section introduces the diners through Latin pseudonyms punning on their names, for example, 'Christoferus vocatus *Torrens* / Et Johannes *Factus*' (p. 50), that is, Christopher Brooke and John Donne; in the second Coryate is served up in the guise of the buffoon; and the third section could be said to be the table talk, a sharper dish of satire.

The indebtedness of the 'Convivium Philosophicum' to an alternative symposiastic tradition is largely signalled by the prominence given to the buffoon at the table. It is a role inhabited by Coryate, and one that he had made his own through performances at taverns, private tables, and at court. Coryate's buffoonery is configured very differently to that of Carlo Buffone in Jonson's *Every Man Out*; Coryate is a welcome guest, and expands rather than transgresses the convivial horizons of the company in a similar manner to the buffoon in Xenophon's *Symposium*. In this seminal symposiastic text, the buffoon, Philip, is an interloper; nonetheless he has a recognised and necessary place at the table, as Callias admits when he invites him to 'take a place, for the guests, though well fed, as you observe, on seriousness, are perhaps rather ill supplied with laughter'.[55] The role of Philip, like the other professional entertainers, is to enliven the conversation, in his case, with jests and ludicrous performances, and so contribute to the relaxed and heightened atmosphere of the *symposium*.[56]

Jesting was characteristic of table talk. Lord John in Guazzo's *Civile Conversation* distinguished between two types of jests: scurrilous jests 'which turne to the empeachment or discredit of any man' and 'deserve (in truth) great blame'; and those 'which bring with them a certaine kinde of pleasure and recreation' and are 'worthy of praise and commendation'.[57] This distinction is founded on a notion of moderation that once again goes back to the classical drinking party. The rules of the *symposium* required the participant to maintain a state halfway between sobriety and drunkenness; a moderate pleasure that did not descend into the riotous excesses of the barbarians, but was not restricted by the dull gravity of the sober. Symposiastic literature was therefore concerned with the permissible expression of collective pleasures and passions as well as social and political tensions – the latter frequently managed through the jest and laughter.[58] Philip's presence in Xenophon's *Symposium* is a stimulus to sharp personal and political satire. Prompted by a female acrobat's performance of a sword dance, Anisthenes makes a general satire on the cowardice of Athenian men; Philip then shifts the satire from the general to the particular, turning it to a personal political attack on an Athenian demagogue, Peisander (2.13).

The buffoon introduces the ludic and theatrical forms of burlesque, alongside satire, into the feast. Philip mimics the dancing of the entertainers, making 'a burlesque out of the performance by rendering every part of his body that was in motion more grotesque than it naturally was' (2.22). Burlesque returns when Socrates is likened to the 'ugliest of all the Satyres ever on the stage' (4.19), recalling Alcibiades' famous comparison of Socrates to the Silenus box, grotesquely decorated on the outside, yet containing rare unguents – a favourite Renaissance topos for the seriocomic literary tradition, which included burlesque, and also used in the mock-encomiastic poems before the *Crudities*.[59] There is a strong ludic aspect to the *symposium*. Value is placed on moderation and temperance; nonetheless, it does not overshadow the equal place given to sensual pleasure in its diverse forms: the pleasures of beauty and physical perfection, wine, perfume, music, dance, and the pleasures of conversation which freely 'mingled raillery and seriousness' (4.28).

The 'Convivium Philosophicum' at the Mitre is similarly held under the ludic influence of Folly encapsulated in the buffoon Coryate, and freely mingles philosophy and play; or rather its philosophy is play. The English version produced by John Reynold, a fellow of New College who died in 1614, moralisingly maintains the decorum of moderate banqueting by turning Coryate into a shameful figure whose ludicrous body, speech and manners displays the deforming effects of immoderate drinking and speech:

Nam facete super illum	For wittily on him, they say,
Sicut malleus in anvillum	As hammers on an anvil play,
Unusquisque ludet.	Each man his jeast may breake.
Coriatus cum potavit,	When Coriate is fudled well,
Lingua regnum peragrabit	His tongue begins to talke pel-mel,
Nec illum quicquam pudet.	He shameth nought to speake.

(p. 51)

The Latin is less censorious: 'Lingua regnum peragrabit' could be translated as 'His tongue will wander the Kingdom', in keeping with his *Crudities*, and denoting the linguistic freedoms of travel.[60] The poem delights in linguistic licence, mixing the vernacular and Latin to produce a satiric accompaniment to the classical banquet, kitchen Latin, evident not only in the punning quality of the poem but also comic formulations such as 'rectum stampum' and 'rampum scampum' (p. 52). Kitchen Latin introduces a lively and satiric strand of vulgarity into the learned proceedings of the *convivium*.[61] The poem parades its promiscuity, the polyphony of its talk linguistically figuring the expansiveness of the banquet as topics of conversation move spatially and satirically from Somerset to Rome, and to London – the city, church, and court. Violence is moderated and jests are good-natured rather than vicious. Reynolds translated the lines describing Coryate's youth – 'Puer fuit expers artis / Et cum fabis et cum fartis / Somersetizatus' – into a fairly innocuous, homely joke about Coryate's Somerset childhood: 'A boy he was devoid of skill / With white-pots and oaten-cakes at will / Somersetized' (p. 51). The Latin is a little more irreverent and playful: 'Fabis' is a plural form of *faba*, the broad bean, and 'fartis' derives from *farcio*, meaning stuffing, mincemeat, yet the internal rhyme concentrates the ear on the aural similarities between fartis and fart. Beans, stuffing, and farts – 'Somersetizatus' therefore seems to be coined as a jesting term for someone puffed-up, full of stuffing or wind.

Jonson was not above experimenting with the role of the buffoon when investigating the full range of convivial and symposiastic vocabularies, particularly their potential for constituting or deforming social identity.[62] As we have seen, the buffoon held a particular fascination for Jonson. He sets a mock-symposiastic scene at the Mitre tavern presided over by Carlo Buffone in his *Every Man Out*. The civilising effect of eating, drinking and talking together is lost through violence and unmannerly excesses of the body. If the *convivium* was a ritual of *communitas*, then Buffone drinks alone, scorning friendship, 'Pish, the title of friend, it's a vain idle thing'

(4.3.109–11); instead his boon companions are his two drinking cups. The scene culminates in ritual violence enacted upon Buffone by Puntarvolo and Maciente, who fill his mouth with wax used for sealing letters. In an ingenious twist on the theme of verbal violence, Buffone is transformed into a type of text, a scurrilous verse, and then expelled from the play. The premise of Jonson's 'Epistle to Arthur Squib', appropriately a teller in the Exchequer, is a wager: 'I am to dine, friend, where I must be weighed / For a just wager, and that wager paid / If I do lose it' (lines 1–3). Like the buffoon, Jonson in a sense must pay for his dinner by performing for the company. He assumes a Socratic and Rabelaisian corporeality akin to the Silenus box, whose grotesque exterior discloses spiritual and intellectual riches, except his grotesque body is, in fact, his riches. The epigram ludically places the external and internal, matter and soul in a state of tension uncertainly secured by a pun on 'good weight' (line 6) which denotes physical size, his 'Full twenty stone, of which I lack two pound' (line 12), economic value, the 'six in silver' (line 13) he lacks, and his moral worth. The problem is his credit 'Stinketh' (line 14). There is a fundamental ambivalence in Jonson's response to the buffoon: this persona permits liberties at the table not usually available to one of his class; yet performing for a wager diminishes one's moral credit even as it provides financial benefits. This importuning epistle plays with the dilemmas of a poet who produced poetry for money and relied on this work for his credit.

The place of the classical *symposium* or *convivium* is the private table within the gentleman's villa. In the case of the 'Convivium Philosophicum', the diners leave their own tables to pay for dinner at the Mitre – so if any man's company should be desired, he shall be 'amerciated', fined forty pence, presumably for his supper ('Protinus amercietur / Pro defaulto fourty-pence') (p. 51). Here is a point of difference between the moderate banqueting Jonson promises in his 'Inviting a Friend to Supper' and the satiric feast provided at the Mitre *convivium*: Jonson's canary wine may come from the Mermaid, but it is drunk at his private table. Given Renaissance principles of decorum, it is likely that once the scene of speaking is altered, new possibilities are opened within the form. While there were clear social distinctions between the tavern and the alehouse, they were not absolute. The plebs may not be able to drink at the tavern, but it was still a place for riotious and uncivil behaviour among the 'better sort'. Possibly more so than the private dining table, the tavern signifies the potential inherent within symposiastic literature for drunken speech to overtake the disciplined conversations of the diners. It is at this point that Rabelais, or rather his English counterpart, Sir John Harington, comes to the feast.[63]

Coryate's tongue loosened by drink becomes capable of fantastic linguistic play. This style of speech is 'Harringizing', the Harington of the *Metamorphosis of Ajax*, that little book of 'skurril and toying matter' composed by a wit noted both for his inability to refrain from a 'scurvey jeste' and for his mirth and 'good conceit'.[64] A society in which Harringizing is the defining idiom of the wit is a society in which Folly reigns supreme. That may be so, yet those listed among the diners, particularly Hoskyns and Martin, were not above 'Harringizing' themselves. In fact, Harington's own mock-encomium on Coryate appears in the 'Panegyricke Verses' before *Coryats Crudities*.

When Jonson does formulate rules for the tavern – his own 'Laws of Drinking' – in his *Leges Convivales* for the Apollo Room in the early 1620s, he turns to the moderate banqueting tradition initiated in 'Inviting a Friend' to create a space for refined, urbane male tavern-clubbing.[65] Even so, he does not exclude the ludic forms of the 'Convivium Philosophicum'. While the violence of Lucian's *Lapiths*, in which the drinking party ended in a drunken brawl, must be avoided, there is a place for play and competitive jesting, as rule 14 states: 'De seriis, aut sacris, poti & saturi ne disserunto' (But let there be more skirmishing in conversation than in wine).[66] In his tavern scenes in plays such as *Every Man Out* and *The Staple of News*, Jonson is open to the burlesque theatricality present within the symposiastic tradition. His own private table is a different matter, and here he refrains from the excesses of the buffoon and burlesque. Its ethos of liberty is defined in terms of 'a private festivity', as Joseph Loewenstein notes, enabling Jonson to strengthen the association of friendship with freedom of speech, permitting the host and his guests to 'speak our minds' in learned fashion, and to debate 'Virgil, Tacitus, / Livy, or of some better book' (lines 21–2). Jonson's is a temperate liberty that is insistently distinguished from licence, and assimilated to an ethos of moderation.[67] Hence the Mermaid's 'pure Cup of rich Canary wine', 'Of this we will sup free, but moderately' (lines 29, 35), is commensurate with the table talk 'uttered at our mirthful board' that will not 'affright / The liberty that we'll enjoy tonight' (lines 40–2). Jonson's liberty has a private, leisurely aspect that he inherits from Martial's epigrams in which a 'public republican discourse exemplifying *libertas* is reduced and reconfigured to be the stuff of private diversion'.[68] The banquet is a sanctioned space identified with liberties of speech and conscience precisely because it is a private space: the speaker and his guest will be amongst friends, a social sphere that is shaped in contradistinction to a corrupt and dangerous public world peopled by men such as 'Poley or Parrot', government informers whose association with religious and political oppression contrasts with the values of learning, liberty and conscience ascribed to the private sphere of friendship. Frank speech is no longer safe in a society policed by Pooleys and Parrots, hence *libertas* finds refuge among friends at the table, and satire becomes private, marginal and secretive.[69]

At the Mitre's 'Convivium Philosophicum', satire is open and freely expressed. By placing the buffoon at the centre of the feast, constant pressure is exerted on the very fine line dividing raillery and civility in symposiastic literature, and gives the impression of freely uttered invective. The diners discuss the efforts of the Lord Chamberlain, Thomas Howard, Earl of Suffolk, to control royal expenditure: 'Et Suffolcius, severe / Regis familiam coercere / Quaerens, defatigatur' ('And Suffolke, seeking, in good sorte, / The king his household to supporte, / Is still defatigated'). Reynolds' translation of 'severe' (gravely, austerely) and 'coercere' (place restraints, limits on) into 'in good sort' and 'to supporte' appears a dramatic understatement of the original. Satire is not confined to the privacy of the table. Just as the poem in formal terms traverses the classical symposiastic lyric and the popular drinking song, so too the railing table talk promiscuously expands to become 'London city' talk that ramps and scamps. It sounds very similar to other forms of early seventeenth-century tavern poetry – sharp epigrams, political satires and libels. When these wits gathered together at the table their talk was of corruption in the city and at court. Henry is said to be frustrated with his lack of real political power, even in Reynold's translation: 'Princeps nescit otiari, / Cupiens materiam dari / Propriae virtuti' ('Prince Henry cannot idly liven, / Desiring matter to be given / To prove his valour good') (p. 52). The parlous state of the royal finances due to James's extravagance had recently been heatedly debated by a number of the diners in parliament, and Hoskyns, in particular, put the blame on James's Scottish courtiers, those Scots 'cum scarfis et cum spanglis' ('With silken scarfes and with spangles') (p. 51). The table talk at this *convivium* gives an anatomised view of a state riven by self-interest at the expense of a wider public good.

What these friends 'were doing that evening in the Mitre Tavern', as Annabel Patterson has pointed out, 'was talking politics'.[70] One could see the revival of the *convivium* by this politicised company of wits as an attempt to find an equivalent discursive space to the classical public forum, a virtuous public sphere in which good men could speak freely and authoritatively on matters affecting the state.[71] The *convivium* was a very appropriate model for the scribal community to construct and present a social identity since it provided a model for conceptualising and organising texts that was both embodied and dialogic. It imagined communities coming together in the exchange of civilities, ideas and opinions, and presupposed the participants' engagement in a wider sphere of dialogue and debate. Yet, these humanist-educated men would have recognised that the table was a different space to the forum. The table, like the tavern, stands adjacent to the public forum as a place where affairs of state can be discussed in a different register. Classical theorists of the *symposium* were quite clear that the persuasive rhetoric employed in the public forum was not appropriate to the private table, where conversation was governed by principles of pleasure and permitted liberties not advisable in more public places. Crato, in Plutarch's *Table Talk*, gave the example of Plato who did not dispute at the table 'and get his customary tight and unbreakable hold, but with simple and easy premises, with examples, and with mythical legends he brings the company into agreement with him'. To make philosophy and politics more palatable they should be mixed with lighter genres, such as jests and satire, and seasoned with entertainments.[72] One of the distinctive features of early modern table talk is the way that it freely mixes politics and play, raillery and seriousness.[73]

The 'Convivium Philosophicum' achieved a degree of fame within scribal communities.[74] Part of its appeal probably arose out of a taste for texts that possessed 'clubbability': jests and puns often rely on privileged knowledge and those able to decipher their meaning gain textual pleasure from the satisfaction of belonging to an exclusive group. It was copied into a miscellany, compiled from around 1600 into the early 1620s, belonging to the Welshman Richard Roberts (Bod., MS. Don.c.54), a lawyer and later a justice on the Welsh circuit who was part of a legal scribal community and had access to a circle of Essex sympathisers in the late 1590s.[75] Some caution does need to be exercised when drawing conclusions about the compilation of the anthology, given that Roberts seems to have copied poems some time after receiving them. Nonetheless, there is evidence of politically motivated compilation and a politicised concept of the scribal community itself: a cluster of pro-Essex and anti-Cecil material (fols. 19r–20v) is followed by a group of texts relating to the period from 1609 to 1613, consisting of 'A peticion to the kinges most exellent Matie from the lower howse of Parliament about imposicions. / 1610' (fols. 20v–21r), the 'Convivium Phoolosophicum' (fols. 21r–22r), and a set of poems 'Upon the earle of Somersett's marriadg withe the earle of Essex wife her husband being alive' (fols. 22v–23r). Given Roberts's legal connections, he may have had access to the scribal community gathered around Hoskyns and Martin – these men spoke loudly against impositions in the Commons and possibly had a hand in the 1610 petition – and collected material during the years when the tavern societies were active.[76] His notes to the 'Convivium

Philosophicum' suggest insider knowledge: the names of those attending are carefully identified in the margin against their Latin pseudonyms; a note is made on the section of political table talk that 'This later part was made by Whittakers', the High Seneschal of the Sireniacs; and the poem is attributed 'per Johannem Hoskins', the information that Hoskyns was made serjeant-at-law in 1624 possibly being added at a later date. While the miscellany does not include any other poems attributed to Hoskyns, there are numerous anonymous libels and epigrams – tavern poems – that are allusively associated with the table talk of the drinking society celebrated in the 'Convivium Philosophicum'.

The 'Convivium Philosophicum' and Jonson's 'Inviting a Friend' illustrate how a symposiastic tradition provided a vocabulary for considering the place and limits of pleasure, liberty and satire. Both draw attention to the scene of speaking and the way it determines who has the authority to speak and the forms of conversation. It does make a difference if the conversation takes place in the classical villa or private house to an exclusive audience of a select few, or in the early modern tavern, a public house in which private societies met, thus opening the private table onto other arenas. The 'Convivium Philosophicum' is a key text in an English tradition of symposiastic poetry because it is an early example of burlesque that makes a space for freely uttered invective in the learned conversation of the diners. Tavern poetry returned the body and its appetites to the table through the forms of embodied satire.[77] In its symposiastic pleasures and satiric anger and corruptions, the body has the potential to disrupt civil conversations because it figures the release of inhibitions regulating public discourse and behaviour. The body was thus simultaneously stigmatised through satires and libels and imagined productively and creatively as the site for new liberties.

CHAPTER FOUR

Wits in the House of Commons

Writing to Sir Edward Phelips from Ajmer, Coryate asked to be remembered to his son, Sir Robert, and 'M. *Martin* also, M. *Christopher Brooke*, whom I thanke still for his no lesse elegant then serious verses: M. *Equinoctiall Pasticrust* [John Hoskyns] of the middle Temple, M. *William Hackwell*, and the rest of the worthy gentlemen frequenting your Honourable table, that favour vertue, and the sacred Muses' (*Traveller*, pp. 8–9). Coryate will send his remembrances once more to these men in his letter addressed to the Sireniacal fraternity. The men Coryate identifies were predominantly Middle Temple and Lincoln's Inn lawyers who sat in the first Jacobean parliament, which met in 1604 and was finally dissolved at the end of 1610 – Sir Edward was Speaker in the House of Commons in this parliament, and Hoskyns, Brooke, Hakewill and Sir Robert would go on to sit in the 1614 'addled' parliament. The company at Sir Edward's table engaged in conversations and practised modes of sociability that were an extension of their complex civic and social identities. They had strong civic credentials as lawyers and members of parliament, as well as connections with Prince Henry's court and the city. When Martin assumed the role of *parrhesiastes* in his speech welcoming James to London, he was authorised to speak frankly both as the representative of the City of London and as a Middle Temple lawyer. Parliament was an institution that intersected with the civic corporate culture at the Inns of Court, extending its communicative practices into the sphere of governance, and fostering forms of political sociability among social élites.

When we look to the recreational forms favoured by these societies then it is noticeable how civil and civic conversations are transformed through ritualised play. This is exemplified with outstanding brio by the popular comic political poem 'The Censure of a Parliament Fart'. It is a poem energised by the practices of commoning: the House of Commons takes on a ludic utopian aspect comparable to the artificial commonwealths of the Inns of Court revels. This mode of political discourse is open to, and not disabled by, parody and burlesque. The kind of political work the poem undertakes cannot be heard fully if we confine our understanding of purposeful communicative practices to the discourses of civic rationality often privileged in studies of the early modern public sphere. The 'Parliament Fart' does describe a political community united by shared values. But the political semantics of the fart are not oriented towards the democratic consensus of public opinion, nor do they produce a rational, civil subject.[1] Both the 'Convivium Philosophicum' and the 'Parliament Fart' are committed to a notion of *communitas* that is enlivened by play and improvisation and receptive to the sounds of political dissonance. The political fart is a rhetorical figure for dissonance, a musical term in which each sound, in the words of Boethius, is 'unwilling to blend together and each somehow strives to be heard unimpaired, and since one interferes with the other, each is transmitted to the sense unpleasantly'. Semantically related to the Greek *diaphonia*, dissonance incorporates the sense of a conflict of opinions and ideologies. In the discordant fart can be heard, as Mikhail Bakhtin says of heteroglossia, 'the co-existence of socio-ideological contradictions' between different communicative practices and interest groups, 'all given a bodily form'.[2] A notion of political dissonance provides a conceptual framework for attending to the historical effect of contesting political meanings that could be heard within the public arenas of the early seventeenth century.

COMPOSITION, PERFORMANCE, CIRCULATION

On the afternoon of 4 March 1607, an event took place that was to inspire one of the most popular comic political poems in the seventeenth century. Sir John Croke had just delivered the message from the Lords to the Commons regarding a conference on the naturalisation of the Scots, those born after James's accession to the throne. At this point Robert Bowyer, clerk to the House of Lords, inserted the following note in the margins of his parliamentary diary:

As the Messenger had spoken the Words (their Lordships) one at the nether end of the House *sonitum ventre emisit*; whereat the Company laughing the Messenger was almost out of Countenance. It is said to have bene young Ludloe; not that this seemeth done in disgrace, for his Father Sir Edward Ludloe before a Committee fell on sleepe and *sonitum ventre emisit*: So this seemeth Infirmity Naturall, not Malice.[3]

Bowyer delights in expounding the fart, and he was certainly not alone. The result was 'A Censure of the Parliament Fart', as it is entitled in several copies, and all copies begin with the same ten or twelve lines, albeit with much internal variation:

> Downe came grave ancient Sr John Crooke
>   And read his Message on a Booke
> fferry well quoth Sr William Morris, soe
>   But Henry Ludlowes taile cried noe
> Upstarte one ffuller (fuller of devotion
>   then eloquent) and said, a verie ill motion
> Not soe neither, quoth Sr Henry Jenkin
>   the motion were good, but for the stinkin
> quoth Sr Henrie Poole tis a verie bold tricke
>   to farte in the nose of the body politicke
> Indeed I confesse too, saith Sr Edward Grivill
>   the matter it selfe was somwhat uncivill[4]

The 'Parliament Fart' is an extended piece of extempore wit by an assembled 'Company laughing the Messenger . . . almost out of Countenance'.

The poem's loose, improvisational structure gives the impression it was composed, in Puttenham's words, in 'tavernes and common tabling houses, where many merry heades meete, and scrible with ynke, with chalke, or with a cole such matters as they would every man should know, and descant upon'.[5] There are stylistic similarities with the 'Convivium Philosophicum'. Whereas the 'Convivium Philosophicum' places the buffoon at the centre of the banquet, the 'Parliament Fart' admits the fart to a meeting of the great council of parliament. In both instances, the effect is to introduce the Rabelaisian body, a site for burlesque, parody and licentious verbal play, thus allowing dissonant voices to be heard in the proceedings. The poems share a four-stress metre with the popular drinking ballad, performed in alehouses and taverns.[6] And there is evidence that the 'Parliament Fart' was sung: the papers of Sir Edward Conway include a ballad ('A furious fight there befell / all about an Oyster shell') headed 'A proper newe ballad intituled the duel of dogs to the tune of downe came grave auntient Sergeant Crooke'.[7] Four-stress metre is an attribute of the poem's radical and unique compositional flexibility: this metre enables improvisation and speaks to the poem's status as a highly accomplished performance text. There is no fixed form to the poem, aside from the set opening lines; rather it is a type of bricolage, a free assemblage of couplets whose organisational principle is extemporisation. The result is a form so radically improvisatory that it could be described as a type of anti-structure. It does not designate an author; instead its origin lies in the communal and collaborative processes of performance. The pleasures of the text reside not in remembering and recreating a fixed text, but in improvising on couplets already in circulation and introducing variants, thereby artfully tuning the poem to the performer's own voice. Extemporised versifying is taken to new heights of craft as some versions announce in the following heading they give to the poem – *'Never was bestowed such art / Upon the tuning of a Fart'*.[8] Blank leaves are left either in the middle or at the end of the poem in some anthologies, allowing the composer to introduce couplets from other versions in circulation.[9] The poem is made and remade through the processes of performance, transcription and circulation. Its content is not fixed in space; instead couplets are constantly on the move and in various states of mutation from one version to the next.

Just as the 'Convivium Philosophicum' opens by naming the diners through Latin puns, the 'Parliament Fart' proceeds in epigrammatic fashion by assembling couplets naming members of the Commons and giving their 'character'. There were couplets in circulation on at least 112 members of James's first parliament. Most couplets have no intrinsic link with each other aside from the occasion, although some are organised in distinct sections, such as the opening lines setting the occasion, and the following sequence on the Speaker, Sir Edward Phelips, and the convivial antiquarians Sir Robert Cotton and John Pory, which sometimes acts as the conclusion:

> Then up riseth the Speaker that noble Ephestion,
> And says, gentlemen, Ile put it to question
> The question was made but the eyes did it loose
> for the major part went cleare with the nose.
> Sr Robert Cotton, a man well read in old storie
> Havinge conferred his notes wth Mr Porrye,
> Can verie well witnesse that these are not fables.
> Yet was it hard to putt a farte in their tables.
>
> (Add. 23,229, fol. 17v)

The well-crafted couplets assembled in the 'Parliament Fart', admirable for their sharp wit and brevity, were composed by writers, like Hoskyns and Martin, highly skilled and well-practised in penning epigrammatic verse. 'Much a doe quoth Sr Peter Manwood for a stenche / my ffather lett a hundred in the benche' (fol. 17v), for example, does not simply equate father and son – Sir Roger had been examined before the Privy Council in 1592 over charges of malpractice – but wittily and pithily incorporates a sense of a legal-parliamentary milieu.[10]

The poem proceeds through *prosopopeia*, comic impersonation. An embodied mode, it attributes a sociocorporeality to the text in which writing is analogous to face-to-face interaction. The poem is thus secured within communities and the performance spaces they inhabit, and located in time as well as space.[11] The fart is an aural and olfactory phenomenon primarily experienced in bodily terms. Collectively heard and smelt by members within the chamber of the House of Commons, it conveys an '*embodied* understanding' of *communitas*, producing an imagined, 'acoustic' community.[12] Textual time is the moment of composition, just after the assembled company hear the fart; yet the couplets carry with them political memories of other events at other times, thus attributing the historical continuities of the past, present and future to the institution of parliament. There is an earlier parliament satire, entitled 'A Rayling libell against those of the p[ar]liament house', that uses a similar although less sophisticated mode of institutional embodiment, and proceeds by satirically naming a Commons committee that met in October 1566 to consider Elizabeth's marriage and the question of succession:[13]

> Mollineux the mover
> Bell the Orato[r]
> Mountsoun the prover
> Ringsmell the Colecto[r]
> Wentforth the Wrangle[r]
> Strange the Religious
> S[t] John the Jangle[r]
> (BL, MS Stowe 354, fol. 18r)

'A Rayling libell' fashions parliament within satire's sharp discourses of moral, social and political judgement. Paradoxically, by attacking the Commons the verse in effect confirms its institutional presence within the commonwealth. Embodied and personified through its elected members, parliament is imagined not simply as an event or an aspect of the royal prerogative, but as a vital institution of governance in its own right.

The initial phase of composition and performance of the 'Parliament Fart' overlapped with the flurry of versifying among the London coteries occasioned by Coryate and his travels. Ludlow's fart was let during the third session of the first Jacobean parliament that ended in July 1607, the fourth session ran from early February to late July 1610, and the fifth from 16 October to 6 December of this year – parliament was dissolved on 9 February 1611, and not recalled until April 1614. For many months preceding the publication of his *Crudities* in March 1611, Coryate and his friends had been soliciting and gathering poems that would be collected in the 'Panegyricke Verses'. The period from around 1607 to late 1612, when the Sireniacs sent Coryate on his travels, thus witnessed a concerted experimentation with burlesque, the mock-encomium, parody, and other classical low and ludic forms.[14] Versifying, as we have seen in the 'Convivium Philosophicum', was a vital element of the sociability practised by these companies. At the end of a version in the Conway papers is the following ditty:

> Ned Jones Dick Martyn, Hopkins, & Brooke
> The fower compilers of this booke,
> fower of like witte, fower of like arte.
> And all fower not worth a farte.
> (Add. 23,229, fol. 17v)

Edward Jones regularly entertained his friends, among them Donne and Martin – and presumably Hoskyns and Brooke – at his house in Essex.[15] The 'fower compilers of this booke' tells us these wits shared a manuscript book in which they composed and copied verses, including the 'Parliament Fart'.

The poem was presumably composed and performed when parliament was in session, or soon after. There are couplets that can be dated to this third session: 'y^t wer noe grievance quoth Mr Hare / If this knave Purvey^r of this ffart had a share' (Bod., MS. Tanner 306/2, p. 256) refers to John Hare, who led the campaign in this session against purveyance, the enforced purchase of goods by the Crown to supply the royal household at less than market value; 'qth Sir Edw: Hobbie alleadgd wth the spiggot, / S^r if you fart at the union reme[m]ber Kitt Piggott' (BL, MS Stowe 962, fol. 67r) refers to the expulsion of Christopher Piggot from the House on 16 February 1607 for his invective against the Scots. Parliament, as Pauline Croft has demonstrated, was 'a social event' bringing over one thousand individuals – members, their households and others – from the counties into London. Sir Edward Hoby organised great feasts held at the Merchant Taylors' Hall on 3 July 1604 and 12 February 1607 at the start of these parliamentary sessions to unite the Commons and the King.[16] Members spent their time in London socialising – conversing, dining, drinking, gaming, and exchanging news, texts and gossip – thereby consolidating social and political networks.[17] The law term also brought lawyers, like Hoskyns and Brooke, and others with legal business from their residences in the counties and provincial towns into the capital. It fostered civic conversations between the capital and the provincial cities: Brooke, for example, wrote to York's Lord Mayor with details of events in the 1606 parliamentary session following the Gunpowder Plot, including tensions between the Bishops and the Commons.[18] At the end of his letter to Whitaker and his fellow Sireniacs, Coryate gave directions as to where his well-wishers could be found when in London: Hoskyns 'of the citie of Hereford', Brooke 'of the city of Yorke', Martin, and Hakewill all resided in chambers at their Inns; Donne at his house on the Strand; Jonson and Sir Robert Cotton at their respective houses in Blackfriars; and Inigo Jones and Holland 'where Maister *Martin* shall direct you'. And when these friends were together, according to Coryate's letters, they met on the first Friday of the month at the Mermaid tavern.[19] By the early seventeenth century, there was a distinct London season that followed the law year: beginning in autumn, ending in June, it reached its height at Christmas.[20] It was a time of socialising when recreation and business – in parliament, the law courts, the city and at court – productively coincided.

Parliament fostered its own distinctive scribal communities. The wits credited with the composition of the 'Parliament Fart' and their close associates were recording speeches and producing studies of parliament and its procedures, particularly the legal issues raised by impositions, taxes on imported goods imposed by the royal prerogative. Martin was not alone in keeping a table book for recording speeches and making notes.[21] His close friend James Whitelocke advised his son that the 'whole proceeding' of the 1610 session 'is otherwise amplye related by the cleark of the parliament', Ralph Ewen, and implied these books were available for study.[22] Speeches of Hakewill and Whitelocke setting out the legal case against impositions quickly passed into the realms of scribal publication. Hakewill in the preface to his *Libertie of the Subject: Against the Pretended Power of Impositions*, eventually published in 1641, spoke of how this text had circulated scribally since 1610, 'entertained in many judicious hands'.[23] The 'Parliament Fart' was copied alongside parliamentary and other political tracts in a miscellany compiled by Ralph Starkey (BL, Add. MS 4149); a London merchant and close associate of Cotton, he systematically collected state papers, especially contemporary legal and parliamentary documents. Satires and political tracts shared the same social and textual space: the 1610 'Petition of Right' for the freedom of speech to debate impositions was copied by the Welsh lawyer Richard Roberts alongside the 'Convivium Philosophicum' and Jacobean libels.[24]

Parliamentary business was disseminated through scribal channels, conversation, and other communicative practices despite the principle of the secrecy of parliamentary business, intended to protect the privileged status of parliament and the principle of freedom of speech. Tensions between this principle and the desire to open parliament to wider discussion were evident in the early seventeenth century.[25] A print-based notion of the public sphere is simply too restrictive to understand how parliament in the early seventeenth century as an institution and a social event facilitated a range of conversations. The 'Parliament Fart' is a case in point. Given its high survival rate in miscellanies, coupled with the sheer range of variants, there must have been hundreds of copies in circulation from 1607 onwards. This means that, in this instance, manuscript was achieving and perhaps even exceeding levels of transmission attributed to print. Still circulating well into the Restoration, the 'Parliament Fart' possessed a popularity and longevity remarkable for a poem tied to specific events and achieved only by a very few similarly occasional printed texts.

Part of its popularity arose out of its structural openness, a feature of scribal and oral publication that is difficult for print to replicate. A number of couplets seem to relate specifically to later events or business in subsequent parliaments.[26] Sir Thomas Monson is given the cryptic lines 'Then gan sage Mounson silence to breake / And said this fart would make an Image speake' (Bod., Mal. 23, p. 8). Accused of complicity in Sir Thomas Overbury's murder, 'sage' Monson did not break his silence; two attempts at arraignment in 1615 were called off, and he was released in 1617 without standing trial.[27] Sir Francis Moore made his name for attacking monopolies in James's first parliament; however, the particular phrasing of his couplet, 'letts this motion repeale / Whats good for the private is oft ill for the comonweale' (p. 3), seems to derive from a speech he delivered in 1614 in which he condemned monopolists for pretending patents were for the public good when they were concerned with 'private gain'.[28] Monopolies were a hot issue again in the 1621 and 1624 parliaments: a variant attributed to Lawrence Hyde has him proclaim 'I like not that fashion / for Monopolies were forbidden by proclamation' (Rosenbach 1083/15, fol. 56r) – in March 1621 James cancelled by proclamation the patents on concealed lands, inns, and gold and silver thread.[29]

The House of Commons in the early seventeenth century was not a democratic public forum. Parliaments were summoned according to the king's necessity, and not as a matter of course in the government of the early modern state. That said, James's long first parliament was in session from 1604 to 1610, and the 1614 parliament met just over three years later.[30] Even though business was frequently prorogued, parliament in effect met relatively regularly over a ten-year period in a similar pattern to Elizabethan parliaments, summoned approximately every three years. This meant that members of the Commons had frequent and regular opportunities to socialise in London, to form associations and to engage in political conversations, thus contributing to a wider culture animated by parliament both as a civic institution and as a sociable event. The parliamentary texts transmitted through scribal communities were social texts that conceptualised a broader community of citizens actively interested in the processes of governance they described. The 'Parliament Fart', in comparable fashion to the Inns of Court revels, employs the forms of ritualised play, attributing a rhetorical and civic authority to the Commons that constitutes the Lower House as a ludic utopian body of state.

HEARING THE 'PARLIAMENT FART'

The 'Parliament Fart' is a festive celebration of the political body of parliament. Farting in early modern medical discourse was necessary for the health and regulation of the body. Just as parliament brings nutriment to the commonwealth, the stomach was the centre of digestion and the organ which cleansed the body of superfluity. Such 'excrementes be none other, but matter superfluouse and unsavery', as Sir Thomas Elyot explained in his *The Castel of Helth* (1541), 'which by natural powers may not be converted in to the fleshe, but remayning in the body corrupt the members, and therefore desireth to have them expelled'.[31] The collective move to censure and expel the noisome fart comedically establishes the central regulatory role of the Lower House within the body politic. Scatology in the poem owes a debt to anticlerical satire and works to secure the moderate Protestant consensus represented by the English parliament. Hence the fart is either puritan or papist, in keeping with Reformation satire:

> Nay quoth S^r: Hugh Beeston and swore by the Masse
> Its rather the braying of some Puritain Asse.
> . . . .
> Then wisely spake S^r: Anthony Cope
> Pray God it be not A Bull from the Pope
> (Mal. 23, pp. 4–5)

The 'Parliament Fart' is not a burlesque or a travesty in that it does not employ the techniques of inversion, using a low style, for example, to treat a high subject. Rather it is a parody that works by the textual processes of transposition and displacement. Like the law sports during the revels, with their exuberant parodies, the 'Parliament Fart' concentrates on procedures and practices specific to the House of Commons. Laughter is not provoked by the irruption of carnivalesque popular energies, but instead arises out of 'an intensification of self-consciousness within the institution itself'.[32]

Lawyers in James's first parliament when faced with political questions legalistically reiterated procedure 'peculiar to the Commons'. In doing so, they gave the 'collective membership . . . a conscious sense of the identity of the House as well as a practical knowledge of its inner workings'.[33] Faced with the procedural problem posed by the fart, the 'Parliament Fart' parodically invokes measures available to the Commons to deal with this noisome interruption of its business. In keeping with the decorum of speaking in the House, members speak only once to the fart when deliberating the House's response, hence Starkey's descriptive headnote to the poem: 'A Censure of a Fart (that was lett in the Parleament howse by m^r Henry Ludlowe) by a worshipfull Jurie each speaking in theire order as foloweth' (Add. 4149, fol. 213r).[34] There is some dispute over precedents in lawyerly fashion: Sir Robert Hitcham, the 'Learned Councell of the Queene', claims 'Such a Fart was never seene'; Mr Peak disagrees, 'I have a President in store / That his Father farted the Session before', to which William Noy, the highly regarded Lincoln's Inn lawyer, adds, ''twas lawfully done / ffor this fart was entaild from father to sonne'; however, as Christopher 'Kitt' Brooke points out, 'Though he has right by discent he has not livery & seizin' (Mal. 23, p. 3). The House deliberates on appropriate action to take in order to deal with the fart. A couplet attributed either to a 'friend' or to Sir Edward Hoby points out that 'ere this be transacted / I feare wee must have this fart enacted', in other words, the House must give their consent to turn the fart into law before the whole business can be brought to a close. Sir John Bennett disagrees and instead argues that 'Wee must have a scelect Committee to penn it' (p. 7). Sir George More, Donne's father-in-law and one of the most senior men in the Commons, warns 'wee suffer this fart . . . more y^n is fitt / T'were goode wee did it to ye Sergeant comitt'. The Serjeant, Roger Wood, 'humbly on's knees' demurs, pointing out that 'farts often breake prison but never pay fees' (this refers to the gratuities paid to the Serjeant by prisoners in his custody) and adding, 'And by your favour ye motion wth out reason sta[nds] / I should be charg'd wth y^t I can not hold in my hand' (CCC 328, fol. 95r). This is precisely the procedural problem posed by the fart – it is immaterial and ephemeral. The impossibility of containing a fart introduces a procedural open-endedness; available measures for censuring the fart are stymied by its effluvial nature. The parodic figure of the fart works by introducing indeterminacy into structures creating a situation in which, in the words of Thomas Greene, 'the group is obliged to wing it'.[35]

There is a literary precedent for the dissonant political acoustics of the parliament fart:

> Why qth Sir Roger Owen if books be noe liers,
> I know on fart devided among'st 12: ffriers.
> (Stowe 962, fol. 67r)

The book is Chaucer's *The Summoner's Tale*, which posed the philosophical problem of how to divide a fart among a dozen friars equally. The fart is 'an extremely complex political sign' in both the *Summoner's Tale* and the 'Parliament Fart' that introduces interpretive and procedural conundrums but does not resolve them.[36] In *The Summoner's Tale*, the Friar brings the legacy of the fart to his lord's table, where those assembled act as a council, each representative proposing a solution to the metaphysical problem put before them:

> Nevere erst er now herde I of swich mateere.
> I trowe the devel putte it in his mynde.
> In ars-metricke shal ther no man fynde,
> Biforn this day, of swich a question.
> Who sholde make a demonstracion
> That every man sholde have yliche his part
> As of the soun or savour of a fart?[37]

Disputation in both texts, as a result of the political acoustics of the fart, sounds like dissonance rather than the harmonious sounds of consensus. In the case of the 'Parliament Fart', its acoustic horizons mark out the House of Commons as a ritualised space in which political differences could be voiced and debated.[38]

One ending given to the 'Parliament Fart' in a miscellany owned by Christopher Wase, a fellow of King's College, Cambridge in the 1640s, is particularly noisy:

> Conclude qth Sr John Hollis ther is no reason lawe or art
> We wise men thus be questioned for a fart
> Wth that each man discharginge his nose
> Willed be gone, and so the Court rose
> When all had well laughed they Concluded by art
> y^t Pliaments of late wear subject to a fart
> Yet they better likte the tricke of the Chollicke
> Then the former blast of the Powder Catholique
> And thus the parliament, in mens opinion
> Hath turnde to a fart the matter of union!
>
> Bod., MS. Rawl.poet.117, fol. 86v

Farts, nose blowing and bomb blasts – the sounds of dissidence heard in different and politically unequal registers. So, for example, the gunpowder plot is distinguished from the 'tricke of the Chollicke', which in turn is the dissonant sound of the debates on the Union. Henry Ludlow's fart on 4 March 1607 was heard at a crucial point in debates over the naturalisation of the *post nati*. Lawyers had led the House in refusing to accept the legal ruling by King's judges granting naturalisation to Scots born after James's accession to the English throne, and negotiations had once again reached stalemate. At the end of March, James complained bitterly to the House about their failure to reach agreement on the Union: 'But now finding many crossings, long disputations, strange questions, and nothing done... so you adde delay unto delay, searching out as it were the very bowels of Curiositie, and conclude nothing.'[39] Turning 'to a fart the matter of union' is the sound of this highly contentious 'nothing' of crossings, long disputions, and strange questions, in other words, the political tactic of delay.

James's 'delay' and 'nothing' was, of course, the House's exercise of its freedom to debate and provide counsel on matters concerning the commonwealth, such as naturalisation and impositions. The couplet attributed to Sir John Holles, 'ther is no reason lawe or art / We wise men thus be questioned for a fart' is an assertion of the House's privilege of free speech even in the face of royal censure. Yet, this equation between free speech and the fart sounds as much like dissonance as it does the consensual sound of counsel. In the fart, it is possible to hear both sides of the argument simultaneously, both James's interpretation of proceedings in the Commons in terms of the voices of dissent, and the argument set out in the Commons' 1610 Petition: 'First, we hold it an ancient, general, and undoubted right of Parliament to debate freely all matters which do properly concern the subject and his right or state; which freedom of debate being once foreclosed, the essence of the liberty of Parliament is withall dissolved.'[40] Freedom of speech was an aspect of parliament's role as the king's 'Great Council'. However, parliament was not only a counsel chamber, it was a legislative body, the supreme court in England. Counsel and council were 'interchangeably spelt' in this period: either word could denote royal advice, an institution and a legal adviser, and so carried multiple meanings. Privy councillors maintained a different notion of counsel to that held by many of lawyers in the House. In James's first two parliaments, it became apparent that the latter saw counsel primarily in terms of debate conducted in the interest of establishing the law, rather than consent secured in the interests of the king. James complained bitterly about the lawyers in parliament who studied his prerogative, and many, like Hakewill, Brooke, Hoskyns, Martin and his friend James Whitelocke, questioned the notion of the *arcana imperii*, since prerogatives were objects of reason rather than mysteries of state.[41] Terms like counsel were sites of contestation as different interests within parliament and the state asserted their authority to speak and debate.

There are versions of the 'Parliament Fart' that seem to give a more sympathetic hearing to the liberties of the House. A version in the Conway papers, given the title 'The Parliament Libell', is more politically pointed in parts than many others. This is also the version ending with the verse claiming its source is a manuscript book compiled by Edward Jones, Martin, Hoskyns and Brooke, and its politics are in keeping with the interests of three of these wits who sat in the Commons – Martin, Hoskyns and Brooke:

> Then quoth feirce Henrye looke to this clause,
> Else farewell England o^r liberty, & lawes.
> Quoth Sandies Sr Edwin marke my progression
> Ile farte yo^u a progect shall last a whole session
> And, quoth Sr Herbert Croffte, Ile second the same,
> To farte in ou^r Countryes cause is noe shame.
> Gentelmen, quoth Lewckno^r, Ile tell yo^u one thinge,
> This farte is misreported to o^r noble kinge.
> naye quoth Sr Rodger, I went from this place,
> and reported it worde for worde to his grace.
> Yo^u did so, quoth Duncombe, but wth an ill intent
> yo^u left but the sense precendent & the sense subsequent
> O wofull tymes, quoth Lawrence Hyde.
> yf once ou^r freedome of speach be denyed.
> Then quoth Hugh Beeston with a stammeringe speach
> Though you^r liberty for you^r tounge, yo^u haue non^e fo^r yor breeche.
> (Add. 23229, fol. 16v)

'Feirce Henry' is a jibe at Sir Henry Yelverton, nicknamed ironically 'Henry the Hardie' or 'Harry the Hardie', as this figure is known in other versions. Once a vocal critic of royal policy in the Commons, he changed his political colours in the 1610 sessions when he argued vehemently for the king's right to impose. Martin was quick to take Yelverton to task for proposing 'an arbitrary, irregular, unlimited and transcendent power of the king in imposing'.[42] When James put his proposals for Union before the Commons in 1604, Sir Edwin Sandys and Sir Herbert Croft were instrumental in making the legal case against Union to the House. Both men, along with Sandys's kinsman Lawrence Hyde, and Brooke, Martin, Hoskyns and Hakewill, were reputed patriots in the Commons – Sir Francis Bacon identified them amongst what he called the 'popular' or 'opposite party'.[43]

The majority of these men were either Middle Temple or Lincoln's Inn lawyers, and the way they gained their reputation as patriots in the Commons, by maintaining the common law against the prerogative and the principle of king-in-parliament, speaks to the emergence of a professional legal culture that we have seen at the Inns of Court and expressed in the idealised lawyer-orator. It may also indicate the presence of a distinctive political culture at these Inns that upheld the authority of the common law and had a particular investment in parliaments. Parliamentary committee meetings were sometimes held in the Great Hall of the Middle Temple; although partly for convenience, this sharing of institutional space also establishes a symbolic and political continuity between the two institutions. The civic ethos of the Inns shaped the lawyers' sense of the institutional role of the House of Commons, while parliament gave these lawyers a 'public forum' in which their practical experience of governance at the Inns could be put to use and the principle of the sovereignty of the common law could be articulated.[44] Martin appears in the 'Parliament Fart' as a parliamentary wit with an authoritative command of rhetoric: 'for all you^r eloquence, quoth Richard Martyn, / Yo^u cannot finde an figure for fartinge' (fol. 16r). He established a reputation in James's first parliament as a learned lawyer-orator, extending the role of *parrhesiastes* he had adopted in his oration on the king's entry into London into the sphere of governance. Highly regarded by the House, he was selected to act as its spokesman in conferences with the Lords in 1610 probably because he combined parliamentary experience with an excellent wit, legal expertise and a thorough command of rhetoric.[45] The lawyer-orators in the Commons by adopting the forms of classical rhetoric to structure the way they set out precedents, compared statutes and argued points of law in their speeches sought to counter the accusation, frequently made by civil lawyers, that the common law was inferior because it lacked method.[46] And they added to the prestige not only of the common law but also of the House of Commons itself.

Behind the couplet attributed to Samuel Lewkenor is a speech he delivered on 6 May 1607, described by Bowyer as 'much approved, of length, and eloquence', which set out the House's concerns about the way its freedom of speech had been compromised by 'private suggestions or reports' delivered to the king. Lewkenor requested that men who had 'expressly been blamed and reprehended by his Majesty for their speeches in the House' be given an opportunity to clear themselves; and that in future the House be able 'with all liberty and freedom and without fear, [to] deliver their opinions in the matter in hand'.[47] The couplet attributed to Hyde in this version affirms that the issue at stake is freedom of speech – other variants have Hyde concur with his fellows and suggest 'that wee may come by it / Weele make a Proviso tyme it, and tye it' (Mal. 23, p. 4). The principle of freedom of speech arises out of the conception of parliament as a 'Great Council', and is based on the premise that it could only fulfil this role if it was able to give its advice and opinion freely, without fear of prosecution outside the House. The sassy interjection 'I went from this place, / and reported it worde for worde to his grace', attributed to Sir Roger Aston, may have behind it the grievance brought before the House on 21 November 1610 alleging that thirty of its members had attended a conference called by the King at Whitehall following the collapse of the Great Contract. Hakewill argued the event set a dangerous precedent allowing the King and the Privy Council to circumvent the body of counsel represented by the Commons.[48] The passage, as a whole, effectively interlinks the sovereignty of the common law, the liberties of the subject embodied in parliament, freedom of speech, and the welfare of the commonwealth in a manner that was highly characteristic of patriot politics in the early Stuart period.[49]

There was a political jest that configured freedom of debate through the fart, and spoke to the dangers of royal foreclosure of this privilege. Sir John Harington provided a translation of Sir Thomas More's epigram on the healthful effects of political farting in his *Metamorphosis of Ajax* as part of a jesting yet serious meditation on satires, libels and liberty of speech:

> my Muse was afraid to translate this Epigram: and she brought me out three or foure sayings against it, both in Latine and English: and two or three shrewd examples, both of this last poet [Sir Thomas More], who died not of the collicke, and of one Collingbourne, that was hanged for a distichon of a Cat, a rat, and a dogge. Yet I opposed *Murus aheneus esto nil conscire sibi*, and so with much a do, she came out with it.
>
> > *To breake a litle winde, sometimes ones life doth save,*
> > *For want of vent behind, some folke their ruine have:*
> > *A powre it hath therefore, of life, and death express:*
> > *A king can cause no more, a cracke doth do no lesse.*[50]

More's epigram sets up a medicopolitical analogy between the power of monarchs and farting on the basis that both have the power over life and death. The epigram suggests that a healthy state is one in which kings are able to hear and tolerate the sound of political dissonance within the body politic – Harington appears to extend this to political satire and libel, suggested by the example of the poet Collingbourne executed by the tyrant Richard III. If one follows through the medicopolitical implications of More's epigram in relation to the 'Parliament Fart', then the ability to debate freely, like breaking wind, is necessary for the continued health of the commonwealth, whereas the royal restriction of debate, like trapped wind, is potentially fatal.

The 'Parliament Fart' is a very clever piece of political wit comparable to More's epigram on kings, farting and the health of the commonwealth, and arises out of a political culture with a sophisticated and politicised taste for vulgarity. The 'Parliament Fart' is an improvisation on political rhetoric, opening its forms to dissonance. The fart, as we have seen in

Jonson's *Bartholomew Fair*, is related to nonsense and both can be described as rhetorical figures for anti-rhetoric.[51] The scatological analogy between the mouth and the anus figured in the fart denotes a disruption of sociolinguistic decorum. It magnifies the impropriety of privileging sound, at the expense of meaning, to create nonsense that is in turn figured in the airy insubstantiality of the fart. Even so, the parliament fart is not a derisory figure; in tune with the poem's radical improvisatory form, it signifies a creative impulse in sociopolitical languages. This dissonant potentiality informs Harington's coining of *cacophonia* as a rhetorical term. *Cacophonia* is simultaneously the sound made on the jakes and the heteroglot nature of language; since different accentual systems co-exist historically, dissonance is generated, causing the pronunciation of words to change over time.[52] The parliament fart is a cacophonic figure that introduces change into established discursive and political structures. It does so through the sounds of dissonance, thereby disrupting established forms of rhetorical consensus – this, in turn, enables the wits in the House of Commons to extemporise political alternatives, allowing contentious views to be heard and debated. The radical openness of the poem's form, which encourages different couplets and hence different members of the House to be introduced, represents parliament as a self-regenerating body, continually reconstituted through a succession of elected members. In this sense, the institutional space described by the 'Parliament Fart' may be improvised, but it is not depicted as provisional.

DISSONANCE, WIT AND THE 1614 'ADDLED' PARLIAMENT

The 1614 'addled' parliament has come to exemplify political dissonance. Even before this parliament sat, it was unsettled by rumours of packing: Stephen Clucas and Rosalind Davies have drawn attention to the 'sense of the *rumorousness* of political life in 1614, and its role in creating events'.[53] Speeches made by Hoskyns and Christopher Neville on 3 June attacking the Scottish bedchamber confirmed James's distrust of parliament, and it was dissolved in July without passing any legislation. Earlier speeches by Thomas Wentworth and Sir Walter Chute had also offended the king, and all four were quickly sent to the Tower. In the aftermath of the dissolution, the term 'wit' was employed in various and competing ways to explain political behaviour. Meditating on recent events in a letter, Sir Henry Wotton used the term 'wit' as an equivalent for 'licentiousness' and 'irreverent discourse':

The second is in for more wit, and for licentiousness baptized freedom. For I have noted in our House, that a false or faint patriot did cover himself with the shadow of equal moderation, and on the other side, irreverent discourse was called honest liberty; so as upon the whole matter, 'no excesses want precious names'.[54]

Wotton distances himself from his old friend, Hoskyns, as well as such talk in parliament. The 'wit' of a 'false or faint patriot' is equated with disingenuous and imprudent speech that fosters dissension, rather than prudent use of rhetoric to persuade men to virtuous action and to achieve consensus. Wotton de-legitimates the way these men were developing the principle of freedom of speech; they are dissemblers who have appropriated and redefined the language of political ethics, 'equal moderation' and 'honest liberty', and it is left to men of judgement like Wotton to discern the violent excesses and 'irreverent discourse' behind these men's recourse to the parliamentary principle of free speech.

Hoskyns gave a rather different and extensive gloss on wit. Responding to 'great ones' fears that he will 'taxe' them on his release, since 'no obligation will bynd my witt',

but yet alass the poor honest gentlema[n] informer of greate ones . . . so much feares a jest & desires to imprison witt . . . and suer he hath reade little history: for no man ever suffered for mere witt: but yf he lived not to requitt it hymselfe, yet the witt of all posterity took penaunce on his name that oppressed hym . . . I can ot be psuaded that any ma[n] that hath witt of his own is afrayd of anothers witt as no good soldier that hath a sword feares another mans sword. and for my part I had rather dy with witt than live without it.[55]

It is interesting how much of his social and political identity Hoskyns invested in his wit. His metaphor of the soldier transfers the codes of a community of honour to an aristocracy of wit identified with intellectual courage, resolution, and liberty of speech.[56] Hoskyns identifies with a politicised tradition of wits and jesters: the wit that 'lived not' may recall the fate of More, the martyr-jester, remembered for 'all posterity' for his fine and singular wit in English studies of rhetoric by writers such as Gabriel Harvey and Thomas Wilson, as well as in Catholic hagiographies.[57] Harington's remembrance of More in his *Metamorphosis of Ajax* is telling in this context. Following More's epigrams on kings and farting, he cited noble precedents of 'men of worth and wit' famous for their jests that began, not surprisingly, with More and his jesting all the way to the scaffold. It initiates a witty meditation on notions of freedom of speech that give liberty not only to the tongue, but also to the breech. If More, the witty author of the epigram on kings and healthful farts, 'died not of the collicke', then following through the political metaphor of farting, he must have died in the cause of free speech. The second jester, John Heywood, indicted for treason for denying Henry the title of 'Supreme Head of the English and Irish Church', 'scaped hanging with his mirth, the King being graciously and (as I thinke) truely perswaded, that a man that wrate so pleasant and harmlesse verses, could not have any harmfull conceit against his proceedings'.[58] Erasmus in his letter to Martin Dorp appended to the *Praise of Folly* defended his mock-encomium on the grounds that it recovered an ancient tradition in which *parrhesia* was delivered with a 'sportive wit', pointing out that 'princes in ancient times introduced licensed fools into their courts so that their freedom of speech might expose and correct lesser faults without offending anyone'.[59] Heywood's fate, whose wit finds grace with the King and is accorded a provisional space within the structures of counsel, sits uncomfortably with the execution of More, which speaks to the impossibility of counsel at courts of costive and tyrannical kings. The liberties claimed for the jester in *Metamorphosis of Ajax* are set within wider arguments relating to religious toleration and freedom of conscience. Harington justifies his decision to include More's epigram on the fart despite concerns about its safety by citing a line from Horace's *Epistle*, 1.1, '*Murus aheneus esto nil conscire sibi*' ('Be this our wall of bronze, to have no guilt at heart'), which upheld the rights of a man of good conscience against tyrannical authorities.[60]

When Hoskyns's friend Hakewill came to define the parliamentary privilege of freedom of speech in his essay on 'Speaking in the House', he introduced an important qualification to the notion of parliamentary decorum, and that was conscience:

> But if the House shall not hold such a man guilty of intemperate and indiscreet speech though he have spoken never so plainly and freely in informing the House against some great officer (so as his information be true) or touching something amiss in the government or in withstanding or redressing some desire or pretended prerogative of the King's which he shall in his conscience conceive may not well stand with the good of the state, or is against the law, and shall discreetly and temperately deliver the reasons of his conscience, he ought not for so speaking be called in question or any wise troubled, neither ought the House to be restrained from free debating of any such matter by any commandment from the King or his council, especially when the matter concerneth the interest of the subject in their good[s], lands or liberties.[61]

Hakewill was reflecting on the events following the 1610 and 1614 parliaments when members of parliament were not held guilty by the House, but were nonetheless 'called in question' and otherwise 'troubled' by the king and the Privy Council for speaking plainly, freely, even intemperately and indiscreetly, but according to the 'reasons of their conscience'. Arguments of conscience frequently arose out of dilemmas relating to political and religious allegiance. Hakewill, like other lawyers in the Commons, argues that since the royal prerogative is an attribute of the king's person, the subject owes a higher allegiance to the laws of God and the land, and a duty to the public good as it is conceived through the common law.[62] It is possible to see in Hoskyns's 'wit' and Hakewill's 'conscience' political subjectivities formed through dissonance, with its complex of conflicting interests and allegiances.[63]

The early seventeenth century sees a situation in which notions of decorum that had been employed to govern political rhetoric were placed under increasing pressure. Whereas Piggott had been sent to the Tower by the House for his inflammatory speeches against the Scottish bedchamber in February 1607, in 1614 men who made violent anti-Scots speeches were not expelled by the House; instead, a provisional space was made for such expressions of dissent within the parliamentary principle of freedom of speech. John Chamberlain was clearly shocked by the noisiness of the House in 1614, particularly following the speeches of Hoskyns and Sir Christopher Neville: 'The truth is yt shold seeme by theyre cariage, and by that I have heard from some of them, that there was never knowne a more disorderly house, and that yt was many times more like a cockpit then a grave counsaile, and many sat there that were more fit to have ben among roaring boyes then in that assemblie.'[64] Roaring boys, figures of riot on the London streets, have made their way into the state disrupting the structures of counsel. It is probable that the sound Chamberlain could hear in these disorderly speeches emerged from a culture of libelling – the cockpit and the streets were spaces frequently associated with such unauthorised modes of discourse. There had been public brawling between the Scots and Inns of Court men in 1612, culminating in the murder of an English fencing master, which generated the following popular libel:

> They beg our goods, our lands, and our lives,
> They whip our Nobles and lie with their wives,
> They pinch our Gentrie, and send for the benchers,
> They stab our sergeants, and pistoll our fencers.
> Leave of proud Scotts thus to undo us,
> Least we make you as poore as when you came to us.[65]

The anti-Scots speeches of Hoskyns and Neville have much in common with contemporary libels put out against the Scottish bedchamber, and draw the violence of their analogies from recent clashes between the English and the Scots at court and on the streets of London.

James also made association between the Commons and libels. Some versions of the 'Parliament Fart' conclude with the lines: 'Come Come quoth the king libelling is not safe / Bury you the fart, I'le make the Epitaph' (Mal. 23, page 10).[66] The allusion is to a poem James was provoked into penning in the early 1620s in response to a highly sophisticated libel said to have been 'put into the hand of Queene Elizabeths statue in Westminster by an unknowne person' in 1621, and entitled 'The humble petition of her now most wretched and most Contemptible, the Com[m]ons of poore distressed England' (p. 32). James made an explicit connection between libelling and the study of his prerogative by his subjects in parliament: both undermine the mystery of state, and instead the people should 'Wounder at kings, and them obey' (p. 49),[67] since:

> Kings cannot comp^{r}hended bee
> In Comon circles. Conjure yee
> All what you cann by teares or termes
> Deny not what your king affirmes
> Hee doth disdaine to cast an eye
> Of Anger on you least you die
>
> (p. 54)

It is extraordinary that the king was impelled to leave himself open in verse in this way. James was not able to end libelling by re-imposing his royal word on the subject, nor could he stop his subjects in the Commons from debating his prerogative, except of course by depriving them of that forum, as he pointed out somewhat peevishly:

> The p[ar]liament I will appoint
> When I see things more out of joynt
> Then will I sett all wry things straight
> And not upon your pleasure waite
>
> (p. 51)

James disliked the Commons and was increasingly distrustful of the lawyers' wit; along with many of his key ministers – particularly Thomas Egerton, Lord Ellesmere, Henry Howard, Earl of Northampton, and Thomas Howard, Earl of Suffolk – he took punitive measures against 'those lawyers who studied the prerogative' on the grounds that subjecting such a central aspect of monarchical government to scrutiny was not safe.[68] Yet, while James was attempting to deprive these lawyers of a legitimate voice outside royal parameters by equating liberty of speech with libel, the composers of the 'Humble Petition' were employing the forms of libel and satire to construct a potent critique of the current 'lamentable' state of the commonwealth.

Private conviviality was integral to political culture in the early seventeenth century. The milieux around the Inns of Court were sites for the sociable activity occasioned by the summoning of parliament, providing stimulating environments in which news was exchanged, conversations were held, alliances and political identities formed and political verses written. The 1614 'addled' parliament decisively shaped the political consciousness of many of its members. It was not just that the parameters of political debate had been extended, but also that different registers were being heard in a manner that both profoundly troubled and excited contemporaries, and set the scene for the 1620s. Many of the various speech acts recorded in texts of this period and heard in taverns and in parliament were sites of dissonance, of contestation and contradiction. The 'Parliament Fart' remained a popular poem well into the second half of the seventeenth century largely because it provided a complex rhetorical figure, that of the political fart, able to comprehend, to censure and at the same time to take pleasure in such sounds of political *cacophonia*.

CHAPTER FIVE

Coryats Crudities *(1611) and the sociability of print*

The subject of this chapter is not Coryate's book of travels as such, but the body of preliminary material that makes up approximately 160 pages at the front of the *Crudities*: William Hole's engraved title page and the accompanying sets of distichs explicating its emblems supplied by Lawrence Whitaker and Jonson; Coryate's dedication to Prince Henry and his epistle to the reader; Jonson's 'Character of the famous *Odcombian*' together with an acrostic; and finally the extensive body of 'Panegyricke Verses', prefaced by Coryate's introduction. It is difficult to know just what to call this material. Preliminary material seems a misnomer since it has expanded beyond all proportion to become a book in itself, in many ways autonomous from the following travels said to provide its occasion. In fact, the 'Panegyricke Verses' were detached from Coryate's travel book, and republished the same year in an unauthorised edition, *The Odcombian Banquet*, by Thomas Thorpe. The front matter to the *Crudities* fashions a self-authorising company of wits, many of whom are familiar from the convivial gatherings at the Mitre and Mermaid taverns, and extends these sociable practices into the arena of print, making highly innovative use of the space at the front of the book to transform itself into a print event.

With the 'Panegyricke Verses', we can see the forms of ritualised play favoured by the wits making their way into the format of the printed book, one effect is to turn the area at the front of the book into an élite performance space. This collection is a self-conscious revival of the mock-encomium that looks back to Erasmus's seminal mock-encomium, *Praise of Folly*. *Crudities* and its sequel, *Coryats Crambe*, testify to the wits' concerted experimentation with low forms, including macaronics and burlesque, alongside the development of new forms, such as nonsense. This serious literary play moves from relatively exclusive performance spaces and scribal communities into the arena of the print marketplace. Here, it becomes available to John Taylor, who popularises these low literary forms in his Coryate-inspired pamphlets. The wits employ the mock-encomium to establish

Coryate as the clownish buffoon partly in order to distinguish between different modes of play along social lines within a broader performance culture. At the same time, the mock-encomium is put to interrogatory uses; the 'Panegyricke Verses' as a whole improvise on the forms of encomiastic poetry, introducing the sounds of dissonance. The paradox encoded by the mock-encomium opens the conventions of encomiastic poetry to improvisatory play and stimulates processes of critique.

PRINT AND SOCIABILITY

Coryate famously paid for the publication of the *Crudities* himself, reinvesting the profits from his wager on his travels in his new book venture. Given his relentless self-promotion, it would be tempting to see Coryate as an entrepreneurial author-publisher eager to capitalise on the new opportunities provided by an expanding print industry. Loewenstein has argued along these lines that 'Coryat seems to have "dared" to pay for the printing in order to profit directly from the sales of the book, an eager embrace of the new mass market in books in preference to the differently chancy pursuit of traditional patronage.'[1] Coryate, however, did not abandon patronage; in fact, his highly sociable book is the product of the transactions between the print marketplace and a patronage economy. His orchestration of a print event is a dramatic example of the sociality of print, its orientation outwards towards the wider community along networks of social exchange rather than inwards towards the proprietorial author and the possessive individual. Margaret Ezell writes of the methodological problems arising out of a 'narrative history of authorship' which prioritises the 'new' technology of print, 'advanced' market economics and a modern democratic press over a 'feudal', 'aristocratic', and ultimately 'anachronistic' manuscript culture.[2] The print coterie assembled at the front of Coryate's book argues against a model of the print marketplace in which the 'anachronistic' sociality of a manuscript culture has been left behind and superseded by the commercial and individualistic relationship between the author and the stationer.

When Coryate in his *Crambe* (1611) railed against the unauthorised publication of the 'Panegyricke Verses' in the *Odcombian Banquet*, he did not evince a proprietary interest in his book: there was no complaint that material was stolen, or about the standard of printing; instead, his primary concern was his reputation, '*because it doth not a litle concerne my credit to cleere my selfe of two very scandalous imputations laide upon me*'.[3] The print market, like other areas of early modern commerce, was constituted by a 'culture of credit': the 'public means of social communication and circulating judgement about the value of other members of communities'. Credit relations place the 'accumulating' possessive individual back within 'the body of the community' and its structures of sociability.[4] The communality of credit lies behind Coryate's well-orchestrated use of the 'front' matter of the printed book for the purposes of advertising.[5] Coryate was making arrangements in 1611 for the second, even more extensive leg of his travels, this time to the East (he left England for Constantinople in late 1612). The *Crudities* was designed, in part, to encourage investment in this new venture by establishing his celebrity and trading on his fame. His earlier European venture was a wagered journey: a local Yeovil linen draper, Joseph Starre, had promised him a return of one hundred marks if he completed his travels. Since his return from Europe, Sir Lionel Cranfield, that consummate early modern businessman, had been handling his finances – Coryate says Cranfield was the first to encourage him to print his book.[6] Cranfield participated in the promotion of Coryate's book: he contributed to the 'Panegyricke Verses' himself, and solicited verses from kin and other associates, including his brother-in-law, Sir John Suckling.[7] Cranfield's poem uses a particularly pertinent metaphor:

> Me thinks when on his booke I cast my eies,
> I see a shop repleate with merchandize,
> And how the owner jelous of his fame,
> With pretious matter garnisheth the same.
> Many good parts he hath, no man too much
> Can them commend, some few I'le only touch.
>
> (sig. e8v)

The metaphor of the book as a shop moves easily between a market-based notion of ownership and accumulation and the circulation of fame and reputation; in fact, commerce and credit speak the same language.

At all stages of publication of the *Crudities*, Coryate drew on the networks of friendship, personal obligations, and clientage available to him both in London and in his home county, Somerset. His book needed to be licensed for the press by the ecclesiastical authorities; to facilitate this, he persuaded his Yeovil neighbour, the Reverend John Seward, to write on his behalf to Dr Richard Mocket, a chaplain in the Archbishop of Canterbury's household, and also asked him to include a letter from his friend Lawrence Whitaker, secretary to Sir Edward Phelips.[8] Coryate then published Whitaker's letter in the *Crudities*, giving its full context in a headnote, so that his book accrued further value through this advertisement of his personal networks of credit, trust and obligation. He tried to get his book licensed quickly, and turned to Sir Michael Hicks, the secretary to Salisbury, whom he had met at a dinner given by Cranfield, 'to intercede for me unto my Lorde Treasurer [Salisbury], y^t it would please his Lordship to give order it may be printed in London with some expedition', pointing out that it had already met with approval from Prince Henry.[9] Sir Edward Phelips, Coryate's long-standing patron, was chancellor to the prince's household, and had probably helped him to a position at his court. The *Crudities* is dedicated to Henry, who is also credited with suggesting – or rather ordering – the publication of the 'Panegyric Verses'. There is a strong showing of members of his court among the contributors, suggesting that participation in this print event was a means of advertising one's proximity to Henry's court.[10]

The collection of 'Panegyricke Verses' was a social event in its own right. Over fifty gentlemen participated, and Coryate, not surprisingly, proudly drew attention to the fact that *such a great multitude of Verses as no booke whatsoever printed in England these hundred yeares, had the like written in praise thereof* (sig. civ). Coryate and his friends, including Whitaker and Holland, orchestrated this event, even commissioning a mock-encomium from the renowned wit Sir John Harington. Poems were solicited and collected through established social networks that testify to the commerce between London, the counties and the universities. The Phelipses had their country estate in Somerset at Montacute House, a short distance from Coryate's village of Odcombe; Coryate's distant kinsman and neighbour George Sydenham contributed a poem, as did another influential Somerset neighbour, John Pawlet.[11] These Somerset men frequently socialised together in London – at the Middle Temple, Prince Henry's court, Phelips's official residence (Rolls House on Chancery Lane) and the taverns. When they appear in the 'Panegyricke Verses', as Melanie Ord has noted, there is a complex interplay between their social identities as local Somerset gentry and as Inns of Court men or servants of the Crown.[12] The summoning of parliament, the law year and the new season, as we have seen, brought gentry into London and provided opportunities for socialising and versifying. Sir Edward Phelips, the Speaker in the recent parliament, may have used his influence on Coryate's behalf to solicit verses from men who had sat in the House and whose social standing placed them at the front of the collection: Sir Henry Neville, his brother-in-law Sir Henry Poole, Lewis Lewkenor and Sir Rowland Cotton. Many of the 'Panegyricke Verses' were probably composed in similar circumstances to the 'Parliament Fart', in company and at convivial gatherings. As news of this gathering of wits in print spread, other verses made their way to Coryate unsolicited from London and the universities: he advertised that the poem by Laurentius Emley (probably Theophilus Emilie) was *'lately sent me by a learned Gentleman of* Magdalen *Colledge in Oxford: who though he never saw me, hath vouchsafed to grace my booke with his Encomiasticks'* (sig. 11r).

The formal openness of the 'Parliament Fart', which allowed the incorporation of new material, was a feature of its communality. Print is less flexible; even so, there is evidence that sections of the front matter to the *Crudities* were circulating while the book was in the process of being printed, thus allowing later contributors to converse with the book and other participants.[13] Several of the mock-encomiastics are an exposition of the frontispiece, often taking their cues from the distichs supplied by Whitaker and Jonson. Coryate himself pointed out that he had inserted an extra set of verses because 'after all these former verses were printed, I was most importunatly perswaded by the[m] that have no small interest in me, to adjoyne these ensuing unto the rest, by way of a supplement or overplus' (sig. 11r). One can imagine the frontispiece and other preliminary material being consulted in William Stansby's shop as the book was being printed – Coryate sends his remembrances to 'M. *William Stansby*, the Printer of my *Crudities* and *Crambe*, at his house in Thames Street' at the end of his letter to the Sireniacs.[14] Donne in his anatomy of Coryate's book has it broken up into separate sheets, and 'Each leafe enough will be / For friends to passe the time, and keepe companie' (sig. d3v). In other words, he imagines the printed page rather than the script circulating among friends, and functioning as a constitutive part of their social exchanges. Later writers refer to earlier contributions. Richard Badley, for instance, who appeared in the second set of 'Panegyricke Verses', printed after the first collection, referred to 'those immortall Rimes ... / Thy honour'd friends compos'd'. The wits therefore were not simply participants in this print event; they were its co-producers, with an investment in its success. As Badley astutely observed, Coryate may have been the immediate occasion, but he is so often displaced by the very act of participating that he could not tell whether the wits' purpose was 'thy name, or theirs t'immortalize' (sig. k1v). Sydenham imagines 'that all the world ... / ... now send post to fetch this raretie' (sig. f2v). It suggests how Coryate's book was constituted as a print event; the 'post' made it possible for the book to travel from the print shop in London to the universities and to Somerset, thus joining communities in London and the provinces within a larger imagined community constituted by the book itself.

The print coterie gathered in front of the *Crudities* overlapped with the drinking societies and scribal communities around the Middle Temple and Lincoln's Inn – around half of the fifty contributors who can be identified were from these Inns. Those who will in a few months be present at the Mitre *convivium*, and remembered by Coryate as his fellow Sireniacs, constitute a distinct grouping within the 'Panegyricke Verses': Donne's poem is followed by verses by Martin, then Whitaker and Holland, and shortly after in quick succession are poems from Brooke, Hoskyns, Cranfield and Inigo Jones. Martin draws on the motifs of banquet literature to imagine the book's milieu. The book successfully transformed the wits into a print community; an effect made apparent in the title given to the unauthorised edition of the 'Panegyricke Verses', *The Odcombian Banquet Dished foorth by Thomas the Coriat, and served in by a number of Noble Wits in prayse of his Crudities and Crambe too*. Print formalised the performance of sociability, turning the open-endedness of the network into the closed form of the circle. That said, while this print coterie may have achieved some fixity in print, it was by no means closed off in the sense Walter Ong attributes to 'cold, nonhuman' mechanics of the printing press.[15] There was at least one reader who decided to follow the wits and take an active role in the volume's composition. Sir Thomas Fairfax, probably a recipient of a presentation copy, wrote his own verse on Coryate's book, inserted at the end of the final set of 'Panegyricke Verses', just before Hermann Kirchner's oration in praise of travel, thus supplementing the gathering.[16] Print technology enabled authors to exploit systematically the physical space of the book. It made available a range of typographical and visual features, including engraved title pages or plates, decorative borders, and a range of fonts to demarcate different spaces within the book. All of these could be reproduced in multiple copies. *Coryats Crudities* fully exploited the resources of the printed book. Its beautifully engraved title page introduces the motif of the man as his book, and the whole of the front matter is built around this figure, visually, typographically and metaphorically. These forms of embodiment simulate face-to-face communication and transform the front of the book into a performance space. Such a concerted exploitation of the resources of the printed book gives Coryate and his book a substantial presence in the public realm and the print marketplace.

Coryate was experimenting with the format and social functioning of the book. Henry Parrot, contemplating the fate of his own book, looked to Coryate as an author who had removed himself from the marketplace by selling his books himself:

> My Epigrams escap'd the Printers hand,
> Eyther on Stationers stal's regardles lye,
> Or must on Posts, for pennance, nayled stand,
> That every one may gaze on, passing by:
> Which to prevent, and therewith purchase pelfe,
> *Tom Coriat* solde the Bookes he made himselfe.[17]

Title pages providing details of where books could be bought were displayed on posts in St Paul's Churchyard and throughout London.[18] It is likely that the sale of Coryate's book was transacted not through the bookseller but through the same social networks and practices of sociability behind its composition. We should not assume that, because the printed book was mechanically reproduced, technology took the book out of the author's hands and sent it alone into the marketplace. Authors expected to profit from their books through the transactions of credit. Books functioned within a complex culture of gift-giving; Jason Scott-Warren reminds us that precisely because the book was a material object it was available as an object of exchange.[19]

Coryate expended much effort and expense in preparing his books for a patronage economy, reserving for his book the kudos of the privately printed and circulated book within an increasingly specialised print marketplace. During late March and early April 1611, he went on his own mock-progress around the royal residences, presenting personalised copies with a keen sense of the theatricality of the occasion. Evidence of surviving copies would support the account he gave in his *Crambe* that he made gifts of his book to the Privy Council, and a large swathe of the nobility and gentry. Prince Henry's copy is particularly fine: it is bound in red velvet and embossed with Henry's arms; Hole's frontispiece and his other engravings illustrating the book are coloured carefully by hand. Such workmanship harks back to the early printed books that were frequently finished by an illuminator; this patina gives the book a level of craftsmanship that marks it out as an object to be collected.[20] John Chapman says of the *Crudities* that it is

> A volume which though t'will not in thy pocket,
> Yet in thy chest thou maist for ever locke it
> For thy childrens children to reade hereafter,
> Being disposed to travell, or to laughter.
>
> (sig. f6r)

Brooke makes a rather convoluted jest: Homer's *Iliad* was so prized it was placed in '*Darius* Casket' but had the *Iliad* been written by Coryate – whose book is even longer and bigger – the Greeks would have to have 'bought a Basket / Of richer stuffe to intombe thy volume large' (sig. e5v). Both jests argue that it is the 'weightiness' of the book, in a very literal and material sense, which will ensure its posterity. The size of the early modern book determined its social uses and the social and symbolic space in which it would circulate.[21] Placed in the chest, the richly worked basket or the cabinet – places for valuable objects – the book is physically and symbolically taken out of the realms of cheaper popular printed books and pamphlets (typically printed in octavo and so small enough to fit in the pocket) and placed in the realms of more socially élite modes of circulation.

Jonson's acrostic, in contrast, wants to return Coryate's book to the popular print marketplace, slyly hinting at a different publishing scenario to the élite story of the privately printed book:

> T rie and trust *Roger*, was the word, but now
> H onest *Tom Tell-Troth* puts downe *Roger, How?*
> O f travell he discourseth so at large,
> M arry he sets it out at his owne charge;
> A nd therein (which is worth his valour too)
> S hewes he dares more then *Paules Church-yard* durst do.
> (sig. b4r).

So too, John Taylor in his *The Eighth Wonder of the World: or, Coriats escape from his supposed drowning*, imagines the Stationers awaiting Coryate's next book:

> But yet I know the *Stationers* are wise,
> And well do know wherein the danger lies:
> For to such inconvenience they'le not enter:
> But suffers *Coriat* to abide th'adventer:
> Because his Gyant volume is so large,
> They'l give sir *Thomas* leave to beare the charge.

The sound business sense of the stationers has determined that Coryate must finance his own bastard book, 'Let him that got and bore the Barne still breed it', so that it does not become a financial burden on the Company.[22] This big book is conceived as waste, and has no value within a print economy based on thrift and 'wise' investments. For many of the wits, print publication raised other issues. While the front matter to the book does attempt to retain the exclusivity of a coterie production, nonetheless print necessarily opens the coterie to a wider public readership. This print event brought the wits, previously habituated to a manuscript culture, face to face with the popular print marketplace and its arenas of performance. The ludic, paradoxical form of the mock-encomium enabled the participants to

110 *The English Wits*

collude in and to resist the unfolding print event, and to put in place a language of social discrimination that sought to regulate this print community and the nature of its readership.

PERFORMING IN PRINT AND THE TALKED BOOK

During the 'Convivium Philosophicum' Coryate was allotted the role of buffoon, a 'game-maker', as David Wiles says of the stage clown, 'who makes play possible' at the table.[23] Coryate's mode of performance, and the styles attributed to him by the wits, draws on a range of entertainers – the classical Greek buffoon; the professional court fool, a position held at James's court by Archibald Armstrong; the courtier-jester, a type represented by Elizabeth's witty godson Harington, who was much admired by the wits; and the stage clown, a profession that found celebrity status in the performances of Richard Tarlton, William Kemp and Robert Armin.[24] As early as 1606, Coryate sought the role of game-maker, acting as a master of ceremonies at an elaborate Whitsun Ale which ambitiously and somewhat eccentrically took the form of a mock-military campaign – thus giving the medieval forms of lay games and entertainments a Roman 'martiall discipline'.[25] He was assisted by Phelips, the local magnate, who lent him his horse; yet, this performance was not driven by patronage but was put on for the benefit of his father's Odcombe parish and the local community. Coryate was eccentric; although he draws on a rich performance tradition, as Jonson noted, 'he treads in no other Mans steps but his owne' (*Crambe*, sig. A2v). Like his martial Whitsun Ale, his mock-progresses to royal households and subsequent orations belong to the modes of ritualised play that we are familiar with from the performances of the wits. Ceremonial forms are opened to the creative forces of improvisation. The oration he delivered before Prince Henry in the Privy Chamber at St James's Palace, printed in the *Crambe*, is excessively euphuistic to the point of parody: his red-velvet-covered book is 'this tender feathered Red-breast. Let his Cage be your Highnesse studie, his pearch your Princely hand, by the support whereof, hee may learne to chirp and sing so lowde, that the sweetnesse of his notes may yeeld a delectable resonancie' (sig. A3v). Such an overly aureate style draws attention to the theatricality of the oration: it is a fantastical performance designed to give pleasure and provoke laughter through the playful dressing of speech, rather than edify through its serious matter. Coryate's social identity was predicated on such performances to the extent that contemporaries jested he was all words and no matter.

In the *Crudities* and its sequel the *Crambe*, the second course to the banquet of the wits, in which mock-encomiastic poems are followed by

Coryate's orations, it is possible to see the making of a celebrity identity through the re-creation of live performance in print.[26] Coryate's very eccentricity as a performer meant that he was free to improvise. The creative freedom he embodied may explain his attractiveness to John Taylor, the waterman turned poet, who was similarly experimenting with translating the forms of live performance into print. Taylor's interest in Coryate, as we have seen, had an aggressive edge. He disdained the more exclusive forms of élite play that Coryate and the wits identified with; his social and cultural investment was in the popular print marketplace, as his mocking of Coryate's privately published book indicates, and he sought to popularise, or perhaps disclose the demotic potential in, the modes of literary play developed by the wits.[27] The advantage of translating live performance into print is that it supplements the original performance and opens out an event that, temporally and spatially, was relatively confined to new audiences. These print performances coincided with a range of performance spaces in London, from alehouses and taverns to courts and the public stage.

It is telling that when Taylor began to leave off his Coryate pamphlets, possibly because of a failure to provoke a response from the wits, he tried an extemporised wit contest on stage, challenging William Fennor, the 'King's Rhyming Poet', to a public wit contest at the Hope theatre in late 1614. Fennor had previously challenged one Kendall (probably Timothy Kendall, a university-educated wit) to a contest at the Fortune, but Kendall failed to show, just as Fennor failed to show for Taylor, leaving Taylor to his own devices on stage. Staged wit contests may derive from the improvised battle of wits performed at the end of plays: a stage practice established by the celebrity clown, Tarlton. As with the game of capping verses, the clown must instantly cap the witty rhyme thrown at him from the audience.[28] Both these amateur and professional wit contests on stage drew on older traditions of flyting as well as forms of pedagogic play.[29] These jests and quips were published in pamphlets – *Tarlton's Jests* (1600) and Armin's *Quips upon Questions* – but the variation introduced in the Taylor/Fennor pamphlets is the sense of the occasion, of a performance (or rather aborted performance) that occurred in time and space. Pamphlet flyting between Taylor and Fennor opened a performance space in print, which supplemented the original 'failed' performance, and enabled the participants to shape a persona in print that was an extension of that available on stage and in performance.[30]

A type of rhetoric of presence is noticeable in Coryate's embodied book as well as the verbal violence of flyting exhibited in the Fennor/Taylor pamphlets, Taylor's Coryate pamphlets, and the personification of 'Coryate' in the 'Panegyricke Verses'. It creates an illusion of face-to-face communication in which the audience is addressed directly and provoked to respond. The outline of this personality or celebrity in print was etched through violent words. It was a style prevalent in the 1590s pamphlet wars and *poetomachia* on stage: through satiric stigmatisation the private man was delineated in grotesque fashion for public consumption. Coryate himself was not averse to this rhetorical strategy that made bodies and books present in the text. His *Crambe* engaged in vituperative attacks on Starre, the Yeovil linen draper; the unnamed editor of the *Odcombian Banquet*, 'that virulent and rancorous pessant, some base lurking pedanticall tenebricous *Lucifuga*', was similarly censured for his unauthorised gulling of Coryate, as opposed to the authorised 'Panegyricke Verses'. Coryate ended with fighting words delivered in a tag from Ovid's 'Litany of Maledictions: Ancient Torments', from his *Ibis*: 'Vtque repertori nocuit pugnacis Iambi, / Sic sit in exitium lingua proterva tuum' ('And as pugnacious iambics harm their creator / May your insolent tongue be your destruction').[31] Vituperation imagines the physical presence of the rival author and his book in a fantasy of face-to-face combat. It gives the impression of a wider controversy or battle of wits that is being waged just outside the pages of the book, and presents print as providing a wider audience with privileged access to these disputes. In this way, the book or pamphlet is constituted as an equivalent arena to the sociable spaces imagined just beyond its pages; a forum in which these disputes could be acted out and a wider populace could hear these voices. The tendency towards serialisation is an inherent aspect of these performances in print because it adds a temporal dimension to the spatialising strategies of these texts. Hence, *Coryats Crudities* was quickly followed by the parodic *Odcombian Banquet*, which in turn was followed and put in its place by *Coryats Crambe*. Similarly, Taylor's wit contest with both Coryate and Fennor was conducted through a series of pamphlets published in relatively quick succession, thereby keeping up narrative momentum. Serialisation presupposes an audience keenly awaiting successive instalments. It therefore imagines a readership that is knowable, possesses a print memory, and has a personal investment in the author.

Coryate's book and Taylor's pamphlets experimented with modes of performance-in-print. They were part of new print genres that were conceptualising arenas where people could imaginatively create and experience different forms of communication and association. The *Crudities* was a 'talked book' – a term that draws attention to the communal act of reading aloud, which had continued well into the seventeenth century. 'At a time when the ability to read silently (at least for the upper classes) had become sufficiently common that understanding a text no longer depended on its being "vocalized"', as Roger Chartier points out, 'reading aloud was no longer a necessity for the reader, but rather an exercise in sociability practised on any number of occasions and to diverse ends.'[32] The talked book functioned as a textual motif which located the book and its consumption within sociable spaces in which people gathered to hear texts performed. The talked book was thus simultaneously read, vocalised, heard and discussed.[33] The motif of the talked book in the *Crudities* tends to locate Coryate's book in the social spaces identified with the wits, such as the tavern and the table. It creates the impression of intimate face-to-face social bonds between participants in the 'Panegyricke Verses', imagines the ways in which this print coterie could be accessible to a readership outside its immediate milieu and, in doing so, puts in place a regulatory economy of consumption.

The talked book was a motif easily incorporated within the feast *topos* – recitations frequently accompanied the literary meal, and were one of the pleasures of the table. Thomas Bastard imagined Coryate and his book as 'table talke' (sig. g1v); Sir Robert Phelips drew on a convivial vocabulary when he declared the purpose of the *Crudities* was 'to delight and recreate thy friends' (sig. c7v). Martin, that consummate tavern wit, composed a rollicking tavern ballad – there are several other songs in the collection that amplify this acoustic community. The headnote to the ballad places Coryate at the tavern, insinuating that he had paradoxically enhanced his reputation by placing himself at the mercy of the wits, 'that by lying at the signe of the Fox doth prove himselfe no Goose' (sig. d4r). The ballad burlesques the bibliophagic analogy between food and words characteristic of banqueting literature: 'these *Crudities* he gobled, / Which since he season'd hath for sundry palats' (sig. d4v). The book is a travelling meal that Coryate has regurgitated to be digested by others. John Jackson's poem, in the shape of an egg to feed Coryate's 'hungry prayses', again uses bibliophagia to imagine the mass consumption of Coryate's book:

> . . . Thy other
> Heliconian friends bring store of Salt, of
> Pepper, and Vineger sowre, to furnish thy
> Italian banquet forth . . .
> . . . .
> Feast *Coryate*, feast the world,
> Still with thy travell, discharge
> The Presse, and care
> Not then who
> Cavell
>
> (sig. h3v)

Glareanus Vadianus (John Sanford) jested that only the tavern wits had strong enough heads (and stomachs) to digest the richness of the *Crudities*'s humour:

> The Pleiade of Poets fell a quaffing
> At Hippocrenes fountaine head,
> London her selfe fell sicke abed
> Surfetted on a jole of laughing.
>
> (sig. h2r)

These ludic and often burlesque images of bibliophagia travesty the humanist analogies between eating and reading, and digestion and acquiring knowledge. Lurking behind Martin's vomited book and other images of surfeit are problems of indiscriminate consumption attributed to the popular print marketplace. As Craik has noted in her study of bibliophagic images in the 'Panegyricke Verses', reading the *Crudities* can make you sick. Bibliophagia is a source of 'ambivalent delights': 'The panegyricists thus implicate themselves in a curious form of textual exchange: even as they willingly take in reading matter they have described as superfluous, they imagine themselves experiencing both delight and affliction.'[34]

Reading the *Crudities* for many of the wits was intimately associated with the making and consumption of their own verses, in other words, with their own performances in print. For many participating in this print event, it was the first and only time they would appear as poets in print, while others such as Donne, Hoskyns and Martin preferred to circulate their texts scribally. The Inns of Court wits, as we have seen, invested heavily in their intellectual capital, which in turn served to establish their gentle status. Many who mocked Coryate – Martin, Hoskyns, Donne, Jones, Jonson and others – had less well-established gentry pedigrees. Coryate's father, George Coryate, was descended from well-established Somerset gentry families, and a distant kinsman of Henry Herbert, second Earl of Pembroke, serving as his chaplain before being appointed Rector of Odcombe. A fellow of New College, Oxford, his son Thomas went up to Gloucester Hall in 1596.[35] Coryate published his father's Latin poetry at the end of his *Crudities*, establishing his own learned legacy. Some would argue that he squandered his patrimony through his eccentric occupations. Coryate threatened the wits' own carefully cultivated reputation. His orations and performances in print, whatever his intent, crossed the threshold dividing the gentleman wit, skilled in oratory, and the low-born buffoon, thereby undermining his social status and leaving him vulnerable to the mimicry of the popular pamphleteer Taylor.

As both traveller and performer, Coryate troubled many of the wits' sense of their occupation, given their own social liminality. A number would soon be undertaking their own travels to Europe. Sir Robert Phelips may have embarked on a gentleman's grand tour in 1613, but the others travelled for employment. Donne departed for France in November 1611, soon after the publication of the *Crudities*, to act as secretary to Sir Robert Drury on his tour of Europe. Jonson left for France and the Low Countries the following summer of 1612 as tutor to the young Walter Raleigh. Inigo Jones, reputed a 'great traveller', was to travel to Italy in the same year, accompanying Charles Howard, Earl of Arundel, on an extended tour of the antiquities, architecture and paintings of Italy. Jones and Coryate shared an intense admiration for Italian culture; but they were very different types of travellers. Jones travelled largely in the service of patrons, and did not publish his travels for a wider market. Unlike his fellow wits, or those numerous English gentlemen he met in Europe, Coryate used his patronage connections to travel independently for his own employment.

A complex set of social distinctions is frequently enforced between Coryate and the London wits because proximity to Coryate potentially compromised their intellectual credibility. One strategy is to translate Coryate into a parodic traveller often through comparisons with fantastic travellers, such as Sir John Mandeville, or the fictitious and comic knight-errant of popular romance, or the Rabelaisian traveller, the giant Pantagruel. A popular comparison is Kemp, famous for the morris dance from London to Norwich that he publicised in his pamphlet *Nine Days Wonder*. Kemp was available as a native English burlesque traveller: his mode of travel is popular, conducted for the purposes of entertainment rather than employment. Before Coryate, he had taken a mock-heroic journey across Europe; although not published, it was recorded in popular ballads.[36] John Strangewayes, like many others, fixates on Coryate's legs and shoes, proclaiming that he has outdone Kemp in the feats of burlesque travel since he 'did go at least nine hundred mile, / With one poore paire of shoes' (*Crudities*, sig. d1v); 'N. T.' in 'Certaine Anacreonticke verses praeambulatory to the most ambulatorie Odcombian Traveller' jests that 'the story of his shoes' has made Coryate 'a nine months wonder' (*Crambe*, sig. b1r); and Henry Peacham produced an emblem and a wonderful encomiastic poem on 'thy shooes so artificially tanned' (sig. k4v). Turning Coryate into a popular burlesque traveller by fetishising the mundane – his shoes – means that he is distanced from élite play, becoming its object for ridicule and parody rather than an equal participant. It attributes to 'Tom Coryate' or 'Don Coryate of Odcombe' (sig. d7r) the characteristics of the Kemp-like stage clown. The entry of the term 'clown' into the Elizabethan cultural vocabulary coincided with the rise of the celebrity stage clowns. It denotes 'the rustic who by virtue of his rusticity is necessarily inferior and ridiculous' and contrasts with the 'gentle' man in neo-chivalric discourse.[37] The play on Coryate's clownish rusticity in the 'Panegyricke Verses' effectively positions him within the realms of popular print alongside Kemp, and at a safe and ironic distance from the urbane coterie play of the wits.[38]

Jonson found Coryate perplexing. His 'Character of the Author' simultaneously recognises Coryate is a novelty and de-legitimises his travels from a humanist standpoint. For Jonson, Coryate was a curiosity at Henry's court: 'hee conditioned to have no office of charge, or neerenesse cast upon him, as the *Remora* of his future travaile; for to that he is irrecoverably addicted' (sig. b2r).[39] Preferring travel to service at courts, this novel and independent traveller separates travel from its conventional humanist rationale of state employment. Coryate's addiction to travel as an end in itself has turned him into a veritable travelling machine:

He is an Engine, wholly consisting of extremes, a Head, Fingers, and Toes. For what his industrious Toes have trod, his ready Fingers have written, his subtle head dictating. He was set a going for *Venice* the fourteenth of *May Anno* 1608 and returned home (of himselfe) the third of *October* following, being wou[n]d up for five moneths, or thereabouts . . . (sig. b1r)

Artificial human beings adorned figure clocks, like the clock above the gate at the end of via Merceria in Venice described by Coryate, 'a clocke with the images of two wilde men by it made in brasse, a witty device and very exactly done' (p. 187), and the far more elaborate and magnificent figure clock in Strasbourg, whose description in the *Crudities* is accompanied by Hole's engraving. Clocks and automata made a strong impression on observers, entering into the European imagination to become powerful metaphors that brought together technology and myth to act as figurative 'mediators between the worlds of magic and rationality'.[40] Coryate, Jonson's travelling 'Engine', is imagined as a figure of awe and wonder, and there is a sense of travel as empirically calculable in the machine-like workings of his toes, fingers and head. Like the 'witty device' of the figure clock, he is cast as an object of delight, a sense also present in the description of Coryate as '*à Deliciis* to the Court' (sig. b1v); a figure that can be put on the table, wound up and set in motion to delight and amuse the assembled company, like the figure clocks that ornamented the well-dressed table. Yet, the metaphor of the automaton also carried negative connotations, and signified a lack of will, like the mindlessness of the jacks that strike the clock. Hence, for the humanist Jonson, Coryate is 'irrecoverably addicted' to travel; he has surrendered himself to travel beyond the bounds of reason, profit and utility, and has turned himself into an emblem of Folly.

Sir John Suckling, meditating on Coryate's relentless self-promotion, made a similar point, although with more sympathy. His sonnet stands out from the surrounding mock-encomia through its avoidance of wit for the plain-spoken sincerity of a friend:

> Whether I thee should either praise or pitty
> My senses at a great *Dilemma* are:
> For when I thinke how thou hast travaild farre,
> Canst Greeke and Latin speake, art curteous, witty,
> I these in thee and thee for them commend;
> But when I thinke how thou false friends to keepe
> Dost weare thy body, and dost leese thy sleepe,
> I thee then pitty and doe discommend.
> Thy feete have gone a painfull piligrimage,
> Thou many nights dost wrong thy hands and eyes
> In writing of thy long Apologies;
> Thy tongue is all the day thy restlesse page.
> For shame intreate them better, I this crave,
> So they more ease, and thou more wit shalt have.
>
> (sig. f1r)

The economical sparseness of the verse contrasts pointedly with Coryate's profligate linguistic excesses. Over-circulation, Suckling warns, will wear out the body and debase his credit. There is consternation that a gentleman of Coryate's education should be promoting himself in this way, diminishing his reputation by perversely translating himself from a learned gentleman into a witless buffoon. Suckling was clearly troubled by the errant career path chosen by this itinerant gentleman.

Hoskyns, Martin and Donne had built reputations on wit within their social milieu. Wit augmented their identity as gentlemen by effortlessly displaying the educational capital acquired at the universities and the Inns of Court. Manuscript enabled these men to exercise their wit in a manner that was often not advisable in print, and it enhanced their credit since it possessed an aura of social exclusivity that print could simulate but not equal. Scribal publication therefore allowed these wits to distinguish themselves from other 'gentlemen' wits of similar social backgrounds, such as Coryate, who were marketing their wit in print and other public performance spaces and, in doing so, risked debasing their credit. Donne's response to print appears to have been to isolate and thereby distinguish himself within the print coterie. His poem ends equivocally, simultaneously affirming and rejecting the textual sociability embodied by Coryate's book. The speaker cannot keep up with Coryate's ability to hold his drink and keep his head during a competitive health-pledging, and so removes himself from the companionship of fellow readers:

> The healths which my braine beares, must be farre lesse;
> Thy Gyant-wit o'rethrowes me, I am gone,
> And rather then reade all, I would reade none.
>
> (sig. d4r)

Donne uses the motif of the talked book to mark out an internal distance within the print coterie, and to put in place discriminations that govern the way his poem will be read in relation to Coryate's book, and the type of print celebrity Coryate has manufactured.

Hoskyns chose the form of octosyllabic doggerel for his third poem in the collection ('No more but so, I heard the crie'), thus subtly reinforcing the association with the demotic forms of popular verse, while simultaneously expressing distaste for joining with the pack.[41] In a witty variation on the conventional profession of inadequacy, 'like an old hound' he joins common voice, only to find 'My mouth decayes much in this kind', punning on old age and the corrupting effect of the popular voice. Infection inspires a distinction between a popular and an élite market for news. He imagines a publishing scenario in which the wits have been 'undone', and 'There is no newes we are more sorry at / Then this strange newes of *Rawbone Coryate*', a Rabelaisian giant generic to popular pamphlet literature. He is then impelled to turn, half mockingly, to an alternative marketplace, 'the newes of learned people / In Pauls Churchyard & neere Pauls steeple' (sig. e7r), which is circulating a more discriminating image. Hoskyns distinguishes between popular and élite cultures. The language of bibliophagia was similarly employed within the 'Panegyricke Verses' to construct an economy of consumption stratified by different tastes. The front matter to the book holds in tension conflicting responses to the print marketplace and the print event itself. Coryate tried to bridge élite and popular cultures by cultivating the image of the orator-buffoon equally at home in prince's courts and 'Fayres and Mercats, to all places, and all societies a *Spectacle* gratefull' (sig. b1v), as Jonson noted. While sincere panegyricists, like Brooke, applauded him for his efforts, many others tried to insulate themselves from the potentially indiscriminate popularity of the printed book by embodying a notion of 'bad taste' in the figure of Coryate's hastily gobbled and just as quickly regurgitated book.

'WITS GARGANTUA COLUME'[42]

The sociable flyting of Coryate in the 'Panegyricke Verses' is not nearly as sharp-tongued as the vicious satiric attacks on Davies and others at the Inns in the late 1590s, and is frequently alleviated by honest praise. Communal energies are channelled into clubbing, which, as we have seen, results in a community stratified and policed by carefully calibrated social distinctions. It is a community committed to reviving the forms of learned literary play. Timothy Raylor has identified the 'Panegyricke Verses' as the primary source for an English tradition of formal burlesque later taken up by Sir John Mennes and James Smith and collected in their anthology, *Musarum Deliciæ, or the Muses Recreation* (1655).[43] The *Crudities* and the *Crambe* showcase a range of low literary forms: the mock-encomium predominates, but there are also other forms, including macaronics, nonsense poems, mock-anacreontics, and burlesquing ballads, such as Whitaker's parodically titled 'Course Musicke plaid upon the Odcombian Hoboy, to attend the second course of Coryats Coleworts, and dittied to the most melodious Comicall ayre, borne and brought up in the Septentrionall suburbs, which the vulgar call, The Punks delight' (*Crambe*, sig. b2r).

Erasmus's *Praise of Folly* revived the mock-encomium after it had been 'practically extinct for a thousand years', thus opening the genre to subsequent generations.[44] The image of Coryate as a modern-day Folly runs throughout the 'Panegyricke Verses' and coalesced in *Traveller for the English Wits*, which includes a verse elaborating Coryate's '*Parallel with Erasmus*' and the *Praise of Folly*, and an accompanying woodcut (*Traveller*, sig. A3v–4r). Just as Erasmus took More's name – because of its proximity to the Greek word for folly, *moria* – as the seriocomic inspiration for his mock-encomium, many of the Coryate poems pun on the fortuitous fact that his home town was called Odcombe. Erasmus's unflinching defence of his *Praise of Folly* against detractors claimed legitimacy for the improvisational energies of the mock-encomium and intellectual game-playing in general. For Erasmus, the ability to 'take great pleasure in jokes' defined More's wit, his 'extraordinary keen intelligence'; it simultaneously placed More 'apart from the common herd' and made him 'able and willing to be a man for all seasons with all men'.[45] Intellectual 'witty' game-playing was part of an élite literature of leisure that allowed participants in the 'Panegyricke Verses' to maintain their social status, while joining in the joke with others in print. Lewis Lewkenor read *Coryats Crudities* as a mock-encomium within a tradition that included '*Apuleius* Asse', Virgil's mock-encomium on the gnat, Homer's *Battle of the Frogs and Mice*, and even his *Iliad*, a classical source for the mock-heroic.⁴⁶ He explicates the genre through the Silenus topos, advising the reader to 'Cracke then the nut, and take the kernell for thy paines' (sig. c5v–6r) – just like the rare curiosity of Homer's *Iliad* in a nutshell cited by Brooke. The box of the Sileni, whose surface was grotesquely carved but which once opened discovered profound truths, was frequently chosen to illustrate the intellectual value and pleasures of the mock-encomium.⁴⁷ The reader with enough wit should therefore look beyond the slight and motley surface of Coryate's book to find the inner kernel of meaning and value. The Silenus topos is appropriate to the freer structure of the mock-encomium, which was not restricted by a set rhetorical form; cracking the nut implies breaking something that is finished, opening its forms to improvisatory play.

Improvisation in the 'Panegyricke Verses' is linguistic as well as formal: there are verses in Latin, Greek, French, quasi-French, Italian, Spanish, Welsh, mock-Irish, and the Utopian tongue. These macaronics, like the *Crudities*, are 'hastily gobled up': macaroni is 'a thick and unrefined rustic dish', hence, as Michel Jeanneret points out, 'macaronic verse should only contain that which is coarse and crude, along with vulgar words'. Macaronics open scholarly, taught languages, as opposed to the vernacular, to creative play and have affinities with nonsense.⁴⁸ The very learned grammarian John Sanford, writing under the pseudonym Glareanus Vadianus, produced macaronic verses in Latin, English, French, Italian and Spanish (sigs. g6v–h3r), as well as a nonsense poem in English using the form of a 'loose verse called by the Italians, *versi sciolti*' (sig. l1v).⁴⁹ These macaronics, like the mock-encomium, laugh at Coryate's oddness – his body, his clothes and, above all, his travel madness. Their effect relies on the pleasurably comic sound of the language itself, achieved through the witty use of alliteration and rhyme. These verses are like '*mosto, / De poca cosecha haga su Agosto*' (sig. h3r), the sweet and delicious, but unfermented and so unfinished grape juice (*mosto*) harvested early in August.

This collection of mock-encomiastic verses relied heavily on Coryate taking on the role of buffoon. Yet, why was he so willing to collude with his seeming detractors and make himself the object of their laughter? The primary function of laughter in classical and Renaissance thought was to express scorn and contempt for the object of ridicule and thereby assert one's own social and ethical superiority.⁵⁰ This is true of many of the mock-encomiastic poems, and yet it is also an oversimplification of their effect. The laughter of the mock-encomium, according to Erasmus, offered 'a way to take the minds of spoiled men by surprise' through its incongruity, thus 'even cure them by means of pleasure'.⁵¹ Laughing at Coryate does not take place within the forms of satire, as such, but rather within the ludic forms of the mock-encomium, burlesque and the 'nonsense' poems of Hoskyns and Sanford. An effect of such incongruity is to produce a state of wonder and admiration: the mind liberated from reason, and indulging in the emotion of laughter, is free to enjoy the effects of nonsense and the fantastic.[52] Coryate is simultaneously the object of ridicule and a figure of wonder: for Phelips, Coryate is the 'travelling *Wonder* of our daies' and his *Crudities*, a 'booke of wonders', whose main effect is to give pleasure (sig. c7r–v). Laughter in the 'Panegyricke Verses' wants to have it both ways. As Craik notes in relation to the corporeal pleasures of the book, the '*Crudities* represents corporeal appetite as simultaneously repellent and desirable; for the traveler, and hence for the reader, Coryat proposes both the indulgence of the senses and the intervention of reason'.[53] These burlesque poems explore realms of pleasure and wonder, states of liberation that were also available in the sociable pleasures of symposiastic literature. By casting Coryate as the buffoon, these writers were able to explore states of excess, while still maintaining a hold on the laughter of ridicule, hence asserting their own superiority, moderation and civility in the face of such excess.

The degree of collusion in producing laughter and promoting Coryate is indicated by Inigo Jones's contribution, turned into a dialogue through Coryate's skilful manipulation of the margins of the book.[54] Jones punningly set out Coryate's correspondence with the Dutch, reputed for their humanism and their drinking:

Next, to the sober Dutch I turne my tale,	
Who doe in earnest write thee Latin letters,	*The modesty of the Author
And thou in good pot paper ne're didst faile	being such, and his temperance
To answere them; so are you neither debters.	in drinking, that he sometimes
But sympathize in all, save when thou drinkst	frowneth when a health is
Thou mak'st a *crab-tree face, shak'st head, and wink'st	drunke unto him.

(sig. f1v–2r)

The Erasmian ideal is quickly degraded into the pot poet, and the civilities of health-pledging into a grotesque display. This, of course, is the effect of drinking which deforms and unmakes the civil gentleman. Coryate is notably quick to refute the charge and insist on his temperance, although in the manner of a mock-innocent which wittily lets the original jest stand. Jones concludes that 'thy booke the Cordiall of sad mindes, / Or rather Cullis of our *Od combe Cocke*' – a cullis both is like a cordial (in that it is a restorative beef broth – or chicken soup in this case) and is a stick to beat someone with, in other words, a satire. Stoicism, which insists the body and its pleasures must be tempered and physicked for the sake of civility, is both held as an ideal by Jones and Coryate and revealed as profoundly limited. Like the other mock-encomiastics, the poem employs Rabelaisian laughter also heard in the epicureanism of banquet literature. Temperance may be an ideal, but excess is liberating. Many of the 'Panegyricke Verses' delight in the Rabelaisian body attributed to Coryate, even as it is invoked in order to confirm their own civil identities, because it offered a figure for imagining the release of inhibitions that regulate public discourse. That said, as Suckling's admonition indicates, the role of buffoon was an inherently difficult position to adopt if one wanted to maintain one's own hold on civility. While some were clearly attuned to the different registers of laughter and explored the dimensions of wonder and the fantastic, others such as Sir Thomas Fairfax clearly only heard the laughter of ridicule, as his contemptuous account of Coryate's wit testifies: 'but he hath witt whie then should men deride it / yet what is witt if that a foule doe guide it'.[55]

Considerable effort went into securing a mock-encomium from Sir John Harington: Holland composed an importuning Latin verse, and Sir Robert Phelips may have also corresponded with him about Coryate.[56] Holland addressed his verse specifically to the author of the *Metamorphosis of Ajax*: another model for the mock-encomium whose *cacophonia* or 'graveolentibus facetiis' ('strong-smelling facetiousness'), as Holland wrote in a note to his verse (sig. e2r), offered the wits a model for liberty of speech.[57] The *Metamorphosis of Ajax* and the 'Panegyricke Verses' share an admiration for Erasmus's *Praise of Folly*, Sir Thomas More and François Rabelais. For Harington, these learned wits and virtuous men paradoxically authorise modes of 'slovenly eloquence' and 'sluttish arguments', rhetorical styles, as Harington's examples illustrate, in which the jest spills over into libel.[58] Rabelais's influence over the 'Panegyricke Verses' turns Coryate's serious observations of Europe into a fantastic traveller's tale more in the manner of *Pantagruel* than More's philosophical commonwealth in *Utopia*.[59] The wits turned to Rabelais for linguistic play and fantastic humour, and because of his reputation as a tavern wit and libeller.[60]

Rabelais's influence is to be found in the dangerously 'sluttish argument' of Harington's mock-encomium for the *Crudities*. Harington wittily and subversively inverts the encomiastic poem, turning it inside out, and turning it into a subtle libel. Following in the footsteps of his *Metamorphosis of Ajax*, he vulgarly delights in the fantastic, the material and the physical, and speculates on the conventions of praise. His poem opens in deflationary mode with a mock-heroic apostrophe to the goose that kept the Roman

Capitol. The homophonic pun on Coryate's 'sory wit' – sorry/soary – hyperbolically takes the speaker up to '*Cinthia's* spheare' and a comparison between Coryate's 'vast wit, and courage so audacious' and that of '*Roland*'. Rumour has it that Cynthia-Elizabeth I insisted that Harington translate *Orlando Furioso* after he circulated lewd verses from the poem among her ladies-in-waiting, and he now exacts his own textual revenge. Sir Robert Cecil warned Harington in a letter composed in October 1603 not to try to curry favour with James by insulting Elizabeth, 'by rayling (as you are accused to doe) of the late Queen of famous memory at your dynners, for if you knew my soveraine lorde as I do you wold quickly find that such woorks are to him unacceptable sacrifices'.[61] Harington is more circumspect in his Coryate mock-encomium. In the context of the mock-heroic magnification of trivial subjects, a similar type of magnification, either under the influence of drink or via the telescope, or both, has meant that 'the learn'd of late in forren parts / Finde *Phœbe's* face so full of wennes and warts' (sig. c5v). The moon in its symbolic and monarchical form of Cynthia-Phoebe is subjected to an anatomising materialism that rationally disproves the metaphoric magnification of panegyric, which can turn queens into celestial bodies, and instead offers an alternative atomistic way of seeing, warts and all.

Harington effectively parodies the encomiastic poem, reducing it to a piece of inconsequentiality, nonsense. The use of the telescope in this context is suggestive. The sixteenth century saw the emergence of an unorthodox strand within Ptolemaic astronomy that questioned the physical existence of the empryean heaven since it 'refused to accept a system containing any sphere void of visible bodies whereby man could directly observe its motions'. Such observations were made possible by the telescope. The empyrean heaven could be accepted as a matter of faith, but it could not be rationally known.[62] The telescope could be said to privilege sceptical enquiry over matters of faith. Arguably, the mock-encomium is itself a potentially sceptical genre since it is an exercise whereby the writer wittily blames through the mechanism of praise, and thus demonstrates how the terms of encomiastic poetry, which incorporated both praise and blame, are easily reversible.[63] Harington's mock-encomium calls into question a language of praise that through hyperbolic inflation attempts to secure political consensus.

Hoskyns's 'No more but so, I heard the crie' enlists the mock-encomium for similar purposes. The second half of the poem is a fantastic flight of fancy in which the winds of fame that carry news of Coryate to the Antipodes are not metaphoric but real: they are the gusts of wind that lift his shoes hung on top of St Paul's steeple, with his name writ large on a piece of parchment tied to the laces, 'That may be read most legibly', and since 'Fame is but winde, thence winde may blow it / So farre that all the world may know it' (sig. e7r). The syllogism wittily dismantles a metaphoric economy central to poems of praise, since 'Fame is but winde'. At the same time, since it is a false syllogism, it questions the truth and persuasive power of such commonplaces, which rely on proverbial consensus rather than arguments that can be proved by logic and reason.[64] The poem as a whole is characterised by scepticism towards excessive encomiastic amplification and, ultimately, the persuasive power of poetry of praise given that it is based on such windy and, by association, flatulent premises. It is a scepticism also conveyed by Harington's poem, and in his case at least it extends to a sceptical view of political analogies and commonplaces that can turn sovereigns into gods on earth.[65] As we have seen, James I made an equation between the dangerous wit of lawyers in the Commons, such as Hoskyns, and writers of sceptical libels on the basis that both demystified the 'wonder' of kings. These wits appear to have had a contemporary reputation as libertines. Toby Mathew later wrote of Donne and Martin 'that they were libertines in themselves; and that the thing for which they could not long endure me was because they thought me too saucy, for presuming to show them the right way, in which they liked not then to go, and wherein they would disdain to follow any other'.[66] Given that Mathews is referring to his then recent conversion to Catholicism, the libertinism he attributes to Donne and Martin refers to free thinking in religious and other matters. Mathews was trying to discredit Donne and Martin; nonetheless his accusation of libertinism does point up the wits' recognition of the limits of reason, their sensitivity to the place of uncertainty and doubt in moral deliberation, and the tensions between decorum and liberty of conscience and speech.[67]

Not all the scepticism displayed towards encomiastic poetry in the 'Panegyricke Verses' was political in orientation. Donne's anatomy of Coryate's book is a meditation on print publication and, ultimately, the humanist culture of the book. Donne's participation in the 'Panegyricke Verses' coincided with his own entry into print: in January 1610 he had published his *Pseudo-Martyr*, dedicated to James I; in early 1611, he published his *Conclave Ignati*, and its English translation; and in November, he printed *The First Anniversary*, followed by *The Second Anniversary* in 1612. Both the Drury poems were published anonymously, and the uncertainties that he expresses in his letters over his 'descent in printing' appear to be attached to the difficulties of writing eulogistic verses and maintaining intellectual credibility and freedom.[68] The motif of the anatomy, breaking an object or concept down into parts, necessarily involves an interrogation of the mechanics of combination, and so was a figure available to hold processes up to investigation. The doubleness of the mock-encomium gave Donne a certain licence to interrogate a language of praise and the status of print publication.

In terms of its governing motifs at least, Donne's anatomy of Coryate's book and its progress in the world bears a resemblance to his *Anatomy of the World: the First Anniversary* and its sequel, *The Second Anniversary: the Progress of the Soul*.[69] The progress of Coryate's book begins by mustering metaphoric riches from the East and the West, but this does not open out the imaginative horizons of the poem in the way that a similar trope functions to do so in 'To his Mistress going to Bed':

> O my America, my new found land,
> My kingdom, safeliest when with one man manned,
> My mine of precious stones, my empery,
> How blessed am I in this discovering thee.
>
> (lines 27–30)

This ecstatic metaphoric land of riches takes the poet into an imaginative and essentially private realm of liberty and licence. The progress of Coryate's book is imagined in a rather more prosaic form:

> To which both Indies sacrifices send;
> The west sent gold, which thou didst freely spend,
> (Meaning to see'it no more) upon the presse.
> The east sends hither her deliciousnesse;
> And thy leav's must embrace what comes from thence.

Trade and its commodities take us to the merchant's storehouse, a place where the leaves of the book are used to wrap 'vaste Tomes of Currans, and of Figs, / Of Medcinall, and Aromatique twigs'. *Copia* is separated from *anima*, the divine breath of inspiration, the soul, and has to make its home on earth. When the book moves lower down the social scale, the leaves are used to wrap 'Home-*manufactures*', 'thicke popular faires'. In a witty and deflationary variation on literary invention as gestation and the literary text as womb, the pages of the book are used to display goods:

> . . . upon warme stals
> They hatch all wares for which the buyer cals,
> Then thus thy leav's we justly may commend,
> That they all kinde of matter comprehend.
>
> (sig. d3v)

Donne's anatomy constantly grounds the literary resources of hyperbolic inflation in the mundanely physical world. The typical encomiastic analogy between the book and 'bravest Heroes' is subject to a radical materialism that does not recognise moralising notions of honour: the bodies of brave heroes and criminals serve the same 'publique good' whether 'Scattered in divers lands' or 'cut in Anatomies', just as all books, good and bad, will be broken 'in peeces' and serve the same ends. The 'progress of the book' is unremittingly materialistic and anatomising. The printed book is a physical object without *anima* or intellectual life and, like the leaves of Coryate's book, its value solely resides in mundane physical uses:

> Some shall wrap pils, and save a friends life so,
>   Some shall stop muskets, and so kill a foe.
> Thou shalt not ease the Critiques of next age
>   So much, at once their hunger to asswage.
> Nor shall wit-pyrats hope to finde thee lie
>   All in one bottome, in one Librarie.
> Some leav's may paste strings there in other books
>
> (sig. d3r–4v)

Pessimism is expressed towards the humanist notion of the printed book and proprietary authorship. The humanist book was a literary artefact to be collected, read, digested and imitated.[70] Coryate's book, by contrast, will be collected, not for posterity and not in the creation of new bibliographic and proprietary authors, but to furnish other books in a very literal sense – it will make up their bindings.

Coryate's use of the front matter to his book was highly innovative: he staged an event, fashioned his own celebrity, and orchestrated a print community by realising and improvising on a contemporary culture of performance within the format of the printed book. The 'Panegyricke Verses' would help to establish a new print genre, the 'drolleries' collected in the *Musarum Deliciæ* (1655). The self-proclaimed gentlemen wits who participated in this event facilitated this process, although many actively resisted their incorporation within a print community. Voices are not harmonised in praise in the 'Panegyricke Verses'; instead, the mock-encomium was an effective medium for dissonance to be expressed in its many forms, from sharp mockery to witty intellectual play and sceptical critique. The vulgar pleasures of the *Crudities* can unmake the man of reason; nonetheless, there is a willingness to push beyond this stoic proposition and enquire into this unsettling prospect. For subsequent readers and writers, citing Coryate and his *Crudities* signified something (and was meant to) about the 'character' of the writer, and set out 'a homosocial claim to shared taste'. The clubbing that energises the front matter would influence the clubs that proliferated in the 1620s and 1630s. *Coryats Crudities* was portrayed as an acquired taste, cultivated among those wits who possessed the style of urbanity that could tolerate crudity in its manifold forms and enjoyed the 'tough-minded' pleasures of political satires and libels.[71] These urbane tastes encompassed the pleasures of travel and, in turn, were part of the constitution of new 'cosmopolite' communities.

CHAPTER SIX

Traveller for the English wits

When Whitaker jested that Coryate would make his *Crudities* as 'famous, as Moore his *Utopia*' (*Crudities*, sig. a2v), he may have been jocularly implying that his travels were a fabrication, but he was also reading Coryate's travel book within the conventions of *lusus*. The play between the 'Panegyricke Verses' and Coryate's travels both imitates and expands on the front matter to More's *Utopia*. The prefatory letters and verses to the *Utopia* identified More's account of this 'philosophical' city as an intellectual game which allowed its participants to play with the idea of travel, opening it to more speculative viewpoints. Coryate's curious travels similarly improvised on the conventions of humanist travel. Recent studies have portrayed Coryate as almost single-handedly initiating a radically novel mode of travel and travel writing.[1] For Anthony Parr, the revolutionary element of the *Crudities* and his letters from East India resides in the way Coryate turned travel into a ludic literary performance, disclosing a 'surplus value' that opened the way to new travel experiences and ways of seeing.[2] When Coryate travelled to Europe in classic humanist fashion he sought out the company of learned men and observed the city's topography, monuments and antiquities. However, his observations are less concerned with the conventional civic topics of Renaissance travel, and instead engage with memorable sights, especially rarities and curiosities. The traditional civic discourse of travel, with its emphasis on the formation of a civil subject profitable to the state, underwent a transformation in this period as notions of civility were slowly extended to the pleasures of observing and experiencing other urbane cultures. James Howell, in his *Instructions for Forreine Travell* (1642), advised that an English gentleman on his European tour would ideally become acculturated to 'more refined Nations, whom Learning and Knowledge did first Urbanise and polish'.[3] Coryate's book appealed to an audience that was reading for pleasure as well as profit, and for whom books and travel provided the type of leisure activity that characterises early modern cultures of consumption.[4]

TRAVEL AND THE CITY

Foreign travel, on the whole, took the traveller to the city.[5] The reader could find within Coryate's weighty volume '*new*' observations of Venice as well as '*the descriptions of other Cities which I survayed in divers countries in my travels*' which '*will yeeld more matter of newes unto him, because none of these Cities have beene described in our language that I could ever heare of*' (sig. a6v). The great European cities were the seats of government; it was here that princes kept their courts, parliaments sat, and the courts of law were held; as Giovanni Botero observed, 'all matters of importance have recourse to that place'. Power, trade and industry, and a multifaceted culture of consumption were expressed in the physical fabric of the city, in its magnificent, 'Gorgeous and gallant buildings'.[6] When humanists considered the intellectual and national benefits of travel, their primary frame of reference was not the New World, but the magnificent cities described by Botero. The nexus of civic life, civility and consumption, the European city offered a valuable education that would equip the young gentleman for future service to the commonwealth.[7]

Coryate presented his own volume to Prince Henry and his court in precisely these terms:

it may perhaps yeeld some litle encouragement to many noble and generose yong Gallants that follow your Highnesse Court, and give attendance upon your Peerlesse person, to travell into forraine countries, and inrich themselves partly with the observations, and partly with the languages of outlandish regions, the principall meanes (in my poore opinion) to grace and adorne those courtly Gentlemen, whose noble parentage, ingenuous education, and vertuous conversation have made worthy to be admitted into your Highnesse Court: seeing thereby they will be made fit to doe your Highnesse and the Country their better service when opportunity shall require. (sig. a4v–5r)

Travel was an aspect of the *vita activa*, not to be undertaken for personal, private ends, but to make the gentleman profitable to his prince and the commonwealth. Robert Dallington made this point very clearly in his *A Method for Travell*, warning readers that the strictest self-government of mind and manners were required, since 'the end of his *Travell* is his ripening in knowledge, and the end of his knowledge is the service of his countrie, which of right challengeth, the better part of us'.[8] A civic humanist discourse of travel is showcased in Hermann Kirchner's oration prefacing Coryate's travel narrative. Kirchner defended travel on the grounds that it produces a commonwealth of civil gentlemen, equipping them with '*all the wayes and meanes that pertaine to a civill life, and the governing of a humane society*' (sig. b8v). His essay offers readers a utopian class of gentlemen-citizens distinguished by their enlightened civil conversations.

There were other types of civil communities, alongside royal courts, to be found in these great European cities: academies and universities, and men of letters. One purpose of travel was to initiate a dialogue with men of learning. 'What a singular and incomparable comfort is it to conferre with those learned men in forraine Universities and noble Cities', Coryate declares in his epistle to the reader, 'whose excellent workes we reade in our private studies at home' (sig. b3r). Intellectual communities took their place alongside other civic institutions within the city, and their attractions could rival that of courts, especially in the case of men, like Coryate, whose social status and connections meant that they had only limited access to the European courts. The vision of civic life embodied by the Republic of Letters, based around the ideal of learned conversations and equality among men of intellect, shaped the cityscape in its own image and created urbane communities.[9] Coryate devotes a great deal of energy on his travels and in his *Crudities* to describing a utopian Republic of Letters brought into being through his conversations with learned and cultivated men. His observations are punctuated by his conversations with hospitable and companionable strangers: the Huguenot community in Paris, those civil young gentlemen in the Italian cities who act as his guides, and the men of learning at the universities in the Swiss republics, German states and the Low Countries. In Paris and in northern Europe, the Republic of Letters is avowedly Protestant, and located within the arena of confessional politics. Coryate recalls his joy at 'the sight and company of that rare ornament of learning *Isaac Causabonus*, with whom I had much familiar conversation at his house, neare unto St. Germans gate within the citie' (p. 31). He includes a brief catalogue of Casaubon's library, 'set forth, to the great benefite and utility of the Common-weale of learning' (p. 32), noting that Casaubon is in now in England, and publishes his plea for a hagiography of Elizabeth I to boost the morale of England's Protestant allies on the continent (pp. 32–3). By comparison, the companionship of learned men in Italy is characterised by civil conversations that cut across religious and national divides: 'For surely many Italians are passing courteous and kinde towards strangers, of whose humanitie I made triall in divers other cities in Italie, as Padua, Venice, Verona, Brixia, Bergomo' (p. 304). The intellectual ties binding learned men within the Republic of Letters take on a distinctly mannered dimension as these courteous and learned men accompany Coryate around the city, showing him all its memorable sights.

Coryate's playful dialogue with the London wits continues beyond the front matter of the *Crudities*, punctuating his travel observations in the form of snippets of witty conversations with Whitaker about Rabelais, codpieces and forks, and the insertion of a jesting letter of recommendation to Sir Henry Wotton, the English ambassador in Venice, written on his behalf by Martin. These London wits have various personal, social and symbolic points of contact with the diverse community of English travellers populating Coryate's travel observations. In Padua, he makes the acquaintance of George Rook, a member of Wotton's household, who accompanies him on his journeys between Venice and Padua; a Mr Moore, a doctor of Physic, and a Mr Willoughby, both studying at Padua university, show him around the city. In Venice, he meets Samuel Slade, a fellow Dorsetshire man and Merton scholar, 'but now a famous traveller abroad in the world' (p. 230). On his return to Padua from Venice, he dined with the young Sir Thomas Wentworth, later Earl of Strafford, in Italy on his Grand Tour; he narrowly missed the young Earl of Essex in Lyons. Early in his travels in France, he converses with an English-speaking Franciscan Friar born in Ireland, and admiringly observes he is 'as well able to discourse of al particular politique and state matters of England, as any man in our company' (p. 18). At Mezolt, he speaks with a Protestant Grison, Joannes Curtabatus, who had lived in Cambridgeshire in the service of an Italian, Sir Horatio Palavicino, and 'found him a man of very courteous behaviour, and indeede he did me a certaine kindnesse, in which respect I thought it fit to name him in my journall' (p. 355). These meetings and remembrances structure Coryate's narrative of his travel experiences. Such complex cross-national exchanges between England and Europe establish points of correspondence between men of courtesy, conversation, wit and intellect that cut across national boundaries to produce a broader community that is defined in terms of its civility, its learning, and its openness to travel and other cosmopolitan exchanges.

The development of travel literature intersected with the emergence of a metropolitan culture. The two came together in the increasingly sophisticated sense of what cities had to offer the traveller. As early as 1575, *The Traveiler of Jerome Turler* noted that the 'viewing of Cityes requyreth muche more diligence' than the countryside, and listed public works, both religious and secular – cathedrals as well as palaces, marketplaces, gardens, theatres, schools, libraries and hospitals – and an array of private works, 'such notable thinges as are seene in the houses of private men, and citizens, as Pictures, Gardaines, Fountaynes, or whatsoever is worthy y^r seing'.[10] The urban landscapes of the Italian cities had long been recognised as offering the traveller a magnificent 'theater of cultural memory'. The ancient ruins, monuments and objects on display in these cities were carefully observed and recorded by the humanist traveller, both as an end in itself and as part of a project to reconstruct the history of the classical city that fed into ongoing debates about civic practices capable of fully realising the *vita activa*.[11] Albert Meier's highly regarded travel guide advised the traveller to search out 'Antiquaries, that is men excellently seene in antiquities and ancient monuments'. Italy's rather more recent Renaissance paintings and architecture and other examples of 'rare and exquisite workmanship' were similarly recommended.[12] Among the paintings at the Ducal Palace in Venice, Coryate noted a fine painting by Tintoretto (p. 203), and in Bergamo, a mural on the ceiling by Franciscus de Ferreomonte (p. 345).

The early modern view of the metropolis was simultaneously expansive and profoundly ambivalent: the great European cities could both make and unmake the civil gentleman. Italy and France were popularly associated with a foreign hyperurbanity: the Englishman returned with affected speech, dress and manner undermining his credit at home and rendering him unfit for public service.[13] Sir Thomas Palmer praised Italy, the 'ancient nurcerie and shop of libertie, the which to the affects of men is precious and estimable', but ended by warning of 'the infinite corruptions, almost inevitable, that invest Travailers after small abode there'. He even translated the rich humanist civic theatre of cultural memory into the forms of debased specular entertainment: 'the speciall gallerie of monuments and olde aged memorials of histories, records of persons and things to bee seene thorowout the Countrey. But this being a fantasticall attracter, and a glutton-feeder of the appetite, rather than of necessarie knowledge, I will mention no further thereof.'[14]

Coryate's famous encounter with the Venetian courtesan is designed to reassure even the most resistant reader, like Palmer, of the educated traveller's ability to withstand Italian urban temptations, and maintain his natural English civility:

as the beames of the Sunne doe penetrate into many uncleane places, and yet are nothing polluted with the impuritie thereof: so did I visit the Palace of a noble Cortezan, view her own amorus person, heare her talke, observe her fashion of life, and yet was nothing contaminated therewith, nor corrupted in maner. Therefore I instantly request thee (most candid reader) to be as charitably conceited of me, though I have at large deciphered and as it were anatomized a Venetian Cortezan unto thee, as thou wouldest have me of thy selfe upon the like request. (p. 271)

This is one of the earliest known usages of 'candid'.[15] Ever the linguist, Coryate is using the word in terms of its Latin root, *candidus*, meaning shining or glittering white, as an analogy to the pure, dazzling beams of the sun penetrating without taint 'uncleane places', while drawing on its associations with character (honest, straightforward), and implying a reflection on his own writing (clear, lucid) and intentions.[16] It is possible to argue that this encounter between a candid Englishman and a Venetian courtesan participates in the constitution of a discourse of 'civic Englishness' within travel literature. Italy and its courtesans in city comedies of the period, Jean Howard has argued, signified the potential within an England newly identified with its 'burgeoning metropolis' to 'spin out of control', and therefore necessitated the formation of a new civic subject, the 'self-regulating Stoic man'.[17]

Yet, Coryate's observations of Venice resist many of the moral imperatives of the self-regulating Stoic man, and his encounter with the courtesan is itself almost comedically overdetermined. Not surprisingly, the readers gathered in the 'Panegyricke Verses' make a point of refusing the civil contract Coryate sought to secure with the 'candid reader'. His Venetian 'anatomy' is read mockingly 'against the grain', and Coryate is given the part of the voyeuristic rather than candid observer. These readers are alert to the tensions between Coryate's assumption of the 'candid' gaze and his 'sluttish' openness to experiences for the sake of novelty and his own fame. Coryate opens a novel perspective on the early modern city. Aspects of his accounts of the courtesan and the 'uncivill and unseemely' (pp. 261–2) dress of Venetian women on the streets do stigmatise the foreign as 'a fantasticall attracter, and a glutton-feeder of the appetite' in a similar manner to moralising travel guides and feed into the formation of a national characteristic of civic Englishness.[18] That said, this stigmatising, self-regulating perspective on the city frequently disappears from view. Coryate's curious eye is distracted by the manifold pleasures of urban sightseeing, thereby complicating his text's relationship to the formation of these ideological and nationalist categories. His account of the 'memorable things to be seene' (p. 295) expands the usual urban topography that the traveller was urged to observe.[19] His observations range from buildings, antiquities, markets and theatres to include novel sights, such as courtesans and mountebanks, which as he tells the curious reader are new to the literature of travel. While travellers were advised to observe dress, manners and social customs, Coryate is so alert to novelty in all its surprising forms that the mundane is continually transformed into the curious, the rare and the novel.

THE CURIOUS AND INDEPENDENT TRAVELLER

The increasingly diversified market for travel literature accompanying the growth of private travel extended the generic possibilities available in the seventeenth century.[20] When Coryate said 'I am a private man and no statist' (sig. b5v) in defence of the attention he paid to epitaphs, inscriptions and architectural details, he set out a new distinction within travel writing between political and ecclesiastical observation of the state and what could be described as cultural or ethnographic observation. Meier's *Certaine Briefe, and Speciall Instructions* advised the traveller to study closely 'Ancient Epitaphs, and inscriptions, cut, graven, carved, or painted' and 'tombs, pictures, pillers, and dyals, of rare and exquisite workmanship' alongside the structures of state and church.[21] Coryate does glance at matters of state, particularly in his observations of France, but only briefly. Instead he concentrates on social customs, manners and novelties (such as parmesan cheese or the use of umbrellas), antiquities and other rarities, as well as aspects of chorography and topography: in particular, as Meier advised, he specifies the 'Length of miles, & dista[n]ce from place to place' and 'geometricall bignesse', the measurement of the breadth, length and height of architectural features. This latter aspect of his observations would be later parodied by those who were 'Coryatizing' their travels.[22]

For Randall Caudill *Coryats Crudities* is an influential text in the emergence of an 'aesthetic of rarity' in the early seventeenth century, a category of taste defining the virtuoso traveller-as-collector.[23] Practices of collecting were the medium through which taste, and other signifiers of cultural capital, could be acquired and put on display. Palmer may have condemned gentlemen travelling to view antiquities and other collections in 1606, but it was a legitimate rationale for private travel by 1634 when Peacham inserted his new essay 'On Antiquities', which defined the virtuoso traveller, in his revised edition of the *Compleat Gentleman*.[24] New practices of travelling and collecting, like reading for pleasure and entertainment, put objects, be they antiquities or books, to different social and cultural uses not fully accounted for and credited within a humanist culture. They attest to an increasingly sophisticated private sphere, which encompassed social activities that may have had an attachment to humanist discourses of civility, especially in relation to the development of categories of taste and urbanity, but not necessarily civic ends.

Coryate tells the reader he is offering Prince Henry and his court something very different to previous studies of the Venetian city-state represented by works like Contarini's *Commonwealth of Venice*, since '*that booke reporteth not halfe so many remarkable matters as mine doth* (absit dicto invidia) *of the antiquities and monuments of that famous Citie, together with the description of Palaces, Churches, the Piazza of* S. Marke' (sig. a6r). Prince Henry, like his mother, Queen Anne, had embarked upon a programme of collecting to establish one of the first English royal collections, following in the footsteps of the European royal courts.[25] Henry collected paintings, sculptures, antiquities and curiosities, employing agents in Europe. In Brussels, William Trumbull began preliminary plans for producing catalogues of sculptures and pictures for the prince. John Finet wrote to him in early 1612 about an 'Italian gentleman' who wanted to sell his perspective glasses to the prince.[26] While merchants and antiquarians, such as Sir Walter Cope, had been assembling important collections since the late sixteenth century, the collections of the royal court gave collecting a new prominence and credibility in the early seventeenth century.[27]

Coryate devotes a lengthy section to Fontainebleau, Henry IV's recently completed royal showcase – presumably of interest to Prince Henry, who was seeking to define his own identity through architectural projects, and to other members of the nobility and gentry similarly engaged in building works. Parr has rightly argued that Coryate's narrative bears little trace of the political and civic themes expressed in the architectural projects of either Henry IV or Prince Henry.[28] At Fontainebleau, there is no sweeping prospect; instead, the reader is rushed from a 'little way off' straight into the 'three or foure goodly courts' (p. 38). Attention is engaged by objects and ornamental details as Coryate walks about recording what he sees: statues, iron railings, fountains and other water features – especially their decorative details – the workmanship of the garden, and the collection of exotic birds including storks and ostriches. A witty account of the Swiss guard at the palace, assisted by Whitaker, is enlivened by an etymology of codpieces, so called 'because it is by that merrie French writer *Rabelais* stiled the first and principall piece of Armour, the Switzers do weare it as a significa[n]t Symbole of the assured service they are to doe to the French King in his Warres, and of the maine burden of the most laborious imployments which lye upon them in time of Peace' (p. 43). The overarching political themes are absent because the narrative is structured to appeal to a collector fascinated by the material and aesthetic dimension of objects in their own right; a collector who possesses an urbane taste able to appreciate the slightly risqué Rabelaisian jest about the priapic Swiss guard, because he is ready to 'winke at some light matters inserted into these my Observations' (sig. b8r).

Collecting and observing architecture and antiquities provided a new form of employment for the private traveller in which he took his place alongside merchants and other agents in Europe, while retaining his connections with his clientele among the gentry and aristocracy. When describing the paving of St Mark's Square in Venice, Coryate says that it would have been 'more glorious' if 'it been paved either with diamond pavier made of free stone, as the halles of some of our great Gentlemen in England are, (amongst the rest that of my Honorable and thrise-worthy Mecœnas Sir *Edward Phillips* in his magnificent house of Mountague, in the County of Somerset within a mile of Odcombe my sweet native soile)' (p. 175). The comparison is clearly intended to flatter his longstanding patron and hint at the expense that has gone into physical fabric of Montacute to produce a great house that rivals, perhaps even exceeds, the finest examples in Europe. Such comparisons of architectural detail are not unusual in the *Crudities*. Elsewhere, he compares water features in gardens in Verona to those in Sir Francis Carew's gardens in Middlesex.[29] Wotton published a treatise, *The Elements of Architecture* (1624), aimed at those English gentlemen, such as Phelips and Carew, busily building or beautifying their great houses.[30]

Coryate's method of narration could be likened to a catalogue: either he obsessively records objects presented in relatively coherent collections, like that of Cardinal Bessarion's room of antiquities in Venice; or he moves through rooms in palaces, churches, and other civic and private buildings, observing both the objects and the physical, decorative fabric, thus effectively turning these civic, religious and familial spaces into something else, into collections of 'rarities and antiquities' (p. 153). The *Crudities* anticipates the late seventeenth- and early eighteenth-century subgenre of the museum catalogue compiled either for the purposes of sale, as a guide for the future traveller, or for study by the sedentary traveller.[31] After recording the many paintings, particularly portraits, on display in a ducal palace in Verona, which Coryate had gained admittance to 'not without some favour' (p. 372 [327]), he turns to the reader, a prospective traveller, with a piece of advice: 'Therefore I counsell thee whatsoever thou art that meanest in thy travels to see Verona, to make meanes to bee admitted into the Palace of Count *Augustinus Justus*, and to see this noble and glorious roome before thou dost come forth of it: for many English gentlemen have seene it, as the Italian told me that shewed it to me' (p. 328) The *Crudities* put on display a European cabinet of curiosities in all its material detail, in a manner designed to appeal to the appetite of domestic consumers eager to add to their own collections.

Coryate walks through the streets and interior spaces of the city. While 'very diligently surveying these antiquities, and writing out inscriptions', he is taken for a certain type of traveller, 'a great admirer and curious observer of aunctent monuments', by a young man who then acts as his guide to Cardinal Bessarion's collection of antiquities. 'Curious' here is being used in the sense of careful attention to detail, accuracy in description; characteristics that were in the process of being attached to a new kind of traveller-as-collector.[32] Coryate says very simply and elegantly of the room he is shown by his guide, 'I observed a little world of memorable antiquities made in Alabaster' (p. 178). The observations that follow read like a catalogue: each statue is briefly identified through its subject, composition, materials and state of preservation (for example, if hands are missing, or only the head survives), and the descriptions continue for a page and a half. In the 'curious observer of aunctent monuments' it is possible to see how antiquarianism reshaped the humanist 'life of memory'. Whereas the humanist historian concentrated on the past as a lesson in exemplarity, the antiquarian reconceptualised the past as a repository of records and material objects that required the development of skills for their preservation, collection and examination.[33] The humanist Republic of Letters is being reconstituted as a Republic of Collectors whose lively 'Commerce and Correspondence' is the observation, collection and preservation of antiquities and other curiosities.[34] Its locus is the early modern museum. Coryate says of his guide to the collection that he was 'like to the keeper of our monuments in Westminster' (p. 180). These monuments were housed alongside four treasuries containing records that keepers had organised and calendared in order to make them more accessible to those researching into legal matters. The preservation and organisation of these documents turned them into public records, held in trust to serve the interests not just of the King, but a wider civic conception of the state, incorporating those involved in governance from privy councillors to lawyers and antiquarians.[35] Coryate tells the reader that because antiquities are held in such high estimation in the Venetian city-state, the collection has been nationalised, 'so that they are now no private and particular mans onely, but belong altogether to the State or Signiory' (p. 179). The equation between cultural richness and civic liberties has quite literally been enshrined in the city-state through such early modern museums, and is offered as a pattern for emulation.[36]

Coryate's observations were praised for their 'curious' attention to detail. Samuel Purchas, the early seventeenth-century compiler of travel literature, was known to Coryate some time before he set sail for Constantinople, and had been entrusted by Coryate with the notes of his travels in the East, many of which he published in a much-edited form in his *Purchas his Pilgrimes* (1625) – Joan-Pau Rubiés describes this collection as a 'kind of natural history'.[37] Purchas praised 'the curious diligence of many of [Coryate's] observations' on his Eastern travels, 'which might to the wisest have proved profitable' if he had survived to publish them on his return.[38] Edward Terry, the chaplain to the English ambassador in Eastern India, Sir Thomas Roe, similarly admired the fact that 'he was very *Particular*, so was he without question a very *Faithful Relator* of things he saw'.[39] Sections of Coryate's careful ethnographic observations on his travels in the East are preserved in *Purchas his Pilgrimes*: he recorded religious rituals; social customs and dress (such as the carrying of fans by both men and women); the sport of boxing; the preparation of food; education; the social infrastructure of parishes, churches, hospitals and so forth; fireflies and butterflies; and, alongside the price of fowl, the practice of sodomy (pp. 1811–12). Terry in his own *Voyage to East India* gives a very brief summary of Coryate's visit to the ruins of Troy noting nothing but ruins; Coryate's own observations are astonishing for how much they do see: the 'ruines of a goodly Fortresse', natural features, how and where pillars are dispersed in the landscape, their measurements; the 'goodly Marble Sepulchers' are observed in similar detail, conjecturing on the evidence before him that robbers had left them in this state of ruin. He speculates on 'whose Monuments these were', but emphasises that he can only 'conjecture', 'I affirme nothing certainely' (pp. 1813–14). In his travels in Europe, Coryate is just as scrupulous in noting the absence of first-hand observation or other forms of verification; it this quality of accurately relating 'things he saw' that was praised by Terry. This fascination with novelty combined with an accurate eye for detail is part of the broader reconfiguration of humanist ideologies of travel in the seventeenth century that positively valued learned curiosity and accurate, independent observation.[40]

SIGHT-SEEING AND 'MEMORABLE OCCURENTS'

Coryate's travel writing is sensitive to its manifold potentialities for education, pleasure and consumption. His observations of European cities and East Indian landscapes introduce a narrative form of sight-seeing that is improvisational, made up: thoroughly antiquarian and experiential, it familiarises the exotic, both European and Eastern, for domestic consumption.[41] When antiquarians transformed the city into rich cultural theatres of memory, they endowed buildings and physical objects with a powerful civic and emotional charge.[42] Peacham defined the virtuoso traveller as one who is skilled in a particular mode of narrating, of bringing to life what he observes: 'there is nothing fairely more delightfull, nothing worthier of observation, than these Copies, and memorials of men and matters of elder times; whose lively presence is able to perswade a man, that he now seeth two thousand yeeres agoe. Such as are skilled in them, are by the *Italians* tearmed *Virtuosi.*'[43] This persuasive rhetoric of 'lively presence' enlivens Coryate's observations. He gains access to the 'very same house wherein [Livy] lived with his family' in Padua (p. 138). The reader is offered an eye-witness account that moves from a detailed description of the gate, its stonework, ornamentation, and inscriptions, step by step through the house and its rooms. Coryate 'throughly glutted mine eyes with surveying all these pleasing objects of the outside' (p. 139); such visual stimulation and pleasure is accompanied by a desire to lose oneself in the contemplation of these objects thought to have enjoyed such personal intimacy with the great man. Collapsing the distance between the observing self and the observed both generates intense pleasures and offers a means of persuading the 'doubtfull reader' (p. 138), who would dispute the antiquity of the house, by giving the strong impression that the ancient world is still tangibly present in such places, and thus making it credible to 'thinke that this inscription was made in the time of *Æneas*, which was almost one thousand two hundred yeares before the incarnation of Christ, even two thousand eight hundred yeares since' (p. 140).

Coryate's letters to Whitaker from Ajmer in East India similarly relate what he terms 'memorable occurents'. Given that he was such an inventive linguist, the choice of this term is significant since it emphasises a visual rhetoric of sight-seeing, of 'lively presence'. Coryate calls his reader's attention to sites in East India that are memorable because they are places to be seen, such as the 'Long Walk', a man-made topographical feature stretching from Lahore to Agra:

a delicate and eeven tract of ground, as I never saw before; and doubt whither the like bee to found within the whole circumference of the habitable world. Another thing also in this way, beeing no lesse memorable then the plainenesse of the ground; a row of Trees on each side of this way where people doe travell, extending it selfe from the townes end of *Lahore*, to the townes end of *Agra*; the most incomparable shew of that kinde, that ever my eies survaied. (*Traveller*, pp. 17–18)[44]

Ethnographic curiosity is intensified by the narrative pleasures of seeing. The reader is offered a textual sight requiring them to locate themselves imaginatively in the visual moment, to experience the landscape through the appreciative traveller's eyes. Coryate's survey of the landscape is not panoptic in that he is not categorising what he sees according to a fixed episteme. What he sees is extraordinary, 'incomparable', and expressed through a rhetoric of wonder that persuades by securing the emotional commitment of the reader, appealing to subjective experience rather than simply reason.[45]

This rhetoric of seeing in the *Crudities* intensifies when faced with the visual splendours of Venice, the monument to Renaissance global mercantilism and paradigm of the city-state. Coryate apprehends the cityscape with the curious eye of a collector: his gaze is met with 'more variety of remarkable and delicious objects then mine eyes ever survayed in any citie before, or ever shall' (p. 160). Although by the time he visited Venice in the early seventeenth century it had long ceased to dominate Mediterranean trade, the pattern of civic opulence and trade in luxury commodities had been enshrined in its very stonework.[46] Venice's wealth for Coryate is encapsulated by St Mark's square, which ravishes the senses through its architectural magnificence and the sheer visual, linguistic and ethnic diversity that makes it the 'marketplace of the world' (p. 173). One might expect to find sections in the *Crudities* where Coryate explicitly and candidly contrasts the Protestant cityscape with the seductive and idolatrous Italian cityscape. Yet, this is precisely not what distinguishes Italy in Coryate's eyes. Rather, a new vocabulary of visual pleasure that is appreciative rather than pejorative enters English travel writing with the *Crudities* and his letters from East India. Coryate frequently describes himself as glutted or ravished by sights, employing the very language used to vilify such modes of travel, particularly in relation to the seductive delights of Italy. The ambivalent pleasures of the *Crudities* register a broader cultural shift that begins to unfix earlier discourses of travel.[47] Robert Burton admitted that collecting curiosities exceeded the dictates of social profit, '(as Vives saith) *artificialia delectant, sed mox fastidimus*, artificial toys please but for a time'. Nonetheless, antiquities, sculptures and paintings are 'a most pleasing sight', and are invested with their own subjective profits and delights.[48] Travel to study such pleasing sights takes on the surplus value that Parr speaks of; it marks the point where private travel parts company with a public, civic discourse of travel, and develops its own narrative perspective that relates the pleasures of sight-seeing.[49]

This process of transformation is recorded topographically in the *Crudities*. When Coryate travels over the Alps from France into Italy there is a fundamental shift in perspective as the process of seeing is loosened from the ideological imperatives of confessional politics. His observations of France are shaped by the recent history of religious conflict, and structured by an actively Protestant gaze which is resistant and often hostile to Roman Catholic civic spectacles. This point of view does not completely disappear in Italy, but it does frequently give way to, or is modified by, his specular and ethnographic fascination with social customs and objects in terms of their new-found curiosity: a term traditionally used to criticise just such an excessive interest in manners and fashion, but employed in the *Crudities* in a consistently affirmative sense. Walking through the Sunday marketplace in Mantua, Coryate is captivated by the sumptuous 'abundance of delectable fruites' and 'odoriferous flowers', delicious and sensual manifestations of the Italian *bonum vir*, which 'did even so ravish my senses, and tickle my spirits with such inward delight that I said unto my selfe, this is the Citie which of all other places in the world, I would wish to make my habitation in'. He pulls back from 'going native' by remembering 'their grosse idolatry and superstitious ceremonies which I detest, and the love of Odcombe in Somersetshire' (p. 120), momentarily securing his national identity at home among his fellow Englishmen. The recurrent interplay between his provincial identity and cosmopolitan tastes and curious eye in both the *Crudities* and his letters from East India safely familiarises the foreign and exotic for the consumption of the English wits at home. That said, this 'stationary' perspective constantly jostles with Coryate's willingness to have his senses ravished, resulting in an errant, eccentric Englishness that is open to the pleasures of seeing and troublingly mobile.[50]

Terry, the travelling Protestant cleric, may have admired Coryate's faithful observations, but he was less certain about his curiosity: 'he was a man of a very coveting *eye, that could never be satisfied with seeing*'.[51] Coryate's 'very coveting *eye*' frequently unsettles Protestant ideology even at the very moment when it seems to be the dominant frame of reference. Witnessing a ceremony on St Bartholomew's day in Brescia, Italy, to consecrate a new statue of the Virgin Mary, Coryate spied 'a great multitude of little waxen idols . . . whereof some were only armes, some thighs, some presented all parts of a mans body'. Although, 'these toyes were no novelties unto me', he 'had a marvailous itching desire to finger one of them, only to this end, to bring it home to England, to shew it to my friends as a token of their idolatry' (*Crudities*, p. 340). This does seem to be a moment when the Protestant traveller's scepticism towards papist idols divests these objects of religious awe, thus returning them to the status of physical objects and asserting the rational powers of Protestant revelation. Nonetheless, what characterises this passage is Coryate's 'very coveting *eye*', and an overwhelming fascination with the object as a curiosity. Protestant scepticism does merge with ethnographic curiosity, but the itchy fingers of the curious collector undermine any serious theological or ideological point to the anecdote. The transformation of the papist idol into a souvenir registers a broader cultural shift within travel away from the model of pilgrimage and towards that of tourism.[52]

Coryate's eccentricity is most evident in his innovation in celebrity travel – his walking. He marvelled at himself in his letter from Ajmer, 'never did I thinke [my desire to travel] would have broken out to such an ambitious vent, as to travel all on foote from *Jerusalem*, so farre as the place where I wrote this Letter' (*Traveller*, p. 4). Coryate, in fact, did not always walk on his travels in Europe or the Middle East and East India. It becomes his signature in the 'Panegyricke Verses' and *Traveller for the English Wits* in homage to Kemp's popular morris dance to Norwich and because its errant, demotic forms disclose alternative spatial and narrative trajectories and ways of seeing within humanist paradigms of travel. As we have seen, walking through the city and observing its monuments in the *Crudities* coincides with sight-seeing and is figured through the rhetoric of 'lively presence'. Walking locates the traveller on the streets and on the ground, and is body-centred in that it denotes the physical experiences of the body in motion and in encounters with others.[53] Walking between cities through the countryside designated non-élite modes of travel, since the gentry and aristocracy rode or travelled by carriage. The 'Panegyricke Verses' joke about Coryate's lousy shirt and tattered clothes and, in doing so, turn this independent gentleman traveller into a vagabond. Coryate often seems only too happy to play this part for his readers: he encounters thieves outside Baden, 'two clownes commonly called Boores . . . in ragged cloathes', and escapes robbery because the mean and 'threed-bare' state of his own clothes allowed him to play very persuasively the part of a beggar (p. 465). The episode is emblematised on the title-page above the image of his lousy clothes adorning a scarecrow, and Coryate playing thief when he took grapes from a vineyard outside Worms. The vineyard episode is similarly written up in his travel narrative in a self-consciously mock-heroic form, in keeping with the burlesque energies of the front matter, and with an eye to how he has 'expressed it in the frontispice of my booke': Coryate stands before the 'German Boore' 'almost as mute as a Seriphian frogge, or an Acanthian grashopper', until he gains courage 'and so discharged a whole volley of Greeke and Latin shot upon him' (pp. 524–5). Coryate occupies an odd place in the history of tourism in that his errant walking and 'delinquent narrativity' does not allow a safe, comfortable spectatorship but is open to the mundane, the contingent, and the physicality of travel.[54] Taylor quite consciously used Coryate to mark out his own place in a tradition of demotic and burlesque pedestrian travel. Although his *Pennyles Pilgrimage, or the Money-lesse perambulation* (1618) closely followed in the footsteps of Jonson's walk to Scotland, its narrative energies are attributed to '*a smacke of* Coriatizing' that places Taylor within a tradition of fantastic travellers – 'Mandevill, Primaleon, Don Quixot, / *Great* Amadis, *or* Huon' – and finally '*Britaines* Odcomb (Zanye *brave* Ulissis)'.⁵⁵ 'Coryatizing' is more than telling tall tales; it signifies an errant, improvisatory narrative mode and the novel conceptual freedoms available to the independent traveller.

When familiarising the foreign for a domestic readership, as these mock-heroic episodes testify, Coryate experimented with the rhetoric of lively presence in order to perform in print, willingly transforming himself into a collectable curiosity. The novel and foreign custom of using a fork, only practised in Italy and by no 'other nation of Christendome' (p. 90), for example, enabled Coryate to turn himself into table talk on his return: 'being once quipped for that frequent using of my forke, by a certaine learned Gentleman, a familiar friend of mine, one *M. Laurence Whitaker*, who in his merry humour doubted not to call me at table *furcifer*, only for using a forke at feeding, but for no other cause' (p. 91). The fork is a version of the toothpick, a similarly foreign import signifying the affected mannerisms of the stereotypical foolish traveller.⁵⁶ Coryate knowingly embraces this piece of folly because it gives him and his travels a wider currency. Translated into an easily digested piece of wit in the *Crudities*, the joke about Coryate and his fork enables a broader readership to participate imaginatively if vicariously in an élite coterie culture and foreign travels that may be familiar to some select readers, but 'exotic' to many others. Like the '*umbrella*', a word and foreign object he is credited with bringing into English usage, such narrative curiosities are designed to be collectable and to appeal to the interests of the English domestic 'armchair' traveller, the 'many that neither have beene' to Europe, 'nor ever intend to goe thither while they live' (p. 111).

While 'rarity' referred to objects, both natural and man-made, it also encompassed a set of narrative conventions deriving from the genre of memorable histories of wonderful events and strange occurrences. Simon Goulart's rarity encyclopaedia, *Admirable and Memorable Histories, Containing the Wonders of our Time* (translated in 1607), narrates strange, miraculous and memorable histories that often involve ordinary men and women. These are intended to evoke wonder, in the sense both of religious awe and of a secular fascination with strange occurrences, events that lie outside the bounds of mundane human experience. Coryate relates just such a macabre memorable event in his *Crudities*. After describing the figure clock and its automata in via Merceria in Venice, he relates:

> a very tragicall and rufull accident on the twenty fifth day of July being munday about nine of the clocke in the morning, which was this. A certaine fellow that had the charge to looke to the clocke, was very busie about the bell, according to his usuall custome every day, to the end to amend something in it that was amisse. But in the meane time one of those wilde men that at the quarters of the howers doe use to strike the bell, strooke the man in the head with his brasen hammer, giving him such a violent blow, that therewith he fel down dead presently in the place, and never spake more. (p. 187)

The tragedy is memorable partly because of the strange irony of murder by an artificial wild man. The anecdote reads like an early modern version of the 'urban myth'; stories that are memorable because of their curious juxtaposition of the mundane and the wonderful, and take on mythic status because of the way that they circulate anonymously through talk, seemingly arising out of the very social fabric of the city.

Coryate's anecdotal 'memorable histories' and 'memorable occurents' in the *Crudities* and his letters from East India are similar to jests and epigrams in that they can be collected, easily lifted from the surrounding narrative and transmitted by means of table talk that circulates around cities, and during other sociable gatherings.[57] These textual curiosities were valued because of the way they moved from the printed and scribal text into the realms of oral performance, and so are highly suited to communal reading or recitation. Designed to be enjoyed in company, curious 'memorable histories' are an example of the social practices implied by the 'talked book'; a deliberate exercise in sociability that implies the audience has the leisure to spend their time 'unprofitably', reading and listening to tales for their curiosity or wit. The early modern travel book helped to create a new type of readership, the 'armchair traveller'.[58] Coryate played a formative role in the popularisation and novelisation of travel for this domestic market. Providing the substance of table talk, the travel book circulated among and served to define new interpretive communities and reading publics.

GREETING FROM THE COURT OF THE GREAT MOGUL

Coryate was determined to turn himself into a travelling wonder with his Eastern travels: 'such is my insatiable greediness of seeing strange countries: which exercise is the very Queene of all the pleasures in the world, that I have determined ... to spend full seaven yeares more, to the ende to make my voyage answerable for the time to the travels of *Ulysses*' (*Traveller*, p. 6). Ulysses, a well-worn allegorical figure who symbolises the 'worldly wisdom' of the curious traveller, is turned into a fantastic measurement of time and distance.[59] When reflecting on Coryate's extraordinary feats, even usually sober Purchas gave himself up to '*a smacke* of Coriatizing': 'the furthest foot English-Traveller that our dayes have had, and the longest English stile which our eares have heard, with many rests for your wearied breath by the way, a stile indeed so high you can hardly get over, HIEROSOLYMITAN-SYRIAN-MESOPOTAMIAN-ARMENIAN-MEDIAN-PARTHIAN-PERSIAN-INDIAN LEGGE-STRETCHER OF ODCOMB'.[60] There are two volumes of Coryate letters from India: *Thomas Coriate traveller for the English Wits: greeting From the court of the Great Mogul* (1616) and *Mr Thomas Coriat to his friends in England sendeth greeting* (1618).[61] Distance and long absence from England, in comparison with his relatively brief European travels, placed particular pressures on his mode of errant Englishness and the ways in which he envisioned the humanist community. Coryate, as we have seen, was still impelled by curiosity and 'memorable occurents', yet the improvisational drive of his travel narrative in his letters from Ajmer and Agra is tempered by anxieties of distance.

Absent from England in the East, Coryate could no longer turn his travels into a print event by directly capitalising on the sociable networks available to him. Nonetheless, he does seem to have had some success in influencing how his image would be circulated in the printed text: his determination 'one day (by Gods leave) to have my picture expressed in my next Booke, sitting upon an Elephant' is carried out in *Traveller for the English Wits*, which uses this image for its frontispiece and to illustrate his observations of the Mogul's court.[62] Coryate needed to ensure that his exploits continued to be talked about, that he was still Tom 'table talke' (*Crudities*, sig. g1v). His letter to Whitaker was intended to be read at a gathering of the Sireniacal fraternity at the Mermaid: he included in the packet a number of copies of a poem addressed to him by the English merchants in India, 'which I have intreated you to distribute for me, but so that the Letters are not sealed upon them; onely they lie loose within the Letters, therefore they are subject to losing, except you have an extraordinary care of them' (pp. 34–5). Coryate placed great value on the commerce of letters to keep himself in circulation among the communities described by the earlier 'Panegyricke Verses', and clearly intended these letters to be made public, either through being read aloud, or copied within the well-established manuscript channels of these communities, or published in print. He continued to be very adept at managing the sociable economy of credit both at home and abroad. Still a highly companionable traveller, from Constantinople to the Middle East he made the acquaintance of, and was accompanied by, a number of Englishmen; in India he cultivated an attachment to English merchants and to their ambassador, Roe, with whom he was previously acquainted through his London networks.[63] These English communities in India became increasingly important to Coryate once his funds ran low and his health deteriorated. His letters to Phelips, Whitaker and the Sireniacs call on them to show hospitality to the letter-bearers and other close acquaintances he has made in India who have returned to England, such as Peter Rogers, chaplain to the English merchants. Through these men, Coryate hoped to activate the bonds of obligation that would ensure that he continued to have a presence among these communities, if only by proxy.

Coryate's travel plans for the East would mean that he was away for ten years, although in fact he never returned, dying in Surat in December 1617 of dysentery. Such lengthy absence posed a real problem for a persona that resided in an overriding commitment to fame and a convivial presence so strongly invested in clientage and acts of sociability. Anxieties cluster around the delivery of letters: he imagines that items will be lost, or he entreats Whitaker to deliver or read letters in person or to make particular remembrances, his lively presence standing in for the now absent Coryate. He fears that former patrons will have forgotten him; he sent several letters to Sir Robert Phelips 'once my *Mecœnas*', and fretted in a letter to Whitaker, 'but how affected to me at this time I know not' (p. 29). By the time the Ajmer letter was published in England, he had been absent for almost four years. Soon after he left for Constantinople, Prince Henry had died, and in late 1614 his long-standing patron, Sir Edward Phelips, had also died; news of his death had not reached Coryate in Ajmer a year later. Terry recounted an anecdote that, although highly critical of Coryate's self-conceit, neatly captures his anxieties that he would not be talked of, or not talked of enough to sustain his credit. When Richard Steele of the East India Company told Coryate of King James's response to news of him, '"*Is that fool yet living?*" which, when our pilgrim heard, it seemed to *trouble* him very much, because the King spake *no more* nor no *better* of him; saying, that *Kings* would speak of poor men what they pleased'.[64]

Thomas Coriat Traveller for the English Wits, as its title suggests, has its point of origin and return in the companies that met at the Mermaid. The central letter addressed to the 'right Worshipfull Fraternitie of Sireniacal Gentlemen, that meet the first Fridaie of every Moneth, at the signe of the

Mere-Maide in Bread-streete' returns repeatedly to 'that incomparable elegant safe-conduct, which a little before my departure from England, your Fraternity with a general suffrage gave me for the security of my future peregrination' (p. 38). The London wits license his travels; the safe-conduct he carries with him provides his point of contact and dialogue 'with the most polite with that the Cities will yeeld' (p. 40). The symbiosis between travel writing and an emergent metropolitan culture that is evident in the *Crudities* continues to structure Coryate's travels in the East.[65] This is one of the earliest usages of 'polite' to define the nature of a particular group of people in terms of their refinement, civility and cultivation – and, by extension, a fashionable taste for wit, eccentricity and travel.[66] Coryate's 'most polite' are not only metropolitan, they are also in a sense 'cosmopolite' or cosmopolitan: he is referring to social and cultural characteristics that transcend national boundaries, although confined to Christian Europe. Once again, the transnational Republic of Letters is undergoing a metamorphosis to encompass aspects later firmly identified with the civil society.

Coryate discovers, or rather re-creates, this 'polite' society on his travels in India. He delightedly tells Whitaker of his meeting with Sir Robert and Lady Teresia Sherley 'just about the Frontiers of *Persia* & *India*', who had just been 'verie graciously received, and enriched with presents of great value' at the 'King of *Persia's* Court' (pp. 14–15). The landscape of the East is both exotic and familiarised through correspondences with European courtly society, with its structures of patronage and favour that enabled men like Sherley and Coryate to navigate their way around the country. The letters to Whitaker and the Sireniacs tend to foreground cultural and social similarities between the Mogul's court and European court society, largely through observations of the structures of patronage, the politics of magnificence and the role of gift-giving. When describing his encounter with the Sherleys, Coryate reproduces for the reader a 'memorable' moment of leisured amusement, civility and polite conversation. To his joy, Sherley is carrying 'both my Bookes neatly kept' (p. 15), presumably his *Crudities* and *Crambe*. These texts become the medium for the favours Sherley promises, and Coryate hopes to capitalise on these convivial books at the court of Shah Abbas as he had in England, with Sherley acting as his translator: 'for he [Shah Abbas I] is such a jocund Prince, that he will not be meanlie delighted with divers of my factious Hieroglyphicks', presumably referring to the frontispiece and other illustrations, 'if they are truelie and genuously expounded unto him' (p. 17).

Both Sherley and Coryate were independent travellers. Sherley was employed by Shah Abbas as an ambassador to the European courts as part of his campaign against the Turks, and as such was regarded with suspicion by the English court and the East India merchants. And both Sherley and Coryate were involved in creating new Anglo-Persian and Anglo-Indian communities abroad. Sherley's lady, fulsomely praised by Coryate for her courtesy, was Circassian, and popularly reputed to be the niece of Shah Abbas. Texts celebrating the adventures of the Sherley brothers, including the play *Travels of the Three English Brothers* (1607), depicted the family as the founders of a new Anglo-Persian dynasty.[67] Coryate resituates the convivial company of English wits in India. He includes in his letter to Whitaker an 'English-Indian Epistle' (p. 34), one of the volleys in a wit contest between Coryate and the English merchants of the East India Company, that is then to be served up by Whitaker for the delight of the Sireniacs (p. 32). The Anglo-Indian community glimpsed in the Ajmer letters takes part in a broader community of wit that is simultaneously cosmopolitan in its urbanity and distinctly English. The list of remembrances closing the letter to the Sireniacs, 'being the lovers of vertue, and literature' (p. 43), provides a social map of a fashionable area of London which implicitly corresponds to the 'most polite with that the Cities will yeeld'. The letters set up a further correspondence between these 'city wits' and the 'English wits' addressed in the title. Travel is accompanied by a desire to establish national distinctions, projecting supposedly 'homogeneous times and spaces selectively, in relation to new transnational flows and cultural forms'.[68] The particular collocation of 'English wits' identifies the urbanity of polite society as a national characteristic or, more precisely, a discriminating characteristic attributed to English social élites with a cosmopolitan taste for travel. The 'English wits' designate a particular mode of independent polite travel that will be formalised towards the end of the century in the virtuoso travel of the Grand Tour – although at this moment it does have other possibilities – and simultaneously signifies the discriminating consumption of travel writing among polite readerships at home.

Cosmopolitanism, as imagined in the Ajmer letters, has distinct borders that confine it to Christian Europe. Coryate, for instance, is very clear that the safe-conduct does not have any currency in the 'Mahometan Countries' (p. 39). That said, while there could be an implied opposition between the 'barbaric' and 'uncultivated' Muslim countries and the 'civilised' and 'polite' European cities, this colonial binarism is not fully articulated. The letters from Ajmer in general do not fit neatly into an orientalist model of cultural encounter organised around a colonial confrontation between West and East. As Kenneth Parker and others have argued, neither England nor these independent English travellers occupied the economic and political position of colonial powers, and in actuality they were highly dependent on securing the patronage of the ruling powers in East India and Persia.[69] Coryate was impressed by the extreme wealth of the Mogul's court, especially the incomparable richness of the presents the Mogul was able to command. *Traveller for the English Wits*, in a similar manner to his compendious *Crudities*, turned the travel account into a cabinet of curiosities. On display at the Mogul's court are 'the strangest beasts of the world' (p. 25), and to a large extent they take the place of the courtesans, clocks, the Great Tun and other curiosities on display in the *Crudities*. The pamphlet incorporates woodcuts of Coryate on an elephant, also used on the frontispiece, a supposed antelope, with a boar's snout and tusks and a lion's tail and tufts, and that definitive curiosity and rarity, a unicorn.[70]

While India, as Barbour points out, does become 'a great arena of spectacular enjoyments for Englishmen', the English were vicarious rather than fully-fledged consumers of such wealth.[71] The English and indeed the Europeans were a peripheral presence in East India at this time. Coryate went to great and characteristic lengths to gain the favour of Jahangir, delivering one of his orations in the style of the orator-buffoon that required the tolerant hospitality of the socially superior audience. Jahangir understood he was observing a highly encoded performance, but not surprisingly did not recognise the cultural codes, instead 'looking upon him as a *Derveese* or Votary, or Pilgrim (for so he called him)', as Terry explained the unsatisfactory financial outcome of the performance for Coryate, 'and such as bear that name in that Countrey seem not much to care for money, and that was the reason ... that he gave him not a more plentiful Reward'.[72] By contrast, Roe, the English ambassador, who probably had witnessed one of Coryate's orations in England, recognised the social game and, as Coryate noted in the letter accompanying the speech, was infuriated 'that one of our Countrey should present himselfe in that beggarly and poore fashion to the King out of an insinuating humor to crave mony of him' (*To his friends in England*, sig. b4v). Coryate's mock-oration unwittingly parodied the role of the English ambassador as a petitioner at the Mogul's court. His 'beggarly and poore fashion' touched too nearly on English credit at this court – Roe bitterly complained he was unable to operate effectively at Jahangir's court because of his inability to present rich gifts.[73]

Coryate spent a number of years travelling by foot in East India, engaging with its peoples, and subjecting himself to the physical hardships of travel. Alongside his knowledge of Turkish and Arabic, he acquired 'some good knowledge in the *Persian* and *Indostan Tongues*, in which study he was alwaies very apt and in little time shewed much proficiency' as Terry noted, 'that it did exceedingly afterwards advantage him in his Travels up and down the *Mogol's* Territories, he wearing alwaies the *Habit* of that Nation, and speaking their *Language*'.[74] Although he was often highly resistant to aspects of Islamic culture, the position of distanced observer was not available to him; instead he occupied a rather more liminal space. Learning other, foreign languages, as Rubiés notes, does at least suggest the effort to 'get involved with other cultures', and offers the possibility of dialogue.[75] Civil and antiquarian conversations, as we have seen, structure his travels in Europe, among the 'most polite with that the Cities will yeeld', and return in his witty exchanges with the gentlemen of the East India Company. His knowledge of Persian did enable him to converse with Jahangir, although the terms of that dialogue were dictated by the Mogul's far superior social status. Coryate includes the oration in a foreign tongue in his letters because 'though the tong it selfe wil seem to an Englishman very strange & uncuth, as having no kind of affinity with any of our Christian languages', yet the curious reader 'wil take some pleasure in reading so rare and unusuall a tongue as this' (*To his friends in England*, sig. B2r). Strange and uncouth stand in an unclearly defined relationship with rare and unusual and, once again, seem to intimate the cultural binarism of orientalism, while taking pleasure in the rarity and curiosity of difference.

The other exchange, published alongside his oration before Jahangir in the Agra letter, a speech 'made to a Mahometan', is less of a dialogue than a type of flyting that replays his earlier European encounters with the Muslim Turk and the Venetian Jew in the *Crudities*. Coryate was able to find a point of correspondence between Islam and Christianity in the courteous and tolerant presence of Jahangir, who 'speaketh very reverently of our Saviour, calling him in the Indian tongue, *Ifazaret Eesa*, that is the great Prophet, Jesus: and all Christians, especiallie us English, he useth so benevolently, as no Mahometan Prince the like' (*Traveller*, pp. 23–4). When insulted by 'a Mahometan' who called him a '*Giaur*, that is infidell', Coryate responded to the 'discurtesie' with invective, violently railing against '*Mahomet* and his accursed Religion'. The oration certainly constructs Islam as the barbarous other; and yet, the framing material tells another story of cultural exchanges between the East and Europe that were part of the economy of East–West trade. Coryate converses with the Mahometan not in Persian but in Italian because 'he had learned good *Italian*', as he relates, during the years he was captive in Livorno after being enslaved on a Florentine galley – slavery was a common practice used by Europeans, Turks and other trading nations. Coryate acknowledges he is able to deliver the speech without fear because of an admirable culture of religious tolerance: 'If I had spoken thus much in *Turky*, or *Persia* against *Mahomet* they would have rosted me upon a spitt; but in the *Mogols* Dominions a Christian may speake much more freely then hee can in any other Mahometan Country in the world' (*To his friends in England*, sig. D1r). Coryate, possibly in common with his contemporaries, saw no irony in juxtaposing praise for the religious tolerance cultivated in the Mogul's dominions with his own invective against the Islamic religion. The letters from East India do articulate views of Islamic cultures that will harden into the binarisms of orientalism. At the same time, his travel writings help to formulate the 'seventeenth-century ideal of independent observation and learned curiosity', developing a rhetoric of sight-seeing in all its early modern eccentricity that will, in turn, be set against a xenophobic insularity in the eighteenth century.[76]

The mid-eighteenth century witnessed a Coryate revival. A new edition of the *Crudities* appeared in 1776 that collected together all of Coryate's extant writings along with Taylor's 'Coryatizing' pamphlets.[77] In 1767, the bibliophile and bookseller Samuel Paterson took the pseudonym Coriat Junior when he published his *Another Traveller! or Cursory Remarks and Tritical Observations made upon a Journey through part of the Netherlands in the latter End of the Year 1766*. Paterson adopted the style and manner of Laurence Sterne, who then accompanies Coryate in authorising the novelisation of travel. 'Coryatizing' is now a highly sociable and eccentric style, its frequent diversions intended to give 'pleasure in the reading'.[78] There is no sense of purpose to this style of travel; rather its diversions and excursions produce leisured time in-between places and destinations. Paterson is rewriting Coryate and, in doing so, has separated 'that joco-serious *unique* of his age' (though 'not over-witty himself, he was the true cause of *that wit was in other men*') from Coryate, the ethnographic 'tombstone traveller'. As the 'Critic' carps in *Another Traveller!*, 'I have not met with a single inscription, if it were but of a tomb stone, from DOVER to BRUSSELS: – a matter which is never omitted by the curious traveller, which costs nothing, may be done by any one, and helps greatly to swell and set off a book'.[79] Learned curiosity has been displaced by a convivial urbanity, and the playful liberties afforded by travel emphasise subjective experience over objective observations. Coryate's errant Englishness was valued in the eighteenth century for its combination of eccentricity and sociability. These qualities enabled the 'sentimental traveller' to shape a different kind of travel identity to that of the xenophobic, stationary Englishman.[80]

The first decade of this century has seen a revival of interest in Coryate in mainstream popular culture. Tim Moore's homage, *The Continental*

Drifter, begins by celebrating Coryate as the first of the Grand Tourists. Yet, as Moore marvels at his mode of travel across Europe, on foot with very little money, Coryate is transformed from Grand Tourist into the first back-packer.[81] This deliberately liminal traveller, who physically experiences other cultures by embracing hardship, confounds the modern touristic impulse towards comfortable spectatorship. The eccentricity of Coryate seems to provide the postmodern travel writer with a figure for circumventing the imperial gaze of the modern tourist. Dom Moraes and Sarayu Srivatsa's decidedly fantastical *The Long Strider: How Thomas Coryate Walked from England to India in the Year 1613* was published specifically for an Indian rather than a British market. It is a *dialogue* between Srivatsa's account of modern India, in which the often violent divisions between the dominant Hindu and marginalised Muslim communities are addressed in her growing friendship with their Muslim researcher, Juzer, and Moraes's richly fabricated historical account of Coryate's travels through early modern East India, in which Hindus were largely invisible.[82] Coryate is the eccentric starting point for an alternative history of cultural encounters that stands adjacent to British imperialism, and finds its expression in the cosmopolitanism of this new Indian community – Hindu, Muslim, and Indo-Portuguese. Coryate, 'who while he lived', as Terry puts it, 'was like a perpetual motion', offered subsequent writers a highly mobile travel identity that made it possible to unsettle established ideologies of travel. In his travel writings and learned curiosity, it is possible to see the wider cultural ramifications of the improvisatory energies of *lusus* for other narrative modes, alongside the mock-encomium and other classically low forms.

CHAPTER SEVEN

Afterlives of the wits

Coryate's letter to the Sireniacs was addressed to a society, and not a collection of named individuals. This distinction is vital because it marks a stage in the history of sociability in the seventeenth century. The second half of this century saw the proliferation of voluntary societies; an innovation in associational practices that is one of the distinguishing features of civil society.[1] The Sireniacal fraternity was more than an informal gathering that simply had an ongoing arrangement to share the cost of wine or a feast at a tavern. Each meeting was a highly ritualised and codified performance. The participants, for the duration of the meeting at the Mermaid tavern, freely and willingly invested their social identity in this self-regulating social formation, with its agreed structure of offices, codes of conduct, social rituals and symbolic practices.

If we look across the seventeenth century, then we can see societies like the Sireniacal fraternity as part of an ongoing transformation of literary and political culture and everyday life. They were the precursors to the later political clubs held at taverns and coffee houses in the second half of the century. Modes of private conviviality were infused by communicative practices that had undergone further rapid and radical transformation during the English revolution. The resulting forms of political sociability brought together and created citizens.[2] The cultural legacy of the Sireniacs is rich and complex. As we have seen, when Gifford looked back to what he called the 'Mermaid Club', he did not see a political club of professional men, but rather the origins of the eighteenth-century private society devoted to *belles lettres*.[3] From this perspective, it is possible to assimilate the sociable practices of the wits to the early stages of the 'civil acculturation' that accompanied the 'civilizing process' – with the recognition, of course, that this trajectory must be heavily qualified. Elias's seminal study, *The Civilizing Process*, obfuscates the contradictions that energised this process, the ways in which civility was contested, rather than the product of a consensus over its forms and practices, and draws our attention away from other 'positive traditions'.[4]

When the wits reinvigorated an older ludic tradition, they enabled a volatile yet creative dialogue between civility and liberty, which credited and licensed the principles of play and their experiments in laughter; rather than simply subdue the body and emotions within a pacified social arena, it made a place for pleasure and the violence of scurrilous words within sociable play and public political discourse. The communicative practices of this society cannot be comprehended solely in terms of the emergence of the discourses of civic rationality said to structure the public sphere. The 'wit, humor, theatricality, and satire' that David Shields has found in the 'sociability of the eighteenth-century public sphere', with its salons, taverns, tables, clubs and assemblies, can be heard earlier in the previous century in such sociable and playful texts like the 'Censure of the Parliament Fart'.[5] The cultural implications of this mode of play spread beyond sociable circles into other discursive fields and dimensions of experience. As we have seen, when Samuel Paterson read Coryate's travel writings in the eighteenth century his attention was drawn to the ludic 'joco-serious' dimension of these texts, and their eccentric ways of seeing and speculative liberties opened the way for the sentimental traveller.

By examining the immediate legacy of the wits in the decades following the publication of the *Crudities* in 1611 it is possible to elucidate the directions taken by the sociable traditions they adopted, and the historical possibilities such practices opened up. Mapping out trajectories of association will serve to locate the wits within broader narratives of cultural change, and draw attention to alternative and competing traditions within the history of early modern sociability. Jonson, who played a part alongside the wits in fashioning a symposiastic space at the Mitre and Mermaid taverns, has been credited with englishing a classical symposiastic literary tradition, and inaugurating a tradition of moderate banqueting that exerted a decisive influence over modes of élite male sociability well into the eighteenth century.[6] When Jonson was refining his symposiastic ideal in the 1620s, he did so in reaction to the boisterous political clubs proliferating in these years. These clubs had a reputation for raillery and violence and, like the earlier meetings of the wits, may have generated many of the libellous and scurrilous verses circulating in this period. Manuscript miscellanies compiled in this period often collect libels and political satires relating to events and personalities of the 1620s – the Spanish Match and George Villiers, Earl of Buckingham – alongside the 'Parliament Fart' and epigrams and other poems associated with the earlier wits. The 'Parliament Fart' finally appears in print in the royalist anthologies *Musarum Deliciæ or, the Muses Recreation* (1655) and *Le Prince d'Amour* (1660), which co-opt this earlier culture of wit and raillery into the service of a consciously Cavalier political identity and sense of community. *Musarum Deliciæ* introduces a new literary category of 'drollery' that politicises the pleasures of drinking and socialising, burlesque and other low comic poems; such 'politics of mirth' are cast in opposition to the renewed civic ideologies of the Commonwealth. While drollery had specific political affiliations in 1660, it also had wider ramifications in terms of the place of ridicule, pleasure and play in the formation of the literary marketplace.

AFTER *CORYATS CRUDITIES*

Coryate gave the Sireniacal fraternity a lively presence in print and, in doing so, ensured its posterity. After 1611, we tend to lose sight of this society. The study of early modern associations is complicated by the fact that records of meetings have survived only in exceptional cases.[7] In the case of the Sireniacs, it is possible to discover faint textual traces after 1611. Jonson's invocation to the canary-drinking wits, those 'Three Cranes, Mitre, and Mermaid men', in *Bartholomew Fair* (1614) would suggest that the Sireniacs were still a presence on the London scene up to 1614. There is a very brief reference to the Mermaid in Jonson's *Devil is an Ass* (1616), when Merecraft criticises Everill for 'Haunting / The Globes and Mermaids, wedging in with lords / Still at the table' (3.3.25–7). References to the Mermaid and the Mitre were made in plays on a regular basis from the time of the 1597–8 Middle Temple Revels until 1614, and then they tail off dramatically – after *Devil is an Ass*, we do not hear of the Mermaid or Mitre again on stage until William Rowley's *Match at Midnight* (1623), which alludes to the Mitre, then there is a brief citing of the Mermaid in Jasper Mayne's *City Match* (1639).

There are other factors which suggest that 1614 marked the end of a phase of formal association among these men. It is likely that meetings of this society took place either when parliament was in session or when preparations were being undertaken for its resumption, and when parliamentary men and lawyers, like Martin, Hoskyns, and Brooke, were resident at their Inns in London. James's first parliament, as we have seen, met at regular intervals from 1604 to 1614. The dissolution of the 'addled' parliament in 1614 marked the beginning of the seven-year period of James's 'personal rule' – parliament was not called again until 1621.[8] Evidence from the circulation and composition of the 'Parliament Fart' suggests how associational activity among the lawyer-wits during the 1610 sessions coincided with and spilled over into the flurry of versifying that accompanied *Coryats Crudities* through the press, and produced a lively literary and social scene in which a symposiastic poetics of literary crudity was refined.

Sir Edward Phelips, the patron at whose table these men often dined, died in disgrace soon after the dissolution of the 1614 parliament.[9] The severity of Hoskyns's treatment for his speeches in this parliament may have taught his fellow wits a lesson in caution. After his release from the Tower in 1615, he made an effort to keep a low political profile, devoting his energies to his legal career and managing his estate. He chose not to put himself forward for the 1621 parliament, even returning to Hereford in late 1620 to ensure his name was not submitted as one of the town's members. His care was not misplaced, and his continued absence from James's parliaments benefited his legal career. In late 1621, Hoskyns was appointed judge on the circuit of Wales, and made serjeant-at-law in 1623.[10] Martin's care for his 'slippery tongue' meant that he did not put himself forward for the 1614 parliament – he still managed to make an ill-judged speech to the Commons on behalf of the Virginia Company.[11] His efforts to restore himself to royal favour by curbing his wit were part of a campaign to secure the office of Recorder of London. In a letter of August 1616, he sought to persuade Buckingham of his loyalty and service to the king. He pointed to his role in the production of court entertainments on behalf of his Inn, including the current barriers for the creation of the Prince of Wales, and defended his behaviour in parliament, denying the talk 'that I was wavering & uncertaine, & that I offended his Ma^{ty} in the end of the first, & beginning of the last parliament'; rather, 'if it can be truly affirmed that I have offended his Ma^{ty} by any malignant, factious, or undutifull practize or combinacon, or by any folly that had his root in malice; lett me have an ill conscience for my daily companion, & perpetuall reproch for my portion'. It is both an eloquent and awkward letter as Martin struggles to reconstrue his own actions in parliament in terms of a narrative of loyal service to the Crown in the effort to secure the Recordership: 'I cannot ymagine any other place that can give me grace, & receave grace by mee, as this place may, wch needs more then a lawyer.'[12] He eventually gained the Recordership through the patronage of his friend Cranfield, a client of Buckingham, who also lent him the money for the office. For both Hoskyns and Martin, after Hoskyns's release in 1615 it may not have been politic to revive a society so closely associated with such dangerous wit.

It was also a decisive point in Donne's career: on 23 January 1615, he was ordained in the Anglican Church, in February appointed royal chaplain, and the next month made Doctor of Divinity at Cambridge. While 1614 certainly does not mark the end of Brooke's friendship with any of these men, it is a year when he too begins to explore other avenues for expression, aligning himself with other causes; when doing so, he used a very different register to the ludic vein of his own performances among the wits. The companionate volumes of eclogues *The Shepheards Pipe* (1614) and *The Shepherds Hunting* (1615) saw Brooke join William Browne and Wither to participate in another print event, this time organised around Wither's imprisonment for *scandalum magnatum*. In the same year, he published his *Ghost of Richard the Third*, prefaced by commendatory verses from Browne, Wither and Jonson.[13] Both these 1614 poems address the question of counsel under tyrant kings, although with less wit and licence than the 'Parliament Fart'. His *Poem on the Late Massacre in Virginia* (1622) similarly raised concerns over the direction of royal foreign policy that he had also voiced in the 1621 parliament.[14]

Despite these various alterations, literary and other familiar exchanges continued among these men throughout their lifetimes. Brooke, Hoskyns and Martin still kept chambers at their Inns – Donne was appointed Divinity Reader at Lincoln's Inn in 1616. This year Lincoln's Inn and Middle Temple co-produced the entertainment at the barriers to honour Charles's creation as Prince of Wales – it must be said to considerably less royal acclaim than that which attended the 1614 *Memorable Masque* – Martin and Hoskyns organised the armour on behalf of the Middle Temple, and Brooke and William Hakewill acted as senior agents for Lincoln's Inn.[15]

Two years later Martin was dead; he succumbed to smallpox on 31 October 1618, and did not, as Aubrey would have it, die 'of a merry Symposiaque with his fellow-Witts'.[16] A monument was erected in the Middle Temple Church. Martin kneels in prayer in the red and black robes of his profession, immortalised as one of the pillars of the English commonweal, an image that Hoskyns affectionately enlivened in his punning Latin inscription.[17] Hoskyns, Brooke and Holland clubbed together to present an engraved portrait of Martin to Cranfield. Holland's extensive use of chiasmus in his Latin poem accompanying the portrait presents a man that bears little resemblance to Aubrey's dead-drunk Martin. Instead, he is the man of balance, embodying the ideal of well-governed moderation: arbiter of the law and eloquence ('Legumque lingua, Lexque dicendi magis'), public voice of the city and dear heart of his inner circle of friends ('Magnae urbis Os, Orbis minoris corculum') united in loss and friendship. Holland presents Martin as worthy of royal favour, from his successful performances before the court as Prince of Love ('Princeps amorum, principum necnon amor') to his sense of civic duty, learning and government of the Virginia Company. Yet, there are perhaps hints of the royal disfavour Martin experienced in the image of his rise and fall that is conveyed by the analogy between his career and the sun rising in the west and falling in the east ('Oriens cadente sole sol, ortu cadens'), and the sense that he was extinguished by his own virtue – which resided in his witty tongue – 'Bono suorum natus, extinctus suo'.[18]

Literary meetings of the remaining wits may have convened at Brooke's house on Drury Lane in the early 1620s. Brooke had married Lady Mary Jacob (the widow of Sir Robert Jacob, former Solicitor General in Ireland) in 1619; around this time he took a house on Drury Lane opposite Donne. Lady Jacob, who died in 1622, was attended in her final illness by Donne. In the Conway papers is an epithalamium written for the couple, 'An Epithalamicall good morrowe to m^r Christopher Brooke', that lightly praises Lady Jacob, 'A mistris, a Companion, and a nurse, / no way defective in person, or in purse'.[19] Brooke is addressed affectionately as 'woorthye neighbour', yet the low, jesting style of the poem sounds more like John Hoskyns than John Donne. A pair of verse epistles is ascribed to a wit contest between Hoskyns and Lady Jacob in at least one manuscript miscellany.[20] The epistle attributed to Hoskyns is written in his characteristic burlesque style. The gravity of the metre, the alexandrine, and the lyric style is playfully violated. Couplets are completed in a dissonant low register, effectively travestying the love lyric, as the first line demonstrates: 'Oh love whose power & might non ever yet wthstood / thou teachest me to wright, come turne about Robin Hood'. The poem is a low parody of the misogynist love complaint intended to provoke and elicit the wit of the reader-as-respondent. The answer attributed to Lady Jacob may be prompted and have its form licensed by Hoskyns's opening, but this is a contest, and the female respondent aims to outwit her male opponent. She overgoes his alexandrines with fourteeners, and returns the dose of clap he threatens her with in kind by amplifying his closing curse 'then y^e Divell take mee':

> my lookes as kinde shalbee as y^e Divells over Lyncoln
> if ever I returne great Queen of Lightninge flashes
> send downe thy fyre & burne his Cod=peece into ashes.
> (fol. 71r)

This exchange goes beyond the 'pretie and pleasant taunts' between the sexes permissible in Renaissance models of civil conversation.[21] The female respondent makes no attempt to curb her wit to suit the dictates of her sex.

Rather, it is an exercise in burlesque that heightens the raillery permitted in answer-poetry, and flouts civility in favour of licentious wit.

This type of answer-poetry, in which the misogynist complaint or praise of woman is disputed by a respondent, was a popular élite literary game that derived from the rhetorical exercise of *in utramque partem*. It was a game in which women participated, displayed their ingenuity, and proclaimed their status as female wits.[22] Lady Jacob was not above engaging in public raillery; she was involved in a dispute in 1622 reminiscent of the earlier quarrel between Davies and the Prince of Love and his court: 'There is a hot suit commenced in the Starchamber', Chamberlain reported, 'twixt Sir John Davies Lady and the Lady Jacob about womanish brabbes, and an uncivill scurrilous letter written by Kit Brooke in his wifes behalf'.[23] While the drinking societies that met at the Mitre and Mermaid were exclusively male, it is possible to catch glimpses of women in scribal communities associated with the Sireniacs. A number of copies of Hoskyns's 'A Dreame' attribute political agency to Benedicta Hoskyns: a headnote to the poem in one copy has Benedicta present it to James, and another manuscript claims: 'upon ye sight of it the Kings ma:^{tie} most graciously granted her suite and her husband was forth with released'.[24] Chamberlain similarly assigned the poem to Benedicta when he included a copy in a letter to Dudley Carleton: 'Hoskins wife that is a poetesse hath ben a longe suitor, and presented the King with a petition in rime which I here send you.'[25]

Whereas the agency attributed to Benedicta derived from her status as proxy for her husband, Lady Jacob had political influence prior to her marriage to Brooke, probably through her first marriage, and was perceived by those at court as capable of exerting influence over her circle. During the 1621 parliament, Buckingham wrote to Lady Jacob to convince her that royal supply must be granted and to petition her to place pressure on her friends and husband. In reply, she adopts the style of the Roman matron, as well as that of a willing court servant, speaking of her 'friends the fathers of the Lower House' and her 'forward disposition to do my Patria and his great Master my best and humblest service'.[26] And she had a public reputation for wit. Arthur Wilson delightedly recalled an anecdote involving Lady Jacob and Count Gondomar, the Spanish ambassador and focus for anti-Spanish sentiment in the early 1620s, in which she turned herself into a type of libel. Lady Jacob stood at a window in her house on Drury Lane, with her mouth gaping, while Gondomar passed below in the street. This bold and uncivil spectacle was intended to parody the Spanish pensioners at court – the gaping mouth signified the avarice and political incontinence of those courtiers who provided Gondomar with information or exerted influence on his behalf in hope of reward.[27]

How does the presence of female wits in such close proximity to the Sireniacs affect our understanding of the modes of sociability they practised? Jonson, as we have seen, produced a scathing satire on female wit in the Ladies Collegiate in his *Epicoene*. Louise Schleiner has argued that Jonson's play and his 'Epigram on the Court Pucelle', which he owned was an attack on Cecilia Bulstrode, a lady-in-waiting to the Queen, satirised a circle of female wits active at Queen Anne's court from around 1605 to 1609. Lucy Russell, Countess of Bedford, her kinswoman Bulstrode, Lady Anne Southwell and Lady Mary Wroth held regular wit contests and played other literary games in the antechamber to Anne's court with a group of male wits, including Donne, Rudyerd, Sir Thomas Overbury, Sir Thomas Roe, Wotton and Jonson, and poetic exchanges continued through scribal channels. It may be that Jonson's own very personal scuffles with these wits, both female and male, were played out in his satires.[28] Yet, there is an ideological dimension to the quarrel: Jonson stigmatises female wit as part of his revival of a Roman style of conviviality that has its social basis in virile, masculine civility. Benedicta Hoskyns was reputed to have delivered her own judgement on Jonson: ''Twas an ingeniose remarque of my lady Hoskyns', reported Aubrey, 'that B. J. never writes of love, or if he does, does it not naturally.'[29] A Jonsonian masculine wit comes to fruition in his own very patrilineal college of wits, the 'Sons of Ben'. The 'Convivium Philosophicum' and the 'Parliament Fart' describe homosocial communities, but are their modes of play inimical to female wit? The household coterie was more discreet than the public tavern; yet, Lady Jacob was certainly not shy of public displays of wit. Hence, it may have been the masculine professional basis of the early tavern fraternities that excluded women. The question remains whether the forms of play practised by the wits were ideologically open to women in a way that Jonson's symposiastic vocabulary was not; or whether women were required to adopt a masculine wit to join in the game. Because of the lively disjunction between ideology and lived practice, it is difficult to arrive at a definitive answer.[30] What we can say is that women did participate in literary games both at court and on the edges of the formal societies in the early seventeenth century, thus establishing a precedent for the female wit who comes to prominence in the second half of the century.[31]

The evidence we have for convivial societies in the late sixteenth and early seventeenth centuries suggests a highly diversified and sophisticated associational culture. Fraternities like the Sireniacs illustrate how pedagogic and sociable practices introduced at the grammar schools and universities continued at the Inns and in other places of association, such as taverns, where they were augmented by professional affiliations and court connections. And they continued at home, through household circles that could provide an alternative arena to the homosociality of an Inns of Court and tavern culture. These coteries were hospitable environments for literary experimentation. A ludic tradition, previously disseminated through a humanist print culture, is developed within scribal communities and a tavern culture; the relative exclusivity this environment provided encouraged participants to challenge decorum and exert considerable intellectual pressure on Renaissance notions of laughter. The result is the development of a distinct tradition of *lusus* that explores the resources of low literary forms, such as burlesque and travesty, and introduces such innovations into the genre as nonsense verse.

CLUBBING IN THE 1620S

Taverns, tables and the societies that gathered at them, as the 'Convivium Philosophicum' and the 'Parliament Fart' illustrate, were sites for political talk and the exchange of news; they functioned as nodal points within scribal networks, the termini at which epigrams, libels, satires and parliamentary treatises were produced and transmitted. The tempo and volume of this exchange accelerated in the 1620s. That is not to say that such a news culture was unprecedented or even novel. The Overbury scandal, with its nine public murder trials, had held public attention throughout 1615 and 1616; as Alastair Bellany argues, it was 'a print sensation of unusual proportions', and generated both an appetite for news and a news culture able to supply these needs, from accounts of the trials to vicious libels and satires.[32] The 1620s were beset by court scandals, corruption trials and impeachments. Parliament was recalled in 1621 after almost seven years, in the context not only of the outbreak of the Thirty Years War, but also of James's 'Proclamation against excesse of Lavish and Licentious Speech of matters of State', which triggered debates in the Commons over freedom of speech. And parliament was once again in session at regular intervals: 1621, 1624, 1625, 1626 and 1628–9. Events in parliament, James's response to the invasion of the Palatinate, the negotiations for the Spanish Match (and its failure), and the fortunes of the royal favourite the Duke of Buckingham, all fuelled a burgeoning news culture.[33] With individuals and communities competing for the authority to speak in this raucous age, the dissonance celebrated in the 'Parliament Fart' was an apt motif for the times, and probably contributed to its continuing popularity in manuscript miscellanies of this period.

The fraternities formed in the 1620s were distinctive in two inter-related aspects: they had their origins in military companies, and were characterised by riotous speech and behaviour.[34] There had been earlier incidents involving riotous companies of young aristocrats: Chamberlain reported that the youthful Knights of Bath, created in 1616 at Charles's inauguration as Prince of Wales, had run amok at celebrations provided for them at Drapers' Hall: they were 'so rude and unruly and caried themselves so insolently divers wayes, but specially in putting citizen wives to the squeake' that they were ejected, and continued their 'quarrells at their severall meetings, but specially at the Miter in Fleetstreet'.[35] Aristocratic riot, particularly when it targets citizens in this way, is a means of asserting superior social status by disregarding the duty of the nobleman to behave courteously towards social inferiors and to recognise civic authority.[36] The fraternities of the 1620s – the 'Tityre-tu', the 'Order of the Bugle', and the 'Order of the Blue' – shared this disregard for civility with aristocratic orders, like the Knights of Bath.[37] Members of these military fraternities had served together; they took oaths and devised orders, elected a mock-prince, clubbed together for formal suppers, and had their own secret language, employing code and passwords. With rumours of Spanish and papist plots, contemporaries suspected they were secret Catholic associations, intent on mischief (the Tityre-tu did in fact originate in the regiment Lord Vaux raised in 1622 to serve with the Habsburgs in the Low Countries), and members were interrogated before parliament in late 1623.[38]

Although these fraternities had Catholic sympathies, were disdainful of Protestant anti-Spanish propaganda and were frequently frustrated younger sons of wealthy families, Raylor argues they were not purposeful political organisations with a coherent agenda; rather, their primary purpose in clubbing together was 'simple good fellowship'. They were, above all, groups of soldiers, and this military dimension carried through into their play. The Order of the Bugle was formed out of the fleet that accompanied Prince Charles and Buckingham from Spain following the collapse of the Spanish marriage negotiations. Once in England, this Order engaged in mock-skirmishes with the Tityre-tu at taverns, which were followed by drinking sessions between the two companies. Not all associations had Catholic sympathies. During the Christmas festivities of 1622–3, a group of Middle Templars took oaths on their swords, passed around a cup of wine, and swore 'to live and die in the service of Elizabeth of Bohemia'.[39] It is possible that the conflicts on the continent were replayed if not on the streets of London, then in the taverns and in rhyming clubs. Railing rhymes and ballads proliferated in company with the fraternities, and professed divergent viewpoints on the conflicts that energised the 1620s.[40]

There are continuities between modes of political sociability and a culture of versifying among the earlier wits and in the 1620s. A ballad written in 1624, 'The Parliament sitts with a Synod of Witts', can be read within the tradition of parliamentary satire famously exemplified by the 'Parliament Fart'. It was composed sometime around May, before the failure of Mansfield's expedition to recover the Palatinate in August and the French marriage treaty in November, reflecting the lively convivial culture that attended parliamentary sessions. A copy in one manuscript is given a contemporary ballad tune, 'To drive the could winter away'; like the 'Parliament Fart', it is written in the rough, freer rhythms of stress-verse, albeit with a jaunty ballad measure of alternating four- and three-beat lines.[41] The opening line, 'The Parliament sitts with a Synode of Witts', remembers and claims fellowship with the earlier parliamentary wits who dominated James's first parliament so memorably. The ballad celebrates a 'Jubily crowninge this yeere':

> The Catholike King hath a litle yong thing
> Call'd Dona Maria his Sister
> Our Prince went to Spayne h^r love to obtayne
> But (god be thanked) hee miss'd her.
> I am glad it is ended w^t was p^{r}tended
> For Spanyard's yet no^r kept th^r word
> But James of great Brittayne, will make them be shit'em
> If once he but draw his sword.[42]

The failure of the Spanish Match has brought about a new Golden Age, thwarting Catholic ambitions and restoring Great Britain to the civic strength of the military state.[43] The ballad rejoices that 'Astraea y^t swore to see us no more / Shall see us once agayne' (p. XIII). The earlier popular political satire, probably composed around 1621, 'The most humble petition of the poore-distressed Commons of long afflicted England', was addressed to Elizabeth I and was said to have been placed in the hand of her funeral effigy at Westminster Abbey. It prompted at least one answer poem, 'A Gracious answere from that blessed Saint to her whilome Subjects with a divine admonition and a prophetique conclusion'.[44] The 'Parliament sitts with a Synode of Witts' arguably also responds to 'The most humble petition' since it turns the earlier piteous moan of the Commons into jubilation. In Bod., MS Malone 19, the 'Parliament sitts' is followed by 'The most humble petition' (pp. XIII–XIV, 1–5). The ballad is not without political cynicism: James has yet to draw his sword, and it is concerned about political credibility in these times of plots and counterplots.

It is easy to imagine this ballad sung by those Middle Templars who swore allegiance to the second Elizabeth during the revels of 1622–3. Hoskyns continued to be closely involved with the Middle Temple throughout the 1620s, regularly sitting in its parliaments and even using his rooms as guest chambers for friends and clients; his son, Benedict, entered his father's Inn in this period. In 1621, he was under suspicion for authorship of a libel on Sir Francis Bacon ('Lord Verulam is very lame'); given his frequent residence at the Middle Temple in this period, it once again suggests a parallel between practices of commoning at Inns and libelling. In 1628, he returned to the Caroline parliament, after an absence of fourteen years, and was vocal in support of the 'Petition of Right'.[45]

It is credible to posit continuities between communities and political cultures at the Inns across a number of years, even generations, which meant later companies had access to verses, memories and other cultural artefacts of the earlier society. These types of institutional continuities are also suggested by miscellanies like Malone 19. It is a commonplace book compiled by a Wykehamist at New College, Oxford who came up from Winchester sometime during the 1630s and 1640s. As well as the 'Parliament sitts' and the 'Humble Petition', it includes sections of libels and poems on the scandals and major political events and personalities of the early seventeenth century – the Somersets and the Overbury trials, the Spanish Match, Buckingham's rise and fall, Raleigh's execution – together with epigrams and epitaphs on Oxford college personalities. Two distinctive features of the anthology are the number of verses composed on the subject of Coryate and its status, as Colclough has identified, as 'one of the chief sources of Hoskyns' poems'.[46] The compiler's interest in both Hoskyns and Coryate possibly arose out of his institutional connections with these two men. Malone 19 is the earliest known miscellany in a sub-genre of Oxford miscellanies identifiable through the number of poems from Wykehamists: these authors include Hoskyns and Ben Stone, a fellow of New College from around 1605 to 1609.[47] The two Coryate poems ('Did aunciente Socrates his fame advance' (p. 81), and 'Tom comminge neere ye Italian coaste' (pp. 82–4)) are Ben Stone's; since Stone also hailed from Somerset, he may have felt this gave him a special purchase on his fellow countryman.[48]

Malone 19 has wider associations with the early seventeenth-century wits. It includes the epigram attributed to Martin, 'The Romane Tarquin in his folly blind' (p. 87), and a section from the 'Convivium Philosophicum' (pp. 20–1). The way this poem is placed in the miscellany is suggestive: it is preceded by the popular satire on the Spanish Match, dating from around 1623, 'All the newes thats stirringe now / Is of the Golden Ladye' (pp. 18–19), which segues almost seamlessly into the section of political satire from the 'Convivium Philosophicum', beginning with the lines 'Rex Religionem curat / Populus ligiantiam jurat' (p. 20), which is immediately followed by another anti-Spanish satire, 'One the Princes goeing to Spayne' (p. 21). The organisation of these texts indicates that from the 1620s through to the 1640s writers were finding literary and political precedents in early Jacobean satires and libels. They did not simply revitalise earlier satires to speak to the times, but began to discover causes for the current crises in earlier events, and in doing so began to reshape political memory through notions of non-providential causality.[49]

Malone 19 was compiled over twenty years after the Mitre meeting in 1611 and many years after the collapse of the Spanish Match. With its Wykehamist affiliations, the anthology points to the role of masters and tutors at schools and universities, as well as families who maintained associations with these institutions across generations, in the transmission and preservation of texts and collections of poetry – particularly political poetry – over often lengthy periods of time.[50] The poems that were copied were also embedded within associational cultures, and we need to pay attention to the role of societies in the transmission of texts. These texts were not only read, they were often performed and thereby incorporated into the lived experience of a community. Performance cultures continued beyond the involvement of the individual participant, and were perpetuated through shared rituals and cultural artefacts including songs and texts. Hence, a political ballad could continue to be performed at institutions and within milieux over a number of years because it had entered the community's repertoire of signs and symbols of belonging.

The Sireniacs look like a very different type of association to the later 1620s military fraternities Raylor has studied: they have the appearance of a society of comparatively sober and civic-minded men bound together through their common professional association with the Inns of Court. That said, the early history of this company of wits does suggest a point of contact with the later fraternities. Many of those engaged in the libellous politics of the 1590s were men who had either served under Essex or were sympathetic to his aristocratic ethos. This military culture shaped the debates over the legitimacy of violent words, and brought into sharp focus the tensions between a masculine honour culture and the dictates of civility.[51] The 1620s saw the reinvigoration of a militarism following decades of Jacobean peace. One consequence, exemplified by these riotous fraternities, was a resurgence of an aggressive culture of masculine honour that deliberately flouted notions of good manners as the badge of gentlemanly freedom from social constraints. These fraternities also adopted low ludic styles that had become the signature of the wits.[52] The Order of the Blue adopted names of Rabelaisian-style giants – Giant Drunckzadoge, Giant Drinkittupall, and Giant Neversober – and the name 'Tityretu' probably incorporated an obscene meaning, given that 'tityros' could denote priapic satyrs.[53] There is a fundamental difference between the liberties claimed by the Sireniacs and the 1620s fraternities. The earlier wits understood the tensions between liberty and licence within a legal and parliamentary framework of *parrhesia*; their experiments with low forms were incorporated into speculative play, and not deliberately cast within emergent forms of anti-civility. The later fraternities, on the other hand, did repudiate the demands of civility for the pleasures of appetite and excess, and thereby helped to formulate a libertine culture of anti-civility.[54]

The 'Tribe of Ben' at the Apollo Room

Jonson seated in state in the famed Apollo Room at the Devil and St Dunstan tavern on Fleet Street, surrounded by his 'Tribe' or 'Sons', is the *arbiter bibendi*.[55] He formulated an English symposiastic poetic tradition in dialogue with Anacreon, Horace and Martial that was then transmitted via his poetic sons to the eighteenth-century gentlemen's clubs in which the Jonsonian anacreontic symposium provided the 'topos of polite sociability'.[56] Jonson may have developed the symposiastic ideal in conversation with his classical fathers, but it was also delineated through his vituperative argument with the political clubs proliferating in the 1620s. His 'Epistle Answering to One that Asked to be Sealed of the Tribe of Ben' and his *Staple of News* (1626) tell us so, positing rivals – the 'covey of wits' and the 'Society of Jeerers' – that threaten to drown out the civil voice of moderation. The language of conviviality he deploys in these texts does not return us to the quiet sanctity of an inner circle, but rather draws these texts into the political conflicts of the times as they were played out in the taverns, at court and in other arenas of association. Jonson's demarcation of the symposiastic space and ethos is not confined to his Anacreontic-Horatian lyrics, but is also conducted through the ludic mock-convivium. The ironic stance encoded within this form allows the speaker to engage in raillery and burlesque, while maintaining the discriminating distance ascribed to the educated man.

Jonson's 'Tribe of Ben' epistle was probably composed in August or September 1623: Martin Butler has drawn attention to the complexity of the political position Jonson adopts in the epistle as he responds to rapidly fluctuating events at a climactic point in the Spanish marriage negotiations.[57] The epistle is a 'self-conscious social *performance*' in which Jonson pits his 'Tribe of Ben' against the 'covey of wits' (line 22), mimicking the factionalism of the 1620s.[58] The epistle is his volley in the tavern skirmishes of the early 1620s – in late 1623 members of the Tityre-tu and the Order of the Bugle would be examined before parliament. Jonson is remarkably circumspect on the precise nature of his 'Tribe', perhaps for politic reasons; there are no details of rituals, orders or devices. That said, the title of the company derives from the Tribe of Benjamin of the *Book of Revelations*, thus nominating a company of just men untainted by the corrupt times, which, together with the image of martyrdom, sets out an adversarial language of politics.[59] This discourse of trial through adversity is concentrated in the Horatian image of Jonson as the embattled yet just man, who will 'dwell as in my centre as I can' (line 60). This just man is the armed patriot; Jonson explicitly adopts codes of military honour as the seal of his tribe, his fraternity.

The 'Tribe of Ben' epistle is about honour, personal integrity and loyalty. One of the reasons why the authorities suspected the fraternities of the 1620s of subversion was because the use of oaths and orders 'specially to be true and faithfull to the societie', as Chamberlain noted, 'and to conceale one anothers secrets' meant that their allegiance to the company was seen to compromise their loyalty to the state.[60] These potentially conflicting loyalties were exacerbated by the aggressive honour culture that gave rise to these fraternities, which advocated the pursuit of honour even at the expense of the rule of law. The 'Tribe of Ben' epistle borrows heavily from Jonson's earlier epigram 'To Captain Hungry' in which the professional soldier, a professed veteran of military campaigns against the French Catholic League and Spain in the 1580s and 1590s, is also a professional newshound. His trafficking in news is emasculating and at the same time places his loyalty to the state in question since it mimics his readiness to serve different military commanders. This association between news and the soldier is also made in Captain Shunfield in the *Staple*, who is not simply a satire on Captain Thomas Gainsford, the early news writer and editor, but also functions to de-legitimate the claims that writers like Gainsford were making for the news as civic discourse. The speaker's own social and civic identity, as well as that of his tribe, is secured by his patriotism and his adherence to a military honour code, which places him above effeminate and emasculating talk and in the world of action:

> But if, for honour, we must draw the sword,
>   And force back that which will not be restored,
> I have a body yet that spirit draws
>   To live, or fall a carcass in the cause.
>
> (lines 39–42)

Jonson fashioned the 'Tribe of Ben' in competition with the fraternities of the 1620s; in doing so, he constructed an alternative site of affirmation and fellowship, not simply amongst friends but within his own fraternity.

In the 1620s, Jonson returned to the language of censure that he had refined during the libellous politics of the 1590s. His favoured mode for attack is the mock-convivium, and he chooses arenas for combat he has made his own. Act 4 of *The Staple of News* is set at the Apollo Room at the Devil and St Dunstan tavern. In the 1620s, the Apollo Room seems to take over from the Mermaid and Mitre taverns, not simply as a fashionable meeting place for gallant company, but as a symposiastic space. Just as the Sireniacs were identified with the Mermaid, so too Jonson and the 'Sons of Ben' took up residence at the Apollo Room, and fashioned it in their image. It had been furnished two years previously with Jonson's *Leges Convivales* over the fireplace – these 'Laws of Dining', as we have seen, define this social space through a classical tradition of moderate banqueting.[61] Jonson overwrites the Apollo Room through layers of self-imitation and learned classical citations, thereby taking possession of this symposiastic space, and marking out its parameters in terms of a tradition of learned play. Thus, the disputation between the poet Madrigal and the cook Lickfinger on the relative merits of the 'quick cellar' and the 'fat kitchen' repeats a dialogue in Jonson's unperformed masque *Neptune's Triumph*, composed in 1624, that in turn derives from Athenaeus' *Deipnosophistae* (The Sophists at Dinner).[62]

The scenes set at the Apollo Room are an extended experimentation with convivial *lusus* comparable with the front matter to *Coryats Crudities*. Gossip Mirth, who oversees the play between acts in the intermean, is a version of Erasmus's Folly. Don McKenzie rightly observed that Mirth is given the role of 'dramatic theorist, literary historian, and sharp reviewer'; the action therefore unfolds in Erasmian fashion under the ironic purview of *lusus*.[63] Jonson keeps this ludic style remarkably close: he has Madrigal crowned by Pennyboy Junior in his own image as Horace, the symposiastic poet, whose 'lyrics and his madrigals . . . / . . . we will have at dinner, steeped in claret, / And against supper, soused in sack' (4.4.96–8); and he caricatures himself as the Rabelaisian 'stewed poet', who overtaken with symposiastic excess 'hath torn the [play]book in a poetical fury, and put himself to silence in dead sack' (*Prologue*, 67, 72–3). The scene at the Apollo rewrites Athenaeus for an English audience, setting in play rival classical theories of the *symposium*: whether inspiration is the effect of the wine drunk during the relaxed drinking session that follows the meal, or comes from the banquet itself. The classics are read through Rabelais to produce a learned travesty of a tradition of moderate banqueting, a tradition that Jonson has made his own. Whereas in Guazzo's *Civile Conversation*, for example, the company converse after dinner to nourish the mind as well as the body, and 'sport and jest discreetly', Fitton proposes that this gathering 'jeer a little'(4.1.4); the topic then shifts to the news, 'Ha' you any news for after dinner? Methinks / We should not spend our time unprofitably'(37–8).[64] The ironic stance made available within learned play enables Jonson to set in place carefully calibrated cultural distinctions that are elaborated through the convivial vocabulary of taste.[65]

The *Staple*, as critics have noted, is a play about the news in all its complexity – manuscript, printed pamphlet, talk and the stage.[66] It dramatises a public sphere that is unregulated not because of an absence of corporations but because there are too many corporations competing for authority. The Society of Jeerers, for example, identify Pennyboy Canter as a potential rival: Captain Shunfield suspects 'He's some primate metropolitan rascal' (4.1.46). The urban terrain of the jeerers travesties ecclesiastically regulated civic space; it suggests schism, an intense urban factionalism, with different denominations battling it out in the metropolis. The Staple, the Society of Jeerers, and the Canters' College are all interrelated, sharing motifs and members, and yet different, suggesting a proliferation of societies without purpose.[67] Jonson's *Staple* dramatises the 'more dynamic, open, and pluralistic world of voluntary societies in Britain', as Peter Clark notes, 'distinguished by the absence, except in a few cases of official sanction and resources'.[68] Through the vocabulary of the *convivium*, which he had mastered and claimed as his own, Jonson marks out his place within this domain, asserting his authority to define and take possession of the symposiastic space, to set the generic parameters for the poetics of play and to wield a discourse of honour.

THE WITS IN PRINT: *MUSARUM DELICIÆ* AND THE *PRINCE D'AMOUR*

The 'Parliament Fart' first appears in print in the Royalist anthologies *Musarum Deliciæ: or, the Muses Recreation* (1655) and *Le Prince d'Amour, or* the *Prince of Love* (1660). Read nostalgically as the *locus classicus* of an earlier Stuart culture which licensed wit and laughter, the poem is thus incorporated into a royalist politics of mirth. Leah Marcus traces the beginnings of a royalist tradition of public mirth to Jonson's masques for James and the Jacobean court. The period from the 1640s through to the Commonwealth and Protectorate sees this royalist tradition take specifically oppositional form.[69] These anthologies, which often collected poetry from the 1590s to the 1630s alongside later poems from the civil wars such as 'Upon Sir John Sucklings 100 horse', sought to establish precedents for royalist culture, providing it with the credibility of literary tradition by appropriating earlier forms of wit, buffoonery and raillery that did not necessarily share its ideological affiliations.[70] *Musarum Deliciæ* commandeers the 'Parliament Fart' into the service of a Cavalier literary and political identity which politicises the pleasures of drinking, socialising and versifying – specifically the composition of low comic poems – as an oppositional mode to the civic ideologies of the Commonwealth. Canonised as an earlier exemplar of literary crudity and burlesque, the 'Parliament Fart' is co-opted within a libertine tradition of low literary forms that sets itself in opposition to the high-minded civic forms of Republican humanism. *Prince d'Amour* reprints the 'Parliament Fart' following an account of the 1597–8 Middle Temple revels; it heads the anthology's *Collection of several Ingenious Poems and Songs by the Wits of the Age*. This republication of earlier texts is part of a Restoration cultural agenda that posits a fundamental break between an earlier monarchical culture and the Republic, a rupture that it seeks to heal by reclaiming these texts for the restored king.

With *Musarum Deliciæ*, the stationer Henry Herringman claimed to have compiled an authoritative edition '*of Sir* John Mennis, *and* Doctor Smiths *Drolish Intercourses*', and in doing so established their style of low comic and burlesque poetry as a new print genre – 'drollery'.[71] The anthology fashions a relatively cohesive print community, with a well-defined social and political identity, out of poetry that had previously circulated in manuscript among a close coterie. Printing royalist coterie poetry in the 1650s had its advantages, as Raylor points out, since 'more public means of circulation was appropriate for broadcasting values, as public gestures of solidarity, and as foci for discontent'.[72] The collection gives the strong impression of an embattled but resilient band of cavaliers with their own distinctive literary culture and sociable practices. Raylor notes how the use of features of coterie publication, such as initials, which comfort the insider in possession of privileged knowledge and tease the outsider with partially disclosed information, fashions a 'readerly community' defined by 'aggressive inclusiveness', which draws the reader into an alliance with these men.[73]

The modes of sociable play and experiments in low literary forms on show in this miscellany are part of a Cavalier rather than humanist culture. These are not the forms of learned relaxation employed by the professional classes, nor is there any sense this play arises out of pedagogic exercises. The men at play are royalist soldiers and not professional lawyers. Friendship is still continuous with the game of wit, but it is expressed within an honour culture familiar from the 1620s fraternities. The volume opens with five epistles exchanged between Mennes and Smith, and other members of their circle, over the two-year period 1640–2. They are written in octosyllabics, the metrical form that had become the group's signature.[74] The first epistle, 'To Parson Weeks. An Invitation to London', addressed by either Mennes or Smith to John Weeks, a friend of Robert Herrick, is a symposiastic invitation poem that despite having an antecedent in Jonson's 'Inviting a Friend to Supper' is not part of this tradition of civil moderate banqueting. Rather than Jonson, the speaker looks to 'Yong *Herric*' that 'took to entertaine / The Muses in a sprightly vein' with his poems on sack, and privileges excess and easy wit over Jonsonian moderation and intellectual labour.[75] The addressee is a rustic ale-drinking clergyman to the speaker's urbane wine-drinking friend from London. The conventional epistolary exchange between the country and city expands the vista of the symposiastic poem; no longer confined to the dining room, the drinker travels on the road, meeting fellow travellers, exchanging jests and drinking. The kindness of witty strangers along the way re-establishes the place of traditions of hospitality in the countryside as a counterpart to the private forms of conviviality among friends in the city, re-feudalising the nation in the name of these Cavalier 'men of honour'. In keeping with its libertine easy wit, the epistle makes light of politics, jesting that Weeks should

> Rather then faile, speak Treason there,
> And come on charges of the Shire;
> A *London* Goal, with friends and drink,
> Is worth your Vicaridge, I think.
>
> (p. 3)

This is not the ludic politics of Sireniacs; instead, serious jesting is cultivated to signify detachment from the civic public political sphere. Political loyalties are re-inscribed elsewhere, in the community of honour that binds friends and the camp.

The speaker imagines Weeks travelling to London 'On Camels back, like *Coryat*: / Imagine that a pack-horse be / The Camell, in his book you see' (pp. 2–3) – the book is Taylor's edition of Coryate's letters, *Mr Thomas Coriat to his friends in England sendeth greeting* (1618). It is a very appropriate choice at a number of levels. Epistolary exchange is refigured and given material embodiment through the books that the friends share; Weeks (and the reader) is asked to take this book from his shelf, open to the woodcut, and share the jest, thus completing the circle of friendship despite physical absence. The epistle asks Weeks, rusticated in his parish in late 1642 at the outbreak of the civil wars like many of his clergymen friends including Smith and Herrick, to recall the pleasures of the London tavern scene; it both expresses nostalgia for an earlier, now threatened culture, and establishes the place of their circle within a tradition of wit and sociability that gives permanence to this community. Coryate and his *Crudities*, as Raylor notes, stand for a 'tradition of clubbing' transmitted through versifying, drinking and conviviality.[76] 'Upon a Surfeit caught by drinking evill Sack, at the George Tavern in Southwark', attributed to Smith, is an exercise in literary crudity reminiscent of the mock-encomiastic verses before the *Crudities* which figured travel-writing through sea-sickness, taking their cue from Coryate's own exuberantly scatological description of vomiting on board the ship bound for France which opens his travels. The speaker of this mock-symposiastic poem, written on the back of a hangover from drinking bad wine, vows to forsake wine, with its élite lyric associations, for the cruder, lowly poetic style of ale and beer, and wishes for 'Old *Johnsons* head' to compose a satire to 'confute / Our Poet Apes, that doe so much impute / Unto the grapes inspirement' (p. 29). Ironically the speaker eschews Jonsonian moderation: bad or impure wine is not invoked to signify the dangers of excess; rather, the speaker will simply change his drink.[77] 'The Lowses Peregrination' is an obscene poem that tells of the louse's travels from 'an old Pedlers haunches' to 'his doxie' (p. 30), thence to 'A Lord of this Land that lov'd a Bum well', and onto Venice and dildos (p. 31). Collected alongside the Mennes–Smith epistles, it suggests the way that Cavalier identity shades into the urbanity of the libertine.

This is the context in which the 'Parliament Fart' first appears in print. It is immediately preceded by Smith's epistle to Mennes, composed around 1640–1, and given the explanatory headnote:

A Letter to Sir *John Mennis*, when the Parliament denied the King Money to pay the Army, unlesse a Priest, whom the King had reprieved, might be executed. Sir *John* at that time wanting the Money for provisions for his troop, desired me by his

Letter to goe to the Priest, and to perswade him to dye for the good of the Army; saying,

> *What is't for him to hang an houre,*
> *To give an Army strength and power?*
> (p. 63)

The Long Parliament had met in November 1640, and quickly moved to impeach Archbishop Laud and the Earl of Strafford – the latter was executed in May 1641. The Catholic priest that is the subject of this jest is John Goodman: as the headnote explains, despite royal reprieve, parliament had refused to vote supply for the northern forces until he was executed. Parliament is portrayed as an arbitrary, tyrannical and absolute political body, yet the poem is silent on the subject of Charles I, so that he both is placed outside parliament's merciless rule, and is passive, ineffectual.[78] The drolling style functions as a politically charged form of black humour, turning the traditional refrain of the folly of the times into a much darker theatre of the absurd.

'The Fart censured in the Parliament House' which follows this epistle, as Raylor observes, is reconstituted as an attack on parliament, which is mockingly presented as disappearing up its own arse through its flurry of legislative activity. This version is markedly different from other versions in that it chooses to rewrite the standard opening of the poem: 'Puffing down coms grave antient Sir *Io. Crook*, / And reads his message promptly without book' (p. 65). Other versions preserve the dignity of the Lords's messenger and the procedure of the House – hence he reads his message in his book – but this version's 'puffing' Sir John who reads 'without book' deliberately eschews decorum to depict hot air (puffing, farting) as the defining condition of parliament. 'But *Harry Ludlows* foysting Arse cry'd no'. Foisting is a synonym for farting, but it also carries the sense of a fart that is surreptitiously and seditiously let. The 'Fart censured in the Parliament House' ends with a variation on the lines attributed in most versions to George More – 'Quoth Sr: George Moore I thincke it / be fitt / That wee this fart to the Seriant Comitt' (Bod., MS Malone 23, p. 3):

> But all at last said, it was most fit,
> The Fart as a Traitor, to the Tower to commit:
> Where as they say, it remaines to this houre,
> Yet not close prisoner, but at large in the Tower.
> (p. 71)[79]

That a fart could be a traitor – and a reprieved priest executed – is a fit symbol for the folly that has taken residence in the Long Parliament.

Underneath the 'Fart Censured' in the second edition of *Musarum Deliciæ*, published in 1656, is the 'Farts Epitaph':

> *Reader, I was borne and cryed,*
> *Crackt so, smelt so, and so dyed.*
> *Like to* Cæsars *was my death,*
> *He in Senat lost his breath;*
> *And alike inter'd doth lye,*
> *The famous* Romulus *and I.*
> *And, at last, like* Floria *faire,*
> *I left the Common wealth mine Aire.*
>
> (p. 71)

All these Roman analogies have a republican dimension that would have had clear political resonances in the 1650s.[80] The 'Farts Epitaph', in this context, re-writes the 'Parliament Fart' within an oppositional Cavalier poetic, which harnesses an older laughter of ridicule to travesty the Commonwealth and its foundations in republican humanism.

The laughter of ridicule was not confined to Royalists, and was in actuality employed by both sides as part of the 'vituperative rhetoric' of the warring broadsheets and pamphlets of the 1640s and 1650s. John Milton in his *Animadversions upon the Remonstrant against Smectymnuss* (1641) defended 'grim laughter' and the use of personal invective as part of the armoury of the orator in religious controversy. John King has traced Milton's zealous laughter to native English medieval and reformation satirists, yet it also continues a vibrant tradition of libellous polemics that entered a new phase in the 1590s and was developed throughout the early seventeenth century.[81] King's study sets out to recuperate burlesque and the laughter of ridicule as significant elements of the generic mix of Milton's *Paradise Lost*. The laughter of derision in Heaven encompasses satanic flatulence: Satan rallies his troops with the cry 'Heaven witness thou anon, while we discharge / Freely our part'.[82] The vocabulary of political flatulence had been expanded considerably and tuned by the 'Parliament Fart'. Milton develops the ironic perspective of *lusus* in Raphael's jocoserious narration of the defeat of Satan.[83] His account of the discovery of gunpowder, in particular, echoes Jonson's complex combination of irony, burlesque and the mock-heroic in 'On a Famous Voyage' as well as his exuberantly atomistic language of matter and ordure:

> in a moment they turned
> Wide the celestial soil, and saw beneath
> The originals of nature in their crude
> Conception; sulphurous and nitrous foam

> They found, they mingled, and with subtle art,
> Concocted and adusted they reduced
> To blackest grain, and into store conveyed:
> (6.509–15)

Gunpowder and farts recall the explosive ending of one version of the 'Parliament Fart' in a miscellany dating from the late 1640s and 1650s that compares this 'tricke of the Chollicke' to the Gunpowder Plot, 'the former blast of the Powder Catholique' (Bod., MS Rawl.Poet.117, fol. 194r). Satanic farting does continue the 'spirit of seventeenth-century resistance writing and its radical Protestant roots', and it is also part of a tradition of *lusus* that incorporates Jonson's 'Famous Voyage' and 'The Parliament Fart'.[84]

Five years after its appearance in *Musarum Deliciæ*, the 'Parliament Fart' was reprinted in the Restoration anthology, *Prince d'Amour* (1660). The title refers to the 1597–8 Middle Temple revels; Martin is, however, a very distant memory – this Prince of Love is clearly meant to compliment Charles II recently returned to the English throne from exile in France: 'A *Prince* for some yeares past in *disguise*, and a stranger to his Native Soil, is now brought to light; and to you he comes, not for *Patronage*, but *welcome*' (sig. A2r–v). The compilers of the anthology wanted to construct a *Stuart* golden age, and hence distanced these revels from their original Elizabethan context. The Prince of Love described in the prefatory material is no longer an Elizabethan – he has more affinities with William Davenant's neo-Platonic *Triumphs of the Prince d'Amour* (1636) than the urbanely Ovidian Prince presiding over the 1597–8 revels. Despite the dedication to the Middle Temple, the preface has nothing to say about lawyers and their law sports, but rather gives a primarily courtly rendition of the revels. The revels have been co-opted to signify the cultivated pleasures of the reign of Charles I and, by contrast, to define the incivility and barbarity of the Commonwealth:

> His *Raign* was short, but prosperous; the *Genius* of the *Nation* being then heightened by all the accesses of *peace, plenty, Wit*, and *Beauty*, in their exact perfection. They who have been borne as it were out of time, and under the sullen influence of this latter ill-natured Age, who look on the past innocent and ingenious pleasures and divertisements wherewith your *Honourable Society* used to entertain it self and the whole glory and *grandeur* of *England* as *Romance* and *Fabulous*, may here reade that exaltation of *Wit*, wherewith all eares were charmed, and wish for the return of those blessed days, wherein you who come not short of your *Predeccesors* in any Ornaments of soul or body, may have the like opportunities of giving your selves and the *Age* you live in, the same excellent entertainments. (sigs. A2v–3r)

This Restoration anthology conflates texts from the late sixteenth and early seventeenth centuries with Royalist poetry from the 1630s onwards, incorporating poems in print as well as those circulating only in manuscript. It is part of the strategic republication project, key to the notion of the restoration, which utilised the resources of print to give the new regime cultural stability and to reinstitute court culture, making it over again by recycling old texts.

The 'Parliament Fart' heads the collection of *Ingenious Poems and Songs by the Wits of the Age*, and is followed by 'A Paradox of a Painted Face', attributed to Donne, and a series of poems and elegies on Elizabethan and Jacobean courtiers and members of the royal family, including Queen Anne, Prince Henry, Cecilia Bulstrode and Sir Philip Sidney. The predominance of elegies heightens the tone, lending decorum to the collection, and provides a context for reading the 'Parliament Fart' that contrasts markedly with that of *Musarum Deliciæ*. The anthology announces itself not as a collection of low drollery, but as one of socially and aesthetically refined wit – there are mild political satires, but no libels or obscene verses like the 'Lowses Peregrinations'. The 'Parliament Fart' is not given a title but instead prefaced by the headnote, found also in Malone 23, '*Never was bestow'd such Art / Upon the tuning of a Fart*' (p. 93). Rather than a political satire deriding parliament, the 'Parliament Fart' is to be read for its art and its wit. The ending of this version, as one might expect, differs considerably from 'The Fart censured in the Parliament House' printed in *Musarum Deliciæ*:

> With many more whom here I omit
> In censuring this fart that busied their Wit.
> Come, come, quoth the King, Libelling is not safe
> Bury you the fart, Ile make the Epitaph.

The wits in parliament, including 'merry Mr. *Hoskins*' (p. 99), join with their king in the artful composition of the poem. The way the poem is framed works to minimise the breach between king and parliament indicated by a number of couplets. Rather than a king who railed against the lawyers in the Commons, the reader instead is left with the merry, jest-loving James I.

The publication of the 'Parliament Fart' in royalist anthologies was politically motivated, yet it marked the entrance of a text so embedded with scribal and performance cultures into the print marketplace. A culture and tradition of play continue to inform the way this poem is read in print. *Musarum Deliciæ* was both an anthology of Cavalier political poetry and the inauguration of a new popular print genre, 'drolleries'; a term attached to anthologies of miscellaneous verse, it generically encompassed raillery, burlesque, lampoons and other classically low forms. Edward Phillips defined the term 'drollery,' in his *The New World of English Words* (1658), as 'a merry, facetious way of speaking or writing.'[85] Drollery, as the full title of the miscellany – *Facetiae. Musarum Deliciæ* – indicates, has its antecedents in the humanist tradition of *facetiae* and the jest book. The genre has expanded from the jest to include a variety of literary forms – lyrics, paradoxes, ballads, satires, and libels – under the broad category of wit. These collections of wit and drolleries, as Adam Smyth has shown, were shaped by and shaped the tastes of new generations of readers, in particular, the young urban male readers.[86] The clubbability of these anthologies, based in their appropriation of the textual artefacts of coterie cultures, established print fellowships which offered readers access to and means of participating in a coterie sociability that did not require personal knowledge of one's fellows. It is part of the democratisation of private modes of sociability: as Shields points out, print enabled 'a middling readership the opportunity to participate imaginatively in a discursive analogue of genteel company'.[87] These print communities provided a mode of sociability in which individuals were bound together through friendship, pleasure and play, and shared tastes and appetites, rather than the traditional communal ties of kinship and patronage. In this aspect, these anthologies are an expression of the accelerating urbanisation of London, as well as the major provincial towns, in the second half of the seventeenth century.[88]

This later literature of sociability had developed out of textual practices and cultures of performance that had entered the literary marketplace earlier in the century in *Coryats Crudities*. The mode of print fellowship inscribed in this volume had in turn developed out of the older 'talked book', a set of sociable printing and reading practices that marks the point of intersection between print and aural and performance cultures. In *Coryats Crudities*, reading functions as a mode of sociability, consumption and performance. The sociability that structures the volume gave rise to textual practices of collecting: jests, anecdotes and verses are designed to be lifted from the front matter and Coryate's travel narrative, and recycled and reconstituted in conversation, play or other texts. The malleability, playfulness and inherent sociability of the literary forms pioneered by this early company of wits ensured their survival as they were reconstituted within changing sociable and textual practices across the seventeenth century.

Notes

INTRODUCTION

1. *Thomas Coriate Traveller for the English Wits: greeting From the court of the Great Mogul* (London, 1616), p. 37.
2. *Poems. The Golden Remains of those so much admired Dramatick Poets, Francis Beaumont and John Fletcher Gent* (London, 1660), sig. L6r. I will use the term 'wits' in this sense to denote those participating in these convivial societies and literary performances.
3. *The Works of Jonson*, ed. William Gifford, 9 vols. (1816), I, pp. lxv–lxvi. Gifford drew on Beaumont's epistle 'The Sun which doth the greatest comfort bring' and John Aubrey's note on Sir Francis Stewart: 'He was a learned gentleman, and one of the club at the Mermayd, in Fryday Street, with Sir Walter Ralegh, etc., of that sodalitie: heroes and witts of that time', '*Brief Lives*', *chiefly of Contemporaries, set down by John Aubrey, between the Years 1669 and 1696*, ed. Andrew Clark, 2 vols. (Oxford: Clarendon Press, 1898), II, p. 239. I. A. Shapiro, 'The "Mermaid Club"', *Modern Language Review* 45 (1950), 6–17; Shapiro and Percy Simpson, '"The Mermaid Club": An Answer and Rejoinder', *Modern Language Review* 46 (1951), 58–63; Michael Strachan, 'The Mermaid Tavern Club: A New Discovery', *History Today* 17 (1967), 533–8; Martin Butler, 'Sir Francis Stewart: Jonson's Overlooked Patron', *Ben Jonson Journal* 2 (1995), 101–27; Mark Bland suggests there may be some truth to the 'Mermaid Club' in his 'Francis Beaumont's Verse Letters to Ben Jonson and the "Mermaid Club"', *English Manuscript Studies, 1100–1700* 12 (2005), 139–79.
4. Thomas Middleton, *Your Five Gallants* (London, 1608), sigs. E4v–F1r (Act 2).
5. Peter Borsay, *The English Urban Renaissance: Culture and Society in the Provincial Towns, 1660–1770* (Oxford: Clarendon Press, 1989).
6. Clark tends to categorise the pre-1640 tavern companies as aristocratic clubs, *British Clubs and Societies 1580–1800: The Origins of an Associational World* (Oxford: Clarendon Press, 2000), pp. vii–ix, 3–8, 47, 49.
7. Pascal Brioist, 'Que de choses avons nous vues et vécues à la Sirène', *Histoire et Civilisation* 4 (1991), 89–132; Timothy Raylor, *Cavaliers, Clubs, and Literary Culture: Sir John Mennes, James Smith, and the Order of the Fancy* (Newark: University of Delaware Press, 1994); Phil Withington and Alexandra Shepard, eds., *Communities in early modern England* (Manchester:

Manchester University Press, 2000); Michelle O'Callaghan, *The 'Shepheards Nation': Jacobean Spenserians and Early Stuart Political Culture* (Oxford: Clarendon Press, 2000); Jennifer Richards, *Rhetoric and Courtliness in Early Modern Literature* (Cambridge: Cambridge University Press, 2003); Phil Withington, *The Politics of the Commonwealth: Citizens and Freemen in Early Modern England* (Cambridge: Cambridge University Press, 2005), esp. Chapter 5.
8. Clark, *British Clubs and Societies*, p. 9.
9. BL, MS Harley 4931, p. 23. The English translation is by a contemporary, John Reynolds (d. 1614).
10. Shapiro identified a 'nucleus'– Brooke, Donne, Hoskyns, Martin and Holland – judged according to the following criteria: long-standing friendships, the study of the law, membership of parliament and the writing of poetry; see 'Mermaid Club', 9–10. See Brioist's study of the connections among these men using the techniques of network analysis, 'Que de choses avons nous vues', 89–132. Both Philip Finkelpearl and Arthur Marotti discuss these companies of wits in relation to the Inns of Court and their chosen subjects, John Marston and John Donne: Finkelpearl, *John Marston of the Middle Temple: An Elizabethan Dramatist in his Social Setting* (Cambridge, MA: Harvard University Press, 1969); Marotti, *John Donne, Coterie Poet* (Madison, Wisconsin: University of Wisconsin Press, 1986).
11. On these Inns' confraternity, see George Buck, *The Third Universitie of England*, appended to John Stow, *The Annales, or Generall Chronicle of England* (London, 1615), p. 973.
12. J. A. Manning, ed., *The Memoirs of Sir Benjamin Rudyerd, Knt.* (London: Boone, 1841), p. 14.
13. Rebecca Weeks More, 'The Rewards of Virtue: Gentility in Early Modern England', unpublished Ph.D. thesis, Brown University (1998), pp. 189–92; T. V. Wilks, 'The Court Culture of Prince Henry and his Circle, 1603–1613', 2 vols., unpublished D.Phil. thesis, University of Oxford (1987), 1, pp. 11–17, 127–9.
14. Marotti, *Donne, Coterie Poet*; James Biester, *Rhetoric and Wit in Renaissance English Poetry* (Ithaca, NY: Cornell University Press, 1997), pp. 63–5, 83–5.
15. David Colclough has recently recovered Hoskyns as a popular scribal poet; see '"The Muses Recreation": John Hoskyns and the Manuscript Culture of the Seventeenth Century', *Huntington Library Quarterly* 61 (2000), 369–400. See also Baird Whitlock, *John Hoskyns, Serjeant-at-law* (Washington: University Press of America, 1982); David Norbrook, 'Rhetoric, Ideology and the Elizabethan World Picture', in Peter Mack, ed., *Renaissance Rhetoric* (Basingstoke: Macmillan, 1996), pp. 140–64. Martin has received very little attention; see Tom Cain, 'Donne and the Prince d'Amour', *John Donne Journal* 14 (1995), 83–111. On Brooke, see O'Callaghan, *Shepheards Nation*; James Doelman, 'Born with Teeth: Christopher Brooke's *The Ghost of Richard III*', *The Seventeenth Century* 14 (1999), 115–29; David Norbrook, *Poetry and Politics in the English Renaissance*, rev. edn (Oxford: Oxford University Press, 2002), pp. 185, 188–96, 211.

16. On humanist fraternities, see Eckhard Auberlen, *The Commonwealth of Wit: The Writer's Image and His Strategies of Self-Representation in Elizabethan Literature* (Tübingen: Narr, 1984), pp. 27–33.
17. Brioist, 'Que de choses avons nous vues', 92, 126–7.
18. Alan Cromartie, 'The Constitutionalist Revolution: The Transformation of Political culture in Early Stuart England', *Past and Present* 163 (1999), 76–85.
19. Brioist describes the wits as an 'aristocracy of intellect', 'Que de choses avons nous vues', 113. Biester equates wit predominantly with courtly sprezzatura, rather than humanist traditions of learned play, *Lyric Wonder*, pp. 75–6.
20. Edward Phillips, *The new world of English words* (London, 1658), sig. p4v. On forms of citizen sociability, see Withington, *Politics of the Commonwealth*, Chapter 5.
21. Edgar Hinchcliffe published a copy of this safe-conduct and an English translation in 'Thomae Coriati Testimonium', *Notes & Queries* n.s. 15 (1968), 370–5.
22. On this distinction, see Joshua Scodel, *Excess and the Mean in Early Modern English Literature* (Princeton: Princeton University Press, 2002), p. 202.
23. *The Civile Conversation of M. Steeven Guazzo*, books 1–3 trans. George Pettie (1581), book 4 trans. Bartholomew Young (1586), ed. Edward Sullivan, 2 vols. (London: Constable; New York: Alfred A. Knopf, 1925), II, pp. 123, 150, 215. See Richards's discussion of this conversational ideal as the basis for sociability in her *Rhetoric and Courtliness*, esp. Chapter 4.
24. B. Ann Tlusty, *Bacchus and Civic Order: The Culture of Drink in Early Modern Germany* (Charlottesville: University Press of Virginia, 2001), pp. 27–9; and Anna Bryson, *From Courtesy to Civility: Changing Codes of Conduct in Early Modern England* (Oxford: Clarendon Press, 1998), p. 146.
25. Clark, *British Clubs and Societies*, pp. 3, 8–9. Withington heavily qualifies this narrative, arguing that traditional communities do not disappear but participate in this process of transformation, *Politics of the Commonwealth*, pp. 125–7.
26. Norbert Elias, *The Civilizing Process: Sociogenetic and Psychogenetic Investigations*, trans. Edmund Jephcott (Oxford: Blackwell, 2000), pp. 369–74.
27. See Anna Bryson's critique of Elias in *From Courtesy to Civility*, Chapter 6.
28. See the discussion of social space in Pierre Bourdieu, *Distinction: A Social Critique of the Judgement of Taste*, trans. Richard Nice (London: Routledge & Kegan Paul, 1984), pp. 94–5.
29. See frontispiece, and Chapter 3, pp. 69–70.
30. Jürgen Habermas, *The Structural Transformation of the Public Sphere: An Inquiry into a Category of Bourgeois Society*, trans. Thomas Burger and Frederick Lawrence (Cambridge, MA: Massachusetts Institute of Technology, 1989), pp. 32–8; Steven Pincus, '"Coffee Politicians Does Create": Coffeehouses and Restoration Political Culture', *The Journal of Modern History* 67 (1995), 807–34; David Zaret, *Origins of Democratic Culture: Printing, Petitions, and the Public Sphere in Early-Modern England* (Princeton: Princeton University Press, 2000). For a critique of this emphasis on communicative rationality, see John L. Brooke, 'Reason and Passion in the Public Sphere: Habermas and the Cultural Historians', *Journal of Interdisciplinary History* 29 (1998), 43–67.

31. Desiderius Erasmus, *The Praise of Folly*, trans. Clarence Miller (New Haven: Yale University Press, 1979), p. 147.
32. Raymond A. Anselment, *'Betwixt Jest and Earnest': Marprelate, Milton, Marvell, Swift and the Decorum of Religious Ridicule* (Toronto: University of Toronto Press, 1979), pp. 3–4. See also Joanna Brizdale Lipking, 'Traditions of the Facetiae and Their Influence in Tudor England', unpublished Ph.D. thesis, Columbia University (1970), pp. 66–99, and George Luck, '*Vir Facetus*: A Renaissance Ideal', *Studies in Philology* 55 (1958), 114–20; Cicero, *De Oratore, Books I–II*, trans. E. W. Sutton and H. Rackham (Cambridge, MA: Harvard University Press, 1942), pp. 372–3, II.lviii.236; Quentin Skinner, 'Hobbes and the Classical Theory of Laughter', *Visions of Politics*, 3 vols. (Cambridge: Cambridge University Press, 2002), III, pp. 166–7.
33. Noel Malcolm, *The Origins of English Nonsense* (London: Harper Collins, 1997), pp. 4–5.
34. Thomas M. Greene, 'Ceremonial Play and Parody in the Renaissance', in Susan Zimmerman and Ronald F. E. Weissman, eds., *Urban Life in the Renaissance* (Newark: University of Delaware Press, 1989), pp. 284–7. On rituals of play, see Johan Huizinga, *Homo Ludens: A Study of the Play Element in Culture* (London: Temple Smith, 1970), pp. 33–46, 78–82. Huizinga's theorising of play is utopian and idealising, rather than historicised.
35. Victoria Kahn, *Rhetoric, Prudence, and Skepticism in the Renaissance* (Ithaca, NY: Cornell University Press, 1985), pp. 27, 47–54.
36. John D'Arms, 'The Roman *Convivium* and the Idea of Equality', in Oswyn Murray, ed., *Sympotica: A Symposium on the Symposion* (Oxford: Clarendon Press, 1990), pp. 312–19; Michel Jeanneret, *A Feast of Words: Banquets and Table Talk in the Renaissance*, trans. Jeremy Whiteley and Emma Hughes (Cambridge: Polity Press, 1991), pp. 28–32, 40–3, 97–102; Reid Barbour, *English Epicures and Stoics: Ancient Legacies in Early Stuart Culture* (Amherst: University of Massachusetts Press, 1998), p. 14.

1 GENTLEMAN LAWYERS AT THE INNS OF COURT

1. Shapiro, 'Mermaid Club', 10–11.
2. Richards, *Rhetoric and Courtliness*, p. 16; Phil Withington, 'Two Renaissances: Urban Political Culture in Post-Reformation England Reconsidered', *The Historical Journal* 44 (2001), 239–67.
3. J. H. Baker, *The Legal Profession and the Common Law: Historical Essays* (London: Hambledon Press, 1986), pp. 45–60.
4. Sir William Dugdale, *The History and Antiquities of the Four Inns of Court* (London, 1780), p. 102.
5. *The Diary of John Manningham of the Middle Temple, 1602–3*, ed. Robert Parker Sorlein (Hanover, New Hampshire: The University Press of New England, 1976), pp. 4, 43, 48, 70, 100, 120, 150, 187, 191–3, 219, 235, 246.
6. See Wilfred Prest on the Inns' essential 'clubbability', *The Inns of Court under Elizabeth and the Early Stuarts, 1590–1640* (London: Longman, 1972), p. 4.

7. Paul Raffield, *Images and Cultures of Law in Early Modern England* (Cambridge: Cambridge University Press, 2004), pp. 5, 44–54. See also C. W. Brooks, 'The Common Lawyers in England, c. 1558–1642', in Wilfred Prest, ed., *Lawyers in Early Modern Europe and America* (London: Croom Helm, 1981), p. 54.
8. Christopher Baker points out that the markedly sharper satire of these revels is a departure within the tradition, 'Ben Jonson and the Inns of Court: The Literary Milieu of *Every Man Out of His Humour*', unpublished Ph.D. thesis, University of North Carolina (1974), Chapter 4.
9. See Kahn, *Rhetoric, Prudence, and Skepticism*.
10. Greene, 'Ceremonial Play', pp. 283–4.
11. See Raffield's analysis of these revels and the civic utopia, *Images and Cultures of Law*, pp. 100–6.
12. Gerard Legh, *The Accedence of Armorie. Newly corrected and augmented* (London, 1612), pp. 216–17.
13. Raffield, *Images and Cultures of Law*, p. 58.
14. Edwin S. Ramage, *Urbanitas: Ancient Sophistication and Refinement* (Norman, Oklahoma: University of Oklahoma Press, 1973), pp. 55–6. On civic urbanity, see Cathy Shrank, 'Civil Tongues: Language, Law and Reformation', in Jennifer Richards, ed., *Early Modern Civil Discourses* (Basingstoke: Palgrave Macmillan, 2003), pp. 20–5; Withington, *Politics of the Commonwealth*, pp. 3–7.
15. Bryson, *From Courtesy to Civility*, pp. 149–50. See also Robert W. Weinpahl, *Music at the Inns of Court during the reigns of Elizabeth, James and Charles* (Ann Arbor, Michigan: University Microfilms International, 1979), pp. 8, 60–4, 79–80.
16. George Buck, *The Third Universitie of England*, appended to John Stow, *The Annales, or Generall Chronicle of England* (London, 1615), p. 968. See also J. P. Cooper, *Land, Men and Beliefs: Studies in Early Modern History*, ed. G. E. Aylmer and J. S. Morrill (London: Hambledon Press, 1983), p. 66. Brook concludes that although 88 per cent of those entering the Inns in this period took the title 'gentleman', they were more likely to be 'of bourgeois or plebeian stock' rather than 'sons of country gentlemen', 'Common Lawyers in England', p. 56.
17. *The Memoirs and Memorials of Sir Hugh Cholmley of Whitby, 1600–1657*, ed. Jack Binns (Woodbridge: Boydell and Brewer, 2000), p. 83.
18. Withington, 'Two Renaissances', 239–67.
19. 'John Hoskyns (1566–1638)', 'Richard Martin (1570–1618)', 'Christopher Brooke (c. 1570–1628)', History of Parliament Trust, London, 1604–29 section, unpublished articles. I am grateful to the History of Parliament Trust for allowing me to see these articles in draft.
20. R. C. Bald, *Donne, A Life* (Oxford: Clarendon Press, 1986), pp. 20–3, 74.
21. Cooper, *Land, Men and Beliefs*, p. 66; More, 'The Rewards of Virtue, p. 6; Raffield, *Images and Cultures of Law*, pp. 80–1.
22. Martin had been censured for riotous behaviour during the 1591 revels, J. B. Williamson, *The History of the Temple, London* (London: John Murray, 1924), pp. 213–14. Hoskyns was expelled from New College, Oxford in 1592 as the

Notes to pages 14–16 183

      result of a misdemeanour during his office as *terrae filius* (according to Anthony à Wood, Hoskyns was too 'bitterly satyrical'), Whitlock, *John Hoskyns*, pp. 79–82.
23. Finkelpearl, *John Marston of the Middle Temple*, pp. 46, 33–4.
24. *Gesta Grayorum 1688*, ed. W. W. Greg (Oxford: Oxford University Press, 1914), p. 2; John Davies, *Orchestra or a Poeme of Dauncing* (London, 1596), sig. A2r.
25. For a discussion of Hoskyns's Oxford career, see Whitlock, *John Hoskyns*, pp. 58–69; see also Warren Boutcher, 'Pilgrimage to Parnassus: Local Intellectual Traditions, Humanist Education, and the Cultural Geography of Sixteenth-Century England', in Niall Livingstone and Yun Lee Too, eds., *Pedagogy and Power: Rhetorics of Classical Learning* (Cambridge: Cambridge University Press, 1998)', pp. 134–45.
26. Quoted in D. S. Bland, 'Rhetoric and the Law Student in Sixteenth-Century England', *Studies in Philology* 54 (1957), 505. On rhetorical training at Inns, see Peter Mack, *Elizabethan Rhetoric: Theory and Practice* (Cambridge: Cambridge University Press, 2002), pp. 50, 58–61. See also Raffield, *Images and Cultures of Law*, pp. 23–6.
27. On James's entrance to London, see Graham Parry, *The Golden Age Restor'd: The Culture of the Stuart Court, 1603–42* (Manchester: Manchester University Press, 1981), pp. 1–21; on the 'parrhesiastic contract', see Michel Foucault, *Fearless Speech*, ed. Joseph Pearson (Los Angeles: Semiotext(e), 2001), pp. 32–3; on early modern *parrhesia*, see David Colclough, '*Parrhesia*: The Rhetoric of Free Speech in Early Modern England', *Rhetorica* 17 (1999), 177–210.
28. Martin, *A Speech Delivered to the Kings Most Excellent Majestie, at his Neere Approach to London, in the Name of the Sheriffs of London and Middlesex* (London, 1603), sig. A4r.
29. Hugh Holland, *Pancharis: The first Booke*, in J. Payne Collier, ed., *Illustrations of Old English Literature*, 3 vols. (London, 1866), II, p. 56.
30. Foucault, *Fearless Speech*, pp. 30–2.
31. These words are engraved around a memorial portrait of Martin; a copy of the text can be found in Aubrey, *Brief Lives*, II, p. 49; Foucault, *Fearless Speech*, pp. 37, 101–3.
32. Richard Ross, 'The Memorial Culture of Early Modern English Lawyers: Memory as Keyword, as Shelter, and Identity, 1560–1640', *Yale Journal of Law and the Humanities* 10 (1998), 250–9.
33. Holland, *Pancharis*, p. 56.
34. See Chapter 4, pp. 91–5, and David Colclough, '"Better Becoming a Senate of Venice"?: The "Addled Parliament" and Jacobean Debates on Freedom of Speech', in Stephen Clucas and Ros Davies, eds., *The Crisis of 1614 and The Addled Parliament: Literary and Historical Perspectives* (Aldershot: Ashgate, 2003), pp. 51–61.
35. Tucker Orbison, ed., *The Middle Temple Documents Relating to Chapman's 'The Memorable Masque'* (Oxford: Oxford University Press, 1983), pp. 3–4; *The Letters of John Chamberlain*, ed. N. E. McClure, 2 vols. (Philadelphia: the American Philosophical Society, 1939), I, p. 414.

36. Roy Strong, *Henry Prince of Wales and England's Lost Renaissance* (London: Thames and Hudson, 1986), pp. 175–9.
37. More, 'Rewards of Virtue', p. 167. Donne was rumoured to have sought the Company's secretaryship in early 1609, Bald, *Donne, A Life*, pp. 162, 435. Other investors connected with this group were Richard Connock, Sir Robert Cotton, Sir Lionel Cranfield, George Garrard, Sir Arthur Ingram, Sir Henry Neville, John Paulet, Sir Thomas Roe, Sir Henry Wotton; see Theodore Rabb, *Enterprise and Empire: Merchant Investment in the Expansion of England, 1575–1630* (Cambridge, MA: Harvard University Press, 1967).
38. More, 'Rewards of Virtue', pp. 153–6, 183–4, 188–9.
39. George Chapman, *The Memorable Maske of the two Honorable Houses or Inns of Court, the Middle Temple, and Lyncolns Inne*, in *The Plays of George Chapman: the Comedies*, ed. Allan Holaday (Urbana, Chicago: University of Illinois Press, 1970), pp. 565–7. Subsequent references will be to this edition. On the progress, see Jerzy Limon, *The Masque of Stuart Culture* (Newark: University of Delaware Press; Toronto: Associated University Presses, 1990), pp. 142–55.
40. On the masque in general, see Stephen Orgel, *The Illusion of Power: Political Theater in the English Renaissance* (Berkeley: University of California Press, 1975), pp. 37–58.
41. Limon, *Masque of Stuart Culture*, pp. 145–6, 148–9.
42. Chamberlain, *Letters*, I, p. 425.
43. *Proceedings in Parliament, 1610*, ed. Elizabeth Read Foster, 2 vols. (New Haven: Yale University Press, 1966), II, p. 344.
44. On the revels, see Raffield, *Images and Cultures of Law*, Chapter 3, esp. pp. 92–3, and 264–5. On Inns of Court drama and structures of counsel, see Jessica Winston, 'Expanding the Political Nation: *Gorboduc* at the Inns of Court and Succession Revisited', *Early Theatre* 8 (2005), 11–34; Dermot Cavanagh, *Language and Politics in the Sixteenth-Century History Play* (Basingstoke: Palgrave Macmillan, 2003), pp. 36–57; Kevin Dunn, 'Representing Counsel: *Gorboduc* and the Elizabethan Privy Council', *English Literary Renaissance* 33 (2003), 279–308.
45. Andrew Fitzmaurice discusses the shift in colonial discourse from 1609 as it co-opts civic humanist notions of the ideal commonwealth, *Humanism and America: An Intellectual History of English Colonisation, 1500–1625* (Cambridge: Cambridge University Press, 2003), pp. 59–87.
46. Pierre Bourdieu, *Outline of a Theory of Practice*, trans. Richard Nice (Cambridge: Cambridge University Press, 1977), pp. 38–9, *Distinction*, pp. 23, 66.
47. Harold Love, *Scribal Publication in Seventeenth-Century England* (Oxford: Clarendon Press, 1993), p. 219; Marotti, *Donne, Coterie Poet*, pp. 10–12.
48. Aubrey, *Brief Lives*, II, p. 49.
49. Michel Montaigne, 'Of three commerces or societies', *The Essayes, or Morall, Politike and Millitarie Discourses*, trans. John Florio (London, 1603), pp. 495–6. Judith Scherer Herz, 'Of Circles, Friendship, and the Imperatives of Literary History', in Claude Summers and Ted-Larry Pebworth, eds., *Literary Circles*

        and Cultural Communities in Renaissance England (Columbia: University of Missouri Press, 2000), p. 13.
50. Raffield, *Images and Cultures of Law*, pp. 73, 81–2. Richards discusses *amicitia* at the Inns from the mid to late sixteenth century, *Rhetoric and Courtliness*, pp. 139–48.
51. Cicero, *De Amicitia*, trans. W. A. Falconer (Cambridge, MA: Harvard University Press, 1923), xii.40–3, xv.52–3, xvii.63–4, xxiv.89–90. Horst Hutter, *Politics as Friendship: The Origins of Classical Notions of Politics in the Theory and Practice of Friendship* (Waterloo, Ontario: Wilfred Laurier University Press, 1978), pp. 133–64.
52. Christopher probably attended Cambridge University, since he claimed to have known the Bishop of Lincoln there; Bald suggests that 'I. L.' is John Legard (*Donne, A Life*, p. 74), while John Carey argues for a relative of Edward Loftus, *John Donne*, ed. Carey (Oxford: Oxford University Press, 1990), p. 420. Subsequent references to Donne's poetry will be from this edition. Bald found no evidence to substantiate Walton's claim that Donne transferred to Cambridge from Hart Hall, Oxford, *Donne, A Life*, pp. 46–7.
53. Margaret Ezell, *Social Authorship and the Advent of Print* (Baltimore: Johns Hopkins University Press, 1999), pp. 39–40.
54. See Christopher Boswell, 'The Culture and Rhetoric of the Answer-Poem, 1485–1625', unpublished Ph.D. thesis, University of Leeds (2003), pp. 207–13.
55. See Elias on an ethos of moderation and the dispassionate ideal, *Civilizing Process*, pp. 372–4.
56. See David Cunnington, 'The Profession of Friendship in Donne's Amatory Verse Letters', in David Colclough, ed., *John Donne's Professional Lives* (Woodbridge: Boydell and Brewer, 2003), pp. 108–9. Cunnington's 'civil dishonesty' is a variant on the 'honest lies' described by Richards in *Rhetoric and Courtliness* (pp. 28–31) since it manages affective outbursts within forms of civil conversation.
57. Bald, *Donne, A Life*, p. 43; Ted-Larry Pebworth and Claude J. Summers, '"Thus friends absent speake": the Exchange of Verse Letters between John Donne and Henry Wotton', *Modern Philology* 81 (1984), 361–77.
58. Paul E. J. Hammer, *The Polarisation of Elizabethan Politics: The Political Career of Robert Devereux, Second Earl of Essex, 1585–97* (Cambridge: Cambridge University Press, 1999), pp. 220, 265–8.
59. Ibid., pp. 222–4; on Essex and honour, see also Richard McCoy, *Rites of Knighthood: The Literature and Politics of Elizabethan Chivalry* (Berkeley: University of California Press, 1989), pp. 79–102.
60. See Marotti's reading of these poems, *Donne, Coterie Poet*, pp. 114–15.
61. Hammer, *Polarisation of Elizabethan Politics*, pp. 9, 389.
62. Malcolm Smuts, 'Court-Centred Politics and the Uses of Roman Historians, c. 1590–1630', in Peter Lake and Kevin Sharpe, eds., *Culture and Politics in Early Stuart England* (Basingstoke: Macmillan, 1994), pp. 25–30.
63. Greene, 'Ceremonial Play', pp. 284–7.

64. On *Utopia* and *lusus*, see Peter R. Allen, '*Utopia* and European Humanism: the Function of the Prefatory Letters and Verses', *Studies in the Renaissance* 10 (1963), 100–7, and Douglas Duncan, *Ben Jonson and the Lucianic Tradition* (Cambridge: Cambridge University Press, 1979), pp. 66–7. I will follow Duncan's usage of the term *lusus* to refer specifically to the concept of learned play as opposed to play (*ludus*) more generally; see p. 24. On the revels and the tradition of learned folly, see W. R. Elton, *Shakespeare's 'Troilus and Cressida' and the Inns of Court Revels* (Aldershot: Ashgate, 2000), Chapter 1.
65. John Elliot, 'Drama', in T. H. Aston, gen. ed., *The History of the University of Oxford*, 8 vols. (Oxford: Clarendon Press, 1984–97), IV, pp. 641–58; Lawrence Clopper, *Drama, Play, and Game: English Festive Culture in the Medieval and Early Modern Period* (Chicago: University of Chicago Press, 2001), pp. 59–61; Bland, 'Rhetoric and the Law Student', 498–508; Alessandro Arcangeli, *Recreation in the Renaissance: Attitudes towards Leisure and Pastimes in European Culture, c. 1425–1675* (Basingstoke: Palgrave Macmillan, 2003), Chapters 2 and 3; Peter Burke, 'The Invention of Leisure in Early Modern Europe', *Past and Present* 146 (1995), 136–50.
66. John Brinsley, *Ludus Literarius (1612)* (Menston: Scolar Press, 1968), pp. 300–1.
67. Clopper, *Drama, Play and Game*, pp. 109, 125. On rituals of play, see Huizinga, *Homo Ludens*, pp. 33–46, 78–82.
68. Intellectual game-playing prepared individuals for public life, and so does not maintain the Kantian 'disinterestedness' that Bourdieu assigns to the academic and cultural capital of a later aesthetic disposition, *Distinction*, pp. 23, 41, 53–6.
69. Ben Jonson, *Every Man Out of His Humour*, ed. Helen Ostovich (Manchester: Manchester University Press, 2001), p. 226 (3.1.168ff); see also p. 35. Francis Beaumont's parody of pedagogic rhetoric in his 'Grammar Lecture', performed at the Inner Temple revels, owes much to Hoskyns; see Mark Eccles, 'Francis Beaumont's *Grammar Lecture*', *Review of English Studies* 16 (1940), 402–14.
70. *Directions for Speech and Style*, in *The Life, Letters and Writings of John Hoskyns*, ed. Louise Osborn (New Haven: Yale University Press, 1937), p. 165.
71. *Le Prince d'Amour, or the Prince of Love* (London, 1660), p. 38.
72. On Hoskyns and the development of early English nonsense, see Malcolm, *Origins of English Nonsense*.
73. David Colclough, '"Of the alleadging of authors": the Construction and Reception of Textual Authority in English Prose, c. 1600–1630. With Special Reference to the Writings of Francis Bacon, John Hoskyns, and John Donne', unpublished D.Phil. thesis, Oxford (1996), pp. 100–1.
74. Kenneth Burke, *A Rhetoric of Motives* (New York: Prentice Hall, 1950), pp. 269–71. Skinner briefly discusses the laughter of the unexpected associated with nonsense, 'Hobbes and the Classical Theory of Laughter', pp. 161–2.
75. Colclough, 'Of the alleadging of authors', p. 101.
76. Legh, *Accedence of Armory*, p. 215.
77. On the Cult of Elizabeth, see Philippa Berry, *Of Chastity and Power: Elizabethan Literature and the Unmarried Queen* (London: Routledge, 1989).

78. On these revels' chivalric burlesque, see Elton, *Troilus and Cressida*, p. 40, n. 3.
79. On libertinism and anti-civility, see Bryson, *From Courtesy to Civility*, pp. 99, 236–7, 245. Many participating in these revels were sympathetic to Essex, a potential rival Prince of Love to Elizabeth. Essex's code of aristocratic independence could and did pose political problems; see McCoy, *Rites of Knighthood*, pp. 12–14, 79–102.
80. Finkelpearl, *John Marston of the Middle Temple*, pp. 56–8; Baker, 'Jonson and the Inns of Court', Chapter 4.
81. Ramage, *Urbanitas*, pp. 65–7.
82. Bryson, *Courtesy to Civility*, p. 130.
83. On Donne's peripatetic satire, see Karen Newman, 'Walking Capitals: Donne's First Satyre', in Henry S. Turner, ed., *The Culture of Capital: Properties, Cities, Knowledge in Early Modern England* (London: Routledge, 2002), pp. 203–21.
84. Quintilian, *Institutio Oratoria*, trans. Donald A. Russell (Cambridge, MA: Harvard University Press, 2001), pp. 56–7, 1.pr.10.
85. *OED*; see 1 and 2 (a).
86. Everard Guilpin, *Skialetheia* (London, 1598), sig. D5r.
87. On 'streetness' and the metropolis, see Newman, 'Walking Capitals', pp. 203–21; Cyndia Wall, *Literary and Cultural Spaces of Restoration London* (Cambridge: Cambridge University Press, 1998), pp. 115–24.
88. Bryson, *Courtesy to Civility*, pp. 129–39.
89. Vanessa Harding, 'London, Change and Exchange', *Culture of Capital*, pp. 130–2.
90. See Ronald Weissman on the cryptic, playful forms occasioned by social uncertainty, 'The Importance of Being Ambiguous: Social Relations, Individualism, and Identity in Renaissance Florence', *Urban Life*, pp. 271–2.
91. *Every Man Out*, p. 33.
92. *An Elizabethan in 1582: The Diary of Richard Madox, Fellow of All Souls*, ed. Elizabeth Story Donno (London: The Hakluyt Society, 1976), pp. 73, 5.
93. *Diary of Richard Madox*, p. 71.
94. Oswyn Murray, 'The Affair of the Mysteries: Democracy and the Drinking Group', *Sympotica*, p. 150.
95. John Heath, *House of Correction: or, Certayne Satyricall Epigrams* (London, 1618), sig. A3r.
96. Cyndia Susan Clegg, *Press Censorship in Elizabethan England* (Cambridge: Cambridge University Press, 1997), pp. 198–215. Many of these libels are published in Andrew McRae and Alastair Bellany, eds., *Early Stuart Libels: an edition of poetry from manuscript sources*, EMLS Text Series 1 (2005), Section A: 'Essex, Ralegh and Late Elizabethan Politics', http://purl.oclc.org/emls/texts/libels/ See also Pauline Croft, 'The Reputation of Robert Cecil: Libels, Political Opinion and Popular Awareness in the Early Seventeenth Century', *Transactions of the Royal Historical Society* 1 (1991), 43–69.
97. Cited in Matthew Steggle, *Wars of the Theatres: The Poetics of Personation in the Age of Jonson* (Victoria, BC: University of Victoria, 1998), p. 18. See also

Alexandra Halasz, *The Marketplace of Print: Pamphlets and the Public Sphere in Early Modern England* (Cambridge: Cambridge University Press, 1997), pp. 85–8.
98. Finkelpearl, *John Marston of the Middle Temple*, p. 55.
99. James L. Sanderson, 'Epigrammes P[er] B[enjamin] R[udyerd] and some more "Stolen Feathers" of Henry Parrot', *Review of English Studies* 17 (1966), 252–4.
100. Rudyerd, *Memoirs*, pp. 11, 16, 17.
101. BL, Add. MS 25303, fol. 184v, see also Bod., MS Malone 16, fols. 73v–74r. Anthony Arlidge, *Shakespeare and the Prince of Love: the Feast of Misrule in the Middle Temple* (London: Giles de la Mare, 2000), p. 84. According to Aubrey, when Hoskyns was in the Tower in 1614–15 along with Raleigh, he was 'Sir Walter's *Aristarchus*, to review and polish stile', *Brief Lives*, I, p. 418.
102. 'Essex, Ralegh and Late Elizabethan Politics', *Early Stuart Libels*, Section A; Steven May, *The Elizabethan Courtier Poets: The Poems and their Contexts* (Columbia, Missouri: University of Missouri Press, 1991), pp. 119–25; Boswell, 'Culture and Rhetoric of the Answer-Poem', pp. 36–8.
103. Manningham, *Diary*, p. 235.
104. Norbrook discusses these epigrams in 'Rhetoric, Ideology and the Elizabethan World Picture', pp. 150–1. On embodied satire and stigmatising libels, see Douglas Bruster, 'The Structural Transformation of Print in Late Elizabethan England', in Arthur Marotti and Michael D. Bristol, eds., *Print, Manuscript and Performance* (Columbus: Ohio State University Press, 2000), pp. 53–4; and Andrew McRae, *Literature, Satire and the Early Stuart State* (Cambridge: Cambridge University Press, 2004), pp. 44–50, 58–75.
105. *The Works of John Davies*, ed. A. B. Grosart, 3 vols. (1869), I, p. 313.
106. Possibly refers to Davies' work on *Nosce Teipsum* first published in 1599.
107. Colclough, '*Parrhesia*', 182, 184, 195–6.
108. Boswell, 'Culture and Rhetoric of the Answer-Poem', pp. 32–44.
109. Anna Nardo discusses play and conflict in *The Ludic Self in Seventeenth-Century English Literature* (Albany, NY: State University of New York Press, 1991), p. 3.

2 BEN JONSON, THE LAWYERS AND THE WITS

1. Aubrey, *Brief Lives*, I, p. 11. Mark Eccles dates this building work to 1588, although Jonson's stepfather, Robert Brett, was employed on repair work at Lincoln's Inn in 1590, 1591, and between 1600 and 1610, 'Jonson and Marriage', *Review of English Studies* 12 (1936), 257–72.
2. Ben Jonson, *Timber, or, Discoveries* in *Ben Jonson*, ed. Ian Donaldson (Oxford: Oxford University Press, 1985), p. 549, lines 1045–8. Subsequent references to Jonson's poetry will be to this edition.
3. His fellow pupils at Westminster School were Holland, also a close friend of Martin, and Cotton, who went on to the Middle Temple after Cambridge. Either through these men, or independently, Jonson became acquainted with the society at Middle Temple and Lincoln's Inn. For details of these associations,

see Kevin Sharpe, *Sir Robert Cotton 1586–1631: History and Politics in Early Modern England* (Oxford: Oxford University Press, 1979), pp. 196–221; Bald, *Donne: A Life*; Whitlock, *John Hoskyns*; and Cain, 'Donne and the Prince D'Amour', 83–111.
4. Tom Cain, '"Satyres, That Girdle and Fart at the Time": *Poetaster* and the Essex Rebellion', in Julie Sanders, with Kate Chedgzoy and Susan Wiseman, eds., *Refashioning Ben Jonson: Gender, Politics and the Jonsonian Canon* (Basingstoke and London: Palgrave Macmillan, 1998), pp. 48–70.
5. Baker, 'Jonson and the Inns of Court', pp. 155–216.
6. 'Dedication to the Folio', *Every Man Out*, pp. 383–4. Ostovich, citing Finkelpearl (*John Marston of the Middle Temple*, pp. 79–80), gives a Bakhtinian reading of liberty.
7. Markku Peltonen, *Classical Humanism and Republicanism in English Political Thought, 1570–1640* (Cambridge: Cambridge University Press, 1995), p. 63.
8. See Colclough on frank speaking and counsel, '*Parrhesia*', 210.
9. *The Case is Alter'd*, in *Works of Ben Jonson*, ed. C. H. Herford, Percy Simpson and Evelyn Simpson, 11 vols. (Oxford: Clarendon Press, 1925–52), III, p. 136, 2.7.42–3, 56–8.
10. Thomas Dekker, *Satiro-mastix or the untrussing of the Humorous Poet* (1602), *The Dramatic Works of Thomas Dekker*, ed. Fredson Bowers, 4 vols. (Cambridge: Cambridge University Press, 1970), I, p. 309.
11. Raffield, *Images and Cultures of Law*, p. 37. Sir Philip Sidney, *A Defence of Poetry*, in *Miscellaneous Prose of Sir Philip Sidney*, ed. Katherine Duncan-Jones and Jan Van Dorsten (Oxford: Clarendon Press, 1973), p. 113. See Raffield's discussion of this passage, *Images and Culture of Law*, p. 39.
12. Skinner, 'Hobbes and the Classical Theory of Laughter', pp. 145–7, 165.
13. Sidney, *Defense of Poesy*, p. 116.
14. Cicero, *De Oratore, Books I–II*, II.58.236.
15. Anselment argues the parameters of serious laughter are only set in the eighteenth century in *Betwixt Jest and Earnest*, pp. 3–4.
16. Cicero, *The Speeches: Pro Caelio, De Provinciis Consularibus, Pro Balbo*, trans. R. Gardner (Cambridge, MA: Harvard University Press, 1958), pp. 510–11. See Quintilian, *Institutio Oratoria, Books 6–8*, p. 65, iv.3.1–3.
17. Katherine A. Geffcken, *Comedy in the Pro Caelio* (Leiden: E. J. Brill, 1973), pp. 9–10.
18. Ben Jonson, *Catiline*, ed. W. F. Bolton and Jane F. Gardner (London: Edward Arnold, 1973), 4.2.435; for Cicero and libels, see 5.4.249–64.
19. Jonson draws on *Pro Caelio* at 1.1.131 and 4.2.70–3. On Cicero's rhetoric, see Richard Dutton, '"What Ministers Men Must, For Practice, Use": Ben Jonson's Cicero', *English Studies* 59 (1978), 324–35.
20. Katharine Eisaman Maus, *Ben Jonson and the Roman Frame of Mind* (Princeton: Princeton University Press, 1984), pp. 30–1.
21. Steggle, *Wars of the Theatres*, p. 24.
22. On this distinction, see Chapter 1, pp. 27–9 and this Chapter, pp. 45–9; Ramage, *Urbanitas*, pp. 65–7; Mary A. Grant, *The Ancient Rhetorical Theories*

of the Laughable: The Greek Rhetoricians and Cicero, University of Wisconsin Studies in Language and Literature, 21 (Madison, Wisconsin, 1924), pp. 91–5.
23. See also, *Case is Alter'd*, 2.7.76–82.
24. For further discussion of the association of the buffoon with the *convivium*, see Chapter 3, pp. 73–8.
25. See the discussion of Erasmus and serious laughter in the Introduction, p. 7.
26. On this miscellany, see Katherine Duncan-Jones, '"Preserved Dainties": Late Elizabethan Poems by Sir Robert Cecil and the Earl of Clanricarde', *Bodleian Library Record* 14 (1992), 136–44.
27. See also Cain's discussion of the association between *Poetaster*, libel and Essex, in his 'Satyres, That Girde', pp. 48–70.
28. See Steggle, *Wars of the Theatres*, 18–21; James Bednarz, 'Representing Jonson: *Histriomastix* and the Origin of the Poets' War', *Huntington Library Quarterly* 54 (1991), 1–30.
29. Halascz, *Marketplace of Print*, pp. 85–8.
30. Foucault, *Fearless Speech*, pp. 32–3.
31. Cain, 'Satyres, That Girde', pp. 49–53.
32. BL, MS Harley 1581, fol. 226r; see Chapter 7, pp. 155–6.
33. On the range of *parrhesia* as a rhetorical figure, see Colcough, '*Parrhesia*', 177–212.
34. Steggle, *Wars of the Theatres*, p. 36.
35. On habitus, see Bourdieu, *Outline of a Theory*, pp. 72–95; *Distinction*, pp. 94–5, 110–12.
36. Harding, 'London, Change and Exchange', pp. 129–32.
37. On *Epicoene* and 'the emergent West End society', see Butler, 'Sir Francis Stewart', 114–15.
38. Cicero, *Letters to Friends*, trans. D. R. Shackleton Bailey, 3 vols. (Cambridge, MA: Harvard University Press, 2001), II, pp. 452–3, Letter 267.2. Ramage, *Urbanitas*, pp. 22–5, 54–67.
39. On urbanity in Jonson, see P. K. Ayers, 'Dreams of the City: The Urban and the Urbane in Jonson's *Epicoene*', *Philological Quarterly* 66 (1987), 73–86.
40. Elias, *Civilizing Process*, pp. 188–90, 367–9; Roger Chartier, *Cultural History: Between Practices and Representations*, trans. Lydia G. Cochrane (Cambridge: Polity Press, 1988), pp. 73–89.
41. Bryson, *From Courtesy*, 132–7.
42. On the continuity between on-stage and 'off-stage' action, see Sean McEvoy, '"Hieronomo's Old Cloak": Theatricality and Representation in Jonson's Middle Comedies', *Ben Jonson Journal* 11 (2004), 67–87. On 'staged parties' in Jonson, see also Jonathan Haynes, *The Social Relations of Jonson's Theater* (Cambridge: Cambridge University Press, 1992), pp. 46–64.
43. Haynes, *Social Relations of Jonson's Theater*, p. 10.
44. Ben Jonson, *Epicoene, or the Silent Woman*, ed. R. V. Holdsworth (London: Ernest Benn, 1979), p. 13, 1.1.38–9.

45. Lorna Hutson, 'Civility and Virility in Ben Jonson', *Representations* 78 (2002), 3, 8, 17.
46. On the Ladies Collegiate as an 'alternative commonwealth of women', see Julie Sanders, *Ben Jonson's Theatrical Republics* (Basingstoke: Macmillan, 1998), pp. 50–67.
47. Butler suggests this place of judgement is offered to the dedicatee, Sir Francis Stewart; see 'Sir Francis Stewart', pp. 115–16.
48. *Bartholomew Fair*, ed. Suzanne Gossett (Manchester: Manchester University Press, 2000), pp. 45–6, 1.1.34–42.
49. See Cedric Brown, 'Sons of Beer and Sons of Ben: Drink as a Social Marker in Seventeenth-Century England', in Adam Smyth, ed., *A Pleasing Sinne: Drink and Conviviality in Seventeenth-Century England* (Woodbridge: Boydell and Brewer, 2004), pp. 18–20.
50. Withington, *Politics of the Commonwealth*, pp. 60–2.
51. Stanley Fish, 'Authors-Readers: Jonson's Community of the Same', in Stephen Greenblatt, ed., *Representing the Renaissance* (Berkeley: University of California, 1988), pp. 231–63.
52. Duncan, *Jonson and the Lucianic Tradition*, esp. pp. 127–8.
53. Arcangeli, *Recreation in the Renaissance*, Chapter 3. On jesting and recreation, see Luck, 'Vir Facetus', 114–20; Lipking, 'Traditions of the Facetiae', pp. 22–31; Chris Holcomb, *Mirth Making: The Rhetorical Discourse on Jesting in Early Modern England* (Columbia, SC: University of South Carolina Press), pp. 155–8.
54. Burke, 'Invention of Leisure', 136–50; Arcangeli, *Recreation in the Renaissance*, I, 118–27.
55. John Harington, 'A Treatise on Playe' (c. 1597), in *Nugae Antiquae*, ed. Thomas Park, selected by Henry Harington, 2 vols. (London, 1804), I, pp. 188, 200.
56. *Ben Jonson*, ed. Herford, Simpson and Simpson, IV, pp. 110–14, 4.3.81–200.
57. Dekker claimed that it was 'missliked' by the court in his *Satiromastix*, 5.3.324.
58. On this metropolitan phenomenon, see Fisher, 'Development of London', pp. 46–7; Harding, 'London, Change', pp. 131–2.
59. See Elias, *Civilizing Process*, pp. 367–9.
60. Arcangeli, *Recreation in the Renaissance*, pp. 14–6.
61. Ibid., p. 118.
62. Clopper, *Drama, Play, and Game*, pp. 12–31.
63. David Wiles, *Shakespeare's Clown: Actor and Text in the Elizabethan Playhouse* (Cambridge: Cambridge University Press, 1987), pp. 14–20. Max W. Thomas concentrates on the commercialisation of entertainment; see 'Kemp's *Nine Daies Wonder*: Dancing Carnival into the Market', *PMLA* 107 (1992), 511–23; Halasz notes that the popular entertainer traverses 'alehouse and court, ordinary people and powerful ones', '"So beloved that men use his picture for their signs": Richard Tarlton and the Uses of Sixteenth-Century Celebrity', *Shakespeare Studies* 23 (1995), 31–2.

64. W. H. Grattan Flood, 'Fennor and Daborne at Youghal in 1618', *Modern Language Review* 20 (1925), 321–2. On medieval travelling entertainers, see Clopper, *Drama, Play, and Game*, pp. 27–31.
65. See Chapter 5, pp. 110–13.
66. Duncan, *Lucianic Tradition*, pp. 44–50.
67. Bruce Boehrer, *The Fury of Men's Gullets: Ben Jonson and the Digestive Canal* (Philadelphia: University of Pennsylvania Press, 1997), p. 192.
68. Crudity was not necessarily a low form in class terms. Francis Willughby recorded a parlour game played in the seventeenth century, the 'Selling of Bargaines', in his 'Book of Games', which involves a series of requests, questions and responses. The first, for example, expresses a wish that 'hee had as manie dogs as there are starres', to which his fellow responds (thinking the request honest) by asking 'what hee would doe with them', and the first 'Sels him a Bargaine' by replying that he would 'Hold up their Teales [tails] while you Kisse their Arses'. The aim is to cap each other's lines by selling the most bargains, and 'All bargaines are either obscene or nastie', *Francis Willughby's Book of Games: A Seventeenth-Century Treatise on Sports, Games and Pastimes*, ed. David Cram, Jeffrey Forgeng and Dorothy Johnson (Aldershot: Ashgate, 2003), pp. 45–6, 198.
69. *Coryats Crudities*, sig. e6r.
70. On the form of the disputation, see Mack, *Elizabethan Rhetoric*, pp. 58–9.
71. Catherine Connors, 'Imperial Space and Time: The Literature of Leisure', in Oliver Taplin, ed., *Literature in the Greek and Roman Worlds: A New Perspective* (Oxford: Oxford University Press, 2000), pp. 495, 508.
72. *OED*, 2.
73. On his use of low forms, see J. G. Nicholls, *The Poetry of Ben Jonson* (London: Routledge & Kegan Paul, 1969), p. 108.
74. On this poem, see Andrew McRae, '"On the Famous Voyage": Ben Jonson and Civic Space', in Andrew Gordon and Bernhard Klein, eds., *Literature, Mapping, and the Politics of Space in Early Modern Britain* (Cambridge: Cambridge University Press, 2001), pp. 181–203; Boehrer, *Fury of Men's Gullets*, pp. 161–7.
75. *The Sculler, rowing from the Tiber to the Thames* (London, 1612), sig. A2v.
76. See, for example, Halasz, *Marketplace of Print*, pp. 191–6.
77. Mikhail Bakhtin recognises the currency of low literary genres and theories of laughter among the educated classes in the Renaissance, rather than simply ascribing them to the popular marketplace, *Rabelais and His World*, trans. Hélène Iswolsky (Bloomington: Indiana University Press, 1984); see, for example, Chapter 1, 'Rabelais in the History of Laughter', pp. 58–107.
78. See Katharine Craik, 'Reading *Coryats Crudities*', *Studies in English Literature, 1500–1900* 44 (2004), 79–84.
79. Bruster, 'Structural Transformation of Print', p. 75.
80. Katharine Craik, 'John Taylor's Pot-Poetry', *The Seventeenth Century*, 20(2005), 185–203.
81. *Discoveries*, lines 629–31. Craik discusses this passage in 'John Taylor', 186.

82. See McRae on Jonson's ambivalence towards popular entertainment, 'The Famous Voyage', pp. 197–8.
83. Richmond Barbour, 'Jonson and the Motives of Print', *Criticism* 40 (1998), 499–528; see also Marjorie Swann, *Curiosities and Texts: The Culture of Collecting in Early Modern England* (Philadelphia: University of Pennsylvania Press, 2001), pp. 158–9.

3 TAVERNS AND TABLE TALK

1. The richest account of this tradition in the Renaissance is Jeanneret, *A Feast of Words*.
2. Peter Goodrich, 'Eating Law: Commons, Common Land, Common Law', *Journal of Legal History* 12 (1991), 249–55; see also Raffield, *Images and Cultures of the Law*, pp. 9–10, 16–20, 87.
3. Jeanneret, *Feast of Words*, pp. 28–30. See Elias on *civilité* and changes in rituals of eating together, *Civilizing Process*, pp. 49–109.
4. Plutarch, *Moralia*, trans. Paul Clement and Herbert Hoffleit, 16 vols. (Cambridge, MA: Harvard University Press, 1969), VIII, pp. 6–7, 1.612.
5. *Civile Conversation*, II, pp. 214–15.
6. Cathy Shrank discusses Thomas Starkey's use of the term 'commyning', which encompasses table talk, in his *Dialogue between Pole and Lupset*, and refreshes and strengthens the commonwealth, '"The commyning of al such vertues": Sixteenth-Century Dialogue and the Commonweal', unpublished paper given at the RSA conference, Cambridge, April 2005.
7. *Gesta Grayorum*, pp. 29–30.
8. Thomas Dekker, *The Gull's Hornbook*, ed. R. B. McKerrow (New York: AMS Press, 1971), p. 57.
9. Haynes, *Social Relations of Jonson's Theatre*, pp. 13–14. See also Alison Findlay, 'Theatres of Truth: Drinking and Drama in Early Modern England', in James Nicholls and Susan Owen, eds., *A Babel of Bottles: Drinkers and Drinking Places in Literature* (Sheffield: Sheffield Academic Press, 2000), pp. 21–39.
10. Stephen Gosson, *The Schoole of Abuse* (London, 1579), p. 23; George Gascoigne, *Glass of Government* (London, 1573), prologue, sig. Aiiiv.
11. Peter Clark, *The English Alehouse: A Social History, 1200–1830* (London: Longman, 1982), p. 2. Shrank discusses a formal dialogue set in an inn, *News from the North* (1579), that employs a notion of community based on the principle of debate, 'Commyning of al such vertues'.
12. Clark, *English Alehouse*, pp. 5–15; Judith Hunter, 'Legislation, Royal Proclamations and other National Directives Affecting Inns, Taverns, Alehouses, Brandy Shops and Punch Houses, 1552 to 1757', unpublished Ph.D. thesis, University of Reading (1994), pp. 10–19, 117.
13. George Wilkins, *Miseries of Enforced Marriage* (London, 1607), sigs. E2r, E3r. For further discussion of the Mitre and Mermaid as a *topos*, see my 'Tavern Societies, the Inns of Court, and the Culture of Conviviality', *A Pleasing Sinne*, pp. 37–51.

14. Tlusty, *Bacchus and Civic Order*, p. 91. Elias, *Civilizing Process*, pp. 369–74.
15. For further discussion of these texts, see my 'Tavern Societies', pp. 43–6.
16. *The Art of Drinking. Three Books by the Author Vincentius Obsopoeus the German*, trans. Helen F. Simpson, in E. M. Jellinek, 'A Specimen of the Sixteenth-Century German Drink Literature – Obsopoeus's *Art of Drinking*', *Quarterly Journal of Studies on Alcohol* 5 (1944–5), 666–72.
17. See also Markku Peltonen's discussion of civil conversation and lying in relation to duelling, in 'Francis Bacon, the Earl of Northampton, and the Jacobean anti-duelling campaign', *Historical Journal* 44 (2001), 4.
18. Clark, *British Clubs and Societies*, p. 22; Tlusty, *Bacchus and Civic Order*, p. 115.
19. *Art of Drinking*, p. 663.
20. *Feast of Words*, p. 98.
21. Oswyn Murray, 'Sympotic History', and Ezio Pellizer, 'Outlines of a Morphology of Sympotic Entertainment', *Sympotica*, pp. 5, 179, 182–3.
22. It could be Coryate's witty conflation of Cyrenaic with Sireniacal, the adjectival form of 'siren' in current usage, and therefore punning on Mermaid – Coryate made a habit of fantastical linguistic compounds. On the Cyrenaics, see Voula Tsouna, *The Epistemology of the Cirenaic School* (Cambridge: Cambridge University Press, 1998). Aristippus was characterised negatively in Richard Edwards's *Damon and Pythias*, performed at Lincoln's Inn in 1565; see *The Works of Richard Edwards: Politics, Poetry and Performance in Sixteenth-Century England*, ed. Ros King (Manchester: Manchester University Press, 2001), pp. 57–8.
23. Thomas Randolph, *The Drinking Academy*, ed. Samuel A. Tannenbaum and Hyder E. Rollins (Cambridge, MA: Harvard University Press, 1930), pp. xii–xiii.
24. Scodel, *Excess and the Mean*, p. 201.
25. Stella Achilleos, 'The *Anacreontea* and a Tradition of Refined Male Sociability', *Pleasing Sinne*, pp. 24–6.
26. George Puttenham, *The Arte of English Poesie. Contrived into three Bookes (1589)*, ed. Edward Arber (London: Murray & Son, 1869), pp. 68–9.
27. *Ben Jonson*, ed. Herford, Simpson and Simpson, III, 2.4.94–5.
28. Bruce Smith, *The Acoustic World of Early Modern England* (Chicago: University of Chicago Press, 1999), pp. 21–5.
29. Christopher Marsh, 'The Sound of Print in Early Modern England: The Broadside Ballad as Song', in Julia Crick and Alexandra Walsham, eds., *The Uses of Script and Print, 1300–1700* (Cambridge: Cambridge University Press, 2004), p. 175.
30. William Camden, *Remaines of a greater work, concerning Britaine* (London, 1605), p. 56.
31. See Colclough's first line index of Hoskyns's poems in manuscript, 'The Muses Recreation', 392–400.
32. The poem is headed 'Martin' in MS CCC. 327, fol. 29r, and also appears in a New College miscellany (Bod., MS Malone 19, p. 95) which has a large number of verses attributed to Hoskyns.

33. This epitaph is attributed to Hoskyns in the Farmer Chetham miscellany, *The Dr. Farmer Chetham MS. Being a commonplace-book in the Chetham library, Manchester. Temp. Elizabeth, James I, and Charles I*, ed. A. B. Grosart, 2 parts (Chetham Society, 1863), II, p. 157. 'Lord Verulam is very lame' is attributed to Hoskyns in Bod., MS Rawl.B.151, fol. 102v.
34. John Donne, *Letters to Several Persons of Honour* (London, 1651), p. 89.
35. Andrew Gordon, 'The Act of Libel: Conscripting Civic Space in Early Modern England', *Journal of Medieval and Early Modern Studies* 32 (2002), 375–97.
36. On libelling among the lower social orders, see Adam Fox, *Oral and Literate Culture in England, 1500–1700* (Oxford: Oxford University Press, 2000), pp. 311–34.
37. See the case involving the riotous behaviour of Sir Edmund Baynham and his 'Damned Crew' at Bread Street Mermaid in 1600, John Hawarde, *Les Reportes del Cases in Camera Stellata, 1593–1609*, ed. W. P. Bailden (London, 1894), pp. 114–15.
38. *Dr. Farmer Chetham MS*, II, p. 150.
39. George Wither, *The Shepherds Hunting* (London, 1615), sig. F2v–3r.
40. In lines 2 and 10 of this passage, subsequent editors emend 'Hard' to 'heard' and 'take' to 'talk': for example, see *The Lyric Poems of Beaumont and Fletcher*, ed. Ernest Rhys (London: Dent, 1897), pp. 133–4.
41. Jeanneret, *Feast of Words*, p. 128.
42. Brioist has argued that the tavern sign portrayed in the engraving is that of the Mermaid tavern, 'Que de choses avons nous vues', p. 103. However, the accompanying verse is dedicated to William Meere, the vintner at the Ship at the Old Bailey.
43. Bourdieu, *Distinction*, p. 56.
44. Shapiro, 'Mermaid Club', 7–8. More has argued that this meeting was held not at the Mitre but at Brasenose College because copies frequently have a headnote attributing the poem to a 'Rodolphus Colfabius' (usually identified with Coryate) of Brasenose College, Oxford; see 'Rewards of Virtue', p. 202. Yet, it just states that the composer was educated at this college, not that the banquet was held there, and the Mitre is specifically mentioned as the meeting-place in the poem.
45. HMC, *Lord Sackville at Knole, Cranfield Papers, 1551–1612*, I, pp. 254–5.
46. The translation is Edgar Hinchcliffe's; see 'Thomae Coriati Testimonium', 370–5.
47. The number and concentration of citings is remarkable – the popular Belsavage is referred to on only four occasions. For allusions in plays, see Edward Sugden, *A Topographical Dictionary to the Works of Shakespeare and His Fellow Dramatists* (Manchester: Manchester University Press, 1925), pp. 341–2, 348–9.
48. HMC, *Marquess of Downshire, Papers of William Trumbull the Elder, 1605–1618*, II, pp. 182–3. On the companies that met at the Mermaid, see my essay 'Patrons of the Mermaid Tavern (fl. 1611)', *Oxford Dictionary of National Biography*.
49. HMC, *Marquess of Downshire*, III, p. 250.

50. Cranfield was banker to Martin, the legal advisor to syndicates run by Ingram and Cranfield; Sir Robert Phelips, Hakewill and Brooke were signatories to legal documents of Cranfield and Ingram, *HMC, Lord Sackville at Knole*, I, pp. 175, 255, 100, 271–2, 255. Both Brooke and Ingram sat for York in James's parliaments.
51. D'Arms, 'The Roman *Convivium* and the Idea of Equality', pp. 312–19. See also Shields on the private society and democratisation, *Civil Tongues*, p. xx.
52. Robert Cummings argues for these dates in his 'Liberty and History in Jonson's "Invitation to Supper"', *Studies in English Literature* 40 (2000), 103, 117, n. 2.
53. On Jonson and the symposiastic lyric, see Scodel, *Excess and the Mean*, pp. 201–11, and Achilleos, '*Anacreonta*', pp. 25–31.
54. All references will be to Clark's edition of the Latin poem and Reynold's English version in his *Brief Lives*, p. 52.
55. Xenophon, *Symposium*, trans. O. J. Todd (Cambridge, MA: Harvard University Press, 1961), pp. 384–5, 1.13.
56. On Philip, see Jeanneret, *Feast of Words*, p. 141.
57. *Civile Conversation*, II, p. 132.
58. Pellizer, 'Outlines of a Morphology', pp. 179, 182–3.
59. See the discussion of Rabelais's use of the Silenus box as a convivial topos in Richard A. Lanham, *The Motives of Eloquence: Literary Rhetoric in the Renaissance* (New Haven: Yale University Press, 1976), pp. 169–71.
60. I am grateful to Bradley Sekedat for the translation from the Latin.
61. See Jeanneret on kitchen Latin, *Feast of Words*, pp. 201–25.
62. Boehrer, *Fury of Men's Gullets*, p. 46.
63. On Rabelais as an authority for a burlesque symposiastic tradition, see Anne Lake Prescott, *Imagining Rabelais in Renaissance England* (New Haven: Yale University Press, 1998), pp. 9–11.
64. Holcomb, *Mirth Making*, pp. 147–8.
65. On the proximity between 'Inviting a Friend' and *Leges Convivales*, see Cummings, 'Liberty and History', 105.
66. See also rules 14, 16, and 17. The translation is Boehrer's, who notes the ambiguity of the *Leges Convivales*, although he does not relate it to the playfulness of a symposiastic tradition, *Fury of Men's Gullets*, pp. 69–70, 72–4.
67. Joseph Loewenstein, 'The Jonsonian Corpulence, or the Poet as Mouthpiece', *ELH* 53 (1986), 492, 499–501. Cummings argues for a notion of the 'historian's liberty' in the context of Jonson's friendship with Camden and Cotton, James's surveillance of the historians, and the failed revival of the 'Society of Antiquaries' in 1614, 'Liberty and History', 112–14.
68. See Connors' discussion of Martial, 'Imperial Space and Time', p. 517.
69. Ibid., p. 518.
70. Annabel Patterson, 'All Donne', in Elizabeth Harvey and Katharine Eisaman Maus, eds., *Soliciting Interpretation: Literary Theory and Seventeenth-Century English Poetry* (Chicago and London: University of Chicago Press, 1990), pp. 42–3.

71. Brioist turns the early modern tavern society into an early form of the Habermasian public sphere, a 'crucible' where the fusion of legal, intellectual, commercial, and political milieux of the court and the city took place, 'Que de choses avons nous vues', pp. 126–7.
72. Jeanneret, *Feast of Words*, pp. 93–4; Plutarch, *Table Talk*, 1.614.
73. A mix of bawdy and scurrilous anecdotes, misogynist jokes about women and marriage, alongside 'serious' discussion of contemporary legal and political issues is evident in the table talk of Sir Roger Wilbraham, *Journal of Sir Roger Wilbraham, Solicitor-General in Ireland and Master of Requests, for the Years 1593–1616*, ed. Harold Spencer Scott (London: Royal Historical Society, 1902), pp. 18–22.
74. Copies can be found in: BL, MS Harley 4931, pp. 22–5 (with Reynold's version); Bod., MS Don. c. 54, fols. 21r–22r, Rawl. poet. 117, fols. 192r–191v (rev.), Malone 19, pp. 34–5 (fragment); State Papers Domestic, 1547–1625, 14/66.
75. *The Poems of Sir John Davies*, ed. Robert Krueger (Oxford: Clarendon Press, 1975), pp. 438–9; Duncan-Jones, 'Preserved Dainties', 141–3; see also Arthur Marotti, *Manuscript, Print, and the English Renaissance Lyric* (Ithaca, NY: Cornell University Press, 1995), pp. 36–7, 93–8, 150, 182, 327.
76. Roberts and Hoskyns promoted Welsh culture – half of the miscellany consists of Welsh poetry. The Welsh poets Henry Perry and John Owen dedicated volumes to Hoskyns – *Egluryn phraethineb* (1595) and *Epigrammatum* (1607) respectively.
77. On embodied satire, see Bruster, 'Structural Transformation of Print', pp. 53–4, and Chapter 1, pp. 31–4.

4 WITS IN THE HOUSE OF COMMONS

1. Zaret prioritises a democratic model of the public sphere, discovering in the English Revolution the origins of 'those democratic tenets ... the importance of consent, open debate, and reason for the authority of opinion in politics'; he tends to sideline alternative forms of communicative practices, arguing that political communication 'was severely restricted' in the early seventeenth century, *Origins of Democratic Culture*. For studies of the discursive and associational possibilities of the period, see Bellany, *Politics of Court Scandal*; McRae, *Literature, Satire and the Early Stuart State*; and Withington, *Politics of the Commonwealth*.
2. Andreas Ballstaedt, '"Dissonance" in Music', in Hans Ulrich Gumbrecht and K. Ludwig Pfeiffer, eds., *The Materialities of Communication*, trans. William Whobrey (Stanford: Stanford University Press, 1994), pp. 157–69. Peter Travis cites Boethius and Bakhtin in 'Thirteen Ways of Listening to a Fart: Noise in Chaucer's *Summoner's Tale*', *Exemplaria* 16 (2004), 17–18. Mikhail Bakhtin, *The Dialogic Imagination: Four Essays by M. M. Bakhtin*, ed. Michael Holquist, trans. Caryl Emerson and Holquist (Austin: University of Texas Press, 1981), p. 291.

3. *The Parliamentary Diary of Robert Bowyer, 1606–1607*, ed. David Harris Willson (Minneapolis: University of Minnesota Press, 1931), p. 213, n. 1.
4. BL, Add. MS 4149, fol. 213r. This version has decorative line endings (./.) which have been removed for clarity.
5. Puttenham, *Arte of English Poesie*, p. 68.
6. On four-stress verse, see Joseph Malof, *A Manual of English Meters* (Westport, Connecticut: Greenwood Press, 1970), pp. 82, 87. See Raylor on this milieu's use of octosyllabic doggerel, *Cavaliers, Clubs and Literary Culture*, pp. 122–5.
7. BL, Add. MS 23229, fol. 19r. This mock-heroic ballad, given Conway's close connections with the Order of the Fancy, probably belongs to this later company.
8. Bod., MS Malone 23, p. 2, and *Prince of Love*, p. 93. For a fuller discussion of the performative qualities of the 'Parliament Fart', see my 'Performing Politics: The Circulation of the "Parliament Fart"', *Huntington Library Quarterly* 69 (2006), 121–38.
9. See BL, MS Sloane 2023, fols. 59v–60r.
10. Donne satirised Sir Roger in his *Courtier's Library*: '*A Manual for Justices of the Peace*, comprising many confessions of poisoners tendered to Justice Manwood, and employed by him in his privy', *The Courtier's Library: or, Catalogus librorum aulicorum incomparabilium et non vendibilium*, ed. E. M. Simpson (London: Nonesuch Press, 1930), p. 49.
11. On textual sociocorporeality, see Love, *Scribal Publication*, pp. 5, 141–60; Jan-Dirk Müller, 'The Body of the Book: The Media Transition from Manuscript to Print', *Materialities of Communication*, pp. 38–44; D. F. McKenzie, 'Speech-Manuscript-Print', *Making Meaning: 'Printers of the Mind' and other Essays*, ed. Peter D. McDonald and Michael F. Suarez, SJ (Amherst: University of Massachusetts Press, 2002), pp. 237–58.
12. Smith, *Acoustic World*, pp. 21–5, 46–7.
13. See G. R. Elton's discussion of this verse, *The Parliament of England, 1559–1581* (Cambridge: Cambridge University Press, 1986), p. 353.
14. The 'Parliament Fart' is embedded within this milieu: Sir Edward Phelips's niece Elizabeth, who lived with the Phelipses in London from 1607 to 1612, married the famous parliament farter, Henry Ludlow (More, 'Rewards of Virtue', p. 186).
15. Bald, *Donne, A Life*, pp. 176, 188–9.
16. I am grateful to Dr Andrew Thrush for this information. See also Chamberlain, *Letters*, I, p. 243, Whitlock, *John Hoskyns*, p. 209.
17. Pauline Croft, 'Capital Life: Members of Parliament outside the House', in Thomas Cogswell, Richard Cust, and Peter Lake, eds., *Politics, Religion and Popularity in Early Stuart Britain: Essays in Honour of Conrad Russell* (Cambridge: Cambridge University Press, 2002), pp. 65–7.
18. York City Archives, York House Book, 33, fols. 24r–26r. Withington points to the way that members of parliament 'were more adept at talking in ways which citizens and their representatives could understand' because of shared

19. *Traveller for the English wits*, pp. 44–6.
20. F. J. Fisher, 'The Development of London as a Centre of Consumption in the Sixteenth and Seventeenth Centuries', *Transactions of the Royal Historical Society* 30 (1948), 41–2, 47.
21. *Proceedings in Parliament, 1610*, I, pp. 331–2.
22. James Whitelocke, *Liber Familicus*, ed. John Bruce (London: Camden Society, 1858), p. 24.
23. Whitelocke, *Liber Familicus*, pp. 24–5; William Hakewill, *Libertie of the Subject: Against the Pretended Power of Impositions. Maintained by an Argument in Parliament An°.7°. Jacobi Regis* (London, 1641), sig. A3r–v. A similar process of transmission is evident in the dissemination of his other essays; see his *The Manner how Statutes are enacted in Parliament by passing of Bills. Collected many yeares past out of the Iournalls of the house of Commons* (London, 1641), sig. A4r; and Elizabeth Read Foster, 'Speaking in the House of Commons', *Bulletin of the Institute of Historical Research* 43 (1970), 35–55.
24. On the Starkey miscellany, see my 'Performing Politics', 129–32; Bod., MS Don.c.54, fols. 20v–24r.
25. Oliver Arnold's dismissal of the notion that this principle was necessary to protect members from the scrutiny of the king and Privy Council as a 'red herring' flies in the face of evidence, 'Absorption and Representation: Mapping England in the early modern House of Commons', *Literature, Mapping, and the Politics of Space*, p. 20. In 1610, James went to great lengths to find out who likened him to King Joram; following the 1607 and 1610 sessions, Thomas Egerton, Lord Ellesmere moved against MPs who had scrutinised the royal prerogative – Nicholas Fuller, Sir Herbert Croft and Whitelocke – as a warning to others, *Proceedings in Parliament, 1610*, I, pp. xxxvi–vii; Neil Cuddy, 'The Conflicting Loyalties of a "vulger counselor": The Third Earl of Southampton' in John Morrill, Paul Slack, and Daniel Woolf, eds. *Public Duty and Private Conscience in Seventeenth-Century England* (Oxford: Clarendon Press, 1993), pp. 132–3; Whitelocke, *Liber Familicus*, pp. 34–8. On tensions between parliamentary principle and practice, see Zaret, *Origins of Democratic Culture*, p. 44.
26. For further explication of the topicality of the couplets assembled in Malone 13, see my edition of the poem, 'The Parliament Fart (1607–)', *Early Stuart Libels*, Section C. In versions I have studied, around 25 per cent of the 112 members who sat in James's first parliament and made an appearance in the 'Parliament Fart' went on to sit in parliaments in the 1620s, while a further 9 per cent of those who sat in 1607 share names with members sitting in the 1620s, and seven individuals share names with members sitting in the 1640s.
27. Bellany, *Politics of Court Scandal*, p. 77.
28. 'Sir Francis Moore, 1559–1621', History of Parliament Trust, London, 1604–29 section, unpublished article. I am grateful to the History of Parliament Trust for allowing me to see this article, and articles cited subsequently in draft, and for the assistance of Dr Andrew Thrush at the Trust.

29. *Stuart Royal Proclamations*, ed. James F. Larkin and Paul L. Hughes, 2 vols. (Oxford: Clarendon Press, 1973), I, pp. 503–5.
30. Pauline Croft discusses the frequent summoning of parliament between 1601 and 1610 ('Capital Life', p. 67).
31. Quoted in Michael Schoenfeldt, 'Fables of the Belly', in David Hillman and Carla Mazzio, eds., *The Body in Parts: Fantasies of Corporeality in Early Modern Europe* (London: Routledge, 1997), p. 250.
32. Malcolm, *Origins of English Nonsense*, p. 119.
33. *Proceedings in Parliament, 1614*, ed. Maija Jansson (Philadelphia: American Philosophical Society, 1988), p. xxi; Alan Cromartie, 'The Constitutionalist Revolution: The Transformation of Political Culture in Early Stuart England', *Past and Present* 163 (1999), 76–80.
34. *The Tudor Constitution: Documents and Commentary*, ed. G. R. Elton, 2nd edn (Cambridge: Cambridge University Press, 1982), p. 253.
35. Greene, 'Ceremonial Play', p. 283.
36. Travis, 'Noise in Chaucer's *Summoner's Tale*', 3.
37. *The Riverside Chaucer*, ed. F. N. Robinson (Oxford: Oxford University Press, 1987), p. 135 (lines 2220–6)
38. See Mack's discussion of parliament as a political community formed through a 'shared experience of disputation', *Elizabethan Rhetoric*, p. 251.
39. James VI and I, *Political Writings*, ed. Johann P. Somerville (Cambridge: Cambridge University Press, 1994), p. 160.
40. *Constitutional Documents of the Reign of James I, 1603–25*, ed. J. R. Tanner (Cambridge: Cambridge University Press), p. 246.
41. Cromartie, 'Constitutionalist Revolution', 96, 106–7.
42. 'Sir Henry Yelverton, 1566–1629', History of Parliament Trust, 1604–29.
43. *The Letters and Life of Francis Bacon*, ed. by James Spedding, 7 vols. (London: 1857–74), IV, pp. 365–6. On these men in parliament, see Cuddy, 'Conflicting Loyalties of a "vulgar counsellor"', pp. 126–47.
44. Raffield, *Images and Cultures of Law*, p. 206.
45. See Cain's discussion of Martin's parliamentary career in his 'Donne and the Prince D'Amour', 85–104.
46. Ross, 'Memorial Culture', 279–80, 304.
47. 'Samuel Lewkenor', History of Parliament Trust, 1604–29.
48. *Proceedings in Parliament 1610*, II, p. 342.
49. See J. H. Hexter, 'Parliament, Liberty, and Freedom of Elections', in Hexter, ed., *Parliament and Liberty: From the Reign of Elizabeth to the English Civil War* (Stanford: Stanford University Press, 1992), pp. 54–5.
50. Sir John Harington, *A New Discourse of a Stale Subject, called the Metamorphosis of Ajax*, ed. Elizabeth Story Donno (London: Routledge & Kegan Paul, 1962), p. 100.
51. As Kahn says, 'Rhetoric becomes the means by which the *possibility* of rhetoric is itself put in question', *Rhetoric, Prudence, and Skepticism*, p. 54.
52. Harington, *Metamorphosis of Ajax*, p. 71.
53. Stephen Clucas and Rosalind Davies, 'Introduction', in Clucas and Davies, eds., *The Crisis of 1614 and the Addled Parliament: Literary and Historical*

Perspectives (Aldershot: Ashgate, 2003), p. 5. See this collection of essays in general for the various forms of disturbance in this year.

54. *The Life and Letters of Sir Henry Wotton*, ed. Logan Pearsall Smith, 2 vols. (Oxford: Clarendon Press, 1907), II, p. 37.
55. Hoskyns, *Life, Letters and Writings*, p. 71. See Colclough's discussion of the meanings of 'wit' in these letters of Wotton and Hoskyns, 'Of the alleadging of authors', pp. 110–11.
56. By October 1614, the following railing rhyme was circulating:

> London's full of rumo^{r}s;
> ffower men in the tower
> of eight severall humou^{r}s:
> Sharpe the divine is soberly mad
> Hoskings the lawyer is merrily sad
> Cornewallis ye ledg^r is popishlie p^{r}cise,
> And Chuit the Carv^r is foolishlie Wise.
> (Bod., MS Sloane 2023, fol. 60v)

57. Lipking, 'Traditions of the Facetiae', pp. 382–5; Holcomb, *Mirth Making*, pp. 145–6.
58. *Metamorphosis of Ajax*, pp. 100–2.
59. Erasmus, *Praise of Folly*, pp. 143, 147–8.
60. Horace, *Satires, Epistles and Ars Poetica*, ed. H. Rushton Fairclough (Cambridge, MA: Harvard University Press, 1970), p. 255 (1.1.60–1).
61. Foster, 'Speaking in the House of Commons', 46–7.
62. Keith Thomas, 'Cases of Conscience in Seventeenth-Century England', in *Public Duty and Private Conscience*, pp. 29–56; Cromartie, 'Constitutionalist Revolution', 107.
63. See also Meg Lota Brown on Donne, casuistry and conscience in *Donne and the Politics of Conscience in Early Modern England* (Leiden: E. J. Brill, 1995).
64. Chamberlain, *Letters*, I, p. 538.
65. Ibid., p. 356. See 'Attacks on the Scots', *Early Stuart Libels*, Section E.
66. Another version has 'Gentlemen quoth Hoskins, to lible is not safe, / Let the ffart bee buried, Ile make ye Epitaph', Add. 58215, fol. 189r – Add. 34218, fol. 21r has another variant.
67. See McRae's discussion of this satire, *Literature, Satire, and the Early Stuart State*, pp. 97–8.
68. Whitelocke, *Liber Familicus*, pp. 36–9; on James's extreme antipathy to the Commons, see Andrew Thrush, 'The Personal Rule of James I, 1611–1620', *Politics, Religion and Popularity*, pp. 97–101.

5 CORYATS CRUDITIES (1611) AND THE SOCIABILITY OF PRINT

1. Joseph Loewenstein, *The Author's Due: Printing and the Prehistory of Copyright* (Chicago and London: University of Chicago Press, 2002), p. 96. Paul J. Voss points out that the kind of 'traditional patronage' Loewenstein describes had disappeared well before the early seventeenth century, 'Books for Sale:

Advertising and Patronage in Late Elizabethan England', *The Sixteenth Century Journal* 29 (1998), 733–4.
2. Ezell, *Social Authorship*, pp. 7–13.
3. *Coryats Crambe, or His Colwort twise Sodden, and now served in with other Macaronicke dishes, as the second course to his Crudities* (London, 1611), sig. H1r.
4. Craig Muldrew, *The Economy of Obligation: the Culture of Credit and Social Relations in Early Modern England* (Basingstoke: Macmillan, 1998), pp. 2–3.
5. Voss, 'Books for Sale', 733.
6. Thomas Coryate, *Coryats Crudities (1611)*, intro. by W. M. Schutte (London: Scolar Press, 1979), sig. a8v. Subsequent references will be to this edition.
7. This Sir John Suckling is the father of the later royalist poet.
8. Mocket was unable to license the *Crudities* since he had responsibility for theological and political works; see Susan Cyndia Clegg, *Press Censorship in Jacobean England* (Cambridge: Cambridge University Press, 2001), pp. 63–4.
9. The letter is pasted into the back cover of Prince Henry's copy of *Coryats Crudities* (British Library, G 6750).
10. Other contributors to the 'Panegyricke Verses' in Prince Henry's service were Sir Robert Phelips, Sir Robert Yaxley, John Pawlet, Inigo Jones, Walter Quin, John Davies of Hereford, John Owen and Jean Loisseau de Tourval. There were other contributors eager to cement their relationship with the Prince: Henry Peacham, who dedicated his Latin translation of James I's *Basilikon Doron* to Henry in 1610, and Michael Drayton, who would dedicate his *Poly-Olbion* to the Prince in 1612.
11. On Coryate's kinship and local connections, see More, 'Rewards of Virtue', p. 201.
12. Melanie Ord, 'Provincial Identification and the Struggle over Representation in Thomas Coryat's *Crudities* (1611)', in Philip Schwyzer and Simon Mealor, eds., *Archipelagic Identities: Literature and Identity in the Atlantic Archipelago, 1550–1800* (Aldershot: Ashgate, 2004), pp. 131–40.
13. Anomalies in the foliation may result from quires being printed for consultation and circulation, possibly on different presses, while printing was still in progress. The distichs and the epistles have the foliation a–b^8; Jonson's 'The Character of the famous Odcombian', and his anacrostic make up b^4, and the next section runs c–g^8 followed by h^4, with '*FINIS*' on h4r, and the foliation continues i–L^4. Kirchner's essay runs across B–C^8, D^1, followed by Whitaker's epistle D^3, and the 'Observations' begin on D2r and continue regularly throughout. Stansby kept three presses in operation; see Loewenstein, *Jonson and Possessive Authorship*, p. 184, fn. 105.
14. He also remembered Edward Blount and William Barratt, the stationers who entered his *Crudities* in the Stationers' Register, among his London network of friends and associates, *Traveller for the English Wits*, p. 46. Poems may have been circulating in manuscript – if so, then their absence from manuscript miscellanies is surprising. Hoskyns's 'Cabalistic Verses' ('Even as the waves of brainlesse butter'd fish') does appear in the later university miscellanies, but it was probably copied from the printed book; see Bod., MS Malone 19, p. 157.

15. Walter Ong, *Orality and Literacy: The Technologizing of the Word* (London: Routledge, 2002), p. 120.
16. Museum of London, 714, fol. 14v, written on blank verso. This Thomas Fairfax was the grandfather of the parliamentary general, and appeared in the 'Parliament Fart' – 'Nay then Masters sayd S^r Th: Fayrfax / it wear high tyme to send for Sr Ajax', Bod., MS Rawl.poet.117, fol. 86r (194v (rev.)).
17. Henry Parrot, *Laquei ridiculosi: or Springes for Woodcocks* (London, 1613), Epigram 144, sig. F4v.
18. Voss, 'Books for Sale', 737. The title-page to the *Crudities* only bears the printer's initials and the date.
19. Jason Scott-Warren, *Sir John Harington and the Book as Gift* (Oxford: Oxford University Press, 2001), pp. 3, 15–17.
20. BL, G6750. N. F. Blake, 'Manuscript to Print', in Jeremy Griffiths and Derek Pearsall, eds., *Book Production and Publication in Britain, 1375–1475* (Cambridge: Cambridge University Press, 1989), pp. 404–5.
21. Roger Chartier, 'Introduction', in Chartier, ed., *The Culture of Print: Power and the Uses of Print in Early Modern Europe*, trans. Lydia G. Cochrane (Princeton: Princeton University Press, 1989), p. 2.
22. John Taylor, *The Eighth Wonder of the World: or, Coriats escape from his supposed drowning* (London, 1613), p. 68.
23. Wiles, *Shakespeare's Clown*, p. 2.
24. On the buffoons, jesters and courtiers see Holcomb, *Mirth Making*, Chapter 3; on stage clowns see Wiles, *Shakespeare's Clowns*, Chapters 2, 3, 10; and Halasz, 'So beloved that men use his picture', 19–38.
25. See Coryate's account in his *Crambe*, sigs. D6r–G2r. This event is remembered in a number of the Coryate poems, including those contributed by his countrymen – Sydenham in the *Crudities* (sig. f2r–v) and William Rich in the *Crambe* (sig. b4v). On the Parish Ale, see Clopper, *Drama, Play, and Game*, pp. 65–6.
26. Halasz argues for the usefulness of celebrity as an early modern category in relation to the stage clown, 'So beloved that men use his picture', 19–38.
27. See Chapter 2 for discussion of his appropriation of the *Crudities* and nonsense, pp. 57–8.
28. William Fennor, *Fennors Defence: Or, I am your First Man* (London, 1615), sig. B3r–4v; Flood, 'Fennor and Daborne at Youghal', 321–2; Wiles, *Shakespeare's Clowns*, p. 14.
29. See Boswell's detailed discussion of the Taylor/Fennor contest as an example of stage-to-pamphlet flyting in his 'Culture and Rhetoric of the Answer-Poem', pp. 141–51; Clopper, *Drama, Play, and Game*, pp. 30–1. This learned element is evident in Armin's *Quips upon Questions*; see Wiles, *Shakespeare's Clowns*, pp. 138–9.
30. It is uncertain whether the original event did take place or was 'improvised' by Taylor; see Boswell, 'Culture and Rhetoric of the Answer-Poem', pp. 143–5.
31. *Coryats Crambe*, sig. H3r.
32. Roger Chartier, 'Leisure and Sociability: Reading Aloud in Early Modern Europe', *Urban Life in the Renaissance*, p. 104.

33. William Nelson, 'From "Listen Lordings" to "Dear Reader"', *University of Toronto Quarterly* 46 (1976–7), 110, 121.
34. Craik, 'Reading *Coryats Crudities*', 92.
35. More, 'Rewards of Virtue', pp. 117–18, 201–2.
36. Wiles, *Shakespeare's Clown*, pp. 26, 36–8.
37. Ibid., pp. 61–2.
38. This differs from Ord's reading of Coryate's 'provinciality' in that she assumes he is of low status: 'It is Coryat's provincial identity, among other things, that enables writers of panegyric verses to point up negotiations between their possession, and Coryat's lack, of scholarly and social status', 'Provincial Identification', p. 138.
39. A remora is a 'sucking-fish believed by the ancients to have the power of staying the course of any ship to which it attached itself', OED, 1.
40. Otto Mayr, *Authority, Liberty, and Automatic Machinery in Early Modern Europe* (Baltimore: Johns Hopkins University Press, 1986), p. xviii.
41. See also Raylor's discussion of this poem in his *Cavaliers, Clubs and Literary Culture*, p. 123.
42. Taylor, *Scullers Travels*, sig. B1r.
43. Raylor, *Cavalier, Clubs, and Literary Culture*, pp. 122–3. As I have argued in the previous chapter, one could add the 'Parliament Fart' to this list and it is also printed in this miscellany. Craik similarly speaks of the *Crudities*, and the 'Panegyricke Verses' in particular, as a self-conscious exercise in 'literary "crudeness"', 'Reading *Coryats Crudities*', 77–8.
44. Miller, 'Introduction', *Praise of Folly*, p. xiv.
45. Erasmus, 'Letter to Thomas More', *Praise of Folly*, pp. 2–4.
46. See Michael West, 'Homer's *Iliad* and the Genesis of Mock-Heroic', *Cithara* 21 (1991), 3–22.
47. Kahn, *Rhetoric, Prudence, and Skepticism*, pp. 91–2, 103.
48. Jeanneret, *A Feast of Words*, p. 217.
49. Brandon Centerwall, 'Identifying "Glareanus Vadianus" as John Sanford', *Cahiers Elisabéthains* 55 (1999), 35–7. See Malcolm's discussion of these poems, *Origins of English Nonsense*, pp. 14–21.
50. Skinner, 'Hobbes and the Classical Theory of Laughter', pp. 145–7.
51. Erasmus, *Praise of Folly*, p. 144.
52. Skinner briefly discusses the laughter of burlesque and nonsense, although he identifies it with the later Augustans, 'Hobbes and the Classical Theory of Laughter', pp. 161–2.
53. Craik, 'Reading *Coryats Crudities*', 90–1.
54. See Evelyn Tribble's discussion of a book's 'collaborative nature, of the conversation between a text and its margins, of the play made possible by the space of the page', *Margins and Marginality: The Printed Page in Early Modern England* (Charlottesville: University Press of Virginia, 1993), pp. 1–2, 7–10.
55. London Museum, 46.78/714.
56. BL, Add. MS 27632, fol. 46r. Scott-Warren, *Sir John Harington*, p. 233.

57. On *Metamorphosis of Ajax* as a mock-encomium, see D. H. Craig, *Sir John Harington* (Boston: Twayne, 1985), pp. 77–81.
58. Harington, *Metamorphosis of Ajax*, p. 65. See Chapter 4, pp. 95–8.
59. For a detailed discussion of Rabelais's influence on the 'Panegyricke Verses', see Prescott, *Imagining Rabelais*, pp. 70–3.
60. *A Pleasant Satyre or Poesie: Wherein is discovered the Catholicon of Spayne, and the chiefe leaders of the League*, trans. T. W. (London, 1595), pp. 203–4; Prescott, *Imagining Rabelais*, p. 59.
61. Quoted in Scott-Warren, *Harington and the Book as Gift*, pp. 192–3.
62. Francis R. Johnson, 'Marlowe's Astronomy and Renaissance Skepticism', *English Literary History* 13 (1946), 247.
63. See Kahn's discussion of the comparable humanist rhetorical practice of argument *in utramque partem* in *Rhetoric, Prudence and Skepticism*, p. 22.
64. See the discussion of the syllogism in ibid., pp. 32–3.
65. Norbrook argues for Hoskyns's scepticism towards political analogies in his 'Rhetoric, Ideology and the Elizabethan World Picture', pp. 148, 153–4.
66. Tobie Mathew, *A True Historical Relation of the Conversion of Sir Tobie Mathew to the Holy Catholic Faith*, ed. A. H. Mathew (London: Burns & Oates, 1904), p. 86.
67. On Donne's casuistry, see Brown, *Donne and the Politics of Conscience*.
68. Graham Roebuck, '*Johannes Factus* and the Anvil of Wits', *John Donne Journal* 15 (1996), 141–4. See also Curtis Perry's discussion of Donne's response to 'the problematic decorum of praise occasioned by James's "stile"', *The Making of Jacobean Culture* (Cambridge: Cambridge University Press, 1997), p. 39.
69. Roebuck, '*Johannes Factus*', 147.
70. Swann, *Curiosities and Texts*, pp. 149–56.
71. I am indebted to Prescott's discussion on the significance of citing Rabelais, *Imagining Rabelais*, pp. 60–1.

6 TRAVELLER FOR THE ENGLISH WITS

1. Andrew Hadfield, *Literature, Travel, and Colonial Writing in the English Renaissance, 1545–1625* (Oxford: Clarendon Press, 1998), pp. 58–68; Richmond Barbour, *Before Orientalism: London's Theatre of the East, 1576–1626* (Cambridge: Cambridge University Press, 2003), Chapter 4.
2. Anthony Parr, 'Thomas Coryat and the Discovery of Europe', *Huntington Library Quarterly* 55 (1992), 579–602.
3. James Howell, *Instructions for Forreine Travell* (London, 1642), pp. 13–14.
4. Barbour, *Before Orientalism*, pp. 105–9.
5. Early modern travellers spent the great majority of their time in urban areas; see Sara Warneke, *Images of the Educational Traveller in Early Modern England* (Leiden: E. J. Brill, 1995), p. 3.
6. Giovanni Botero, *The Magnificence and Greatness of Cities (1606)*, trans. Robert Peterson (Amsterdam: Theatrum Orbis Terrarum, 1979), pp. 48, 61–2, 65.

7. Warneke, *Educational Traveller*, pp. 44–6.
8. Robert Dallington, *A Method for Travell* (London, c. 1605), sig. B1r.
9. The internationalism of the Republic of Letters resists geographical fixity, and it is certainly not possible to argue that its primary locus was the city in this period; nonetheless, if a gentleman wanted to contact learned men on his travels, then he was more likely to accomplish this in cities; see Peter N. Miller, *Peiresc's Europe: Learning and Virtue in the Seventeenth Century* (New Haven: Yale University Press, 2000), p. 2.
10. *The Traveiler of Jerome Turler (1575)* (Gainesville, Florida: Scholars' Facsimiles & Reprints, 1951), pp. 54–5.
11. Anthony Grafton, *Bring Out Your Dead: The Past as Revelation* (Cambridge, MA: Harvard University Press, 2001), pp. 1, 11.
12. Albert Meier, *Certain briefe, and speciall instructions for gentlemen, merchants, students, souldiers, marriners, &c. employed in services abroad*, trans. Philip Jones (London, 1589). Gabriel Harvey in his copy of *The Traveiler of Jerome Turler*, a gift from Edmund Spenser, praised the 'excellent tract of Albert Meier; intituled, *Special Instructions for gentlemen travelers*' (sig. A7r).
13. Warneke, *Images of the Educational Traveller*, pp. 44–6, 258–60.
14. Sir Thomas Palmer, *An Essay of the Meanes how to make our Trauailes, into forraine Countries, the more profitable and honourable (London, 1606)* (Amsterdam: Theatrum Orbis Terrarum, 1972), pp. 42–4.
15. The first recorded usage in the OED is 1630.
16. Ann Rosalind Jones, 'Italians and Others: *The White Devil* (1612)', in David Scott Kastan and Peter Stallybrass, eds., *Staging the Renaissance: Reinterpretations of Elizabethan and Jacobean Drama* (London: Routledge, 1991), pp. 259–60.
17. Jean Howard, 'Civic Institutions and Precarious Masculinity in Dekker's *The Honest Whore*', *Early Modern Culture: An Electronic Seminar*, issue 1, paragraphs 2, 9, 18 http://eserver.org/emc/1-1/howard.html
18. Jones and Barbour posit an analogy between the erotic and orientalist gaze in their studies of Coryate in Venice: Jones, 'Italians and Others', pp. 259–60; Barbour, *Before Orientalism*, pp. 128–9.
19. See, for example, the lists provided in *Traveiler of Jerome Turler* and Albert Meier's *Certain Briefe, and Speciall Instructions*.
20. Robin Myers and Michael Harris, 'Introduction', in Myers and Harris, eds., *Journeys Through the Market: Travel, Travellers and the Book Trade* (New Castle, Delaware: Oak Knoll Press; Folkestone: St Paul's Bibliographies, 1999), p. vii.
21. Meier, *Certaine Briefe, and Speciall Instructions*, pp. 17–18.
22. Ibid., pp. 5, 7. 'Coryatizing' is a term coined by John Taylor in his *The Pennyles Pilgrimage, or the Money-lesse perambulation, of John Taylor, Alias the Kings Majesties Water-Poet* (London, 1618), sig. E2r.
23. Randall L.-W. Caudill, 'Some Literary Evidence of the Development of English Virtuoso Interests in the Seventeenth Century, with particular reference to the literature of travel', unpublished D.Phil. thesis, Oxford (1976), pp. 2–3, 116, 34.

24. Ibid., p. 10.
25. Strong, *Henry Prince of Wales*, pp. 184–7; Swann, *Curiosities and Texts*, p. 2.
26. HMC, *Marquess of Downshire* III, p. 238; Trumbull may have also been attempting to interest the Prince in a 'witty and worthy invention' for cataloguing a cabinet of curiosities (p. 239); Wilks, 'Court Culture of Prince Henry', pp. 180–1, 198.
27. On collecting in this period, see Swann, *Curiosities and Texts*, pp. 5–27, and Edward Chaney, ed., *The Evolution of English Collecting: Reception of Italian Art in the Tudor and Stuart Periods* (London and New Haven: Yale University Press, 2003).
28. Parr, 'Coryat and the Discovery of Europe', 590.
29. See *Crudities*, pp. 316, 329.
30. Edward Chaney points out the significance of Coryate's accounts of architectural detail in his *Crudities* in the context of his friendship with Inigo Jones and Sir Henry Wotton; see *The Evolution of the Grand Tour: Anglo-Italian Cultural Relations since the Renaissance*, 2nd edn (London and Portland, Oregon: Frank Cass, 2000), pp. 13, 207–8, 256.
31. On early museum catalogues, see Caudill, 'Development of English Virtuoso Interests', pp. 47–8.
32. OED, 2c and 3a.
33. Ross, 'Memorial Culture', pp. 241–2.
34. The phrase derives from a description of the Republic of Letters associated with Nicolas-Claude de Peiresc; see Miller, *Peiresc's Europe*, p. 2.
35. Ross, 'Memorial Culture', 241.
36. On the early modern museum in England, see Swann, *Curiosities and Texts*, 5–8, 50–4.
37. Joan-Pau Rubiés, *Travel and Ethnology in the Renaissance: South India through European Eyes, 1250–1625* (Cambridge: Cambridge University Press, 2000), p. 349.
38. Samuel Purchas, *Purchas his Pilgrimes. In Five Bookes* (London, 1625), Pt II, Bk X, p. 1820.
39. Terry shared a tent with Coryate for a number of months when Coryate was residing with Roe, *A Voyage to East India* (London, 1655), pp. 58–9.
40. Jás Elner and Joan-Pau Rubiés, *Voyages and Visions: Towards a Cultural History of Travel* (London: Reaktion, 1999), pp. 36–7, 40, 46, 49–50. Roe used information supplied by Coryate to compile the first English map of India, Michael Strachan, *The Life and Adventures of Thomas Coryate* (London: Oxford University Press, 1962), p. 257.
41. See Barbour's discussions of the paradoxical impulses of this traveller, *Beyond Orientalism*, pp. 123–4, 132.
42. Grafton, *Bring Out Your Dead*, pp. 11, 35–7.
43. Peacham, *The Compleat Gentleman* (London, 1634), p. 105; Caudill, 'Development of English Virtuoso Interests', p. 12.
44. See also the summary of Coryate's account in Terry, *Voyage to East India*, p. 68.

45. A comparison can be made to the rhetorical effect of laughter; see Skinner, 'Classical Theory of Laughter', pp. 166–7.
46. Lisa Jardine, *Worldly Goods: A New History of the Renaissance* (London: Macmillan, 1996), p. 119.
47. Craik, 'Reading *Coryats Crudities*', 92–3; Warneke records this shift that takes place over the course of the seventeenth century in her *Educational Traveller*.
48. Robert Burton, *The Anatomy of Melancholy*, 3 vols. (London and Toronto: Dent; New York: Dutton, 1932), II, pp. 86–7; Caudill, 'Development of English Virtuoso Interests', p. 9.
49. Parr, 'Coryat and the Discovery of Europe', 583.
50. Barbour describes 'stationary voyaging' as an 'obsessional mobility that would capture foreignness without suffering self-transformation', in contrast to the compulsive mobility of Coryate's experiential ethos, *Beyond Orientalism*, pp. 109, 131–2.
51. Terry, *Voyage to East India*, p. 71.
52. See Barbour, *Beyond Orientalism*, Chapter 4, 'Thomas Coryate and the Invention of Tourism'.
53. Michel de Certeau, *The Practice of Everday Life*, trans. Steven F. Rendall (Berkeley: University of California Press, 1984), p. 130.
54. Ibid., pp. 129–30.
55. Taylor, *Pennyles Pilgrimage*, sig. E2r.
56. Warneke, *Educational Traveller*, pp. 259–61.
57. See Swann on the social function of the 'wonder book', *Curiosities and Texts*, p. 26; Parr has written of the 'anecdotal vigor' of many of the episodes in the *Crudities*, which derives from Coryate's novel 'adaptation of an essentially satiric or jest-book mode to the demands of descriptive travel writing', 'Coryat and the Discovery of Europe', p. 591.
58. Barbour, *Beyond Orientalism*, pp. 105–9.
59. Elner and Rubiés, *Voyages and Visions*, p. 46.
60. Samuel Purchas, *Purchas his Pilgrimage. Or relations of the World and the Religions observed in all ages and places discovered, from the Creation unto this Present* (London, 1626), p. 530.
61. The editor of *Traveller for the English Wits* is unknown, though it is likely that Purchas was involved given his close acquaintance with Coryate: Henry Fetherstone and William Jaggard put out this collection at a time when Fetherstone was working with Stansby, the printer of the *Crudities* and *Crambe*, on the editions of *Purchas his Pilgrimes*. Taylor edited the second collection from Agra, thus completing his corpus of Coryate pamphlets that had begun in 1612 with *The sculler, rowing from Tiber to Thames*.
62. For Barbour this 'Orientalist' image 'assures readers that the East is now a thrill, not a threat: India is a great arena of spectacular enjoyments for Englishmen', *Before Orientalism*, pp. 142, 144.
63. The poem that closes *Traveller* bears the initials 'R. R.', perhaps Robert Rugge, the author of the extempore verses recited during Coryate's mock-knighting at

the ruins of Troy. Roe was a close friend of Donne, and an associate of Brooke, Martin and Hoskyns; see Bald, *Donne, A Life*, pp. 162, 286.
64. Terry, *Voyage to East India*, pp. 72–3.
65. See Katherine Turner on the metropolis and eighteenth-century travel writing, *British Travel Writers in Europe, 1750–1800: Authorship, gender and national identity* (Aldershot: Ashgate, 2001), p. 6.
66. The OED (2 (b)) lists Wadsworth, 1629 as the earliest usage; Coryate's usage of the term in this letter comes close to our modern definition of the word in terms of urbanity and refined manners (2 (c)), which according to the OED began to emerge in the mid-eighteenth century.
67. Anthony Parr, 'Foreign relations in Jacobean England: the Sherley brothers and the "voyage of Persia"', in Jean-Pierre Maquerlot and Michèle Willems, eds., *Travel and Drama in Shakespeare's Time* (Cambridge: Cambridge University Press, 1996), pp. 14–29.
68. James Clifford, *Routes: Travel and Translation in the Late Twentieth Century* (Cambridge, MA: Harvard University Press, 1997), p. 10.
69. Kenneth Parker, ed., *Early Modern Tales of Orient: A Critical Anthology* (London: Routledge, 1999), pp. 3–9; see also Parr, 'Foreign relations in Jacobean England', pp. 19–20.
70. The horn of the narwhal was frequently said to be a unicorn's horn, and one had been on display at Windsor from the late sixteenth century. By the end of the seventeenth century, the unicorn's horn was the definitive falsified rarity (Caudill, 'Development of English Virtuoso Interests', pp. 153–5).
71. Barbour, *Before Orientalism*, p. 144.
72. Terry, *Voyage to East India*, p. 70.
73. Barbour, *Before Orientalism*, pp. 168–70; Sir William Foster, ed., *Letters Received by the East India Company from its Servants in the East, 1602–17*, 6 vols. (London: Sampson Low, 1896–1902), v, p. 332.
74. Terry, *Voyages in East India*, p. 69.
75. Rubiés, *Travel and Ethnology in the Renaissance*, p. xvii.
76. Elner and Rubiés, *Voyages and Visions*, p. 50.
77. *Coryat's Crudities; reprinted from the Edition of 1611. To which are now added His Letters from India, &c. and extracts relating to him, from various authors: being A more particular Account of his Travels (mostly on Foot) in different Parts of the Globe, than any hitherto published. Together with his Orations, Character, Death, &c.*, 3 vols. (London, 1776).
78. Coriat Junior (Samuel Paterson), *An Entertaining journey to the Netherlands, containing a curious and diverting Account of the manners and customs of Antwerp, Alost, Breda . . . the Whole Written in the Manner and Stile of the Late Lawrence Sterne*, 3 vols. (London, 1782), i, p. vii.
79. Coriat Junior, *Another Traveller! or Cursory Remarks and Tritical Observations made upon a Journey through part of the Netherlands in the latter End of the Year 1766*, 2nd edn, 2 vols. (London, 1769), i, pp. 2, 113–14.
80. Turner, *British Travel Writers*, pp. 101, 104.

81. Tim Moore, *Continental Drifter: Taking the Low Road with the First Grand Tourist* (London: Abacus, 2001).
82. Dom Moraes and Sarayu Srivatsa, *The Long Strider: How Thomas Coryate Walked from England to India in the Year 1613* (New Delhi: Penguin, 2003).

7 AFTERLIVES OF THE WITS

1. Clark, *British Clubs*, pp. vii–viii.
2. Pincus, 'Coffee Politicians Does Create', 807–34.
3. See Introduction, pp. 1–2.
4. Bryson, *Courtesy to Civility*, pp. 196–7.
5. Brooke, 'Reason and Passion in the Public Sphere', 43–67, esp. 52; Shields, *Civil Tongues*, pp. xii–vi, xxvii.
6. Scodel, *Excess and the Mean*, pp. 201–2; Achilleos, 'The *Anacreontea*', pp. 21–35.
7. Clark, *British Clubs*, p. 9. See also 'Introduction', pp. 2–3.
8. Thrush, 'Personal Rule', pp. 84–102.
9. On his death and disgrace, see Whitelocke, *Liber Familicus*, p. 43; Chamberlain, *Letters*, I, p. 556.
10. Whitlock, *John Hoskyns*, pp. 555, 578, 587–9.
11. Chamberlain reported in April 1614 that Martin was 'loth to venter his rising fortune upon his slipperie tongue', *Letters*, I, p. 525.
12. BL, MS Harley 1581, fol. 226r–v.
13. See O'Callaghan, *Shepheards Nation*, pp. 26–85.
14. Ibid., pp. 197–203.
15. Shapiro, 'Mermaid Club', 14; Chamberlain, *Letters*, II, p. 33.
16. Aubrey, *Brief Lives*, II, 49; see also James Whitelocke's account of his friend's death, *Liber Familiacus*, p. 63.
17. See Whitlock's translation, *John Hoskyns*, p. 539.
18. A copy of the inscription and verse to Martin's engraved portrait is in Aubrey, *Brief Lives*, II, p. 49. I am grateful to Bradley Sekedat for assistance with the translation.
19. BL, MS Add. 23229, fol. 35r.
20. BL, MS Add. 25303, fols. 70v–71r.
21. See Guazzo, *Civile Conversation*, pp. 156, 161–2.
22. On answer-poetry and women's participation in scribal communities, see Marotti, *Manuscript, Print*, pp. 56–9; Elizabeth Heale, *Wyatt, Surrey and Early Tudor Poetry* (London: Longman, 1998), pp. 39–49, 58–63; and Boswell, 'Culture and Rhetoric of the Answer-Poem', pp. 247–76.
23. Chamberlain, *Letters*, II, p. 444.
24. Colclough, 'Muses Recreation', pp. 383–4.
25. Chamberlain, *Letters*, I, pp. 581–2.
26. BL, MS Harleian 1581, fol. 240r. On the political role of gentry and aristocratic women, see Barbara J. Harris, *English Aristocratic Women, 1450–1550: Marriage, Property and Careers* (Oxford: Oxford University Press, 2002), p. 209.

27. Bald, *Donne, A Life*, pp. 266–7.
28. Louise Schleiner, *Tudor and Stuart Women Writers* (Bloomington and Indianapolis: Indiana University Press, 1994), Chapter 5. Donne and Jonson successfully sought the patronage of Bedford, and Wroth was also Jonson's patron; see Barbara Lewalski, *Writing Women in Jacobean England* (Cambridge, MA: Harvard University Press, 1993).
29. Aubrey, *Brief Lives*, II, p. 13.
30. That said, the careful study of manuscript anthologies compiled by women, such as that owned by Margaret Bellasys, which collected poems like the 'Parliament Fart' and other railing rhymes, may tell us something about reading habits. On Bellasys's miscellany, see Ian Frederick Moulton, *Before Pornography: Erotic Writing in Early Modern England* (Oxford: Oxford University Press, 2000), pp. 57–62; Sasha Roberts, *Reading Shakespeare's Poems in Early Modern England* (Basingstoke: Palgrave Macmillan, 2003), pp. 16, 48, 176, 179–83, and 'Feminism and the New Formalism: Early Modern Women and Literary Engagement', in Dympna Callaghan, ed., *The Impact of Feminism in Renaissance Literary Studies* (Palgrave Macmillan, forthcoming).
31. See Fidelis Morgan, ed., *The Female Wits: Women Playwrights on the London Stage, 1660–1720* (London: Virago, 1981).
32. Bellany, *Politics of Court Scandal*, Chapter 2, esp. p. 113.
33. On the political culture of the 1620s, see McRae, *Literature, Satire*, esp. Chapters 3 and 4; Thomas Cogswell, *The Blessed Revolution: English Politics and the Coming of War, 1621–1624* (Cambridge: Cambridge University Press, 1989); Norbrook, *Poetry and Politics in the English Renaissance*, Chapter 9; and O'Callaghan, *Shepheards Nation*, Chapter 5.
34. Raylor provides a full and definitive discussion of these fraternities in his *Cavaliers, Clubs, and Literary Culture*, pp. 75–83. He views the fraternity as distinct from the club in that the latter inaugurated a tradition of moderate banqueting, while the former 'indulged in debauched behaviour', p. 83. See also Thornton Shirley Graves on the 1620s fraternities, 'Some Pre Mohock Clansmen', *Studies in Philology* 20 (1923), 399–408.
35. Chamberlain, *Letters*, II, p. 35.
36. Bryson, *Courtesy to Civility*, pp. 245–6.
37. Thomas Carew was squire to one of the Knights of Bath, and named among the later Order of the Bugle, Chamberlain, *Letters*, II, p. 31.
38. Ibid., p. 230; also cited in Raylor, *Cavaliers, Clubs, and Literary Culture*, p. 76 (see also pp. 75–8).
39. Raylor, *Cavaliers, Clubs, and Literary Culture*, pp. 78, 82.
40. See 'Early Stuart Libels', Section N, 'The Spanish Match crisis (c1618–1623)'.
41. A copy with the tune is held in the archives of the Dean and Chapter of Ripon (No. 298), A. J. Smurthwaite, 'A Satirical Ballad of 1624', *Notes and Queries* 27 (1980), 321–2.
42. Bod., MS Malone 19, p. XIII.
43. See also J. D. Alsop's reading of this ballad, 'The Cult of Elizabeth-Astraea and the Anti-Catholic "Jubilye" of 1624', *Cahiers Elisabéthains* 22 (1982), 93–4.

44. The headnote to the poem in Bod., MS Malone 23 claims that it is 'The Coppie of a Libell put into the hand of Queene Elizabeths statue in Westminster by an unknowne person', and gives two dates for the poem – 1621 and end of March 1623 (p. 32). It is followed by the answer poem, 'A Gracious answere from that blessed Saint' (pp. 14–48 (the page order has been disrupted in binding)). On these poems, see Bellany and McRae, *Early Stuart Libels*, Section N.
45. Whitlock, *John Hoskyns*, pp. 557–8, 586, 615, 626; on other accusations of libelling, see Colclough, 'Muses Recreation', 372–4, 382.
46. Colclough, 'Muses Recreation', 378, fn. 39, 390.
47. Mary Hobbs, *Early Seventeenth-Century Verse Miscellany Manuscripts* (Aldershot: Scolar Press, 1992), p. 87.
48. Ben Stone matriculated at New College in October, 1605 – nine years after Coryate entered Gloucester Hall, Oxford – and was made B.A. in May 1609.
49. On non-providential causation and a new historicism, see Ross, 'Memorial Culture', 240–2.
50. See also Boutcher, 'Pilgrimage to Parnassus', 38–45.
51. See Chapter 1, pp. 21–3, 32–4.
52. Hoskyns's mode of nonsense had been adopted by Taylor, who published his *Sir Gregory Nonsense* in the 1620s (see P. N. Hartle, '"All his Workes Sir": John Taylor's Nonsense', *Neophilologus* 86 (2002), 155–69), and Richard Corbett, a friend of Jonson (Raylor, *Cavaliers, Clubs, and Literary Culture*, pp. 99–100).
53. Raylor, *Cavaliers, Clubs, and Literary Culture*, pp. 76, 81.
54. On anticivility, see Bryson, *Courtesy to Civility*, Chapter 7.
55. Percy Simpson, 'Ben Jonson and the Devil Tavern', *Modern Language Review* 34 (1939), 367–73; Scodel, *Excess and the Mean*, p. 199.
56. Achilleos, '*Anacreontea*', pp. 21–35; Scodel, in contrast, sees the process of transmission in terms of a movement away from Jonson's moderate symposiastic ideal, *Excess and the Mean*, Chapters 7 and 8.
57. Butler, 'The Dates of Three Poems by Ben Jonson', *Huntington Library Quarterly* 55 (1992), 284–6.
58. Robert Evans, '"Men that are Safe, and Sure": Jonson's "Tribe of Ben" Epistle in its Patronage Context', *Renaissance and Reformation* n.s. 9 (1985), 240, 242–3.
59. Ibid., 239.
60. Chamberlain, *Letters*, II, p. 530; Raylor, *Cavaliers, Clubs, and Literary Culture*, p. 82.
61. On the *Leges Convivales*, see Chapter 3, p. 77.
62. *The Staple of News*, ed. Anthony Parr (Manchester: Manchester University Press, 1988), pp. 195–8, 4.2.3–41.
63. D. F. McKenzie, '"The Staple of News" and the Late Plays', in William Blisset, Julian Patrick and R. W. Van Forsten, eds., *A Celebration of Ben Jonson* (Toronto and Buffalo: University of Toronto Press, 1973), pp. 92, 98–9.
64. Guazzo, *Civile Conversation*, p. 162.
65. Don E. Wayne argues that the play sets in place distinctions based on an emergent notion of intellectual capital, '"Pox on Your Distinction!": Humanist Reformation and Deformations of the Everyday in *The Staple of News*', in

Patricia Fumerton and Simon Hunt, eds., *Renaissance Culture and the Everyday* (Philadelphia: University of Pennsylvania Press, 1999), pp. 69–91.
66. Stuart Sherman, 'Eyes and Ears, News and Plays: The Argument of Ben Jonson's *Staple*', in Brendan Dooley and Sabrina Baron, eds., *The Politics of Information in Early Modern Europe* (London and New York: Routledge, 2001), pp. 24, 27–9. See also Wayne, 'Pox on Your Distinction', pp. 71–2.
67. On this triad, see Richard Levin, '*The Staple of News*, the Society of Jeeres, and Canters' College', *Philological Quarterly* 44 (1965), 445–53. The Canters' College is thought to satirise Gresham College, which had been dogged by problems of regulation since its foundation: the court sought to use College professorships as part of its machinery of patronage, while the City of London wanted to secure men who would carry out their vision of a civic academy providing the citizens of London with practical education. See Parr, 'Introduction', *Staple of News*, p. 47; I. R. Adamson, 'The Administration of Gresham College and its Fluctuating Fortunes as a Scientific Institution in the Seventeenth Century', *History of Education* 9 (1980), 14–19.
68. Clark, *British Clubs*, p. 16.
69. Leah Marcus, *Politics of Mirth: Jonson, Herrick, Milton, and Marvell, and the Defense of Holiday Pastimes* (Chicago: University of Chicago Press, 1986).
70. 'Upon Sir John Sucklings 100 horse', *Le Prince d'Amour, or the Prince of Love. With a Collection of several Ingenious Poems and Songs by the Wits of the Age* (London, 1660), pp. 148–9.
71. *Musarum Deliciae (1655) and Wit Restored (1658)*, ed. Tim Raylor (New York: Scholars' Facsimiles, 1985), sig. A3v.
72. Raylor, *Cavaliers, Clubs, and Literary Culture*, pp. 202–3. Herringman possibly had political sympathies with these Cavaliers: at the Restoration, he published William Davenant's *Poem upon His Sacred Majesties most happy return to his dominions* (1660), and Henry King's sermons on the inauguration of Charles II and the 1664 anniversary of the 'martyrdom' of Charles I.
73. Ibid., pp. 203–4.
74. Ibid., pp. 123, 125, 128.
75. On Herrick, see Scodel, *Excess and the Mean*, pp. 217–23; Marcus, *Politics of Mirth*, pp. 140–68; and Brown, 'Sons of Beer', pp. 3–11.
76. Raylor, *Cavaliers, Clubs, and Literary Culture*, p. 88.
77. On the symbolism of impure wine, see Scodel, *Excess and the Mean*, pp. 204–5.
78. See Raylor's reading of this epistle, and Smith's reworking of the 'Parliament Fart' in his epistle on the death on Mennes's landlady, *Cavaliers, Clubs, and Literary Culture*, pp. 166–8.
79. This appears to be associated, perhaps a variant on other more common couplets: 'Then sayth Sr William Boulstreed lookeinge very sowre / this ffarte desearues to be com[m]itted to the Tower' (Bod., MS Tanner 306–2 A, fol. 254v); 'Then all in anger sayd Sr Will: Lower / Wee may by our p[r]ivilidge Comitt to the Tower' (BL, MS Add. 34218, fol. 21r).
80. Julius Caesar was famously murdered by the Republican Brutus; Romulus, the founder of the Roman Republic, disappeared in a storm and thus lacked

a grave; Flora, a Roman courtesan, left her wealth to the Republic on the condition her birthday was publicly celebrated.
81. John King, *Milton and Religious Controversy: Satire and Polemic in Paradise Lost* (Cambridge: Cambridge University Press, 2000), pp. 2–16; Raymond Anselment sees the Marprelate pamphlets as an early landmark in this tradition, *Betwixt Jest and Ridicule*, pp. 3–6. More was also skilled in the use of the laughter of ridicule in religious controversy; see Lipking, 'Traditions of Facetiae', pp. 345–85.
82. John Milton, *Paradise Lost*, ed. Alastair Fowler (Essex: Longman, 1971), p. 337, 6.564–5.
83. King, *Milton and Religious Controversy*, pp. 110–13, 123–8.
84. David Loewenstein, '"An Ambiguous Monster": Representing Rebellion in Milton's Polemics and *Paradise Lost*', *Huntington Library Quarterly* 55 (1992), 295–315; also cited in King, *Milton and Religious Controversy*, p. 127. Jonson vehemently disliked Reformation polemic, preferring an Erasmian discourse of religious moderation; see Scodel, *Excess and the Mean*, p. 206.
85. *Musarum Deliciae (1655) and Wit Restored (1658)*, pp. 5–10. Phillips is cited in Courtney Craig Smith, 'The Seventeenth-Century Drolleries', *Harvard Library Bulletin* 6 (1952), 40, fn. 2.
86. Adam Smyth, *'Profit and Delight': Printed Miscellanies in England, 1640–82* (Detroit: Wayne State University Press, 2004), pp. 32–7.
87. Shields, *Civil Tongues*, pp. 33, 12.
88. Ibid., p. 31; Clark, *British Clubs*, pp. vii–ix, 3–9.

Bibliography

PRIMARY SOURCES

MANUSCRIPTS

Bodleian Library, Oxford

Don.c.54	Malone 23	Tanner 306/2
Malone 16	Rawl.b.151	
Malone 19	Rawl.poet.117	

Corpus Christi College Library, Oxford

CCC. 327

British Library

Add. 4149	Add. 34218	Sloane 2023
Add. 23229	Add. 58215	Stowe 354
Add. 25303	Harley 1581	Stowe 962
Add. 27632	Harley 4931	

Rosenbach Library, Philadelphia

1083/15

York City Archives

York House Book, 33

PRINTED BOOKS

Aubrey, John, *'Brief Lives', chiefly of Contemporaries, set down by John Aubrey, between the Years 1669 and 1696*, ed. Andrew Clark, 2 vols. (Oxford: Clarendon Press, 1898)
Bowyer, Robert, *The Parliamentary Diary of Robert Bowyer, 1606–1607*, ed. David Harris Willson (Minneapolis: University of Minnesota Press, 1931)
Brathwaite, Richard, (Blasius Multibibus), *A Solemne Joviall Disputation, Theoreticke and Practicke; briefly shadowing the Law of Drinking* (London, 1617)
Brinsley, John, *Ludus Literarius (1612)* (Menston: Scolar Press, 1968)
Buck, George, *The Third Universitie of England*, appended to John Stow, *The Annales, or Generall Chronicle of England* (London, 1615)
Burton, Robert, *The Anatomy of Melancholy*, ed. Holbrook Jackson, 3 vols. (London: Dent, 1932)
Beaumont, Francis and Fletcher, John, *Poems. The Golden Remains of those so much admired Dramatick Poets, Francis Beaumont and John Fletcher Gent* (London, 1660)
Chamberlain, John, *The Letters of John Chamberlain*, ed. N. E. McClure, 2 vols. (Philadelphia: The American Philosophical Society, 1939)
Chapman, George, *The Memorable Maske of the two Honorable Houses or Inns of Court, the Middle Temple, and Lyncolns Inne*, in *The Plays of George Chapman: the Comedies*, ed. Allan Holaday (Urbana, Chicago: University of Illinois Press, 1970)
Cholmley, Hugh, *The Memoirs and Memorials of Sir Hugh Cholmley of Whitby, 1600–1657*, ed. Jack Binns (Woodbridge: Boydell and Brewer, 2000)
Cicero, Marcus Tullius, *De Amicitia*, trans. W. A. Falconer (Cambridge, MA: Harvard University Press, 1923)
  De Oratore, Books I–II, trans. E. W. Sutton and H. Rackham (Cambridge, MA: Harvard University Press, 1942)
  Letters to Friends, trans. D. R. Shackleton Bailey, 3 vols. (Cambridge, MA: Harvard University Press, 2001)
  The Speeches: Pro Caelio, De Provinciis Consularibus, Pro Balbo, trans. R. Gardner (Cambridge, MA: Harvard University Press, 1958)
Coryate, Thomas, *Coryats Crudities (1611)*, intro. by W. M. Schutte (London: Scolar Press, 1979)
  Coryats Crambe, or His Colwort twise Sodden, and now served in with other Macaronicke dishes, as the second course to his Crudities (London, 1611)
  Thomas Coriate Traveller for the English Wits: greeting From the court of the Great Mogul (London, 1616)
  Mr Thomas Coriat to his friends in England sendeth greeting, ed. John Taylor (London, 1618)
Dallington, Robert, *A Method for Travell* (London, c. 1605)

Davies, John, *Orchestra or a Poeme of Dauncing* (London, 1596)
  The Poems of Sir John Davies, ed. Robert Krueger (Oxford: Clarendon Press, 1975)
Dekker, Thomas, *The Dramatic Works of Thomas Dekker*, ed. Fredson Bowers, 4 vols. (Cambridge: Cambridge University Press, 1970)
Donne, John, *Letters to Several Persons of Honour* (London, 1651)
  The Courtier's Library: or, Catalogus librorum aulicorum incomparabilium et non vendibilium, ed. E. M. Simpson (London: Nonesuch Press, 1930)
  John Donne, ed. John Carey (Oxford: Oxford University Press, 1990)
Erasmus, Desiderius, *The Praise of Folly*, trans. Clarence Miller (New Haven: Yale University Press, 1979)
Fennor, William, *Fennors Defence: Or, I am your First Man* (London, 1615)
Gesta Grayorum 1688, ed. W. W. Greg (Oxford: Oxford University Press, 1914)
Guazzo, Stefano, *The Civile Conversation of M. Steeven Guazzo*, books 1–3 trans. George Pettie (1581), book 4 trans. Bartholomew Young (1586), ed. Edward Sullivan, 2 vols. (London: Constable; New York: Alfred A. Knopf, 1925)
Guilpin, Everard, *Skialetheia* (London, 1598)
Harington, Sir John, *A New Discourse of a Stale Subject, called the Metamorphosis of Ajax*, ed. Elizabeth Story Donno (London: Routledge & Kegan Paul, 1962)
  'A Treatise on Playe' (c. 1597), in *Nugae Antiquae*, ed. Thomas Park, selected by Henry Harington, 2 vols. (London, 1804)
Holland, Hugh, *Pancharis: The first Booke*, in J. Payne Collier, ed., *Illustrations of Old English Literature*, 3 vols. (London, 1866), vol. II
Hoskyns, John, *The Life, Letters and Writings of John Hoskyns*, ed. Louise Osborn (New Haven: Yale University Press, 1937)
James VI and I, *Political Writings*, ed. Johann P. Somerville (Cambridge: Cambridge University Press, 1994)
Jonson, Ben, *The Works of Jonson*, ed. William Gifford, 9 vols. (London, 1816)
  Works of Ben Jonson, ed. C. H. Herford, Percy Simpson and Evelyn Simpson, 11 vols. (Oxford: Clarendon Press, 1925–52)
  Ben Jonson, ed. Ian Donaldson (Oxford: Oxford University Press, 1985)
  Bartholomew Fair, ed. Suzanne Gossett (Manchester: Manchester University Press, 2000)
  Catiline, ed. W. F. Bolton and Jane F. Gardner (London: Edward Arnold, 1973)
  Epicoene, or the Silent Woman, ed. R. V. Holdsworth (London: Ernest Benn, 1979)
  Every Man Out of His Humour, ed. Helen Ostovich (Manchester: Manchester University Press, 2001)
  The Staple of News, ed. Anthony Parr (Manchester: Manchester University Press, 1988)
Legh, Gerard, *The Accedence of Armorie. Newly corrected and augmented* (London, 1612)
Le Prince d'Amour, or the Prince of Love. With a Collection of several Ingenious Poems and Songs by the Wits of the Age (London, 1660)

Madox, Richard, *An Elizabethan in 1582: The Diary of Richard Madox, Fellow of All Souls*, ed. Elizabeth Story Donno (London: The Hakluyt Society, 1976)

Manningham, John, *The Diary of John Manningham of the Middle Temple, 1602–3*, ed. Robert Parker Sorlein (Hanover, New Hampshire: The University Press of New England, 1976)

Martin, Richard, *A Speech Delivered to the Kings Most Excellent Majestie, at his Neere Approach to London, in the Name of the Sheriffs of London and Middlesex* (London, 1603)

Meier, Albert, *Certain briefe, and speciall instructions for gentlemen, merchants, students, souldiers, marriners, &c. employed in services abrode*, trans. Philip Jones (London, 1589)

Montaigne, Michel, *The Essayes, or Morall, Politike and Millitarie Discourses*, trans. John Florio (London, 1603)

Musarum Deliciae (1655) and Wit Restored (1658), ed. Tim Raylor (New York: Scholars' Facsimiles, 1985)

Obsopoeus, Vincentius, *The Art of Drinking. Three Books by the Author Vincentius Obsopoeus the German*, trans. Helen F. Simpson, in E. M. Jellinek, 'A Specimen of the Sixteenth-Century German Drink Literature – Obsopoeus's *Art of Drinking*', *Quarterly Journal of Studies on Alcohol* 5 (1944–5), 647–700.

Palmer, Sir Thomas, *An Essay of the Meanes how to make our Travailes, into forraine Countries, the more profitable and honourable (London, 1606)* (Amsterdam: Theatrum Orbis Terrarum, 1972)

Paterson, Samuel, (Coriat Junior), *Another Traveller! or Cursory Remarks and Tritical Observations made upon a Journey through part of the Netherlands in the latter End of the Year 1766*, 2nd edn, 2 vols. (London, 1769)

  An Entertaining journey to the Netherlands, containing a curious and diverting Account of the manners and customs of Antwerp, Alost, Breda . . . the Whole Written in the Manner and Stile of the Late Lawrence Sterne, 3 vols. (London, 1782)

Plutarch, *Moralia*, trans. Paul Clement and Herbert Hoffleit, 16 vols. (Cambridge, MA: Harvard University Press, 1969)

Proceedings in Parliament, 1610, ed. Elizabeth Read Foster, 2 vols. (New Haven: Yale University Press, 1966)

Proceedings in Parliament, 1614, ed. Maija Jansson (Philadelphia: American Philosophical Society, 1988)

Purchas, Samuel, *Purchas his Pilgrimes. In Five Bookes* (London, 1625)

  Purchas his Pilgrimage. Or relations of the World and the Religions observed in all ages and places discovered, from the Creation unto this Present (London, 1626)

Puttenham, George, *The Arte of English Poesie. Contrived into three Bookes (1589)*, ed. Edward Arber (London: Murray & Son, 1869)

Quintilian, Marcus Fabius, *Institutio Oratoria*, trans. Donald A. Russell (Cambridge, MA: Harvard University Press, 2001)

Rudyerd, Benjamin, *The Memoirs of Sir Benjamin Rudyerd, Knt.*, ed. J. A. Manning (London: Boone, 1841)

Sidney, Sir Philip, *Miscellaneous Prose of Sir Philip Sidney*, ed. Katherine Duncan-Jones and Jan Van Dorsten (Oxford: Clarendon Press, 1973)

Stuart Royal Proclamations, ed. James F. Larkin and Paul L. Hughes, 2 vols. (Oxford: Clarendon Press, 1973)

Taylor, John, *The Sculler, rowing from the Tiber to the Thames* (London, 1612).
 Laugh and be fat, or a commentary upon the Odcombyan banket (London, 1612)
 Odcombs Complaint: or Coriatts Funeral Epicedium (London, 1613)
 The Eighth Wonder of the World: or, Coryate's escape from his supposed drowning (London, 1613)
 The Pennyles Pilgrimage, or the Money-lesse perambulation, of John Taylor, Alias the Kings Majesties Water-Poet (London, 1618)

Terry, Edward, *A Voyage to East India* (London, 1655)

Turler, Jerome, *The Traveiler of Jerome Turler (1575)* (Gainesville, Florida: Scholars' Facsimiles & Reprints, 1951)

Whitelocke, James, *Liber Familicus*, ed. John Bruce (London: Camden Society, 1858)

Willughby, Francis, *Francis Willughby's Book of Games: A Seventeenth-Century Treatise on Sports, Games and Pastimes*, ed. David Cram, Jeffrey Forgeng and Dorothy Johnson (Aldershot: Ashgate, 2003)

Xenophon, *Symposium*, trans. O. J. Todd (Cambridge, MA: Harvard University Press, 1961)

ELECTRONIC

McRae, Andrew and Bellany, Alastair, eds., *Early Stuart Libels: An Edition of Poetry from Manuscript Sources*, EMLS Text Series 1 (2005), http://purl.oclc.org/emls/texts/libels/

SECONDARY SOURCES

Achilleos, Stella, 'The *Anacreontea* and a Tradition of Refined Male Sociability', in Adam Smyth, ed., *A Pleasing Sinne: Drink and Conviviality in Seventeenth-Century England* (Woodbridge: Boydell and Brewer, 2004), pp. 18–20

Allen, Peter R., '*Utopia* and European Humanism: The Function of the Prefatory Letters and Verses', *Studies in the Renaissance* 10 (1963), 91–107

Anselment, Raymond A., *'Betwixt Jest and Earnest': Marprelate, Milton, Marvell, Swift and the Decorum of Religious Ridicule* (Toronto: University of Toronto Press, 1979)

Arcangeli, Alessandro, *Recreation in the Renaissance: Attitudes towards Leisure and Pastimes in European Culture, c. 1425–1675* (Basingstoke: Palgrave Macmillan, 2003)

Arlidge, Anthony, *Shakespeare and the Prince of Love: The Feast of Misrule in the Middle Temple* (London: Giles de la Mare, 2000)

Arnold, Oliver, 'Absorption and Representation: Mapping England in the early modern House of Commons', in Andrew Gordon and Bernhard Klein, eds., *Literature, Mapping, and the Politics of Space in Early Modern Britain* (Cambridge: Cambridge University Press, 2001), pp. 15–34

Baker, Christopher, 'Ben Jonson and the Inns of Court: The Literary Milieu of *Every Man Out of His Humour*', unpublished Ph.D. thesis, University of North Carolina (1974)

Baker, J. H., *The Legal Profession and the Common Law: Historical Essays* (London: Hambledon Press, 1986)

Bakhtin, Mikhail, *The Dialogic Imagination: Four Essays by M. M. Bakhtin*, ed. Michael Holquist, trans. Caryl Emerson and Holquist (Austin: University of Texas Press, 1981)

Rabelais and His World, trans. Hélène Iswolsky (Bloomington: Indiana University Press, 1984)

Bald, R. C., *John Donne, A Life* (Oxford: Clarendon Press, 1986)

Ballstaedt, Andreas, '"Dissonance" in Music', in Hans Ulrich Gumbrecht and K. Ludwig Pfeiffer, eds., *The Materialities of Communication*, trans. William Whobrey (Stanford: Stanford University Press, 1994), pp. 157–69

Barbour, Richmond, *Before Orientalism: London's Theatre of the East, 1576–1626* (Cambridge: Cambridge University Press, 2003)

Blake, N. F., 'Manuscript to Print', in Jeremy Griffiths and Derek Pearsall, eds., *Book Production and Publication in Britain, 1375–1475* (Cambridge: Cambridge University Press, 1989), pp. 403–32

Bland, D. S., 'Rhetoric and the Law Student in Sixteenth-Century England', *Studies in Philology* 54 (1957), 498–508

Bland, Mark, 'Francis Beaumont's Verse Letters to Ben Jonson and the "Mermaid Club"', *English Manuscript Studies, 1100–1700* 12 (2005), 139–79

Boswell, Christopher, 'The Culture and Rhetoric of the Answer-Poem, 1485–1625', unpublished Ph.D. thesis, University of Leeds (2003)

Bourdieu, Pierre, *Outline of a Theory of Practice*, trans. Richard Nice (Cambridge: Cambridge University Press, 1977)

Distinction: A Social Critique of the Judgement of Taste, trans. Richard Nice (London: Routledge & Kegan Paul, 1984)

Boutcher, Warren, 'Pilgrimage to Parnassus: Local Intellectual Traditions, Humanist Education, and the Cultural Geography of Sixteenth-Century England', in Niall Livingstone and Yun Lee Too, eds., *Pedagogy and Power: Rhetorics of Classical Learning* (Cambridge: Cambridge University Press, 1998), pp. 110–47

Brioist, Pascal, 'Que de choses avons nous vues et vécues à la Sirène', *Histoire et Civilisation* 4 (1991), 89–132

Brooke, John L., 'Reason and Passion in the Public Sphere: Habermas and the Cultural Historians', *Journal of Interdisciplinary History* 29 (1998), 43–67

Brooks, C. W., 'The Common Lawyers in England, c. 1558–1642', in Wilfred Prest, ed., *Lawyers in Early Modern Europe and America* (London: Croom Helm, 1981), pp. 42–64

Brown, Cedric, 'Sons of Beer and Sons of Ben: Drink as a Social Marker in Seventeenth-Century England', in Adam Smyth, ed., *A Pleasing Sinne: Drink and Conviviality in Seventeenth-Century England* (Woodbridge: Boydell and Brewer, 2004), pp. 3–20

Brown, Meg Lota, *Donne and the Politics of Conscience in Early Modern England* (Leiden: E. J. Brill, 1995)

Bruster, Douglas, 'The Structural Transformation of Print in Late Elizabethan England', in Arthur Marotti and Michael D. Bristol, eds., *Print, Manuscript and Performance* (Columbus: Ohio State University Press, 2000), pp. 49–89

Bryson, Anna, *From Courtesy to Civility: Changing Codes of Conduct in Early Modern England* (Oxford: Clarendon Press, 1998)

Burke, Kenneth, *A Rhetoric of Motives* (New York: Prentice Hall, 1950)

Burke, Peter, 'The Invention of Leisure in Early Modern Europe', *Past and Present* 146 (1995), 136–50

Butler, Martin, 'The Dates of Three Poems by Ben Jonson', *Huntington Library Quarterly* 55 (1992), 279–94

'Sir Francis Stewart: Jonson's Overlooked Patron', *Ben Jonson Journal* 2 (1995), 101–27

Cain, Tom, 'Donne and the Prince d'Amour', *John Donne Journal* 14 (1995), 83–111

'"Satyres, That Girdle and Fart at the Time": *Poetaster* and the Essex Rebellion', in Julie Sanders, with Kate Chedgzoy and Susan Wiseman, eds., *Refashioning Ben Jonson: Gender, Politics and the Jonsonian Canon* (Basingstoke: Palgrave Macmillan, 1998), pp. 48–70

Caudill, Randall L.-W., 'Some Literary Evidence of the Development of English Virtuoso Interests in the Seventeenth Century, with Particular Reference to the Literature of Travel', unpublished D.Phil. thesis, Oxford (1976)

Certeau, Michel de, *The Practice of Everday Life*, trans. Steven F. Rendall (Berkeley: University of California Press, 1984)

Chaney, Edward, *The Evolution of the Grand Tour: Anglo-Italian Cultural Relations since the Renaissance*, 2nd edn (London and Portland, Oregon: Frank Cass, 2000)

Chartier, Roger, *Cultural History: Between Practices and Representations*, trans. Lydia G. Cochrane (Cambridge: Polity Press, 1988)

'Leisure and Sociability: Reading Aloud in Early Modern Europe', trans. Carol Mossman, in Susan Zimmerman and Ronald F. E. Weissman, eds., *Urban Life in the Renaissance* (Newark: University of Delaware Press, 1989), pp. 103–20

Chartier, Roger, ed., *The Culture of Print: Power and the Uses of Print in Early Modern Europe*, trans. Lydia G. Cochrane (Princeton: Princeton University Press, 1989)

Clark, Peter, *The English Alehouse: A Social History, 1200–1830* (London: Longman, 1982)

British Clubs and Societies, 1580–1800: The Origins of an Associational World (Oxford: Clarendon Press, 2000)

Clegg, Cyndia Susan, *Press Censorship in Elizabethan England* (Cambridge: Cambridge University Press, 1997)

Clopper, Lawrence, *Drama, Play, and Game: English Festive Culture in the Medieval and Early Modern Period* (Chicago: University of Chicago Press, 2001)

Clucas, Stephen and Davies, Rosalind, eds., *The Crisis of 1614 and the Addled Parliament: Literary and Historical Perspectives* (Aldershot: Ashgate, 2003)
Colclough, David, '"Of the alleadging of authors": The Construction and Reception of Textual Authority in English Prose, c. 1600–1630. With Special Reference to the Writings of Francis Bacon, John Hoskyns, and John Donne', unpublished D.Phil. thesis, Oxford (1996)
  '*Parrhesia*: The Rhetoric of Free Speech in Early Modern England', *Rhetorica* 17 (1999), 177–210
  '"The Muses Recreation": John Hoskyns and the Manuscript Culture of the Seventeenth Century', *Huntington Library Quarterly* 61 (2000), 369–400
  '"Better Becoming a Senate of Venice"?: The "Addled Parliament" and Jacobean Debates on Freedom of Speech', in Stephen Clucas and Ros Davies, eds., *The Crisis of 1614 and The Addled Parliament: Literary and Historical Perspectives* (Aldershot: Ashgate, 2003), pp. 51–61
Cooper, J. P., *Land, Men and Beliefs: Studies in Early Modern History*, ed. G. E. Aylmer and J. S. Morrill (London: Hambledon Press, 1983)
Craik, Katharine, 'Reading *Coryats Crudities* (1611)', *Studies in English Literature* 44 (2004), 77–96
  'John Taylor's Pot-Poetry', *The Seventeenth Century*, 20 (2005), 185–203.
Croft, Pauline, 'The Reputation of Robert Cecil: Libels, Political Opinion and Popular Awareness in the Early Seventeenth Century', *Transactions of the Royal Historical Society* 1 (1991), 43–69
  'Capital Life: Members of Parliament outside the House', in Thomas Cogswell, Richard Cust and Peter Lake, eds., *Politics, Religion and Popularity in Early Stuart Britain: Essays in Honour of Conrad Russell* (Cambridge: Cambridge University Press, 2002), pp. 65–83
Cromartie, Alan, 'The Constitutionalist Revolution: The Transformation of Political Culture in Early Stuart England', *Past and Present* 163 (1999), 76–120
Cuddy, Neil, 'The Conflicting Loyalties of a "vulger counselor": The Third Earl of Southampton', in John Morrill, Paul Slack and Daniel Woolf, eds., *Public Duty and Private Conscience in Seventeenth-Century England* (Oxford: Clarendon Press, 1993), pp. 121–50
Cummings, Robert, 'Liberty and History in Jonson's "Invitation to Supper"', *Studies in English Literature* 40 (2000), 103–22
Cunnington, David, 'The Profession of Friendship in Donne's Amatory Verse Letters', in David Colclough, ed., *John Donne's Professional Lives* (Woodbridge: Boydell and Brewer, 2003)
D'Arms, John, 'The Roman *Convivium* and the Idea of Equality', in Oswyn Murray, ed., *Sympotica: A Symposium on the Symposion* (Oxford: Clarendon Press, 1990), pp. 308–20
Duncan, Douglas, *Ben Jonson and the Lucianic Tradition* (Cambridge: Cambridge University Press, 1979)
Duncan-Jones, Katherine, '"Preserved Dainties": Late Elizabethan Poems by Sir Robert Cecil and the Earl of Clanricarde', *Bodleian Library Record* 14 (1992), 136–44

Elias, Norbert, *The Civilizing Process: Sociogenetic and Psychogenetic Investigations*, trans. Edmund Jephcott (Oxford: Blackwell, 2000)
Elner, Jás, and Rubiés, Joan-Pau, *Voyages and Visions: Towards a Cultural History of Travel* (London: Reaktion, 1999)
Elton, W. R., *Shakespeare's 'Troilus and Cressida' and the Inns of Court Revels* (Aldershot: Ashgate, 2000)
Evans, Robert, '"Men that are Safe, and Sure": Jonson's "Tribe of Ben" Epistle in its Patronage Context', *Renaissance and Reformation* n.s. 9 (1985), 235–54
Ezell, Margaret, *Social Authorship and the Advent of Print* (Baltimore: Johns Hopkins University Press, 1999)
Finkelpearl, Philip, *John Marston of the Middle Temple: An Elizabethan Dramatist in his Social Setting* (Cambridge, MA: Harvard University Press, 1969)
Fish, Stanley, 'Authors-Readers: Jonson's Community of the Same', in Stephen Greenblatt, ed., *Representing the Renaissance* (Berkeley: University of California, 1988), pp. 231–63
Fisher, F. J., 'The Development of London as a Centre of Consumption in the Sixteenth and Seventeenth Centuries', *Transactions of the Royal Historical Society* 30 (1948), 37–50
Fitzmaurice, Andrew, *Humanism and America: An Intellectual History of English Colonisation, 1500–1625* (Cambridge: Cambridge University Press, 2003)
Flood, W. H. Grattan, 'Fennor and Daborne at Youghal in 1618', *Modern Language Review* 20 (1925), 321–2
Foster, Elizabeth Read, 'Speaking in the House of Commons', *Bulletin of the Institute of Historical Research* 43 (1970), 35–55
Fox, Adam, *Oral and Literate Culture in England, 1500–1700* (Oxford: Oxford University Press, 2000)
Foucault, Michel, *Fearless Speech*, ed. Joseph Pearson (Los Angeles: Semiotext(e), 2001)
Geffcken, Katherine A., *Comedy in the Pro Caelio* (Leiden: E. J. Brill, 1973)
Gordon, Andrew, 'The Act of Libel: Conscripting Civic Space in Early Modern England', *Journal of Medieval and Early Modern Studies* 32 (2002), 375–97
Grafton, Anthony, *Bring Out Your Dead: The Past as Revelation* (Cambridge, MA: Harvard University Press, 2001)
Grant, Mary A., *The Ancient Rhetorical Theories of the Laughable: The Greek Rhetoricians and Cicero*, University of Wisconsin Studies in Language and Literature, 21 (Madison, Wisconsin, 1924)
Graves, Thornton Shirley, 'Some Pre-Mohock Clansmen', *Studies in Philology* 20 (1923), 395–421
Greene, Thomas M., 'Ceremonial Play and Parody in the Renaissance', in Susan Zimmerman and Ronald F. E. Weissman, eds., *Urban Life in the Renaissance* (Newark: University of Delaware Press, 1989), pp. 281–93
Habermas, Jürgen, *The Structural Transformation of the Public Sphere: An Inquiry into a Category of Bourgeois Society*, trans. Thomas Burger and Frederick Lawrence (Cambridge, MA: Massachusetts Institute of Technology, 1989)

Hadfield, Andrew, *Literature, Travel, and Colonial Writing in the English Renaissance, 1545–1625* (Oxford: Clarendon Press, 1998)
Halasz, Alexandra, '"So beloved that men use his picture for their signs": Richard Tarlton and the Uses of Sixteenth-Century Celebrity', *Shakespeare Studies* 23 (1995), 19–38
  The Marketplace of Print: Pamphlets and the Public Sphere in Early Modern England (Cambridge: Cambridge University Press, 1997)
Hammer, Paul E. J., *The Polarisation of Elizabethan Politics: The Political Career of Robert Devereux, Second Earl of Essex, 1585–97* (Cambridge: Cambridge University Press, 1999)
Harding, Vanessa, 'London, Change and Exchange', in Henry S. Turner, ed., *The Culture of Capital: Properties, Cities, Knowledge in Early Modern England* (London: Routledge, 2002), pp. 129–38
Haynes, Jonathan, *The Social Relations of Jonson's Theater* (Cambridge: Cambridge University Press, 1992)
Hexter, J. H., 'Parliament, Liberty, and Freedom of Elections', in Hexter, ed., *Parliament and Liberty: From the Reign of Elizabeth to the English Civil War* (Stanford: Stanford University Press, 1992), pp. 21–55
Herz, Judith Scherer, 'Of Circles, Friendship, and the Imperatives of Literary History', in Claude Summers and Ted-Larry Pebworth, eds., *Literary Circles and Cultural Communities in Renaissance England* (Columbia: University of Missouri Press, 2000), pp. 10–23
Hinchcliffe, Edgar, 'Thomae Coriati Testimonium', *Notes & Queries* n.s. 15 (1968), 370–5
Holcomb, Chris, *Mirth Making: The Rhetorical Discourse on Jesting in Early Modern England* (Columbia, SC: University of South Carolina Press)
Hunter, Judith, 'Legislation, Royal Proclamations and other National Directives Affecting Inns, Taverns, Alehouses, Brandy Shops and Punch Houses, 1552 to 1757', unpublished Ph.D. thesis, University of Reading (1994)
Hutson, Lorna, 'Civility and Virility in Ben Jonson', *Representations* 78 (2002), 1–27
Huizinga, Johan, *Homo Ludens: A Study of the Play Element in Culture* (London: Temple Smith, 1970)
Jeanneret, Michel, *A Feast of Words: Banquets and Table Talk in the Renaissance*, trans. Jeremy Whiteley and Emma Hughes (Cambridge: Polity Press, 1991)
Jones, Ann Rosalind, 'Italians and Others: *The White Devil* (1612)', in David Scott Kastan and Peter Stallybrass, eds., *Staging the Renaissance: Reinterpretations of Elizabethan and Jacobean Drama* (London: Routledge, 1991), pp. 251–62
Kahn, Victoria, *Rhetoric, Prudence and Skepticism in the Renaissance* (Ithaca, NY: Cornell University Press, 1985)
Limon, Jerzy, *The Masque of Stuart Culture* (Newark: University of Delaware Press; Toronto: Associated University Presses, 1990)
Lipking, Joanna Brizdale, 'Traditions of the Facetiae and Their Influence in Tudor England', Unpublished Ph.D. thesis, Columbia University (1970)

Loewenstein, Joseph, 'The Jonsonian Corpulence, or the Poet as Mouthpiece', *ELH* 53 (1986), 491–518
  The Author's Due: Printing and the Prehistory of Copyright (Chicago and London: University of Chicago Press, 2002)
Love, Harold, *Scribal Publication in Seventeenth-Century England* (Oxford: Clarendon Press, 1993)
Luck, George, '*Vir Facetus*: A Renaissance Ideal', *Studies in Philology* 55 (1958), 107–21
Mack, Peter, *Elizabethan Rhetoric: Theory and Practice* (Cambridge: Cambridge University Press, 2002)
McCoy, Richard, *Rites of Knighthood: The Literature and Politics of Elizabethan Chivalry* (Berkeley: University of California Press, 1989)
McKenzie, D. F., '"The Staple of News" and the Late Plays', in William Blissett, Julian Patrick and R. W. Van Forsten, eds., *A Celebration of Ben Jonson* (Toronto and Buffalo: University of Toronto Press, 1973), pp. 83–128
  Making Meaning: 'Printers of the Mind' and other Essays, ed. Peter D. McDonald and Michael F. Suarez, SJ (Amherst: University of Massachusetts Press, 2002)
McRae, Andrew, '"On the Famous Voyage": Ben Jonson and Civic Space', in Andrew Gordon and Bernhard Klein, eds., *Literature, Mapping, and the Politics of Space in Early Modern Britain* (Cambridge: Cambridge University Press, 2001), pp. 181–203
  Literature, Satire and the Early Stuart State (Cambridge: Cambridge University Press, 2004)
Malcolm, Noel, *The Origins of English Nonsense* (London: Harper Collins, 1997)
Marcus, Leah, *Politics of Mirth: Jonson, Herrick, Milton, and Marvell, and the Defense of Holiday Pastimes* (Chicago: University of Chicago Press, 1986)
Marotti, Arthur, *John Donne, Coterie Poet* (Madison, Wisconsin: University of Wisconsin Press, 1986)
  Manuscript, Print, and the English Renaissance Lyric (Ithaca, NY: Cornell University Press, 1995)
Marsh, Christopher, 'The Sound of Print in Early Modern England: The Broadside Ballad as Song', in Julia Crick and Alexandra Walsham, eds., *The Uses of Script and Print, 1300–1700* (Cambridge: Cambridge University Press, 2004), pp. 171–90
Maus, Katharine Eisaman, *Ben Jonson and the Roman Frame of Mind* (Princeton: Princeton University Press, 1984)
Miller, Peter N., *Peiresc's Europe: Learning and Virtue in the Seventeenth Century* (New Haven: Yale University Press, 2000)
More, Rebecca Weeks, 'The Rewards of Virtue: Gentility in Early Modern England', unpublished Ph.D. thesis, Brown University (1998)
Muldrew, Craig, *The Economy of Obligation: The Culture of Credit and Social Relations in Early Modern England* (Basingstoke: Macmillan, 1998)
Müller, Jan-Dirk, 'The Body of the Book: The Media Transition from Manuscript to Print,' in Hans Ulrich Gumbrecht and K. Ludwig Pfeiffer, eds., *The*

Materialities of Communication, trans. William Whobrey (Stanford: Stanford University Press, 1994), pp. 32–44

Murray, Oswyn, 'The Affair of the Mysteries: Democracy and the Drinking Group' in Murray, ed., *Sympotica: A Symposium on the Symposion* (Oxford: Clarendon Press, 1990), pp. 149–61

Newman, Karen, 'Walking Capitals: Donne's *First Satyre*', in Henry S. Turner, ed., *The Culture of Capital: Properties, Cities, Knowledge in Early Modern England* (London: Routledge, 2002), pp. 203–21

Norbrook, David, 'Rhetoric, Ideology and the Elizabethan World Picture', in Peter Mack, ed., *Renaissance Rhetoric* (Basingstoke: Macmillan, 1996), pp. 140–64

Poetry and Politics in the English Renaissance, rev. edn (Oxford: Oxford University Press, 2002)

O'Callaghan, Michelle, *The 'Shepheards Nation': Jacobean Spenserians and Early Stuart Political Culture* (Oxford: Clarendon Press, 2000)

'Tavern Societies, the Inns of Court, and the Culture of Conviviality', in Adam Smyth, ed., *A Pleasing Sinne: Drink and Conviviality in Seventeenth-Century England* (Woodbridge: Boydell and Brewer, 2004), pp. 37–51

'Performing Politics: The Circulation of the "Parliament Fart"', *Huntington Library Quarterly* 69 (2006), 121–38

Ong, Walter, *Orality and Literacy: The Technologizing of the Word* (London: Routledge, 2002)

Ord, Melanie, 'Provincial Identification and the Struggle over Representation in Thomas Coryat's *Crudities* (1611)', in Philip Schwyzer and Simon Mealor, eds., *Archipelagic Identities: Literature and Identity in the Atlantic Archipelago, 1550–1800* (Aldershot: Ashgate, 2004), pp. 131–40

Parr, Anthony, 'Thomas Coryat and the Discovery of Europe', *Huntington Library Quarterly* 55 (1992), 579–602

'Foreign Relations in Jacobean England: The Sherley Brothers and the "Voyage of Persia"', in Jean-Pierre Maquerlot and Michèle Willems, eds., *Travel and Drama in Shakespeare's Time* (Cambridge: Cambridge University Press, 1996), pp. 14–29

Patterson, Annabel, 'All Donne', in Elizabeth Harvey and Katharine Eisaman Maus, eds., *Soliciting Interpretation: Literary Theory and Seventeenth-Century English Poetry* (Chicago and London: University of Chicago Press, 1990), pp. 37–67

Pellizer, Ezio, 'Outlines of a Morphology of Sympotic Entertainment', in Oswyn Murray, ed., *Sympotica: A Symposium on the Symposion* (Oxford: Clarendon Press, 1990), pp. 177–84

Peltonen, Markku, *Classical Humanism and Republicanism in English Political Thought, 1570–1640* (Cambridge: Cambridge University Press, 1995)

Pincus, Steven, '"Coffee Politicians Does Create": Coffeehouses and Restoration Political Culture', *The Journal of Modern History* 67 (1995), 807–34

Prescott, Anne Lake, *Imagining Rabelais in Renaissance England* (New Haven: Yale University Press, 1998)

Prest, Wilfred, *The Inns of Court under Elizabeth and the Early Stuarts, 1590–1640* (London: Longman, 1972)
Raffield, Paul, *Images and Cultures of Law in Early Modern England* (Cambridge: Cambridge University Press, 2004)
Ramage, Edwin S., *Urbanitas: Ancient Sophistication and Refinement* (Norman, Oklahoma: University of Oklahoma Press, 1973)
Richards, Jennifer, *Rhetoric and Courtliness in Early Modern Literature* (Cambridge: Cambridge University Press, 2003)
Roebuck, Graham, '*Johannes Factus* and the Anvil of Wits', *John Donne Journal* 15 (1996), 141–52
Ross, Richard, 'The Memorial Culture of Early Modern English Lawyers: Memory as Keyword, as Shelter, and Identity, 1560–1640', *Yale Journal of Law and the Humanities* 10 (1998), 229–326
Rubiés, Joan-Pau, *Travel and Ethnology in the Renaissance: South India through European Eyes, 1250–1625* (Cambridge: Cambridge University Press, 2000)
Sanderson, James L., '*Epigrammes P[er] B[enjamin] R[udyerd]* and some more "Stolen Feathers" of Henry Parrot', *Review of English Studies* 17 (1966), 241–55
Scodel, Joshua, *Excess and the Mean in Early Modern English Literature* (Princeton: Princeton University Press, 2002)
Scott-Warren, Jason, *Sir John Harington and the Book as Gift* (Oxford: Oxford University Press, 2001)
Shapiro, I. A. 'The "Mermaid Club"', *Modern Language Review* 45 (1950), 6–17
Simpson, Percy, 'Ben Jonson and the Devil Tavern', *Modern Language Review* 34 (1939), 367–73
Simpson, Percy and Shapiro, I. A., '"The Mermaid Club": An Answer and A Rejoinder', *Modern Language Review* 46 (1951), 58–63
Sharpe, Kevin, *Sir Robert Cotton 1586–1631: History and Politics in Early Modern England* (Oxford: Oxford University Press, 1979)
Sherman, Stuart, 'Eyes and Ears, News and Plays: The Argument of Ben Jonson's *Staple*', in Brendan Dooley and Sabrina Baron, eds., *The Politics of Information in Early Modern Europe* (London and New York: Routledge, 2001), 23–40
Shrank, Cathy, 'Civil Tongues: Language, Law and Reformation', in Jennifer Richards, ed., *Early Modern Civil Discourses* (Basingstoke: Palgrave Macmillan, 2003), pp. 19–34
Skinner, Quentin, 'Hobbes and the Classical Theory of Laughter', *Visions of Politics*, 3 vols. (Cambridge: Cambridge University Press, 2002)
Smyth, Adam, '*Profit and Delight': Printed Miscellanies in England, 1640–82* (Detroit: Wayne State University Press, 2004)
Smith, Bruce, *The Acoustic World of Early Modern England* (Chicago: University of Chicago Press, 1999)
Steggle, Matthew, *Wars of the Theatres: The Poetics of Personation in the Age of Jonson* (Victoria, BC: University of Victoria, 1998)
Strachan, Michael, *The Life and Adventures of Thomas Coryate* (London: Oxford University Press, 1962)
  'The Mermaid Tavern Club: A New Discovery', *History Today* 17 (1967), 533–8

Strong, Roy, *Henry Prince of Wales and England's Lost Renaissance* (London: Thames and Hudson, 1986)
Swann, Marjorie, *Curiosities and Texts: The Culture of Collecting in Early Modern England* (Philadelphia: University of Pennsylvania Press, 2001)
Thomas, Keith, 'Cases of Conscience in Seventeenth-Century England', in John Morrill, Paul Slack and Daniel Woolf, eds., *Public Duty and Private Conscience in Seventeenth-Century England* (Oxford: Clarendon Press, 1993), pp. 29–56
Thrush, Andrew, 'The Personal Rule of James I, 1611–1620', in Thomas Cogswell, Richard Cust and Peter Lake, eds., *Politics, Religion and Popularity in Early Stuart Britain: Essays in Honour of Conrad Russell* (Cambridge: Cambridge University Press, 2002), pp. 84–102
Tlusty, B. Ann, *Bacchus and Civic Order: The Culture of Drink in Early Modern Germany* (Charlottesville: University Press of Virginia, 2001)
Travis, Peter, 'Thirteen Ways of Listening to a Fart: Noise in Chaucer's *Summoner's Tale*', *Exemplaria* 16 (2004), 1–19
Turner, Katherine, *British Travel Writers in Europe, 1750–1800: Authorship, Gender and National Identity* (Aldershot: Ashgate, 2001)
Voss, Paul J., 'Books for Sale: Advertising and Patronage in Late Elizabethan England', *The Sixteenth Century Journal* 29 (1998), 733–56
Warneke, Sara, *Images of the Educational Traveller in Early Modern England* (Leiden: E. J. Brill, 1995)
Wayne, Don E., '"Pox on Your Distinction!": Humanist Reformation and Deformations of the Everyday in *The Staple of News*', in Patricia Fumerton and Simon Hunt, eds., *Renaissance Culture and the Everyday* (Philadelphia: University of Pennsylvania Press, 1999), pp. 67–91
Weinpahl, Robert W., *Music at the Inns of Court during the Reigns of Elizabeth, James and Charles* (Ann Arbor, Michigan: University Microfilms International, 1979)
Weissman, Ronald, 'The Importance of Being Ambiguous: Social Relations, Individualism, and Identity in Renaissance Florence', in Susan Zimmerman and Ronald F. E. Weissman, eds., *Urban Life in the Renaissance* (Newark: University of Delaware Press, 1989), pp. 269–80
Whitlock, Baird, *John Hoskyns, Serjeant-at-law* (Washington: University Press of America, 1982)
Wiles, David, *Shakespeare's Clown: Actor and Text in the Elizabethan Playhouse* (Cambridge: Cambridge University Press, 1987)
Wilks, T. V., 'The Court Culture of Prince Henry and his Circle, 1603–1613', 2 vols., unpublished D.Phil. thesis, University of Oxford (1987)
Winston, Jessica, 'Expanding the Political Nation: *Gorboduc* at the Inns of Court and Succession Revisited', *Early Theatre* 8 (2005), 11–34
Withington, Phil, 'Two Renaissances: Urban Political Culture in Post-Reformation England Reconsidered', *The Historical Journal* 44 (2001), 239–67
  The Politics of the Commonwealth: Citizens and Freemen in Early Modern England (Cambridge: Cambridge University Press, 2005)
Zaret, David, *Origins of Democratic Culture: Printing, Petitions, and the Public Sphere in Early-Modern England* (Princeton: Princeton University Press, 2000)

Index

alehouse
    and social class, 7, 49, 58, 69–70
    as *topos*, 61–2
Anne, Queen Consort, 160, 176
Armin, Robert, 110, 111
Armstrong, Archibald, 110
Aubrey, John, 35, 157, 160

Bacon, Sir Francis, 93, 164
Badley, Richard, 106
Bakhtin, Mikhail, 82, 192
banquet literature, 61, 64, 168
    bibliophagia, 113–14
    feast *topos*, 113
Barbour, Richmond, 58, 149
Bastard, Thomas, 113
Beaulieu, Jean, 71–2
Beaumont, Francis
    epistle to Jonson, 1, 45, 68–9
    and 'Mermaid club', 1
Bellany, Alastair, 161
Best, Charles, 25
Boehrer, Bruce, 54
Borsay, Peter, 2
Botero, Giovanni, 129
Bowyer, Robert, 82
Boyle, Robert, Earl of Cork, 53
Brathwaite, Richard, *Solemne Joviall Disputation*, 62–4, 70, 72
    and William Marshall's engraving, 'Lawes of Drinking', 7, 69–70, 72
Brinsley, Richard, *Ludus Literarius*, 23–4
Brooke, Christopher
    friendships, 11, 18, 19, 21, 22, 157, 158
    as lawyer-wit, 4, 35, 36, 155
    marriage to Lady Jacob, 158, 159
    and *Memorable Masque*, 15
    at Mitre convivium, 3, 72, 73
    and 'Panegyricke Verses', 107, 108–9, 118, 120
    and parliament, 17, 81, 86–7, 92, 93, 157
    and 'Parliament Fart', 86, 90, 93
    and the Spenserians, 157
    social status, 13
    and Virginia Company, 16
Brooke, Henry, Lord Cobham, 42
Brooke, Samuel, 4, 19
Browne, William, 157
Buck, Sir George, *Third Universitie of England*, 13
buffoon or *scurra*
    classical, 73–4
    Coryate as, 8, 58, 71, 73, 74–5, 78, 110, 149
    Davies as
    and Jonson, 41, 44, 45, 53–4, 75–6, 77
    and social status, 7, 103
Bulstrode, Cecilia, 160, 176
Burke, Kenneth, 25–6
Butler, Martin, 167
burlesque
    chivalric, 26–7, 34
    English tradition of, 119
    libertine, 2, 9, 10, 26, 158–9, 170
    as *lusus*, 7, 12, 23, 67, 174
    'On the Famous Voyage', 56, 58
    symposiastic, 63–4, 73, 74, 77, 80
    in travel literature, 115, 142
Burton, Robert, *Anatomy of Melancholy*, 140

Cain, Tom, 36, 42
Calvert, George, 71
Calvert, Samuel, 71–2
Camden, William, *Remaines*, 66
Carleton, Dudley, 159
Casaubon, Isaac, 130
Caudill, Randall, 134
Cecil, Robert, Earl of Salisbury, 123
    and factions, 22, 32
    and libels, 31, 42, 79
    as patron, 71, 105
Cecil, William, Lord Burghley, 22
Chamberlain, John, 99, 159, 162, 167

Charles I, 173, 175
  as Prince of Wales, 162
Chaucer, Geoffrey, *Summoner's Tale*, 91
Chapman, George, 16
  Memorable Masque, 15–17, 157
Chapman, John, 108
Chartier, Roger, 113
Cholmley, Sir Hugh, 13
Chute, Sir Walter, 96
Cicero
  De Amicitia, 19
  De Oratore, 38–9, 41
  and laughter, 7, 38–9, 40–1
  Letters to Friends, 45
  Pro Caelio, 39–40
  see also urbanitas
civility
  and anti-civility, 159, 162, 166
  and civil society, 6
  and drink literature, 62–4, 65, 121
  and Inns of Court, 13, 27, 34, 37
  and satire and libel, 33
  and urban culture, 29
  'virile civility', 47
civil society, concept of, 2, 6, 7, 13, 153
'civilizing process', 6, 46, 62, 153
Clark, Peter, 2, 169
clubs
  clubbing, commoning and the revels, 9, 11, 30, 60, 71
  clubbing in the 1620s, 9, 161–9
  Kit-Cat Club, 2, 4
  Mermaid Club, 1
  October Club, 2
  origins of, 30
  political clubs, 4
  tavern-clubbing, 2–3, 9, 65, 77, 172
  as term of association, 5
Clucas, Stephen, 96
coffee-houses, 2, 153
Colclough, David, 25, 26, 164
community, 2
  acoustic, 66, 113
  as ideal of fellowship, 29–30, 82
  print, 2, 8, 105–7, 110, 170–1, 177
  scribal, 2, 19, 20–21, 78–9, 89, 102, 107
  speech, 45, 47
Connock, Richard, 4, 72
Connors, Catherine, 55
convivial societies
  as association, 1, 4, 5
  in early seventeenth century, 10, 18, 49, 61, 160–1
  'holy crew', 71–72
  Mitre convivium, 1, 3–4, 10, 70–2, 73, 107, 159

Sireniacal fraternity, 1, 3, 5, 10, 61, 64, 70–2, 80, 81, 85, 107, 145–8, 153–5, 159–60, 165
social rituals, 2, 3–4, 61, 62, 72
convivium
  classical, 5, 6, 8, 60, 72, 75, 78
  mock-convivium, 8, 73, 168
  see also symposium
'Convivium Philosophicum', poem, 1, 3, 7, 71, 72, 73, 74–7, 78–80, 82, 83–4, 86, 110, 160, 161, 165
Conway, Sir Edward, 83
Cope, Sir Walter, 135
Coryate, George, 114
Coryate, Thomas, 102–26, 164
  Coryats Crambe, 8, 56, 102, 103, 110, 112, 119, 147
  Coryats Crudities, 1, 7–9, 56–7, 70–1, 74, 77, 85, 102–27, 128–44, 147, 149, 151, 154, 156, 168, 172, 177
  eccentricity, 6, 110–11, 114–18
  and Mitre convivium, 3, 70, 72–77
  as performer, 53, 110–11; *see also* buffoon
  and print, 103–9
  and Sireniacs, 64, 70–1, 81
  social status, 114
  To his Friends in England, 145, 150–1, 172
  and tradition of clubbing, 172
  as traveller, 104, 115–17, 128–52
  Traveller for the English Wits, 1, 119, 139–40, 142, 145–50
coteries, 18, 49
court, 2
  and exclusivity, 56, 57
  household, 160–1
  at Inns of Court, 18–19, 36
  and print, 107, 109, 170, 177
Cotton, Sir Robert, 3, 84, 87
Craik, Katharine, 58, 114, 121
Cranfield, Sir Lionel, 3, 70, 72, 104–5, 107, 156, 157
Croft, Pauline, 86
Cunnington, David, 20

Dallington, Robert, *Method for Travell*, 129
Davies, John, 159
  Epigrams, 32
  and libels and satires, 10, 31–3, 67, 119
  Orchestra, 14
Davies, Rosalind, 96
Dekker, Thomas
  Gulls Hornbook, 61
  Satiromastix, 38, 42, 44, 54, 65, 66
Devereux, Robert, Earl of Essex, 21, 32, 165
  and libels, 11, 31, 42, 79
  rebellion of, 10, 42

Index 231

dissonance
  as *cacophonia*, 96
  concept of, 82
  and *lusus*, 7–8, 83, 103, 119, 126
  and 'Parliament Fart', 90–1, 92, 95–6, 161
Donne, John, 4, 13, 86, 87, 114–15, 124, 156–8, 160
  Anatomy of the World, 124–5
  'The Calm' and 'The Storm', 21–2
  at Inns of Court, 10–11, 19, 35
  and 'Mermaid Club', 1
  on libels, 67
  and Mitre convivium, 72, 73
  and 'Panegyricke Verses', 106, 107, 124–6
  'Satire 1', 27–9, 45
  'Satire 2', 33
  Second Anniversary, 124–5
  'To his Mistress going to Bed', 125
  verse epistles, 19–21, 23
drollery, 9, 126, 155, 170, 176–7
Duncan, Douglas, 50
Drayton, Michael, 65
drink literature (*Trinkliteratur*), 62; *see also* Obsopoeus, *Ars Bibendi*

Edmondes, Sir Thomas, 71–2
Egerton, Sir Thomas, 21, 31
Elias, Norbert, 54; *see also* 'civilizing process'
Elizabeth I, 16, 22, 26–7, 42, 53, 85, 123
Elyot, Sir Thomas, 14, 89
Epicureanism, 64
Erasmus, Desiderius, 54
  Praise of Folly, 7, 41, 50, 56, 98, 102, 119, 120, 168
Ezell, Margaret, 103

Fairfax, Sir Thomas, 107, 122
fart, semiotics of, 55, 89, 91, 95–6, 101, 172–5, 176; *see also* dissonance
Fennor, William, 53, 111
Fish, Stanley, 49
Fletcher, John, 1
fraternity, 160
  as civil ideal, 72
  and Inns of Court, 3, 10
  military, 162–3, 165–6, 167–8
  Order of the Blue, 162, 166
  Order of the Bugle, 162, 167
  Sireniacs as, 5
  Tityre-tu, 162, 166, 167
friendship
  impassioned, 19–23, 29
  at Inns of Court, 18–19
  royalist, 171–2
  at the table, 77–8

Gager, William, 23
Gainsford, Thomas, 167
Gascoigne, George, *Glass of Government*, 61
Gifford, William, 1, 153
Goodrich, Peter, 60
Goodyer, Sir Henry, 3, 72
Gordon, Andrew, 67
Gosson, Stephen, *School of Abuse*, 61
Goulart, Simon, *Admirable and Memorable Histories*, 143–4
Greene, Thomas, 90
Guazzo, Stefano, *Civile Conversation*, 5, 60, 74, 169
Guilpin, Everard
  Skialetheia, 28, 29, 31, 32, 39

Hakewill, William
  at Inns of Court, 10, 157
  and parliament, 87, 92–3, 95
  and Sireniacs, 3, 81, 87
  'Speaking in the House', 98–9
Halasz, Alexandra, 42
Harding, Vanessa, 29
Harington, Sir John, 110
  Metamorphosis of Ajax, 77, 95–6, 97–8
  and 'Panegyricke Verses', 105, 122–3, 124
  'Treatise on Playe', 51, 52
Harvey, Gabriel, 42, 97
Haynes, Jonathan, 47
Henry, Prince of Wales, 146
  in 'Convivium Philosphicum', 78
  and *Coryats Crudities*, 105, 108, 116, 129, 134–5
  household, 4, 16, 72, 81
Henry IV, King of France, 135
Herrick, Robert, 171–2
Heywood, John, 98
Holland, Hugh
  and friendships, 18, 49, 87, 157–8
  at Mitre convivium, 3, 72–3
  and 'Panegyric Verses', 105–7
  and *parrhesia*, 15
Horace, *Satires*, 28–9
Hoskyns, Benedicta, 159, 160
Hoskyns, John
  Directions for Speech and Style, 24–5, 33–4
  epitaphs, 66–7, 84
  and friendships, 18, 157
  'Fustian Answer to a Tufftaffeta Speech', 24–6, 27
  and Inns of Court, 10–11, 14, 164
  as lawyer-wit, 4, 31, 35–6, 49
  at Mitre convivium, 3, 4, 72–3, 80
  and nonsense, 7–8, 54–5, 57
  and 'Panegyricke Verses', 107, 118, 123–4

Hoskyns, John (*cont.*)
  and parliament, 17–18, 78, 92–3, 99, 155–6
  and 'Parliament Fart', 176
  and Sireniacs, 81, 86–7
  and social status, 13, 114
  verse exchange with Lady Jacob, 158
  and Virginia Company, 16
  and wit, 97–9, 117
  see also manuscripts, Bod. MS Malone 19
Howard, Jean, 133
Howard, Thomas, Earl of Suffolk, 78
Howell, James, *Instructions for Forreine Travell*, 128
Hutson, Lorna, 47

Ingram, Sir Arthur, 3, 72
Inns of Court, 3–4, 8, 10–37, 44
  associational culture, 10–11, 60, 101, 161, 164
  civic ideal, 12, 16–18, 35–7, 81
  Lincoln's Inn, 3, 10, 15–16, 19, 31, 35, 81, 90, 93, 107, 157
  Middle Temple, 3–4, 10, 15–16, 31–2, 81, 90, 107, 157, 162, 164

Jeanneret, Michel, 120
Jackson, John, 113
Jacob, Lady Mary, 158–60
James I, 14–15, 16–17, 91–2, 100, 146, 156, 161, 164, 176
jests, 7, 50, 74, 79, 97–8, 177
Jones, Edward, 86
Jones, Inigo, 3–4, 15, 72–3, 87, 107, 114–15, 121–2
Jonson, Ben, 35–59, 160
  Alchemist, 55
  Bartholomew Fair, 49, 54–5, 58, 62, 96, 155
  The Case is Alter'd, 38, 50
  Catiline, 40
  and *Crudities*, 102, 106, 109, 110, 114–15, 116–17, 118
  Cynthia's Revels, 50, 51, 54
  Devil is an Ass, 155
  Discoveries, 35, 37–8, 42, 58
  Epicoene, 6, 45, 47–8, 50, 52, 160
  'Epigram on the Court Pucelle', 160
  'Epistle Answering . . . Tribe of Ben', 166–8
  'Epistle to Arthur Squib', 76
  Every Man in His Humour, 66
  Every Man Out of His Humour, 22, 24, 36–42, 45–6, 48, 50, 75–6
  'Inviting a Friend to Supper', 73, 76, 77–8, 80, 171
  Leges Convivales, 77, 168
  and *lusus*, 6, 50–9
  and 'Mermaid Club', 1
  'On a Famous Voyage', 56, 58, 174–5
  Poetaster, 35–6, 38, 42–4
  and Sireniacs, 3, 87
  'Sons of Ben', 65, 160
  Staple of News, 77, 166, 167–9
  and symposiastic poetry, 65, 154, 166–9, 172
  'To Captain Hungry', 167
  'Tribe of Ben', 9, 167–8

Kemp, William, 53, 110, 115–16, 142
Kendall, Timothy, 111
King, John, 174–5
Kirchner, Hermann, 129–30

laughter, 7, 25, 38–41, 50, 120–1, 161, 174; *see also* Cicero
Legh, Gerard, *Accedence of Armorie*, 12–13, 18, 26
Lewkenor, Lewis, 105, 119–20
libels, 31–4, 39–40, 67–8, 99–101, 154, 163–5
  and factional politics, 31–4, 42–3
libertinism, 9, 26–7, 124, 166, 170, 172
Loewenstein, Joseph, 77, 103
Lucian, *Lapiths*, 77

Madox, Richard, 30
Manningham, John, 10, 32
manuscripts
  Bod. MS Don.c.54 (Richard Roberts), 42, 79–80, 87
  Bod. MS Malone 19, 163–5
Marcus, Leah, 170
Marston, John, 31, 42
Martin, Richard
  epigrams and libels, 67, 164
  friendships, 18–34, 157–8
  and Inns of Court, 10–11, 14, 15–17, 31
  as lawyer-wit, 35–6, 49, 117, 131, 155–6, 175
  as libertine, 124
  at Mitre convivium, 3, 72
  and 'Panegyricke Verses', 107, 113–14
  in parliament, 87, 92–3, 94, 156
  and 'Parliament Fart', 55, 84, 86
  as parrhesiastes, 14–15, 43, 81
  and Sireniacal fraternity, 81, 87
  social status, 13, 114
  and Virginia Company, 16–17, 156
Mathew, Toby, 124
Mayne, Jasper, *City Match*, 155
Maus, Katharine, 40
Meier, Albert, *Certaine Briefe and Speciall Instructions*, 132, 134
Mennes, Sir John, 170–2
Middleton, Thomas, *Your Five Gallants*, 2
Milton, John, 174–5
Mock-encomium, 6, 7, 56, 102–3, 109, 119–26
Montaigne, Michel, *Essais*, 18

Index

Moore, Tim, *Continental Drifter*, 151–2
Moraes, Dom, 152
More, Ann, 21
More, Sir George, 21, 90
More, Sir Thomas, 54
  on farting, 95
  as jester, 97–8, 119
  Utopia, 12, 23, 128–30
  'The most humble petition', 100, 163, 164
Musarum Deliciæ: or, the Muses Recreation, 9, 119, 126, 155, 169–74, 176–7

Nashe, Thomas, 42
Neville, Christopher, 96, 99
Neville, Sir Henry of Abergavenny, 105
nonsense, 7, 24, 25, 54–6, 57, 96, 120

Obsopoeus, Vincentius, *Ars Bibendi*, 62–4
The Odcombian Banquet, 102, 103, 107, 112
Ong, Walter, 107
Ord, Melanie, 105
Ostovich, Helen, 30
Overbury, Sir Thomas, 32, 88, 160, 161, 164
Ovid
  Ars Amatoria, 26
  Heroides, 20
  Ibis, 112

Palmer, Sir Thomas, 132, 134
Parker, Kenneth, 148
Parliament, 4, 8, 85–9, 92, 98–101, 161
  and legal culture, 81, 93–5
  1604–10, 15, 17, 78, 81–2, 85, 91–2
  1614, 9, 71, 92, 96, 99, 155–6
  1621, 157, 161
  Long, 173
'Parliament Fart', 7–8, 9, 55, 71, 81–96, 100, 101, 154–5, 160, 161, 163, 169–70, 172–6
  members named in: Croft, Sir Herbert, 93; Hare, John, 86; Hitcham, Sir Robert, 90; Hoby, Sir Edward, 86, 90; Holles, Sir John, 92; Hyde, Lawrence, 88, 93, 94; Lewkenor, Samuel, 94; Ludlow, Henry, 198; Manwood, Sir Peter, 84; Monson, Sir Thomas, 88; Moore, Sir Francis, 88; Noy, William, 90; Piggot, Christopher, 86; Pory, John, 84; Sandys, Sir Edwin, 93; Yelverton, Henry, 93
'Parliament sits with a Synod of Witts', 163–4
parody, 89
Parr, Anthony, 128, 135, 140
parrhesia, or frank speech, 14–15, 98, 166
  and the satirist, 7, 37, 41, 43–4
Parrot, Henry, 107

Paterson, Samuel (Coriat Junior), *Another Traveller*, 151
Patterson, Annabel, 78
Pawlet, John, 105
Peacham, Henry, 115, 134, 138–9
Phelips, Sir Edward
  and *Memorable Masque*, 15–17
  and 'Panegyricke Verses', 105
  and 'Parliament Fart', 84
  as patron, 4, 81, 110, 136, 146, 156
Phelips, Sir Robert, 3, 4, 16, 81, 110, 113, 115, 121, 146
performance, 8, 53, 56–7, 59, 61–2, 103, 110–15
  extemporised, 7, 23, 24, 66, 84
  print, 8, 102, 111–12, 117
  play, 7–8, 12–22, 27, 50–9, 74, 81–2, 110, 154
    humanist traditions of, 6, 7, 23–6, 34, 35–6, 50–1, 54–5, 59, 168–9
    literary forms of, 7–8, 23, 55, 57, 71, 83, 86, 119–20, 152, 166, 171–5
Plutarch
  Morals, 47
  Table Talk, 60, 79
Poole, Sir Henry, 105
Le Prince d'Amour, or the Prince of Love, 9, 155, 169–70, 175–7
'Precepts of Urbanity', 67–8
print, 57, 176
  sociability of, 8, 102–110
  see also community and performance
private society, concept of, 34, 48, 153–4
public sphere, concept of, 7, 82, 87, 154, 197
Purchas, Samuel, *Purchas his Pilgrimes*, 137–8, 145
Puttenham, George, 65–6, 67

Quintilian, 38–41, 58
  Institutio Oratoria, 28, 40, 44

Rabelais, François, 76, 83, 115, 118, 135, 166, 169, 196
Raffield, Paul, 38
'A Rayling libel against those of the p[ar]liament house', 85
Raleigh, Sir Walter, 1, 31, 42, 164
Randolph, Thomas, 65
Raylor, Timothy, 119, 162, 165, 170–1, 172, 173
revels, 5, 23–4
  Inns of Court, 12, 14, 17, 23–4, 30, 37, 60; 1561–2 Inner Temple, 12, 26; 1594–5 Gray's Inn, 14, 61; 1597–8 Middle Temple, 4, 7, 8–9, 11, 14, 23–7, 28–9, 31, 34, 36, 45, 61, 71, 80, 175
  University, 30
Reynold, John, 74
Roe, Sir Thomas, 138, 146, 149, 160

Rowlands, Samuel, 56
Rowley, William, *Match at Midnight*, 155
Rubiés, Joan-Pau, 138, 150
Rudyerd, Sir Benjamin, 3, 31–2, 36, 160
Russell, Lucy, Countess of Bedford, 160

Sanford, John (Glareanus Vadianus), 114, 120
satire, 4, 27, 30–1, 33, 44, 74, 78
    as flyting, 6, 31, 33, 35, 56, 111–12, 150
Scodel, Joshua, 65
Scott-Warren, Jason, 108
Shakespeare, William, 1
Shapiro, I. A., 3, 70
Sherley, Sir Robert, 147–8
Sherley, Lady Teresia, 147–8
Shields, David, 154, 177
Sidney, Sir Philip, 38, 176
Smith, Bruce, 66
Smith, James, 170–2
Smyth, Adam, 177
Southwell, Lady Anne, 160
Srivatsa, Sarayu, 152
Stansby, William, 106
Starkey, Ralph, 87, 90
Steggle, Matthew, 44
Sterne, Laurence, 151
Strangewayes, John, 115
Suckling, Sir John, the elder, 104, 117, 122
Sydenham, George, 105, 106
symposium
    classical, 5, 64, 69–70, 79, 166, 169
    symposiastic literary tradition, 73–8

table, topos of, 8, 58, 61, 76–8, 79–80, 81
table talk, 60, 73, 79–80, 144
talked book, 112–13, 118, 144
Tarlton, Richard, 53, 110, 111
tavern
    Devil and St Dunstan, 9, 65, 68, 166, 168
    Mermaid, 1–2, 27, 49, 56, 68–9, 71, 87, 155
    Mitre, 1–2, 27, 45, 49, 62, 70, 71, 155
    poetry, 9, 66–70, 76, 78, 80, 83, 113
    topos of, 7, 49, 58, 61, 62, 65, 66, 67–70, 76–7, 79–80
Taylor, John, 6, 57–8, 62, 102, 111–12, 114, 151
    Eighth Wonder of the World, 57, 109
    Laugh and be Fat, 57
    Odcombs Complaint, 57

Pennyles Pilgrimage, 142–3
The Sculler, 56–8
Terry, Edward, 138, 141, 146, 149, 150, 152
travel and travel-writing, 115–17, 128–52
    and collecting, 134–7
    and curiosity, 133–8, 141–2, 143–5, 150, 151
    and the 'English wits', 147–8
    Humanist traditions of, 116, 128–30
    and Republic of Letters, 130–1, 137
    as sight-seeing, 8, 128, 133, 138–41
    and walking, 142–3
Trumbull, William, 71–2, 135
Turler, Jerome, *Traveiler of Jerome Turler*, 131

urbanity, 1, 21, 29, 45–9, 61, 127, 148
    satiric, 6, 27–9, 34, 41, 45–6, 48
    urbanitas, 12, 27, 39, 40–1, 45, 48

Villiers, George, Duke of Buckingham, 154, 156, 159, 161, 162, 164
violence
    and clubbing, 30
    and honour, 6, 62–3, 165–6
    and satire, 32, 67, 77, 112
Virginia Company, 4, 16, 17, 61, 71, 156, 158

Weeks, John, 171–2
West, John, 72
Whitaker, Lawrence, 5, 61, 71, 80, 86, 102, 104–7, 119, 131, 135, 143, 145–6
Whitelocke, Sir James, 87, 92
Wiles, David, 110
Wilkins, George, *Miseries of Enforced Marriage*, 62
Wilson, Thomas, 97
wit, 5, 59, 68–9, 96–9, 117, 124, 176
Wither, George, 68, 157
Withington, Phil, 49
wits
    'English wits', 148
    female wits, 159–60
    as social type, 1, 44–9, 68, 69–70
Woodward, Rowland, 13, 19
Woodward, Thomas, 13, 19
Wotton, Sir Henry, 21–2, 96–7, 131, 136, 160
Wroth, Lady Mary, 160

Xenophon, *Symposium*, 60, 73–4